THE ESSENTIAL mediterranean COOKBOOK

THE ESSENTIAL
mediterranean
COOKBOOK

bay books

Published by Bay Books, an imprint of Murdoch Magazines Pty Ltd.
GPO Box 1203 Sydney NSW Australia 1045
Phone: (612) 4352 7000 Fax: (612) 4352 7026

Series Editor: Wendy Stephen. Editorial Director: Diana Hill. Designer: Wing Ping Tong.
Design Concept: Marylouise Brammer. Food Editor: Christine Osmond. Food Director: Jane Lawson.
Stylists (cover and special features): Marie-Hélène Clauzon, Mary Harris.
Photographers (cover and special features): Craig Cranko, Brett Stevens.
Home Economists: Jo Glynn, Justine Poole.
Picture Librarian: Anne Ferrier.

CEO: Juliet Rogers
Publisher: Kay Scarlett
Production Manager: Kylie Kirkwood

National Library of Australia Cataloguing-in-Publication Data
The essential Mediterranean cookbook. Includes index. ISBN 1 74045 033 7 (cased edition)
1 74045 034 5 (pbk) 1. Cookery, Mediterranean. (Series: Essential series (Sydney, N.S.W.)). 641.591822
A catalogue record of this book is available from the British Library.

Printed by Toppan Printing Hong Kong Co. Ltd.
PRINTED IN CHINA

First published in 2001. Reprinted 2003.
©Text, design, photography and illustrations Murdoch Books® 2001

You may find cooking times vary depending on the oven you are using. For fan-forced ovens, as a general rule,
set the oven temperature to 20°C lower than indicated in the recipe.
We have used 20 ml tablespoon measures. If you are using a 15 ml tablespoon, for most recipes the difference will not be
noticeable. However, for recipes using baking powder, gelatine, bicarbonate of soda, small amounts of flour and
cornflour, add an extra teaspoon for each tablespoon specified. We have used 60 g (Grade 3) eggs in all recipes.

IMPORTANT: Those who might be at risk from the effects of salmonella food poisoning
(the elderly, pregnant women, young children and those suffering from immune deficiency
diseases) should consult their GP with any concerns about eating raw eggs.

OUR STAR RATING: When we test recipes, we rate them for ease of preparation.
The following cookery ratings are used in this book:
☆ A single star indicates a recipe that is simple and generally quick to make—perfect for beginners.
☆☆ Two stars indicate the need for just a little more care, or perhaps a little more time.
☆☆☆ Three stars indicate special dishes that need more investment in time,
care and patience—but the results are worth it. Even beginners can make these
dishes as long as the recipe is followed carefully.

MEDITERRANEAN

In this book we take you on a culinary journey along the shores of the sparkling blue Mediterranean. Food ideas from Greece, Turkey, Italy, France, Spain, North Africa and the Middle East are all explored. Examples of the diverse tastes of each country are the delicacies enjoyed as part of the meze in Greece, antipasto in Italy and tapas in Spain. Wonderful recipes from all the countries reflect the cooking styles, eating habits and customs of the people of the Mediterranean. Many of the spices, herbs, vegetables and other ingredients are common throughout these beautiful places that sit on the rim of the sea. However, the rich history and interesting origins of the charming peoples has led to a difference in the way these ingredients are utilized. Along our journey, this remarkable approach to cooking is brought out in the recipes we explore with you.

CONTENTS

SPECIAL FEATURES

MEDITERRANEAN CUISINE

The Mediterranean region is linked not only by the sea and a temperate climate, but also the long and tumultuous history of conquests and occupations. The Phoenicians, Egyptians, Greeks, Carthaginians, Persians and Romans all wove a part in the fabric of the Mediterranean, leaving behind visible remnants of trade routes and great civilisations. For centuries, the Mediterranean Sea was a very active trading route and this resulted in a rich history of cultural exchange. It is not surprising that food ideas crossed national boundaries and were adapted to suit people with different needs.

This book reflects this history because many recipes seem remarkably similar. Dishes such as stuffed peppers (capsicums), baked eggplants (aubergines), fish stews and filo pastries all appear in many versions, scattered throughout the book as we travel along the Mediterranean. On the other hand, many recipes such as such the Provençal Pissaladière (page 162) or Greek Moussaka (page 44) lead us unmistakably to the country of origin. Many of these 'national' dishes appear with numerous variations throughout their homelands but still retain their cultural identity.

The Mediterranean region is rich in resources and varied in landscape and the geographical and culinary focus in this book stretches from Spain down to Morocco and Algeria, then follows the shores of the Mediterranean to cover Tunisia, Libya, Egypt, Israel, Lebanon, Syria and Turkey in the east and Greece, Italy and southern France in the north.

The Arabs had a great impact upon the food of the Mediterranean. Travelling along the trade routes, they brought with them fragrant rose and orange blossom waters, pomegranates, citrus fruits, pine nuts, walnuts, eggplants (aubergines) and zucchini (courgettes). They also brought spices such as saffron, cumin and cinnamon.

WHAT IS MEDITERRANEAN CUISINE?

There is no one Mediterranean cuisine. Because of the history of the region, it remains one of the most colourful and vibrant collections of cuisines in the world. However you could almost define the Mediterranean landscape by the cultivation of olive trees and the use of olive oil. Other quintessential ingredients are vegetables such as zucchini (courgettes), tomatoes, eggplants (aubergines), peppers (capsicums) and garlic, as well as fruits, pulses and grains, pasta, fresh herbs, spices and nuts. The heavy reliance upon seafood is a natural one while the supply of red meat is sometimes more problematic due to the often inhospitable hilly terrain further inland, which makes farming of livestock difficult. A glass of wine is an integral part of the meal for many Mediterranean countries. Generally, the flavours of the Mediterranean are strong and robust and natural flavours are not drowned or masked by butter or creamy, rich sauces.

The Mediterranean diet has received a lot of attention over the past decade from dietitians and nutritionists. At present, there is much research into the theory that the incorporation of olive oil and abundant seafood and fresh fruit and vegetables into the diet, combined with minimal consumption of red meat and animal fats in the

form of butter, cream and lard, may be associated with a low incidence of coronary heart disease, obesity, diabetes and cancer.

In this book you will find a selection of the most classic Mediterranean recipes. We have not included recipes from the north of Italy which embrace influences from the colder countries, sometimes making them unrecognisable as having the same heritage. If you ask an Italian about Italian food, you would find that no one cuisine exists. Instead you would learn of regional cuisines linked closely to the history of the people and the land. So rather than Italian cooking, locals talk of Venetian, Florentine, Neapolitan or Sicilian cooking, to name a few. The chapter on France focuses upon Provence, a region isolated not only historically but also climatically from the rest of France. Provence enjoys more hours of sunlight than any other region in France and the fact that it is warmed by the sun and lapped by the Mediterranean draws it closer to its southern cousins. Nearly all the recipes in this book are derived from resourceful peasant cuisines with powerful basic ingredients such as saffron, garlic and anchovies, to enhance the flavour of fresh vegetables and simple cuts of meat.

A FEW TIPS FOR SUCCESS

● Use top-quality ingredients, preferably when they are in season. Tomatoes are a prime example so, wherever possible, use fresh tomatoes which have been ripened on the vine. Otherwise, use good-quality canned tomatoes such as Italian Roma which are regarded as superior because they are processed when they are at their peak.

● Use fresh herbs where possible. If you have to buy them, choose those with erect stalks and leaves that are not dark or limp. To store fresh herbs such as parsley, basil and coriander, rinse them briefly in cold water, then shake dry and wrap in damp paper towels.

● Some recipes such as Liver with oregano (page 26) or Barbecued quail (page 30) call for dried herbs. Try to buy dried wild herbs, usually still on the branches, from speciality delicatessens, as they have much more flavour and are truly evocative of the wild Mediterranean hills.

● Ground spices differ in flavour if you toast and grind them yourself. Toast and grind a small amount and put them in an airtight container. If you have to rely on pre-ground spices, remember that they lose their flavour and scent with age.

● To plan a meal using this book, you can put together an all Spanish feast or a totally Moroccan meal, but you can also use dishes from different countries. A feast of small dishes, from Dolmades (page 19) to Hummus (page 64) and Italian Stuffed sardines (page 92), all served with bread, would not look at all unusual. Indeed, the beauty of these small dishes is that they are so versatile. Plan the meal using seasonal, quality produce and garnish in the traditional Mediterranean way with roughly chopped herbs, toasted almonds or pine nuts, olives or a simple drizzle of extra virgin olive oil. Keep the presentation simple. You may like to serve wines from the same regions as the food.

MEDITERRANEAN PANTRY

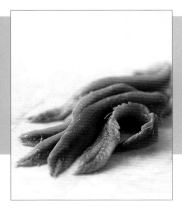

ANCHOVIES
A small fish from the herring family found mainly in southern European waters. Although anchovies can be eaten fresh, they are rarely found outside Mediterranean fishing ports as they are delicate and need to be eaten or processed quickly. More commonly, anchovies are cured and packed in oil, salt or brine and are readily available in cans or jars.

ARBORIO RICE
A short-grained plump rice imported from Italy. Used in both sweet and savoury dishes, arborio rice is particularly suitable for making risotto because the grains absorb a lot of liquid and become creamy but still retain their firmness.

ARTICHOKE HEARTS
The fleshy centres or 'heart' of the thistly artichoke head. They are available whole or quartered, canned or in jars, chargrilled or plain, in olive oil or brine.

BOCCONCINI
Small mozzarella balls are known as bocconcini or *baby mozzarella*. A smooth, mild, unripened cheese originally made from buffalo milk but now usually made from cow's milk, bocconcini should be refrigerated covered in the whey in which it is sold. They will last for three weeks but should be discarded if they show signs of yellowing. Drained and sliced, they are used in salads, as pizza or bruschetta toppings, or in pasta dishes.

BORLOTTI BEANS
Slightly kidney-shaped, this large bean is a beautifully marked pale, pinkish brown with burgundy specks. Popular in Italy, borlotti beans have a nutty flavour and are used in soups, stews and salads. They are sometimes available fresh, otherwise dried or canned can be used.

BURGHUL
Also known as *bulgar* or *cracked wheat*, burghul is wheat which has been hulled, boiled or steamed, then dried and cracked. It is a staple in the Middle East and requires little or no cooking. Sold coarsely or finely ground.

CALASPARRA RICE
This white medium-grained Spanish rice is traditionally used to make paella. If it is not available, arborio, carnaroli or vialone nano can be used instead.

CANNELLINI BEANS
These white, kidney-shaped beans are also known as *Italian haricot beans* or *white kidney beans*. Mildly flavoured and slightly fluffy in texture when cooked, they are good all-purpose beans for use in soups, casseroles, stews and salads. Available fresh, dried or canned.

CAPERS
The pickled buds of a shrub which grows wild in many parts of the Mediterranean. Capers have a sharp, sour taste and are sold in seasoned vinegar or packed in salt which needs to be rinsed off before use.

CHICKPEAS
One of the most versatile and popular legumes in many parts of the world, chickpeas were first grown in the Levant and ancient Egypt. There are two kinds of chickpea, the large white garbanzo and the smaller brown dessi. Some of the most popular Middle Eastern dishes, including hummus, have chickpeas as their basis. They can be boiled, roasted, ground, mashed and milled and are available dried or canned.

COUSCOUS
This cereal is processed from semolina and coated with wheat flour. Instant couscous cooks in 5 minutes. Couscous is used in much the same way as rice is in Asia — as a high-carbohydrate accompaniment to meat and vegetable dishes.

FILO PASTRY
Filo or *phyllo* is a paper-thin pastry made from flour and water. It is used widely in Eastern Mediterranean countries for the making of both sweet and savoury dishes. The paper-thin layers are lightly greased and are either stacked to make things such as baklava, or otherwise one or two layers are rolled up to enclose a filling as for cheese triangles.

CEDRO
This is a citrus fruit, also known as *citron*, which looks like a large, rough lemon. It dates back to ancient times and is grown especially for the thick peel which is removed and candied. Cedro is available in some speciality shops.

FETA CHEESE
A soft, white cheese ripened in brine. Originally made from the milk of sheep or goats, but often now made with the more economical cow's milk. Feta cheese tastes sharp and salty and can be eaten as an appetizer, cooked or marinated. It is an ingredient in traditional Greek salad.

FRISEE
Part of the chicory family, frisee is also known as *curly endive* or *endive*. Frisee is a winter salad green and has a mild, bitter flavour. It is well-matched with robust flavours such as bacon, walnuts or mustard.

CHORIZO
A Spanish sausage, with many regional varieties, based on pork, paprika and garlic. Chorizo is sliced and served as tapas and is also cooked in paellas, stews and soups.

HALOUMI
A salty Middle Eastern cheese made from ewe's milk. The curd is cooked, then matured in brine, often with herbs or spices. It is most often grilled or fried but can also be used in salads or on bread.

LENTILS DU PUY
This tiny, dark green lentil is considered a delicacy in France and is relatively expensive. Unlike most other lentils, lentils du puy keep their shape and have a firm texture after cooking. They are used mostly for making salads and side dishes.

MELOKHIA
The deep green leaves of this plant are used as a vegetable in many Mediterranean countries. In Egypt it is used to make one of the national dishes, a soup of the same name. The leaves give the soup a gelatinous texture. Melokhia is available from speciality food stores and comes fresh, dried or frozen.

NIGELLA SEEDS
Also called *black onion seeds*, these seeds have a nutty, peppery flavour. They are used in the Middle East and India as a seasoning for vegetables, legumes and breads. Often confused with black cumin.

KEFALOTYRI CHEESE
A very hard, scalded and cured sheep or goat's milk cheese with a mild flavour. Its use depends on its age. When young, it is a table cheese, at six months old, it is used in cooking, and when more mature, it makes an excellent grating cheese. Parmesan or pecorino can be substituted.

MARSALA
A fortified wine from Marsala in Sicily that comes in varying degrees of dryness and sweetness. Dry Marsalas are used in savoury dishes and drunk as an aperitif. Sweet ones are suitable for putting in dessert dishes such as zabaglione and are also served with desserts.

MOZZARELLA
A smooth, fresh white cheese with a mild, slightly sweet flavour. Traditionally made from buffalo milk, it is now made with cow's milk. Used as a table cheese as well as in cooking, it melts well and is good for pizzas. Shapes vary from pear to block.

OKRA
Also known as *ladies' fingers* because of the shape, this green, slightly curved, ridged pod is popular in the Eastern Mediterranean. It has a lot of small seeds and has a very glutinous texture which can be lessened considerably by soaking in lemon juice mixed in salt water before cooking. Okra is a natural thickening agent, so is useful in casseroles. Available fresh or canned.

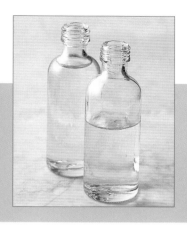

ORANGE BLOSSOM WATER

Sometimes called *orange flower water*, this is an essence made by distilling the blossoms of the bitter Seville orange. The oil rises to the top and is used in perfumery while the watery part is used extensively in Eastern Mediterranean countries to perfume pastries, puddings, syrups and drinks.

PARMESAN

A hard cow's milk cheese widely used in Italian cooking, either grated and added to dishes or shaved to use as a garnish. Always buy Parmesan in a chunk and grate it as you need it, rather than use ready-grated. Parmigiano Reggiano, from Parma in Northern Italy, is the most superior Parmesan.

POLENTA

Also known as *cornmeal*, these ground, dried corn kernels are a staple in Northern Italy. Polenta is most often made into a porridge and flavoured by mixing in butter and Parmesan. After it is cooked, it can also be spread into a thin layer in a dish, then allowed to set before frying or grilling and being served with vegetables or with toppings as an appetizer.

PORCINI MUSHROOMS

Used in Italian and French cooking, these have a brown cap and a thick white stem. Also known as *cep mushrooms*, they come fresh or dried. Soak dried ones in warm water, then rinse. The strained soaking water can be used. Dried porcini have a strong flavour and should be used sparingly. Good in risottos and omelettes.

PANCETTA

This is the belly of the pig that has been cured in salt and spices. There are many regional variations, some matured longer than others, or with different aromatics. It is usually sold rolled into a sausage shape and cut into very thin slices and is popular in many pasta dishes.

PECORINO

One of Italy's most popular cheeses, with virtually every region producing its own variety, pecorino is made from sheep's milk, always using the same method. The ageing time and flavour of the milk varies.

POMEGRANATE MOLASSES

Also sold as pomegranate syrup or concentrate, this is the boiled-down juice of a sour variety of pomegranate used in Syria and Lebanon. The molasses has an unusual sweet-and-sour flavour and is used in sauces and dressings.

PRESERVED LEMONS

These are lemons pickled in salt and spices. They need to be rinsed before use and the pulp removed and discarded. They are used mainly in North African cuisine to flavour couscous and traditional tagine dishes.

PROSCIUTTO

An Italian ham that has been cured by salting then drying in the air. Aged for up to ten months, it is then sliced thinly. It doesn't require cooking. Prosciutto di Parma is the classic Italian ham traditionally served as an antipasto and also used extensively, diced or shredded, in cooking.

RAS-EL-HANOUT

A North African spice blend comprising up to twenty-seven ingredients including powdered cumin, cinnamon, cardamom, ginger, turmeric, nutmeg, cloves, rosebuds, peppercorns and oregano. Traditionally, it also contains aphrodisiacs such as the Spanish fly beetle.

ROSEWATER

This distilled essence, extracted from roses, is used in the eastern Mediterranean to perfume sweets such as Turkish delight and other sweet dishes, as well as drinks.

SALT COD

Cod fillets which have been salted and dried. Needs to be soaked for at least two days before use. Available from speciality shops.

PROVOLONE

A golden yellow Italian cheese with a glossy rind, provolone is often moulded into a pear shape before being hung to mature. While it is young, provolone is mild and delicate and often used as a table cheese. As it matures, the flavour becomes sharper and it can be used for grating. Provolone is often smoked.

ROCKET

This salad green, also known as *arugula*, *rugula* or *roquette* is native to the Mediterranean. The peppery flavour increases as the leaves grow. Served over cooked pizzas, or in a mixed green salad.

SAFFRON

The thread-like stigma of a violet crocus, this is the most expensive spice because of the hard work involved in extracting it from the flowers. Luckily, only a small amount is needed to impart the distinctive flavour and colour to a dish. The colour and flavour varies according to the origin and quality. Saffron is sold as threads or in powdered form but the latter is often adulterated with dyes.

SEMOLINA

This is the product obtained from the first milling of wheat, usually the very hard durum wheat. Semolina can be coarse, medium or fine and is used for making pasta, gnocchi and some puddings or cakes. Although it is tough and doesn't break down into mush when cooked, it still manages to produce a light texture.

SILVERBEET

Also known as *Swiss chard*, silverbeet is often confused with spinach. The large, crinkly leaves have more texture than spinach and are suited to longer cooking because they don't collapse like spinach. Both the leaves and stems can be eaten but need to be blanched before being braised, gratinéed or used as pie fillings.

SUN-DRIED TOMATOES

These are widely available either dry and loosely packed, or in jars in oil. The dry variety need to be rehydrated before use. To do this, cover them with boiling water and leave for about ten minutes. If buying sun-dried tomatoes in oil, choose the variety in olive oil as you can use the oil for cooking to add extra flavour to your dish.

TARAMA

Salted and dried grey mullet roe used to make the popular Greek dip taramosalata. Cod roe is more readily available so it is often used as a substitute for grey mullet roe when making taramosalata.

VINE LEAVES

Young leaves from the grape vine, blanched then preserved in brine. Available in packets, jars and cans.

ZA'ATAR

Popular in Turkey and North Africa, this spice blend is a mixture of toasted sesame seeds, dried thyme, sumac and salt. The proportions vary from region to region. It is used as a seasoning for meats and vegetables and is also mixed with oil to dip bread into, or sprinkled on flatbread, such as Lebanese or pitta bread, that has been brushed with olive oil and then lightly toasted.

SUMAC

The reddish berry has a sour, fruity flavour and is processed to form various grades of powder. Used mainly in Syria and Lebanon, where lemons are rare, for adding to or sprinkling on meat, especially kebabs, fish and vegetables, to add flavour and colour.

TAHINI

An oily paste made from ground sesame seeds, tahini adds a strong nutty flavour and is popular in the eastern Mediterranean.

TOMATO PASSATA

This is a bottled tomato sauce commonly used in Italian cooking and many Mediterranean recipes. The sauce is made with fresh, ripe tomatoes which are peeled, seeded and slowly cooked down with basil, onion and garlic. The thickened sauce is then passed through a sieve before being bottled.

GREECE

Dreaming of lazing in a taverna, with the sparkling waters of the Mediterranean and brilliant blue skies as a captivating backdrop, sets the mood for a Greek cooking adventure. Greek people approach healthy, hearty eating with a similar vitality to that which pervades all aspects of their lives. Traditionally, in many parts of Greece, the sea was one of the main sources of food, but these days lamb and beef, as well as fresh herbs, fruit and vegetables all play a vital role in the cuisine. Kalamata olives, dolmades and taramosalata are quintessentially Greek and can be part of a meze spread to whet the appetite. We have given just a sampling of Greek dishes so you can adapt them as cooks in Greece would do.

GARLIC

One of the smallest members of the onion family, garlic is also the most pungent. Indispensable, its essence imparts a crucial depth of flavour to many dishes such as skordalia. As well as its unique flavour, garlic has the advantage of being rich in minerals and vitamins. As a general rule, the finer that garlic is crushed, the more of its pungent oil is released, hence the popularity of garlic presses. When choosing garlic look for hard, large, round bulbs and always check underneath for any signs of unwanted mould.

ABOVE: Tzatziki

TZATZIKI
(Cucumber and yoghurt dip)

Preparation time: 10 minutes
  + 15 minutes standing
Total cooking time: Nil
Makes 2 cups

☆

2 Lebanese cucumbers (about 300 g/13 oz)
400 g (13 oz) Greek-style natural yoghurt
4 cloves garlic, crushed
3 tablespoons finely chopped fresh mint
1 tablespoon lemon juice
chopped fresh mint, extra, to garnish

1 Cut the cucumbers in half lengthways, scoop out the seeds with a teaspoon and discard. Leave the skin on and coarsely grate the cucumber into a small colander. Sprinkle with a little salt and leave to stand over a large bowl for 15 minutes to drain off any bitter juices.
2 Meanwhile, stir together the yoghurt, garlic, mint and lemon juice in a bowl.
3 Rinse the cucumber under cold water then, taking small handfuls, squeeze out any excess moisture. Combine the cucumber with the yoghurt mixture and season, to taste. Serve immediately or refrigerate until ready to serve.

Garnish with mint. Can be served as a dip with flatbread or as a sauce for seafood and meat.

SKORDALIA
(Garlic sauce)

Preparation time: 15 minutes
Total cooking time: 10 minutes
Makes 2 cups

☆

500 g (1 lb) floury potatoes (desiree, King Edward), cut into 2 cm ($^3/_4$ inch) cubes
5 cloves garlic, crushed
ground white pepper, to taste
$^3/_4$ cup (185 ml/6 fl oz) olive oil
2 tablespoons white vinegar

1 Bring a large saucepan of water to the boil, add the potato and cook for 10 minutes, or until very soft. Drain thoroughly and mash until quite smooth.
2 Stir the garlic, 1 teaspoon salt and a pinch of white pepper into the potato, then gradually pour in the olive oil, mixing well with a wooden spoon. Stir in the vinegar and season, to taste. Serve warm or cold with crusty bread or crackers as a dip, or with grilled meat, fish or chicken.

DOLMADES
(Stuffed vine leaves)

Preparation time: 40 minutes
  + 15 minutes soaking
Total cooking time: 45 minutes
Makes 24

☆ ☆ ☆

200 g (6½ oz) packet vine leaves in brine
1 cup (250 g/8 oz) medium-grain rice
1 small onion, finely chopped
1 tablespoon olive oil
60 g (2 oz) pine nuts, toasted
2 tablespoons currants
2 tablespoons chopped fresh dill
1 tablespoon finely chopped fresh mint
1 tablespoon finely chopped fresh flat-leaf parsley
⅓ cup (80 ml/2¾ fl oz) olive oil, extra
2 tablespoons lemon juice
2 cups (500 ml/16 fl oz) chicken stock

1 Soak the vine leaves in cold water for 15 minutes, then remove and pat dry. Cut off any stems. Reserve some leaves to line the saucepan and discard any that have holes or look poor. Meanwhile, soak the rice in boiling water for 10 minutes to soften, then drain.
2 Place the rice, onion, olive oil, pine nuts, currants, herbs and salt and pepper, to taste, in a large bowl and mix well.
3 Lay some leaves vein-side-down on a flat surface. Place 1 tablespoon of filling in the centre of each, fold the stalk end over the filling, then the left and right sides into the centre, and finally roll firmly towards the tip. The dolmades should resemble a small cigar. Repeat with the remaining filling and leaves.
4 Use the reserved vine leaves to line the base of a large, heavy-based saucepan. Drizzle with 1 tablespoon olive oil. Add the dolmades, packing them tightly in one layer, then pour the remaining oil and the lemon juice over them.
5 Pour the stock over the dolmades and cover with an inverted plate to stop the dolmades moving around while cooking. Bring to the boil, then reduce the heat and simmer, covered, for 45 minutes. Remove with a slotted spoon. Serve warm or cold. These can be served with lemon wedges.
NOTE: Unused vine leaves can be stored in brine in an airtight container in the fridge for up to a week.

DOLMADES

Fold the sides of the vine leaf into the middle and roll up towards the tip.

Pack the dolmades tightly into the pan and pour on the oil and lemon juice.

When the dolmades are cooked, remove from the pan with a slotted spoon.

LEFT: Dolmades

TARAMA
Tarama, the salted, dried and pressed grey mullet roe, has been considered a great delicacy for centuries. Traditionally, intact roes were salted, dried in the sun until very firm, coated with beeswax, then eaten thinly sliced with bread, or skinned and used to make taramosalata. Combined with mashed potato and seasonings, tarama also makes delicious rissoles.

TARAMOSALATA
(Fish roe purée)

Preparation time: 10 minutes + soaking
Total cooking time: Nil
Makes 1 1/2 cups

5 slices white bread, crusts removed
1/3 cup (80 ml/2 3/4 fl oz) milk
100 g can tarama (grey mullet roe)
1 egg yolk
1/2 small onion, grated
1 clove garlic, crushed
2 tablespoons lemon juice
1/3 cup (80 ml/2 3/4 fl oz) olive oil
pinch of ground white pepper

1 Soak the bread in the milk for 10 minutes. Press in a strainer to extract excess milk, then mix in a food processor with the tarama, egg yolk, onion and garlic for 30 seconds, or until smooth. Mix in 1 tablespoon lemon juice.
2 With the motor running, slowly pour in the olive oil. The mixture should be smooth. Add the remaining lemon juice and white pepper. If the dip tastes too salty, add another piece of bread.
NOTE: Grey mullet roe is traditional but smoked cod's roe also gives a lovely flavour.

MELITZANOSALATA
(Puréed roasted eggplant/aubergine salad)

Preparation time: 25 minutes
  + 3 hours refrigeration
Total cooking time: 1 hour
Serves 6

2 large eggplants (aubergines)
2 cloves garlic, roughly chopped
4 tablespoons chopped fresh flat-leaf parsley
1 small onion, grated
1/2 red pepper (capsicum), seeded and chopped
1 large ripe tomato, finely chopped
2 small fresh red chillies, seeded
3/4 cup (60 g/2 oz) soft white breadcrumbs
1/3 cup (80 ml/2 3/4 fl oz) lemon juice
1/2 cup (125 ml/4 fl oz) good-quality olive oil
1–2 tablespoons olive oil, extra, optional
6 black olives

1 Preheat the oven to moderate 180°C (350°F/ Gas 4). Prick both the eggplants with a fork a few times and bake on a baking tray for 1 hour. Remove the skin, then roughly chop the flesh and place in a sieve to drain any excess moisture.
2 Place the eggplant, garlic, parsley, onion, red pepper, tomato, chilli, breadcrumbs, and salt and

RIGHT: Taramosalata

pepper, to taste, in a food processor and process until combined but still a little coarse.

3 With the motor running, add the lemon juice and olive oil alternately, in a steady stream, as if making mayonnaise. The mixture will thicken.

4 Transfer to a large bowl, cover and refrigerate for 3 hours to firm the mixture and infuse the flavours. To serve, spread on a large shallow serving platter, drizzle with the extra oil, if desired, and garnish with black olives.

LATHOLEMONO
(Oil and lemon dressing)

In a bowl, combine ½ cup (125 ml/4 fl oz) olive oil with ¼ cup (60 ml/2 fl oz) lemon juice and 2 teaspoons chopped fresh oregano. Season well with salt and pepper and combine again just before serving. This dressing is a perfect companion for steamed green beans, zucchini, cauliflower or any greens. It can be used to baste meat or seafood when grilling.

Makes ¾ cup (185 ml/6 fl oz).

SAGANAKI HALOUMI
(Fried haloumi cheese)

Preparation time: 5 minutes
Total cooking time: 2 minutes
Serves 6

400 g (13 oz) haloumi cheese
olive oil, for shallow-frying
2 tablespoons lemon juice

1 Pat the haloumi dry with paper towels and cut into 1 cm (½ inch) slices.

2 Pour oil into a large frying pan to 5 mm (¼ inch) depth and heat over medium heat. Add the cheese and fry for 1 minute each side, or until golden. Remove the pan from the heat and pour the lemon juice over the cheese. Season with ground black pepper. Serve straight from the pan or on a serving plate, as part of a meze spread, with crusty bread to mop up the lemon and olive oil mixture.

NOTE: Saganaki refers to the two-handled frying pan in which this dish is traditionally served.

HALOUMI
Originating in Cyprus, this salty, semi-hard sheep's milk cheese is a popular table cheese. It is often served sprinkled with mint or sliced thickly and grilled or fried, then served with a squeeze of lemon juice.

ABOVE: Saganaki haloumi

TIROPITAKIA

Mix the Gruyère, egg and pepper into the feta.

Fold the pastry over the filling to form a triangle and continue folding.

OPPOSITE PAGE, FROM TOP: Keftedes; Quail in vine leaves; Tiropitakia

KEFTEDES
(Meatballs)

Preparation time: 15 minutes
 + 1 hour refrigeration
Total cooking time: 15 minutes
Serves 4

1 egg, lightly beaten
1/2 cup (40 g/1 1/4 oz) fresh breadcrumbs
1 brown onion, finely chopped
2 tablespoons chopped fresh flat-leaf parsley
3 tablespoons chopped fresh mint
500 g (1 lb) beef or lamb mince
2 tablespoons lemon juice
plain flour, for coating
vegetable oil, for shallow-frying
lemon wedges, for serving

1 In a large bowl, mix the egg, breadcrumbs, onion, herbs, mince and lemon juice until well combined. Season well, then with wet hands, shape the mixture into large walnut-sized balls and flatten slightly. Place on a tray, cover and refrigerate for 1 hour.
2 Roll the balls in flour, shaking off any excess. In a large frying pan, heat the oil until very hot. Fry the meatballs for 3–4 minutes on each side, or until crisp and brown, being careful not to overcrowd the pan. Drain on crumpled paper towels and serve with lemon wedges.

QUAIL IN VINE LEAVES

Preparation time: 15 minutes
Total cooking time: 25 minutes
Serves 4

12 black grapes
1 tablespoon olive oil
1 clove garlic, crushed
4 large quail
8 fresh or preserved vine leaves
4 slices prosciutto
black grapes, extra, for garnish

1 Preheat the oven to moderate 180°C (350°F/ Gas 4). Cut each grape in half and toss them all with the oil and crushed garlic. Place 6 grape halves in the cavity of each quail.

2 If you are using fresh vine leaves, blanch them for 1 minute in boiling water, then remove the central stem. If using preserved vine leaves, wash them under running water to remove any excess preserving liquid.
3 Wrap each quail in a piece of prosciutto and place each on top of a vine leaf. Place another vine leaf over the top of each quail and wrap into parcels, tying with string to secure. Bake on a baking tray for 20–25 minutes, depending on the size of the quail. Serve garnished with the whole grapes.
NOTE: Vine leaves are available from speciality food stores.

TIROPITAKIA
(Cheese triangles)

Preparation time: 35 minutes
Total cooking time: 20 minutes
Makes 30

250 g (4 oz) Greek feta
180 g (6 oz) Gruyère cheese, grated
2 eggs, lightly beaten
white pepper, to taste
15 sheets filo pastry
1/2 cup (125 ml/4 fl oz) olive oil
125 g (4 oz) butter, melted

1 Preheat the oven to moderate 180°C (350°F/ Gas 4). Place the feta in a bowl and mash with a fork. Add the Gruyère, egg and pepper and mix.
2 Cut the filo sheets in halves widthways. Keep the unused pastry covered with a damp tea towel to prevent it drying out. Place one half of one sheet lengthways on a work surface. Brush with the combined oil and butter, then fold into thirds lengthways. Brush with the oil and butter.
3 Place 1 tablespoon of the cheese mixture on the corner of the pastry strip. Fold this corner over the filling to edge of pastry to form a triangle. Continue to fold until the filling is enclosed and the end of pastry is reached. Repeat with the remaining pastry and filling.
4 Place the triangles on a lightly greased baking tray and brush them with the oil and butter mixture. Bake for 20 minutes, or until crisp.
NOTE: You can easily adapt these pastries to suit your personal taste. Try using ricotta instead of gruyère and adding your favourite fresh herbs, finely chopped. Flat-leaf parsley, mint or thyme are all suitable.

4 cloves garlic, crushed
1/3 cup (50 g/1 3/4 oz) toasted pine nuts
2 tablespoons chopped fresh mint
2 tablespoons chopped fresh flat-leaf parsley
1 tablespoon chopped currants
1 cup (250 ml/8 fl oz) olive oil, extra
1/3 cup (80 ml/2 3/4 fl oz) lemon juice
extra virgin olive oil, to drizzle
lemon wedges, for serving

1   Heat the oil in a saucepan, add the onion and cook over medium heat for 10 minutes, or until golden. Add the allspice, cumin and nutmeg, and cook for 2 minutes, or until fragrant. Remove from the pan.

2   Bring a very large saucepan of water to the boil and add the bay leaves. Cut the tough outer leaves and about 5 cm (2 inches) of the core from the cabbage, then carefully add the cabbage to the boiling water. Cook it for 5 minutes, then carefully loosen a whole leaf with tongs and remove. Continue to cook and remove the leaves until you reach the core. Drain, reserving the cooking liquid and set aside to cool.

3   Take 12 leaves of equal size and cut a small 'V' from the core end of each to remove the thickest part. Trim the firm central veins so the leaf is as flat as possible. Place three-quarters of the remaining leaves on the base of a very large saucepan to prevent the rolls catching.

4   Combine the mince, onion mixture, rice, garlic, pine nuts, mint, parsley and currants in a bowl and season well. With the core end of the leaf closest to you, form 2 tablespoons of the mixture into an oval and place in the centre of the leaf. Roll up, tucking in the sides. Repeat with the remaining 11 leaves and filling. Place tightly, in a single layer, in the lined saucepan, seam-side-down.

5   Combine 2 1/2 cups (625 ml/20 fl oz) of the cooking liquid with the extra olive oil, lemon juice and 1 teaspoon salt, and pour over the rolls (the liquid should just come to the top of the rolls). Lay the remaining cabbage leaves over the top. Cover and bring to the boil over high heat, then reduce the heat and simmer for 1 hour 15 minutes, or until the mince and rice are cooked. Carefully remove from the pan with a slotted spoon, then drizzle with extra virgin olive oil. Serve with lemon wedges.

NOTE: Cabbage rolls are also delicious served with Saltsa avgolemono from page 37. You can use the cooking liquid from the cooked rolls instead of the chicken stock to make the sauce.

LAHANO DOLMATHES
(Cabbage rolls)

Preparation time: 30 minutes
Total cooking time: 1 hour 35 minutes
Makes 12 large rolls

☆ ☆ ☆

1 tablespoon olive oil
1 onion, finely chopped
large pinch of allspice
1 teaspoon ground cumin
large pinch of ground nutmeg
2 bay leaves
1 large head of cabbage
500 g (1 lb) lamb mince
1 cup (250 g/8 oz) short-grain white rice

ABOVE: Lahano dolmathes

BEETROOT WITH SKORDALIA

Preparation time: 25 minutes
Total cooking time: 55 minutes
Serves 6–8

1 kg (2 lb) medium-sized beetroot, including leaves
1/4 cup (60 ml/2 fl oz) extra virgin olive oil
1 tablespoon red wine vinegar
half quantity of skordalia (page 18), for serving

1 Cut the stems from the beetroot bulbs, leaving a short piece attached. Trim any tough tops from the leaves, then cut the leaves and stem lengths into halves or thirds and wash well.
2 Brush the bulbs to remove any dirt. Cook the beetroot in boiling salted water for 30–45 minutes, depending on their size, until tender when pierced with a sharp knife. Remove with a slotted spoon and cool slightly.
3 Return the water to the boil, add the leaves and stems, and more water if necessary, and boil for 8 minutes, or until tender. Drain and squeeze excess water from the leaves using your hands.
4 Wear rubber gloves and peel the skin from the bulbs. Cut the bulbs in halves and then into thick slices. Arrange the leaves and sliced bulbs on a serving plate. Combine the oil and vinegar and season, to taste. Drizzle over the leaves and bulbs, and serve the skordalia on the side.

PICKLED CAULIFLOWER

Preparation time: 10 minutes
Total cooking time: 10 minutes
Serves 4–6

2 cups (500 ml/16 fl oz) white wine vinegar
1 tablespoon yellow mustard seeds
1/2 teaspoon cumin seeds
3 bay leaves
3/4 cup (185 g/6 oz) caster sugar
400 g (13 oz) cauliflower, cut into florets

1 Put the white wine vinegar, mustard seeds, cumin seeds, bay leaves and sugar into a saucepan. Stir over medium heat until the sugar has dissolved. Bring to the boil, then reduce the heat and add the cauliflower. Simmer for 4 minutes, or until just tender, but still firm. Remove from the heat and leave the cauliflower to cool in the liquid. Can be served chilled or at room temperature.
NOTE: To store the cauliflower, wash a glass jar with a lid in hot soapy water, then rinse thoroughly in hot water. Place the jar in a very slow 120°C (250°F/Gas 1/2) oven to dry for about 20 minutes, or until you are ready to use it. Don't dry it with a tea towel. Put the hot liquid and cauliflower in the jar and seal while still hot. Will keep unopened for up to three months.

PICKLED VEGETABLES
The ancient art of pickling is particularly important in countries such as Greece, where seasonal availability and high temperatures make preserved foods an integral part of the diet. Born of necessity, pickles are also prized for their crisp texture and diversity, as most commonly available Mediterranean vegetables can easily be pickled. They are invariably served as part of a meze selection or as an accompaniment to main meals.

LEFT: Beetroot with skordalia

OFFAL
Although in Greece offal dishes are often associated with religious festivals such as Easter, they were historically regarded as poor people's food and formed the basis of many traditional meals. Offal such as liver and brains are suited to poaching, sautéeing, grilling and frying, although care must be taken not to overcook liver as it toughens easily.

LIVER WITH OREGANO

Preparation time: 15 minutes
Total cooking time: 10 minutes
Serves 6–8

 ☆ ☆

500 g (1 lb) lamb's liver
1/4 cup (30 g/1 oz) plain flour
1/2 teaspoon paprika
2 tablespoons olive oil
2 tablespoons lemon juice
1 teaspoon dried or chopped fresh oregano

1 Trim off any fatty deposits from the liver. Pat the liver dry with paper towels, cut into 2 cm (3/4 inch) slices and cut the larger slices in half or into thirds.
2 In a shallow dish, combine the flour, paprika and 1/2 teaspoon each of salt and cracked black pepper. Heat the oil in a frying pan over medium heat. Toss a third of the liver in the flour, shake off the excess and fry for 1 minute on each side, or until browned, but still pink inside. Drain on crumpled paper towels and place on warm plate. Repeat with the remaining liver. Cover with foil to keep it warm.
3 Remove the pan from the heat and pour in the lemon juice — it should bubble in the hot pan. When the bubbles subside, pour the pan juices over the liver and sprinkle with oregano. Serve hot.

MIALA TIGANITA
(Fried brains)

Preparation time: 20 minutes + soaking
Total cooking time: 20 minutes
Serves 6

☆

6 lamb's brains
1 tablespoon lemon juice
1/4 teaspoon whole white or black peppercorns
plain flour, seasoned, for coating
olive oil, for frying
chopped fresh flat-leaf parsley,
   to garnish
lemon wedges, for serving

1 Soak the brains in cold, salted water for 30 minutes. Drain, then peel off the membrane and discard all the bloody parts. Place the rest in a saucepan. Cover with cold water and add the lemon juice, peppercorns and 1 teaspoon salt. Bring to a gentle simmer, cover and cook for 15 minutes, or until tender. Do not boil.
2 Drain the brains and pat dry with paper towels. Cut into 1 cm (1/2 inch) slices and coat with the flour. Pour the oil into a heavy-based frying pan to a depth of 1 cm (1/2 inch), heat the oil and fry the brains until golden brown. Drain on paper towels, then season, to taste. Sprinkle with parsley and serve with lemon wedges.

RIGHT: Liver with oregano

KALAMARIA TOURSI
(Pickled squid)

Preparation time: 25 minutes
+ 1 week maturing
Total cooking time: 5 minutes
Serves 4

1 kg (2 lb) small squid
4 fresh bay leaves
4 sprigs of fresh oregano
10 whole black peppercorns
2 teaspoons coriander seeds
1 small fresh red chilli, halved and seeded
2¹/₂ cups (625 ml/20 fl oz) good-quality
  white wine vinegar
2–3 tablespoons olive oil, to top up the jar

1 To prepare the squid, grasp each squid body in one hand and the head and tentacles in the other and pull apart to separate them. Cut the tentacles from the head by cutting below the eyes. Discard the head. Push out the beak and discard. Pull the quill from inside the body and discard. Under cold running water, pull away the skin (the flaps can be used). Cut into 7 mm (³/₈ inch) rings.

2 Place 2 litres water and 1 bay leaf in a large saucepan. Bring to the boil and add the calamari and 1 teaspoon salt. Reduce the heat and simmer for 5 minutes. Drain and dry well.

3 Pack the squid rings into a clean (see Note), dry 2 cup (500 ml/16 fl oz) jar with a sealing lid. Add the oregano, peppercorns, coriander seeds, chilli and remaining bay leaves. Cover completely with the vinegar then gently pour in enough olive oil to cover by 2 cm (³/4 inch). Seal and refrigerate for 1 week before opening. When you are ready to serve, remove from the marinade, place on a serving dish and garnish with lemon wedges and chopped fresh parsley.

NOTE: Wash the storage jar and lid in hot soapy water, rinse them well in hot water and then dry in a very slow 120°C (250°F/Gas ¹/2) oven for 20 minutes. Do not dry with a tea towel.

NATURAL YOGHURT

Pour 1 litre of milk into a saucepan, bring slowly to the boil over low heat and simmer for 5 minutes, stirring frequently. Remove from the heat and set aside to cool until lukewarm. Gently stir ¹/4 cup (60 ml/ 2 fl oz) of natural yoghurt into the milk, then pour into a large bowl. Cover the bowl with plastic wrap and wrap the bowl in a thick cloth or towel. This keeps the heat in, thus helping the culture in the yoghurt to ferment the milk. Leave in a warm place for up to 12 hours, until the yoghurt has thickened. Don't leave the yoghurt to stand any longer because it will progressively become more acidic. Refrigerate for at least 4 hours before using. Makes 1 litre. To make another lot of yoghurt, you can use ¹/4 cup (60 g/2 oz) of your home-made yoghurt as a starter.

ABOVE: Kalamaria toursi

GREEK SALAD
What is widely known as Greek salad is but one of the numerous salads served in Greece. Its Greek name, *salata horiatiki*, translates as Greek country or village salad. It is a rustic salad with tomato, cucumber, feta cheese, olives and peppers (capsicums) as its staple ingredients, although cos lettuce, anchovy fillets, flat-leaf parsley, capers and a sprinkle of oregano are not unusual additions.

ABOVE: Greek salad

SALATA HORIATIKI
(Greek salad)

Preparation time: 20 minutes
Total cooking time: Nil
Serves 4

☆

1 telegraph cucumber, peeled
2 green peppers (capsicums)
4 vine-ripened tomatoes, cut into wedges
1 red onion, finely sliced
16 Kalamata olives
250 g (8 oz) Greek feta, cubed
24 fresh flat-leaf parsley leaves
12 whole fresh mint leaves
1/2 cup (125 ml/4 fl oz) good-quality olive oil
2 tablespoons lemon juice
1 clove garlic, crushed

1 Cut the cucumber in half lengthways and discard the seeds. Cut into bite-sized pieces. Cut each pepper in half lengthways, remove the membrane and seeds and cut the flesh into 1 cm (1/2 inch) wide strips. Gently mix the cucumber, green pepper, tomato, onion, olives, feta, parsley and mint leaves in a large salad bowl.
2 Place the oil, lemon juice and garlic in a screw top jar, season and shake well. Pour over the salad and serve.

EGGPLANT (AUBERGINE) SALAD

Preparation time: 20 minutes + 30 minutes draining
Total cooking time: 1 hour 35 minutes
Serves 6

☆

1 kg (2 lb) large eggplants (aubergines)
1/2 cup (125 ml/4 fl oz) olive oil
1 brown onion, finely chopped
1/2 teaspoon ground cinnamon
4 cloves garlic, crushed
2 x 400 g (13 oz) cans good-quality crushed tomatoes
2 tablespoons chopped fresh coriander
3 tablespoons chopped fresh flat-leaf parsley
1 tablespoon lemon juice
2 tablespoons chopped fresh mint
150 g (5 oz) Greek-style natural yoghurt
25 g (3/4 oz) toasted pine nuts

1 Cut the eggplants into 2 cm (3/4 inch) cubes, place in a colander over a bowl and sprinkle generously with salt. Leave for 30 minutes, rinse under cold water, then pat dry with a tea towel.
2 Heat 2 tablespoons oil in a large frying pan and fry batches of eggplant until golden, adding more oil if necessary. Drain on paper towels.
3 Heat another 2 tablespoons oil in the pan and fry the onion for 1 minute. Add the cinnamon

and half the garlic, cook for 1 minute, then add the tomato. Add the eggplant and simmer, uncovered, for 1 hour, or until the mixture is quite dry. Add half of each of the coriander and parsley. Stir and leave to cool.

4 Mix 2 tablespoons of oil with the lemon juice and add the remaining crushed garlic and all the mint, then stir into the yoghurt.

5 Gently toss the pine nuts through the salad and garnish with the remaining fresh herbs. Serve at room temperature with the garlic yoghurt dressing.

HALOUMI WITH SALAD AND GARLIC BREAD

Preparation time: 20 minutes
Total cooking time: 5 minutes
Serves 4

4 firm, ripe tomatoes
1 Lebanese cucumber
140 g (4¹/₂ oz) rocket (arugula)
¹/₂ cup (80 g/2³/₄ oz) Kalamata olives
1 loaf crusty unsliced white bread

5 tablespoons olive oil
1 large clove garlic, cut in half
400 g (13 oz) haloumi cheese
1 tablespoon lemon juice
1 tablespoon chopped fresh oregano

1 Preheat the oven to moderate 180°C (350°F/ Gas 4). Heat the grill to high.

2 Cut the tomatoes and cucumber into bite-sized chunks and place in a serving dish with the rocket and olives. Mix well.

3 Slice the bread into eight 1.5 cm (⁵/₈ inch) slices, drizzle 1¹/₂ tablespoons of the olive oil over the bread and season with salt and pepper. Grill until lightly golden, then rub each slice thoroughly with a cut side of the garlic. Wrap loosely in foil and keep warm in the oven.

4 Cut the haloumi into 8 slices. Heat ¹/₂ tablespoon of the oil in a shallow frying pan and fry the haloumi slices for 1–2 minutes on each side, until crisp and golden brown.

5 Whisk together the lemon juice, oregano and remaining olive oil to use as a dressing. Season, to taste. Pour half the dressing over the salad and toss well. Arrange the haloumi on top and drizzle with dressing. Serve immediately with the warm garlic bread.

KALAMATA OLIVES
Hailing from Kalamata in the southern Peloponnese, these almond-shaped olives are considered to be Greece's best due to the fruity, rich flavour and firm flesh. Packed in either olive oil or wine vinegar to accentuate their robust taste, they are often found on a meze plate, and in salads, sauces and breads.

LEFT: Haloumi with salad and garlic bread

BARBECUED QUAIL

Using poultry shears, cut down the sides of the backbones of the quails.

Place the quails on the work surface and gently press them down flat.

Cut each quail in half through the breast, then cut each half in half again.

BARBECUED QUAIL

Preparation time: 30 minutes
+ 3 hours chilling
Total cooking time: 10 minutes
Serves 6

☆ ☆

6 quails
1 cup (250 ml/8 fl oz) dry red wine
2 sticks celery, including tops, chopped
1 carrot, chopped
1 small onion, chopped
1 bay leaf, torn into small pieces
1 teaspoon allspice
1 teaspoon dried thyme
2 cloves garlic, crushed
2 tablespoons olive oil
2 tablespoons lemon juice
1 lemon, cut into wedges,
   for serving

1   To prepare the quails, use poultry shears to cut down either side of the backbone on each quail, then discard the backbone. Remove the innards, wash the insides of the quails and pat dry with paper towels. Place the quails breast-side-up on the bench, open them out flat and gently press to flatten. With the poultry shears, cut each quail in half through the breast, then cut each quail half in half again, into the thigh and drumstick piece and breast and wing piece.

2   In a non-metallic bowl, combine the wine, celery, carrot, onion, bay leaf and allspice. Add the quail and stir to coat. Cover and marinate in the refrigerator for 3 hours, or preferably overnight, stirring occasionally. Drain and sprinkle with thyme and some salt and pepper.

3   Whisk the garlic, oil and lemon juice together in a small bowl.

4   Heat a lightly oiled barbecue plate until hot or heat a grill to its highest setting. Reduce the heat to medium and cook the quail breast pieces for 4–5 minutes on each side and the drumstick pieces for 3 minutes on each side, or until tender and cooked through. Brush frequently with the lemon mixture during cooking. Serve hot, with lemon wedges.

NOTE: The golden rule with quail is not to overcook them, otherwise the flesh becomes hard and tough. When cooked correctly quail will be still pink on the breast. If quail are unavailable you can use squab, which can be prepared in exactly the same manner and require a similar cooking time.

RIGHT: Barbecued quail

LENTIL AND BURGHUL FRITTERS WITH YOGHURT SAUCE

Preparation time: 20 minutes
+ 1 hour 30 minutes standing
Total cooking time: 1 hour
Makes 35

3/4 cup (140 g/4 1/2 oz) brown lentils, rinsed
1/2 cup (90 g/3 oz) burghul
1/3 cup (80 ml/2 3/4 fl oz) olive oil
1 onion, finely chopped
2 cloves garlic, finely chopped
3 teaspoons ground cumin
2 teaspoons ground coriander
3 tablespoons finely chopped fresh mint
4 eggs, lightly beaten
1/2 cup (60 g/2 oz) plain flour
1 teaspoon sea salt

YOGHURT SAUCE
1 small Lebanese cucumber, peeled
1 cup (250 g/8 oz) Greek-style natural yoghurt
1–2 cloves garlic, crushed

1 Place the lentils in a saucepan with 2 1/2 cups (625 ml/20 fl oz) water. Bring to the boil over high heat, then reduce the heat and simmer for 30 minutes, or until tender. Remove from the heat and top up with enough water to just cover the lentils. Pour in the burghul, cover and leave to stand for 1 1/2 hours, or until the burghul has expanded.

2 For the yoghurt sauce, halve the cucumber lengthways, remove the seeds with a teaspoon and discard. Grate the flesh and mix in a bowl with the yoghurt and garlic.

3 Heat half the oil in a large frying pan over medium heat, add the onion and garlic and cook for 5 minutes, or until soft. Stir in the cumin and coriander. Add the onion mixture, mint, eggs, flour and sea salt to the lentil mixture and mix well. The mixture should hold together enough to drop spoonfuls into the frying pan. If the mixture is too wet, add flour to bind.

4 Heat the remaining oil over medium heat in the cleaned frying pan. Drop heaped tablespoons of mixture into the pan (the fritters should be about 5 cm/2 inches in diameter) and cook for 3 minutes each side, or until browned. Drain on crumpled paper towels, season with salt and serve with the yoghurt sauce.

BAKED SARDINES

Preheat the oven to hot 210°C (415°F/ Gas 6–7). Clean 6 fresh whole sardines by scraping a small knife along the body of the sardine, starting from the tail end to remove any scales (this is best done under running water). Make a slit along the gut. Cut the head, leaving it slightly attached, and pull away slowly — the intestines should come away with the head. Open the gut cavity and clean away any remaining intestines. Pat dry and drain on paper towels. Put the sardines in an ovenproof dish, large enough to fit them snuggly in one layer, and season with salt and 1/2 teaspoon pepper. Drizzle with 3 tablespoons oil and 2 tablespoons lemon juice and sprinkle with 1 small chopped clove garlic and 1 1/2 teaspoons dried oregano. Turn to coat, then bake, uncovered, in the top half of the oven for 12–15 minutes, or until the flesh flakes and starts to come away from the bones. Serve hot or warm with lemon wedges. Serves 6.

ABOVE: Lentil and burghul fritters with yoghurt sauce

CHICKPEAS

Legumes play a vital role in the famed health-enhancing Mediterranean diet. Chickpeas were first grown in the Levant and ancient Egypt and have become an important food in many countries. They are the basis of many very popular Mediterranean dishes. Dried chickpeas should be soaked in cold water before they are cooked. This reduces the cooking time.

FRIED CHICKPEAS

Preparation time: 30 minutes
  + overnight soaking
Total cooking time: 15 minutes
Serves 6

☆☆

1¼ cups (275 g/9 oz) dried chickpeas
oil, for deep-frying
½ teaspoon paprika
¼ teaspoon cayenne pepper

1 Soak the chickpeas overnight in plenty of cold water. Drain well and pat dry with paper towels.
2 Fill a deep saucepan one third full of oil and heat to 180°C (350°F), or until a cube of bread dropped into the oil browns in 15 seconds. Deep-fry half the chickpeas for 3 minutes. Remove with a slotted spoon, drain on crumpled towels and repeat with the rest of the chickpeas. Partially cover the saucepan as some of the chickpeas may pop. Don't leave the oil unattended.
3 Deep-fry the chickpeas again in batches for 3 minutes each batch, or until browned. Drain well again on crumpled paper towels. Combine the paprika and cayenne pepper with a little salt and sprinkle the mixture over the hot chickpeas. Allow to cool before serving.

ABOVE: Fried chickpeas

FAVA

(Split pea purée)

Preparation time: 5 minutes
Total cooking time: 1 hour 15 minutes
Serves 4–6

☆

3 tablespoons olive oil
1 brown onion, finely chopped
1½ cups (330 g/11 oz) dried yellow split peas, rinsed
1–2 tablespoons lemon juice
2 tablespoons baby capers, rinsed, to garnish
60 g (2 oz) Greek feta, crumbled, to garnish
2 tablespoons extra virgin olive oil, for serving
1 lemon, cut into small wedges, for serving

1 Heat the oil in a large heavy-based saucepan over medium heat and cook the onion for 5 minutes, or until softened.
2 Add the split peas and 1.25 litres water to the pan and bring to the boil. Reduce the heat, then cover and simmer, stirring frequently to prevent catching on the base of the saucepan, for 45–50 minutes, or until the peas are very tender and falling apart. Uncover and cook for 15–20 minutes, or until the mixture has reduced and thickened. Season with salt and pepper, to taste, and stir in the lemon juice.

3 Serve warm or at room temperature, garnished with capers and feta. Drizzle olive oil over the top. Serve with lemon wedges. Delicious served with crusty bread.

MUSSELS SAGANAKI

Preparation time: 45 minutes
Total cooking time: 25 minutes
Serves 6

750 g (1 1/2 lb) black mussels
1/2 cup (125 ml/4 fl oz) dry white wine
3 sprigs of fresh thyme
1 bay leaf
1 tablespoon olive oil
1 large onion, finely chopped
1 clove garlic, finely chopped
420 g (14 oz) ripe tomatoes, peeled and very finely chopped
2 tablespoons tomato paste (tomato purée)
1/2 teaspoon sugar
1 tablespoon red wine vinegar
70 g (2 1/4 oz) Greek feta, crumbled
1 teaspoon fresh thyme leaves

1 Scrub the mussels with a stiff brush and pull out the hairy beards. Discard any broken mussels, or open ones that don't close when tapped on the bench. Rinse well.
2 Bring the wine, thyme and bay leaf to the boil in a large pan, add the mussels and cook for 4–5 minutes, or until just opened. Pour the mussel liquid through a strainer into a heatproof jug and reserve. Discard any unopened mussels. Remove the top half shell from each mussel and discard.
3 Heat the oil in a saucepan, add the onion and stir over medium heat for 3 minutes. Add the garlic and cook for 1 minute, or until turning golden. Pour in the reserved mussel liquid, increase the heat and bring to the boil, then boil for 2 minutes, or until almost dry. Add the tomato, tomato paste and sugar, then reduce the heat and simmer for 5 minutes. Add the vinegar and simmer for another 5 minutes.
4 Add the mussels to the saucepan and cook over medium heat for 1 minute, or until heated through. Spoon into a warm serving dish. Top with the crumbled feta and fresh thyme leaves. Serve hot.
NOTE: Saganaki refers to the utensil used to cook the food in. It is a frying pan with two handles, used for cooking a range of meze as it can be transferred from stovetop to table. Any pan of a suitable size can be used.

MUSSELS SAGANAKI

Fresh mussels must be thoroughly scrubbed with a stiff brush to remove any grit or weed.

After scrubbing, pull out the hairy beards. Discard any broken or open mussels, or those that don't close when tapped on the bench.

LEFT: Mussels saganaki

MEZE

Like Spain's tapas and Italy's antipasto, the countries of the Middle East and Levant have a tradition of little dishes to be eaten before a meal or as a meal in their own right. Whether they are enjoyed as mezethakia in Greece, meze in Turkey and the Middle East or mukabalatt in the Maghreb countries of Morocco, Tunisia and Algeria, meze play a part in the culture of communal eating and entertaining.

ORIGINS OF MEZE
Derived from the word meaning 'half', meze refers to individual dishes as well as the style of eating. In the region's non-Muslim communities, the habit of eating a variety of small dishes originated from the custom of not drinking alcohol without having food to nibble on. Even in bars and restaurants, wine, beer, raki, ouzo and arak are accompanied by a few dishes such as slices of melon, feta cheese, olives and bread. Visitors to Greece are pleasantly surprised, when ordering ouzo in a bar, to receive a complimentary mezethakia plate with feta, olives and sliced tomato. In Greece there is a specific grade of taverna called mezepoulio, which only serve mezethakia. The close connection between eating and drinking is also demonstrated in Turkey where a meze table is commonly referred to as a raki table.

In communities where alcohol is not consumed, meze platters are served with coffee or syrups. It is not uncommon for Jewish families to share a meze table after the Sabbath or festival morning services.

Meze are integral to the Levantine lifestyle and many social gatherings are conducted around a meze table. Once they were only eaten in wealthy households or restaurants and for special occasions such as religious holidays and weddings. However, today they are a common feature of everyday household hospitality. Many modern larders contain the fundamentals of a meze selection including cheeses, sausages, olives, home-made pickles and dips, fresh tomatoes and

cucumbers in readiness for unexpected guests. The homes of keen cooks often contain freezers filled with bread doughs and filled filo pastries which can be heated as required.

Meze dishes are an ideal showcase for the Mediterranean region's quintessential flavours such as olives, olive oil, eggplant (aubergine), garlic, cheese, chickpeas, yoghurt, nuts, tomatoes and seafood. Many of the most popular meze dishes have crossed over from street food, with felafel, hummus, meatballs and baba ghannouj being some of the more well-known examples.

The mixture of textures, tastes and aromas are limitless so it is important to consider a contrast of colours and flavours when choosing a meze selection. It is also common to combine cooked and uncooked dishes. Some dishes are served hot and others at room temperature.

The dishes range from salads, dips, breads, nuts, pastries, stuffed vine leaves, marinated or pickled seafood and suitable condiments.

WHAT CONSTITUTES MEZE?

Essentially, any regional dish that can be served in small portions can be part of a meze table. Many meze dishes double as accompaniments to main dishes, making the crossover between courses of a meal more fluid and flexible. Many restaurants in the region compete with the number of meze dishes offered, with some serving upwards of seventy dishes to lure customers.

Although intended as appetizers, the ritual of nibbling meze can stretch over several hours, especially at parties where the range of dishes is so inviting.

While meze can be as simple as a bowl of mixed fresh herbs accompanied by nuts, more elaborate dishes often feature. Dishes such as Keftedes (Meatballs) (page 22) and the Turkish speciality Cerkes tavagu (Circassian chicken) (page 78) are fiddly to make but more filling.

Although the choices are endless, it may be necessary to limit the number of dishes, especially when serving before a large meal, as they are meant to whet the appetite, not satisfy it. Depending on the number of dishes, meze can, however, constitute a whole meal or can be eaten with drinks at any time of the day.

CLOKWISE, FROM TOP LEFT:
Skordalia (page18); Lubyi bi zayt (page 66);
Saganaki haloumi (page 21); Taramosalata
(page 20); Dolmades (page 19); Hummus
(page 64); Kalamaria tiganita (page 49)
AT BACK: Turkish bread

KAKAVIA

Although bouillabaise is the most famous of a large number of Mediterranean fish stew or soup dishes, there are many others, including the Greek version, Kakavia. It is named after the kakavi, a three-legged cooking pot taken by ancient Ionians on their fishing expeditions. This version was always filled with the smallest fish from the catch, olive oil, onions and saffron. Today, it is still made with whatever small fish are available but tomatoes, rather than saffron, are used for colour.

KAKAVIA

Preparation time: 20 minutes
Total cooking time: 20 minutes
Serves 6

2 onions, finely sliced
400 g (13 oz) can good-quality chopped tomatoes
750 g (1 1/2 lb) potatoes, cut into 5 mm (1/4 inch) slices
1 teaspoon chopped fresh oregano
150 ml (5 fl oz) olive oil
2 litres fish or vegetable stock
1.5 kg (3 lb) white fish fillets, such as cod, jewfish or snapper, cut into chunks
500 g (1 lb) raw prawn meat
1/2 cup (125 ml/4 fl oz) lemon juice
chopped fresh flat-leaf parsley, to garnish

1 Layer the onion, tomato and potato in a large heavy-based saucepan, seasoning with salt, pepper and oregano between each layer. Add the oil and stock and bring the mixture to the boil. Reduce the heat and simmer for 10 minutes, or until the potato is cooked through and tender.
2 Add the fish and prawn meat and cook for 5 minutes, or until the seafood is cooked. Add the juice, spoon into bowls and top with parsley.

CANNELLINI BEAN SOUP

Preparation time: 20 minutes + overnight soaking
Total cooking time: 1 hour 15 minutes
Serves 8

500 g (1 lb 2 oz) dried cannellini beans
2 tablespoons olive oil
2 onions, chopped
2 cloves garlic, crushed
450 g (1 lb) ripe tomatoes, peeled and chopped
3 tablespoons tomato passata
2 large carrots (400 g/13 oz), diced
2 sticks celery, (200 g/7 oz), trimmed and diced
1.75 litres vegetable or chicken stock
2 bay leaves
2 tablespoons lemon juice
1/2 cup (30 g/1 oz) chopped fresh flat-leaf parsley

1 Place the beans in a bowl, cover with cold water and leave to soak overnight.
2 Drain the beans and rinse under cold water. Heat the oil in a 5 litre saucepan. Add the onion, reduce the heat and cook gently for 10 minutes, stirring occasionally. Stir in the garlic and cook for 1 minute.
3 Add the cannellini beans, chopped tomato, passata, carrot, celery and stock. Stir and add the

RIGHT: Kakavia

bay leaves. Bring to the boil, then reduce the heat to medium–low and simmer, covered, for 45–60 minutes, or until the beans are tender.

5 Stir in the lemon juice and season, to taste, with salt and pepper. Stir in some of the parsley and use the rest as a garnish.

NOTE: This soup makes a perfect entertaining option. It can be made a day ahead as the flavour improves with time. Reheat over low heat and if too thick, add a little water.

AVGOLEMONO SOUP WITH CHICKEN

Preparation time: 20 minutes
Total cooking time: 30 minutes
Serves 4

☆ ☆

1 onion, halved

2 cloves

1 carrot, cut into chunks

1 bay leaf

500 g (1 lb) chicken breast fillets

1/3 cup (75 g/2 1/2 oz) short-grain rice

3 eggs, separated

3 tablespoons lemon juice

2 tablespoons chopped fresh flat-leaf parsley

4 thin lemon slices, to garnish

1 Stud the onion with the cloves and place in a large saucepan with 1.5 litres water. Add the carrot, bay leaf and chicken and season with salt and freshly ground black pepper. Slowly bring to the boil, then reduce the heat and simmer for 10 minutes, or until the chicken is cooked.

2 Strain the stock into a clean saucepan, reserving the chicken and discarding the vegetables. Add the rice to the stock, bring to the boil, then reduce the heat and simmer for 15 minutes, or until the rice is tender. Meanwhile, tear the chicken into shreds.

3 Whisk the egg whites in a clean dry bowl until stiff peaks form, then beat in the yolks. Slowly beat in the lemon juice. Gently stir in about 150 ml (5 fl oz) of the hot (not boiling) stock and beat thoroughly. Add the egg mixture to the stock and heat gently, but do not let it boil otherwise the eggs may scramble. Add the chicken and season with salt and black pepper.

4 Set aside for 2–3 minutes to allow the flavours to develop, then sprinkle the parsley over the top. Garnish with the lemon slices.

SALTSA AVGOLEMONO
(Egg and lemon sauce)

Bring 1 1/2 cups (375 ml/12 fl oz) chicken stock to the boil in a small saucepan. Mix 1 tablespoon cornflour with enough cold water to make a paste. Add to the stock and stir until the mixture thickens. Simmer for 2–3 minutes, then remove from the heat and cool slightly. Separate 3 eggs and beat the whites in a large bowl until stiff peaks form. Add the yolks and beat until light and fluffy. Mix in 2–3 tablespoons lemon juice. Gradually pour in the thickened stock, beating constantly. Return the sauce to the pan and cook over low heat, stirring constantly for 1–2 minutes. Season, to taste, remove from the heat and stir for 1 minute. Pour immediately over the dish it is to dress. Serve with Dolmades (page 19), Lahano Dolmathes (page 24), poached fish or steamed vegetables. Serves 4.

ABOVE: Avgolemono soup with chicken

PSARI PLAKI
(Baked fish with tomato and onion)

Preparation time: 20 minutes
Total cooking time: 45 minutes
Serves 4

1/4 cup (60 ml/2 fl oz) olive oil
2 onions, finely chopped
1 small stick celery, finely chopped
1 small carrot, finely chopped
2 cloves garlic, chopped
400 g (13 oz) can good-quality chopped tomatoes
2 tablespoons tomato passata
1/4 teaspoon dried oregano
1/2 teaspoon sugar
50 g (2 oz) white bread, preferably one day old
500 g (1 lb 2 oz) white fish fillets or steaks, such as snapper or cod
3 tablespoons chopped fresh flat-leaf parsley
1 tablespoon fresh lemon juice

1 Preheat the oven to moderate 180°C (350°F/ Gas 4). Heat 2 tablespoons of the oil in a heavy-based frying pan. Add the onion, celery and carrot and cook over low heat for 10 minutes, or until soft. Add the garlic, cook for 2 minutes, then add the chopped tomato, passata, oregano and sugar. Simmer for about 10 minutes, stirring occasionally, until reduced and thickened. Season, to taste.

2 To make the breadcrumbs, chop the bread in a food processor for a few minutes, until fine crumbs form.

3 Arrange the fish in a single layer in a baking dish. Stir the chopped parsley and the lemon juice into the sauce. Season, to taste, and pour over the fish. Scatter the breadcrumbs all over the top and drizzle with the remaining oil. Bake for 20 minutes, or until the fish is just cooked.

SPANAKORIZO
(Spinach rice)

Preparation time: 15 minutes
Total cooking time: 30 minutes
Serves 6

400 g (13 oz) English spinach
6 spring onions
2 tablespoons olive oil
1 large onion, chopped
2 cloves garlic, crushed

ABOVE: Psari plaki

1½ cups (330 g/11 oz) short- or
   medium-grain rice
2 tablespoons lemon juice
1 tablespoon chopped fresh dill
1 tablespoon chopped fresh flat-leaf parsley
1½ cups (375 ml/12 fl oz) vegetable stock

1 Wash the spinach in several changes of water,
tear the leaves and chop the stalks. Finely chop
the spring onions, including the green tops.
2 Heat the olive oil in a large, wide casserole
dish. Add the onion and garlic and cook for
5–7 minutes over medium heat, until soft.
Add the spring onion and rice, stir to coat
and cook for 2 minutes, stirring constantly.
Add the spinach, 1 tablespoon lemon juice
and the herbs. Season well. Stir in the stock
and 1½ cups (375 ml/12 fl oz) water. Cover,
bring to the boil, then reduce the heat to low
and cook for 15 minutes.
3 Remove from the heat and set aside for
5 minutes. Stir in the remaining lemon juice
and adjust the seasoning.
NOTE: Silverbeet (Swiss chard) can be used as an
alternative to English spinach. Rinse the silverbeet,
then cut off the thick stems and roughly chop
the leaves. Blanch the leaves in a large pan of
boiling, salted water. Rinse under cold water.

LEMONY CHICKEN

Preparation time: 10 minutes
Total cooking time: 45 minutes
Serves 4

3 tablespoons olive oil
1 kg (2 lb) chicken drumsticks, seasoned
1 large leek, halved, washed and thinly sliced
4 large strips lemon rind, white pith removed
½ cup (125 ml/4 fl oz) fresh lemon juice
1 cup (250 ml/8 fl oz) dry white wine
500 g (1 lb) baby carrots, trimmed

1 In a large heavy-based frying pan, heat the
oil and sauté the chicken in two batches, for
6–8 minutes each batch, or until brown and
crispy. Return all the chicken to the pan, add
the leek and cook until the leek is just wilted.
Add the lemon rind and cook for 1–2 minutes.
2 Pour the lemon juice and wine into the pan
and allow the flavours to combine for a few
seconds. Stir, add the carrots, then cover and
cook for 30–35 minutes, stirring occasionally,
until the chicken is cooked. Remove the rind,
then taste and adjust the seasoning if necessary.

LEMONS
Lemons pervade all
elements of Greek cooking,
as they do in the cooking
in many other parts of the
Mediterranean. The juice is
used when roasting and
stewing meat, poultry and
vegetables, and as a key
ingredient in Avgolemono
soup, the Greek egg and
lemon soup. Wedges of
lemon are squeezed over
cooked or raw vegetables
and grilled or fried seafood,
meat or cheese. The peel is
preserved in sugar and used
as sweetmeats. To extract
the most juice, choose
lemons with thin skins, then
soften them by rolling with
the palm of your hand on
a benchtop.

LEFT: Lemony chicken

STIFATHO
(Spiced beef and onions)

Preparation time: 15 minutes
Total cooking time: 1 hour 30 minutes
Serves 4

1 kg (2 lb) chuck steak
1/4 cup (60 ml/2 fl oz) olive oil
750 g (1 1/2 lb) whole baby onions
3 cloves garlic, cut in half lengthways
1/2 cup (125 ml/4 fl oz) red wine
1 cinnamon stick
4 whole cloves
1 bay leaf
1 tablespoon red wine vinegar
2 tablespoons tomato paste (tomato purée)
2 tablespoons currants

1   Trim the meat of excess fat and sinew, then cut into bite-sized cubes. Heat the oil over medium heat in a large heavy-based saucepan.

Add the onions and stir for 5 minutes, or until golden. Remove from the pan and drain on paper towels.
2   Add the meat all at once to the pan and stir over high heat for 10 minutes, or until the meat is well browned and almost all the liquid has been absorbed.
3   Add the garlic, wine, spices, bay leaf, vinegar, tomato paste, 1/4 teaspoon cracked black pepper, some salt and 1 1/2 cups (375 ml/12 fl oz) water to the pan and bring to the boil. Reduce the heat, cover and simmer for 1 hour, stirring occasionally.
4   Return the onions to the saucepan, add the currants and stir gently. Simmer, covered, for 15 minutes. Discard the cinnamon before serving. Serve with rice, bread or potatoes.
NOTE: For a richer flavour, use 1 1/2 cups (375 ml/12 fl oz) beef or veal stock instead of water in this recipe, or 1 cup (250 ml/8 fl oz) each of wine and water.

SOFRITO
(Veal cooked with vinegar)

Preparation time: 10 minutes
Total cooking time: 1 hour 50 minutes
Serves 6–8

1/2 cup (60 g/2 oz) plain flour
large pinch of cayenne pepper
1 kg (2 lb) veal steaks
1/4 cup (60 ml/2 fl oz) olive oil
1 bay leaf
5 cloves garlic, crushed
2/3 cup (170 ml/5 1/2 fl oz) red wine vinegar
2 1/2 cups (625 ml/20 fl oz) beef stock
chopped flat-leaf parsley, for serving

1   Combine the flour with the cayenne and season well with salt and pepper. Lightly coat the veal with the flour, shaking off any excess.
2   Heat the oil in a large, deep frying pan over high heat and cook the veal a few pieces at a time for 1 minute on each side, or until lightly browned. Remove from the pan and set aside.
3   Add the bay leaf, garlic, red wine vinegar and stock to the pan and bring to the boil, scraping up any residue from the base of the pan. Reduce the heat to low and return the veal and any juices back to the pan. Cover and cook, stirring gently occasionally, for 1 1/2 hours, or until the veal is very tender and sauce is thickened. If the

BELOW: Stifatho

sauce is too watery, carefully transfer the veal to a serving platter and boil the sauce until it is the consistency of a smooth gravy. Sprinkle with parsley before serving.

CHICKEN PIE

Preparation time: 30 minutes
Total cooking time: 1 hour 10 minutes
Serves 6

1 kg (2 lb) boneless skinless chicken breasts
2 cups (500 ml/16 fl oz) chicken stock
60 g (2 oz) butter
2 spring onions, trimmed and finely chopped
1/2 cup (60 g/2 1/2 oz) plain flour
1/2 cup (125 ml/4 fl oz) milk
8 sheets filo pastry (40 x 30 cm/16 x 12 inches)
60 g (2 oz) butter, extra, melted
200 g (7 oz) feta, crumbled
1 tablespoon chopped fresh dill
1 tablespoon chopped fresh chives
1/4 teaspoon ground nutmeg
1 egg, lightly beaten

1 Cut the chicken into bite-sized pieces. Pour the stock into a saucepan and bring to the boil over high heat. Reduce the heat to low, add the chicken and poach gently for 10–15 minutes, or until the chicken is cooked through. Drain, reserving the stock. Add water to the stock to bring the quantity up to 2 cups (500 ml/ 16 fl oz). Preheat the oven to moderate 180°C (350°F/Gas 4).

2 Melt the butter in a saucepan over low heat, add the spring onion and cook, stirring, for 5 minutes. Add the flour and stir for 30 seconds. Remove the pan from the heat and gradually add the chicken stock and milk, stirring after each addition. Return to the heat and gently bring to the boil, stirring. Simmer for a few minutes, or until the sauce thickens. Remove from the heat.

3 Line a baking dish measuring 25 x 18 x 4 cm (10 x 7 x 1 1/2 inches) with 4 sheets of filo pastry, brushing one side of each sheet with melted butter as you go. Place the buttered side down. The filo will overlap the edges of the dish. Cover the unused filo with a damp tea towel to prevent it drying out.

4 Stir the chicken, feta, dill, chives, nutmeg and egg into the sauce. Season, to taste, with salt and freshly ground black pepper. Pile the mixture on top of the filo pastry in the dish. Fold the overlapping filo over the filling and cover the top of the pie with the remaining 4 sheets of filo, brushing each sheet with melted butter as you go. Scrunch the edges of the filo so they fit in the dish. Brush the top with butter. Bake for 45–50 minutes, or until the pastry is golden brown and crisp.

NOTE: If you prefer, you can use puff pastry instead of filo. If you do so, bake in a hot 220°C (425°F/Gas 7) oven for 15 minutes, then reduce the temperature to moderate 180°C (350°F/ Gas 4) and cook for another 30 minutes, or until the pastry is golden.

ABOVE: Chicken pie

RED MULLET IN VINE LEAVES

Preparation time: 20 minutes
  + 30 minutes draining
Total cooking time: 15 minutes
Serves 4 as a first course

☆ ☆

4 large vine-ripened tomatoes
2 cloves garlic, crushed
4 anchovy fillets, chopped
4 tablespoons chopped fresh flat-leaf
  parsley
2 tablespoons chopped fresh basil
4 Kalamata olives, pitted and chopped
4 red mullet (about 250 g/8 oz each),
  cleaned and scaled
8 preserved vine leaves
1 tablespoon olive oil
1 tablespoon lemon juice
lemon wedges, to garnish

1 Score a cross in the base of each tomato.
Place the tomatoes in a bowl of boiling water
for 10 seconds, then plunge into cold water and
peel each down from the cross. Scoop out the
seeds with a teaspoon. Finely chop the flesh,
then place the tomatoes in a sieve over a bowl
and leave to drain for 30 minutes to remove
excess moisture. Preheat the oven to moderate
180°C (350°F/Gas 4).
2 Discard the drained liquid, then place the
tomatoes in the bowl and add the garlic,
anchovies, parsley, basil and olives. Season
with salt and pepper.
3 Season the fish well inside and out, then
stuff each fish with ½ tablespoon of the
tomato mixture.
4 Rinse the vine leaves well and pat dry.
Place two vine leaves together slightly
overlapping. Divide the remaining tomato
mixture into 4 portions. Spread half of one
portion over the vine leaves, place a fish on
top and spread the other half of the filling
portion on top of the fish. Fold the leaves
over to form a parcel, leaving some of the
fish head and tail exposed. Repeat to make
three more parcels.
5 Mix the oil and lemon juice in a small bowl.
Place the fish parcels in a non-metallic baking
dish and brush all over with the lemon and oil
(especially the tails, which burn easily). Bake
for 15 minutes, then carefully lift onto serving
plates and garnish with lemon wedges.

GARITHES ME FETA

(Baked prawns with feta)

Preparation time: 20 minutes
Total cooking time: 30 minutes
Serves 4 as a first course

☆

300 g (10 oz) raw large prawns
2 tablespoons olive oil
2 small red onions, finely chopped
1 large clove garlic, crushed
350 g (11 oz) ripe tomatoes, diced
2 tablespoons lemon juice
2 tablespoons fresh oregano
  or 1 teaspoon dried
200 g (6½ oz) feta
extra virgin olive oil, for drizzling
cracked black pepper, for sprinkling
chopped fresh flat-leaf parsley, to garnish

1 Peel the prawns, leaving the tails intact.
Gently pull out the dark vein from each prawn
back, starting at the head end.
2 Preheat the oven to moderate 180°F (350°F/
Gas 4). Heat the olive oil in a saucepan over
medium heat, add the onion and cook, stirring
occasionally for 3 minutes, or until softened.
Add the garlic and cook for a few seconds,
then add the tomato and cook for 10 minutes,
or until the mixture is slightly reduced and
thickened. Add the lemon juice and oregano.
Season, to taste.
3 Place half the sauce into a 3 cup (750 ml/
24 fl oz) baking dish, about 15 cm (6 inches)
square. Place the prawns on top. Spoon on the
remaining sauce, then crumble the feta over it.
Drizzle with extra virgin olive oil and sprinkle
with freshly cracked black pepper.
4 Bake for 15 minutes, until the prawns are just
cooked. Serve immediately with lightly toasted
bread to soak up the juices.

Stuff a portion of the
tomato mixture into
each fish.

Spread some of the tomato
mixture on top of each fish.

OPPOSITE PAGE:
Garithes me feta (top);
Red mullet in vine leaves

2 large ripe tomatoes, peeled and chopped
2 tablespoons tomato paste (tomato purée)
1/2 cup (125 ml/4 fl oz) white wine
3 tablespoons chopped fresh flat-leaf parsley

CHEESE SAUCE
60 g (2 oz) butter
1/2 cup (60 g/2 oz) plain flour
2 1/2 cups (625 ml/20 fl oz) milk
pinch of ground nutmeg
1/3 cup (35 g/1 1/4 oz) finely grated kefalotyri
    or Parmesan
2 eggs, lightly beaten

1   Lay the eggplant on a tray, sprinkle with salt and leave to stand for 30 minutes. Rinse under water and pat dry. Preheat the oven to moderate 180°C (350°F/Gas 4).
2   Heat 2 tablespoons olive oil in a frying pan, add the eggplant in batches and cook for 1–2 minutes each side, or until golden and soft. Add a little more oil when needed.
3   Heat 1 tablespoon olive oil in a large saucepan, add the onion and cook over medium heat for 5 minutes. Add the garlic, allspice and cinnamon and cook for 30 seconds. Add the mince and cook for 5 minutes, or until browned, breaking up any lumps with the back of a spoon. Add the tomato, tomato paste and wine, and simmer over low heat for 30 minutes, or until the liquid has evaporated. Stir in the chopped parsley and season, to taste.
4   For the cheese sauce, melt the butter in a saucepan over low heat. Stir in the flour and cook for 1 minute, or until pale and foaming. Remove the saucepan from the heat and gradually stir in the milk and nutmeg. Return the saucepan to the heat and stir constantly until the sauce boils and thickens. Reduce the heat and simmer for 2 minutes. Stir in 1 tablespoon of the cheese until well combined. Stir in the egg just before using.
5   Line the base of a 3 litre ovenproof dish measuring 25 x 30 cm (10 x 12 inches) with a third of the eggplant. Spoon half the meat sauce over it and cover with another layer of eggplant. Spoon the remaining meat sauce over the top and cover with the remaining eggplant. Spread the cheese sauce over the top and sprinkle with the remaining cheese. Bake for 1 hour. Leave to stand for 10 minutes before slicing.
NOTE: You can substitute an equal quantity of sliced, shallow-fried zucchini or potatoes, or any combination of these vegetables for the eggplant (aubergine).

MOUSSAKA

Preparation time: 20 minutes
    + 30 minutes standing
Total cooking time: 2 hours
Serves 6

☆ ☆

1.5 kg (3 lb) eggplants (aubergines),
    cut into 5 mm (1/4 inch) slices
1/2 cup (125 ml/4 fl oz) olive oil
2 onions, finely chopped
2 large cloves garlic, crushed
1/2 teaspoon ground allspice
1 teaspoon ground cinnamon
750 g (1 1/2 lb) lamb mince

ABOVE: Moussaka

STUFFED PEPPERS (CAPSICUMS)

Preparation time: 25 minutes
Total cooking time: 1 hour 15 minutes
Serves 6

175 g (4¹/2 oz) long-grain white rice
1¹/4 cups (315 ml/10 fl oz) chicken stock
6 medium-sized red, yellow or orange
    peppers (capsicums)
60 g (2 oz) pine nuts
¹/3 cup (80 ml/2³/4 fl oz) olive oil
1 large onion, chopped
¹/2 cup (125 g/4 oz) tomato passata
60 g (2 oz) currants
2¹/2 tablespoons chopped fresh flat-leaf parsley
2¹/2 tablespoons chopped fresh mint leaves
¹/2 teaspoon ground cinnamon

1 Put the rice and stock in a saucepan and bring to the boil over medium heat. Reduce the heat to medium–low, cover tightly and cook for 15 minutes, or until tender. Remove from the heat and set aside, covered.

2 Bring a large saucepan of water to the boil. Cut off the tops of the peppers, reserving the lids. Remove the seeds and membrane from the peppers and discard. Blanch the peppers in the boiling water (not the lids) for 2 minutes, then drain and leave upturned to dry on paper towels.

3 Preheat the oven to moderate 180°C (350°F/Gas 4). Toast the pine nuts in a small frying pan over low heat until golden brown, then remove from the pan and set aside. Increase the heat to medium and heat 2 tablespoons of oil. Add the onion and cook for 10 minutes or until soft, stirring occasionally.

4 Add the tomato passata, currants, parsley, mint, cinnamon, cooked rice and toasted pine nuts to the pan. Stir for 2 minutes, then season, to taste, with salt and pepper.

5 Stand the peppers in a baking dish in which they fit snugly. Divide the rice mixture among the pepper cavities. Replace the lids.

6 Pour 100 ml (3¹/2 fl oz) boiling water into the dish and drizzle the remaining oil over the top of the peppers. Bake for 40 minutes, or until the peppers are just tender when tested with the point of a small knife. Serve warm or cold.

STUFFED VEGETABLES
Yemista, or stuffed vegetables, are an important feature of Greek gastronomy, and are popular in tavernas across Greece. Vegetarian versions are stuffed with rice, herbs, currants or raisins, and nuts. The addition of finely minced meat to this mixture is an example of Greek improvisation in making a small amount of meat go a long way, using it just as a flavouring.

LEFT: Stuffed peppers

SWEET-AND-SOUR
DISHES
While most often
associated with Chinese
food, the tradition of
sweet-and-sour dishes
also has roots in the
classical cooking of the
Mediterranean, where
the blending of opposite
flavours and textures
reflected mythological
beliefs in achieving
equilibrium among
opposing forces. For
example, meat has been
cooked with fruit for
centuries. Originally, fruit
was used to tenderize
tougher cuts of meat, but
in the recipe on this page,
the flavour of the figs
blends beautifully with
the spices and lemon.

KOTOPOULO ME SYKO
(Chicken with figs)

Preparation time: 20 minutes
Total cooking time: 1 hour 10 minutes
Serves 4

1.5 kg (3 lb) chicken, cut into 8 even-sized pieces
1 tablespoon olive oil
12 fresh figs (not too big), or 12 dried figs,
    soaked in hot water for 2 hours
10 whole cloves garlic
1 large onion, thinly sliced
1/2 teaspoon ground coriander
1/2 teaspoon ground cinnamon
1/2 teaspoon ground cumin
pinch of cayenne
3 bay leaves
1 1/2 cups (375 ml/12 fl oz) ruby port
1 teaspoon finely grated lemon rind
2 tablespoons lemon juice

1 Preheat the oven to moderate 180°C (350°F/ Gas 4). Remove any excess chicken fat. Reserve the chicken giblets if there are any. Lightly season the chicken. Heat the olive oil in a large heavy-based frying pan over high heat and cook the chicken in batches, skin-side-down, for 5 minutes, or until the skin is golden.
2 Remove from the pan and place skin-side-down in a single layer in a 33 x 23 cm (13 x 9 inch) baking dish with the giblets. Place the figs between the chicken pieces. Scatter the garlic and onion over the top, carefully pressing them into any gaps and being careful not to squash the figs. Sprinkle the spices over the top, tuck in the bay leaves, then pour in the port. Cover and bake for 25 minutes, then turn the chicken. Uncover and bake for another 20 minutes, or until the chicken is just tender. Stir in the lemon rind and juice and bake for another 15 minutes, or until the chicken is very tender.

ARNI YAHNI
(Lamb stew)

Preparation time: 25 minutes
Total cooking time: 2 hours 15 minutes
Serves 4

3 tablespoons olive oil
1 kg (2 lb) boneless lamb shoulder,
    cut into 2 cm (3/4 inch) cubes
1 onion, chopped

RIGHT: Kotopoulo me syko

2 cloves garlic, crushed

2 sticks celery, chopped

1 large carrot, chopped

4 ripe tomatoes, peeled, deseeded and chopped

2 tablespoons tomato paste (tomato purée)

1 teaspoon sugar

3/4 cup (185 ml/6 fl oz) red wine

2 bay leaves

3 cloves

1/4 teaspoon ground cinnamon

250 g (8 oz) baby onions

350 g (11 oz) zucchini (courgettes),
  thickly sliced

chopped fresh flat-leaf parsley, for serving

1 Heat 1 tablespoon of oil in a large saucepan, then brown the meat on all sides, in batches, adding more oil when necessary. Set aside.

2 Heat another tablespoon of oil, add the chopped onion, cook for 4 minutes or until soft, then add the garlic, celery and carrot and cook for 1 minute before adding the tomato, tomato paste, sugar, red wine, bay leaves, cloves, cinnamon and 1½ cups (375 ml/12 fl oz) water. Return the meat to the pan. Cover, bring to the boil, then reduce the heat and simmer for 1½ hours.

3 In a separate frying pan, heat the remaining olive oil and cook the baby onions until golden brown and tender. Add them to the stew, along with the zucchini, and cook for another 30 minutes. Sprinkle with chopped parsley and serve immediately.

SOUVLAKE
(Skewered lamb)

Preparation time: 20 minutes + overnight
  marinating + 30 minutes standing
Total cooking time: 10 minutes
Serves 4

1 kg (2 lb) boned leg lamb, trimmed, cut
  into 2 cm (3/4 inch) cubes

1/4 cup (60 ml/2 fl oz) olive oil

2 teaspoons finely grated lemon rind

1/3 cup (80 ml/23/4 fl oz) lemon juice

1/2 cup (125 ml/4 fl oz) dry white wine

2 teaspoons dried oregano

2 large cloves garlic, finely chopped

2 fresh bay leaves

1 cup (250 g/8 oz) Greek-style natural yoghurt

2 cloves garlic, crushed, extra

1 Place the lamb in a non-metallic bowl with 2 tablespoons oil, the lemon rind and juice, wine, oregano, garlic, bay leaves and some black pepper. Toss, then cover and refrigerate overnight.

2 Place the yoghurt and extra garlic in a bowl, mix well and leave for 30 minutes.

3 Drain the lamb. Thread onto 8 skewers and cook on a barbecue or chargrill plate, brushing with the remaining oil, for 7–8 minutes, or until done to your liking. Serve with the yoghurt, bread and a salad.

LAMB
The popularity of lamb in Greece is linked to the country's hilly, often barren landscape. This terrain is not naturally suitable for cattle so, instead, sheep and goats are usually reared, both for their meat and milk. As meat was historically scarce and expensive, it is a food traditionally associated with religious feast days and other special occasions. During Easter, the most important religious festival for Orthodox Greeks, it is customary to spit roast an entire lamb, including its entrails. As with all their meat, Greeks generally prefer lamb to be well done, so that it falls off the bone, but the recipes we have given can be cooked to your liking.

ABOVE: Souvlake

47

1 Rinse and drain the silverbeet thoroughly. Discard the stems and shred the leaves. Heat the olive oil in a large frying pan, add the onion and cook, stirring, over medium heat for 5 minutes, or until softened. Add the spring onion and silverbeet and cook, covered, over medium heat for 5 minutes. Add the dill and cook, uncovered, for 3–4 minutes, or until most of the liquid has evaporated. Remove from the heat and cool to room temperature.

2 Preheat the oven to moderate 180°C (350°F/ Gas 4) and lightly grease a 20 x 25 cm (8 x 10 inch) 2.5 litre baking dish. Place the feta, cottage and kefalotyri cheeses in a large bowl. Stir in the silverbeet mixture and add the nutmeg. Gradually add the eggs and combine well. Season, to taste.

3 Line the base and sides of the baking dish with a sheet of filo pastry. (Keep the rest covered with a damp tea towel to prevent drying out.) Brush with butter and cover with another sheet of filo. Butter the sheet and repeat in this way, using five sheets of pastry. Spoon the filling into the dish and level the surface. Fold the exposed pastry up and over to cover the top of the filling. Cover with a sheet of pastry, brush with butter and continue until all the sheets are used. Roughly trim the pastry with kitchen scissors then tuck the excess inside the wall of the dish.

4 Brush the top with butter. Using a sharp knife, score the surface into squares. Sprinkle a few drops of cold water on top to discourage the pastry from curling. Bake for 45 minutes, or until puffed and golden. Rest at room temperature for 10 minutes before serving.
NOTE: You can use pecorino cheese if kefalotyri is unavailable.

SPANOKOPITA
(Silverbeet and cheese filo pie)

Preparation time: 25 minutes + cooling
Total cooking time: 1 hour
Serves 4–6

☆ ☆

1.5 kg (3 lb) silverbeet (Swiss chard)
3 tablespoons olive oil
1 white onion, finely chopped
10 spring onions, chopped (include some green)
1½ tablespoons chopped fresh dill
200 g (6½ oz) Greek feta, crumbled
125 g (4 oz) cottage cheese
3 tablespoons finely grated kefalotyri
¼ teaspoon ground nutmeg
4 eggs, lightly beaten
10 sheets filo pastry
80 g (2¾ oz) butter, melted, for brushing

ABOVE: Spanokopita

RICE PILAF

In a heavy-based saucepan, melt 60 g (2 oz) butter over low heat, then add 1 finely chopped brown onion and cook, stirring frequently, for 5 minutes, or until softened. Add 2 cups (400 g/13 oz) long-grain rice and stir well to coat. Add 1 litre hot chicken or vegetable stock to the saucepan. Bring to the boil, stirring frequently, then reduce the heat to low, cover tightly and cook for 10 minutes. Remove from the heat and set aside for 10 minutes. Fluff the rice with a fork and serve immediately. Pilaf can be pressed into individual oiled moulds and then turned out onto a serving dish. Serves 6–8.

OKTAPODI KRASATO
(Octopus in red wine stew)

Preparation time: 15 minutes
Total cooking time: 1 hour 10 minutes
Serves 4–6

1 kg (2 lb) baby octopus
2 tablespoons olive oil
1 large onion, chopped
3 cloves garlic, crushed
1 bay leaf
3 cups (750 ml/24 fl oz) red wine
1/4 cup (60 ml/2 fl oz) red wine vinegar
400 g (13 oz) can good-quality crushed
    tomatoes
1 tablespoon tomato paste (tomato purée)
1 tablespoon finely chopped fresh oregano
1/4 teaspoon ground cinnamon
small pinch of ground cloves
1 teaspoon sugar
2 tablespoons chopped fresh flat-leaf parsley

1 To prepare each octopus, using a small knife, cut between the head and tentacles, just below the eyes. Grasp the body and push the beak out and up through the centre of the tentacles with your fingers. Cut the eyes from the head by slicing a small round off with a small sharp knife. Discard the eye section. Carefully slit through one side of the head and remove any gut from inside. Thoroughly rinse all the octopus under running water.
2 Heat the oil in a large saucepan, add the onion and cook over high heat for 5 minutes, or until starting to brown. Add the garlic and bay leaf and cook for another minute. Add the octopus and stir to thoroughly coat in the onion mixture.
3 Add the wine, vinegar, tomato, tomato paste, oregano, cinnamon, cloves and sugar. Bring to the boil, then reduce the heat to low and simmer for 1 hour, or until the octopus is tender and the sauce has thickened slightly. Stir in the parsley and season.
NOTE: The cooking time for octopus varies according to the size. Generally the smaller octopus are not as tough as the larger ones and will take less time to cook.

KALAMARIA TIGANITA
(Fried squid)

Preparation time: 20 minutes
Total cooking time: 15 minutes
Serves 4

1 kg (2 lb) small squid
flour for coating, well-seasoned
oil, for deep-frying
lemon wedges, for serving
skordalia (see page 18), for serving

1 To clean the squid, gently pull the tentacles away from the hoods and remove the intestines and the transparent quills. Trim off the tentacles below the eyes and detach the beaks. Under cold running water, pull away the skin. Rinse the bodies and detach the side wings. Slice the bodies into 5 mm (1/4 inch) rings. Pat dry the rings, wings and tentacles.
2 Heat the oil in a deep, heavy-based frying pan to 180°C (350°F), or until a cube of bread browns in 15 seconds. Toss the squid in the flour and shake off any excess. Fry in batches, for 2–3 minutes each batch, or until golden. Serve with lemon wedges.

COOKING SEAFOOD
The general rule for cooking seafood such as squid or octopus is that it should either be cooked for a very short time or for a very long time, as anything in between causes the seafood to become tough. Barbecued, fried or char-grilled squid and octopus take a matter of minutes to cook, otherwise they are excellent stewed in liquid for an hour or longer.

BELOW: Oktapodi krasato

ROAST LAMB WITH
LEMON AND POTATOES

Cut small slits in the lamb
and insert the garlic slivers
into the slits.

Sprinkle the potatoes with
oregano and seasoning.

*OPPOSITE PAGE: Roast
lamb with lemon and
potatoes (top and front);
Lima bean casserole*

BRAISED ARTICHOKES WITH BROAD BEANS

Preparation time: 25 minutes
Total cooking time: 35 minutes
Serves 4

☆ ☆

1 lemon

6 large globe artichokes

75 ml (2¹/₂ fl oz) extra virgin olive oil

4 spring onions, thinly sliced

300 g (10 oz) fresh, shelled broad beans

3 tablespoons fresh dill, chopped

1 Squeeze the lemon into a large bowl of water and put the skin shells in the water to make acidulated water. Using a small sharp knife, remove the choke from each artichoke and peel away the prickly outer leaves. Trim the bases. Cut each artichoke into quarters and put them in the acidulated water, to prevent them browning, while you prepare the rest.
2 In a large heavy-based, non-aluminium saucepan, heat the oil and cook the spring onion for 1–2 minutes, or until just softened. Add the drained artichokes, beans and dill and add just enough water to cover the vegetables. Cover and simmer for 30 minutes, or until tender. Drain excess water, season and serve warm, or at room temperature.

ROAST LAMB WITH LEMON AND POTATOES

Preparation time: 20 minutes
Total cooking time: 3 hours
Serves 6

☆

2.5–3 kg (5–6 lb) leg of lamb

2 cloves garlic

¹/₂ cup (125 ml/4 fl oz) lemon juice

3 tablespoons dried oregano

1 brown onion, sliced

2 sticks celery, sliced

40 g (1³/₄ oz) butter, softened

1 kg (2 lb) potatoes, quartered

1 Preheat the oven to moderate 180°C (350°F/Gas 4). Cut small slits in the lamb and cut the garlic into slivers. Insert the garlic into the slits. Rub the entire surface with half the lemon juice, sprinkle with salt, pepper and half the oregano. Place in a baking dish and bake for 1 hour.
2 Drain the fat from the pan and add the onion, celery and 1 cup (250 ml/8 fl oz) hot water. Spread the butter on the lamb, reduce the oven to warm 160°C (315°F/Gas 2–3) and cook for 1 hour. Turn during cooking to brown evenly.
3 Add the potatoes to the pan, sprinkle with the remaining oregano and lemon juice and some salt and pepper. Bake for another hour, adding more water if required and turning the potatoes halfway through cooking. Cut the lamb into chunks. Skim any excess fat from the pan and serve the juices with the potatoes and lamb.

LIMA BEAN CASSEROLE

Preparation time: 20 minutes + overnight soaking
Total cooking time: 2 hours
Serves 6–8

☆ ☆

1 cup (185 g/6 oz) dried lima beans

¹/₄ cup (60 ml/2 fl oz) olive oil

1 large onion, halved and sliced

1 clove garlic, chopped

1 small carrot, chopped

1 small stick celery, chopped

400 g (13 oz) can good-quality crushed tomatoes

1 tablespoon tomato paste (tomato purée)

2 teaspoons chopped fresh dill

extra virgin olive oil, for serving

1 Cover the lima beans with plenty of cold water and leave to soak overnight. Drain well.
2 Bring a large pan of water to the boil, add the beans and return to the boil, then reduce the heat to medium and cook, partially covered, for 45–60 minutes, or until the beans are tender but not mushy. Drain. Preheat the oven to moderate 180°C (350°F/Gas 4).
3 Heat the oil in a 2.5 litre heatproof casserole dish over medium heat. Add the onion, garlic, carrot and celery, and cook for 5 minutes, or until the onion is translucent. Add the crushed tomato, tomato paste and ¹/₂ cup (125 ml/4 fl oz) water. Bring to the boil, then reduce the heat and simmer for 3 minutes.
4 Add the lima beans and dill to the casserole dish, then season, to taste. Bring back to the boil, then cover and bake for 50 minutes, or until the sauce is thick and the lima beans are soft. Serve hot or at room temperature, drizzled with the oil.

VEGETABLES IN THE GREEK DIET

Greeks enjoy more vegetables in their diet than most Europeans and eat them raw, pickled or cooked in endless ways. Restaurant menus in Greece usually list numerous vegetable dishes as courses in their own right, not just as accompaniments to meat. In tavernas across Greece it is still possible for patrons to enter the kitchen and peer into the cooking pots and baking trays to choose the dishes that most take their fancy.

BRIAMI
(Potato and zucchini/courgette casserole)

Preparation time: 20 minutes
Total cooking time: 1 hour 45 minutes
Serves 4–6

1 large red pepper (capsicum)
1/4 cup (60 ml/2 fl oz) olive oil
2 onions, sliced
2 cloves garlic, crushed
400 g (13 oz) zucchini (courgettes), thickly sliced
400 g (13 oz) small waxy potatoes (pontiac, kipfler, desiree), unpeeled, cut into 1 cm (1/2 inch) slices
1 kg (2 lb) ripe tomatoes, peeled and roughly chopped
1 teaspoon dried oregano
2 tablespoons chopped fresh flat-leaf parsley
2 tablespoons chopped fresh dill
1/2 teaspoon ground cinnamon

1 Preheat the oven to moderate 180°C (350°F/Gas 4). Remove the seeds and membrane from the red pepper and cut the flesh into squares.
2 Heat 2 tablespoons of the olive oil in a heavy-based frying pan over medium heat. Add the onion and cook, stirring frequently, for 10 minutes. Add the garlic and cook for another 2 minutes. Place all the other ingredients in a large bowl and season generously with salt and pepper. Add the softened onion and garlic and toss everything together. Transfer to a large baking dish and drizzle the remaining oil over the vegetables.
3 Cover and bake for 1–1½ hours, or until the vegetables are tender, stirring every 30 minutes. Insert the point of a small knife into the potatoes. When the knife comes away easily, the potato is cooked.
NOTE: This vegetable casserole dish is delicious served warm with grilled meat, chicken or fish, or it can be served at room temperature as part of a meze selection.

RIGHT: Briami

TOMATES YEMISTES
(Rice-stuffed tomatoes)

Preparation time: 30 minutes
Total cooking time: 1 hour
Makes 8

☆☆

8 medium tomatoes
1/2 cup (110 g/3 1/2 oz) short-grain rice
2 tablespoons olive oil
1 red onion, finely chopped
1 clove garlic, crushed
1 teaspoon dried oregano
1/4 cup (40 g/1 1/4 oz) pine nuts
1/4 cup (35 g/1 1/4 oz) currants
1/2 cup (30 g/1 oz) chopped fresh basil
2 tablespoons chopped fresh flat-leaf parsley
1 tablespoon chopped fresh dill
olive oil, for brushing

 Lightly oil a large baking dish. Preheat the oven to warm 160°C (315°F/Gas 2–3). Slice the top off each tomato and reserve the tops. Spoon out the flesh, place in a strainer to drain the juice, reserving the juice, and then finely dice the flesh. Reserve the juice and flesh in separate bowls. Drain the tomato shells upside-down on a rack.

2 Cook the rice in a saucepan of lightly salted rapidly boiling water for 10–12 minutes, or until just tender. Drain and set aside to cool.

3 Heat the olive oil in a frying pan. Fry the onion, garlic and oregano for 8 minutes, or until the onion is tender. Add the pine nuts and currants and cook for another 5 minutes, stirring frequently. Remove from the heat and stir in the basil, parsley and dill. Season, to taste, with salt and freshly ground black pepper.

4 Add the onion mixture and reserved tomato flesh to the rice and mix well. Fill the tomato shells with the rice mixture, piling it up over the top. Spoon 1 tablespoon of the reserved tomato juice on top of each tomato and replace the tomato tops.

5 Lightly brush the tomatoes with the olive oil and arrange them in a baking dish. Bake for 20–30 minutes, or until cooked and heated through. Serve warm or cold.

RICE-STUFFED TOMATOES
Like much Greek food, stuffed vegetables can be eaten either hot or cold. In fact, eating food piping hot as soon as it has been cooked is more of a modern habit in Greece, as historically most homes, except those of the wealthiest, did not have their own ovens. Instead, foods were cooked at the local bakery then eaten at room temperature later in the day.

ABOVE: Tomates yemistes

1 tablespoon olive oil

2 spring onions, chopped

1 1/2 cups (280 g/9 oz) cold, cooked rice
  (see Note)

60 g (2 oz) pine nuts

75 g (2 1/2 oz) currants

2 tablespoons chopped fresh flat-leaf parsley

2 teaspoons finely grated lemon rind

1 egg, lightly beaten

1 kg (2 lb) medium squid hoods

1 Preheat the oven to warm 160°C (315°F/ Gas 2–3). For the tomato sauce, score a cross in the base of each tomato, soak them in a bowl of boiling water for 10 seconds, then plunge them into cold water and peel the skin from the cross. Chop the flesh. Heat the oil in a frying pan. Add the onion and garlic and cook over low heat for about 2 minutes, stirring frequently, until the onion is soft. Add the tomato, wine and oregano and bring to the boil. Reduce the heat, then cover and cook over low heat for 10 minutes.

2 Meanwhile, for the stuffing, mix all the ingredients except the egg in a bowl. Add enough egg to moisten the ingredients.

3 Wash the squid and pat dry with paper towels. Three-quarters fill each hood with the stuffing and secure the ends with toothpicks or skewers. Place in a single layer in a casserole dish.

4 Pour the tomato sauce over the squid, cover the dish and bake for 20 minutes, or until the squid are tender. Cut the squid into thick slices. Spoon the sauce over just before serving.

NOTE: You will need to cook 1/2 cup (100 g/ 3 1/2 oz) rice for this recipe. The cooking time for the squid will depend upon the size. Choose small squid because they are more tender.

KALAMARIA YEMISTA
(Stuffed squid)

Preparation time: 40 minutes
Total cooking time: 35 minutes
Serves 4

TOMATO SAUCE

4 large ripe tomatoes

1 tablespoon olive oil

1 onion, finely chopped

1 clove garlic, crushed

1/4 cup (60 ml/2 fl oz) good-quality
  red wine

1 tablespoon chopped fresh oregano

ABOVE: Kalamaria yemista

BABY ZUCCHINI
(COURGETTE) SALAD

Trim the stems off 1 kg (2 lb) very small zucchini (courgettes). Cook them whole in boiling salted water for 5 minutes, or until tender but still firm to the bite. Drain and place in a bowl with 1 thinly sliced small red onion, 3 tablespoons chopped fresh flat-leaf parsley and one quantity of Oil and lemon dressing (page 21). Toss well. Serve at room temperature with grilled meats or fish. Serves 6–8.

PASTITSIO
(Meat and pasta bake)

Preparation time: 40 minutes + standing
Total cooking time: 1 hour 30 minutes
Serves 6

☆ ☆

150 g (5 oz) elbow macaroni
40 g (1 1/4 oz) butter
1/4 teaspoon ground nutmeg
60 g (2 oz) kefalotyri or Parmesan, grated
1 egg , lightly beaten

MEAT SAUCE
2 tablespoons oil
1 onion, finely chopped
2 cloves garlic, crushed
500 g (1 lb) beef mince
1/2 cup (125 ml/4 fl oz) red wine
1 cup (250 ml/8 fl oz) beef stock
3 tablespoons tomato paste (tomato purée)
1 teaspoon chopped fresh oregano

BÉCHAMEL SAUCE
40 g (1 1/4 oz) butter
1 1/2 tablespoons plain flour
pinch of nutmeg
1 1/2 cups (375 ml/12 fl oz) milk
1 egg, lightly beaten

1   Preheat the oven to moderate 180°C (350°F/ Gas 4). Lightly grease a 1.5 litre ovenproof dish. Cook the macaroni in a large saucepan of boiling salted water for 10 minutes, or until *al dente*. Drain and return to the pan. Melt the butter in a small saucepan until golden, then pour it over the macaroni. Stir in the nutmeg and half the cheese and season, to taste. Leave until cool, then mix in the egg and set aside.

2   For the meat sauce, heat the oil in a large frying pan, add the onion and garlic and cook over medium heat for 6 minutes, or until the onion is soft. Increase the heat, add the beef and cook, stirring, for 5 minutes or until the meat is browned. Add the wine and cook over high heat for 1 minute, or until evaporated. Add the stock, tomato paste, oregano, salt and pepper. Reduce the heat, cover and simmer for 20 minutes.

3   Meanwhile, to make the béchamel sauce, melt the butter in a small saucepan over low heat. Stir in the flour and cook for 1 minute, or until pale and foaming. Remove from the heat and gradually stir in the milk. Return to the heat and stir constantly until the sauce boils and thickens. Reduce the heat and simmer for 2 minutes. Add the nutmeg and some salt and pepper. Allow to cool a little before stirring in the beaten egg. Stir 3 tablespoons of the béchamel into the meat sauce.

4   Spread half the meat sauce in the dish, then layer half the pasta over it. Layer with the remaining meat sauce and then the remaining pasta. Press down firmly with the back of a spoon. Spread the béchamel sauce over the pasta and sprinkle the remaining cheese on top. Bake for 45–50 minutes, or until golden. Let it stand for 15 minutes before serving.

NOTE: Tubular bucatini, which is available in varying thicknesses, can be used as a substitute for the elbow macaroni. Choose one that is a little thicker than spaghetti.

BELOW: Pastitsio

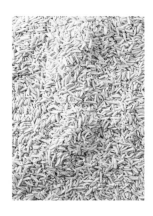

KOURAMBIETHES
(Almond shortbreads)

Preparation time: 25 minutes
+ 10 minutes cooling + 1 hour refrigeration
Total cooking time: 15 minutes
Makes 22

☆ ☆

250 g (8 oz) unsalted butter
100 g (3¹/₂ oz) slivered almonds
2 cups (250 g/8 oz) plain flour
1 teaspoon baking powder
³/₄ cup (90 g/3 oz) icing sugar, sifted
1 egg yolk
1 teaspoon vanilla essence
1 tablespoon ouzo
4 tablespoons almond meal
¹/₂ cup (60 g/2 oz) icing sugar, extra, for dusting

KOURAMBIETHES
Kourambiethes are a Christmas speciality in Greece. Mounds of the biscuits are found in homes and the windows of pastry stores at this time, then by New Year all that remains is a pile of sugar dust. While this recipe has many versions, the constants are that it is always made with unsalted butter and has a low proportion of sugar in the dough so that it retains its characteristic dense texture. The biscuits are dusted liberally with icing sugar after baking.

1 Gently melt the butter over low heat in a small heavy-based saucepan, without stirring or shaking the pan. Carefully pour the clear butter into another container, leaving the white sediment in the pan to be discarded. Refrigerate for 1 hour.

2 Preheat the oven to warm 170°C (325°F/ Gas 3) and line two baking trays with baking paper. Grind the slivered almonds to a medium-fine meal. In a bowl, sift the flour and baking powder together.

3 Using electric beaters, beat the chilled butter until light and fluffy. Gradually add the icing sugar and combine well. Add the egg yolk, vanilla and ouzo and beat until just combined. Fold in the flour, ground almonds and the almond meal.

4 Shape heaped tablespoons of mixture into crescents, place on the baking trays and bake for 12 minutes, or until lightly coloured. Remove from the oven and dust liberally with icing sugar. Leave to cool on the trays for 10 minutes.

5 Line a baking tray with baking paper and dust the paper with icing sugar. Lift the warm biscuits onto this and dust again with icing sugar. When the biscuits are cool, dust them once again with icing sugar before storing them in an airtight container.

RIGHT: Kourambiethes

KATAIFI ME AMIGTHALA
(Shredded pastries with almonds)

Preparation time: 45 minutes
   + 2 hours standing
Total cooking time: 50 minutes
Makes 40 pieces

☆ ☆

500 g (1 lb) kataifi pastry (see Note)
250 g (8 oz) unsalted butter, melted
1 cup (125 g/4 oz) ground pistachios
2 cups (230 g/7½ oz) ground almonds
2½ cups (625 g/1 lb 5 oz) caster sugar
1 teaspoon ground cinnamon
¼ teaspoon ground cloves
1 tablespoon brandy
1 egg white
1 teaspoon lemon juice
5 cm (2 inch) strip lemon rind
4 cloves
1 cinnamon stick
1 tablespoon honey

1   Allow the kataifi pastry to come to room temperature, still in its packaging. This will take about 2 hours and makes the pastry easier to work with.
2   Preheat the oven to warm 170°C (325°/ Gas 3). Brush a 20 x 30 cm (8 x 12 inch) baking dish or tray with some melted butter.
3   Place the nuts in a bowl with ½ cup (125 g/ 4 oz) caster sugar, the ground cinnamon, cloves and brandy. Lightly beat the egg white with a fork and add to the mixture. Stir to make a paste. Divide the mixture into 8 portions and form each into a sausage shape about 18 cm (7 inches) long.
4   Take a small handful of the pastry strands and spread them out fairly compactly with the strands running lengthways towards you. The pastry should measure 25 x 18 cm (10 x 7 inches). Brush the pastry with melted butter. Place one of the 'nut' sausages along the end of the pastry nearest to you and roll up into a neat sausage shape. Repeat with the other pastry portions.
5   Place the rolls close together in the baking dish and brush them again with melted butter. Bake for 50 minutes, or until golden brown.
6   While the pastries are cooking, place the remaining sugar in a small saucepan with 2 cups (500 ml/16 fl oz) water and stir over low heat until dissolved. Add the lemon juice, rind, cloves and cinnamon and boil together for 10 minutes. Stir in the honey, then set aside until cold.
7   When the pastries come out of the oven, pour the syrup over the top. Leave them to cool completely before cutting each roll into 5 pieces.
NOTES: Kataifi, a shredded pastry, is available from Greek delicatessens and other speciality food stores.

   It is very important that the syrup is cold and the kataifi hot when pouring the syrup over, otherwise the liquid will not be absorbed as well or as evenly.

   These pastries keep for up to a week if you cover them. Don't refrigerate them.

ABOVE: Kataifi me amigthala

GALATOBOUREKO
(Custard pie)

Preparation time: 35 minutes + cooling
Total cooking time: 1 hour
Serves 6–8

☆☆

1 vanilla pod, sliced in half lengthways
3 cups (750 ml/24 fl oz) milk
110 g (4 oz) caster sugar
110 g (4 oz) semolina
1 tablespoon finely grated lemon rind
1 cinnamon stick
40 g (1 1/2 oz) unsalted butter, cubed
4 large eggs, lightly beaten
12 sheets filo pastry (40 x 30 cm/16 x 12 inches)
60 g (2 oz) unsalted butter, extra, melted

SYRUP

75 g (3 oz) caster sugar
1/2 teaspoon ground cinnamon
1 tablespoon lemon juice
5 cm (2 inch) strip lemon rind

1 Scrape the vanilla pod seeds into a saucepan. Add the pod, milk, sugar, semolina, lemon rind and cinnamon stick and gently bring to the boil, stirring constantly. Reduce the heat to low and simmer for 2 minutes so the mixture thickens. Remove from the heat. Mix in the butter. Cool for 10 minutes, then remove the cinnamon stick and pod and gradually mix in the egg. Preheat the oven to moderate 180°C (350°F/Gas 4).
2 Cover the filo with a damp tea towel. Remove a sheet, brush one side with melted butter and place buttered-side-down in a 30 x 20 x 3 cm (12 x 8 x 1 1/4 inch) baking tin. The filo will overlap the edges. Repeat with 5 more sheets, buttering one side of each as you go.
3 Pour the custard over the filo and cover the top with the remaining pastry, brushing each sheet with butter as you go. Brush the top with butter. Using a small sharp knife, trim the pastry to the edges of the tin. Bake for 40–45 minutes, or until the custard has puffed up and set and the pastry has turned golden brown. Leave to cool.
4 Mix all the syrup ingredients with 75 ml (2 1/2 fl oz) water in a saucepan. Slowly bring to the boil, then reduce the heat to low and simmer for 10 minutes. The syrup will thicken. Remove from the heat and cool for 10 minutes.
5 Remove the lemon rind. If the filo has risen above the edges of the tin, flatten the top layer with your hand, then pour the syrup over the pie. This will prevent the syrup running over the sides. Allow to cool again before serving.

MELOMAKARONA
(Honey biscuits)

Preparation time: 20 minutes + cooling
Total cooking time: 35 minutes
Makes 20

☆☆

1 2/3 cups (210 g/7 oz) plain flour
1 teaspoon baking powder
1 tablespoon finely grated orange rind
1 teaspoon ground cinnamon
1/2 cup (60 g/2 oz) walnuts, finely chopped
60 g (2 oz) unsalted butter, softened
1/4 cup (60 g/2 oz) caster sugar
1/4 cup (60 ml/2 fl oz) olive oil
1/4 cup (60 ml/2 fl oz) orange juice

SYRUP

75 g (3 oz) caster sugar
2 tablespoons runny honey
1 teaspoon ground cinnamon
2 tablespoons orange juice

1 Preheat the oven to moderate 180°C (350°F/Gas 4). Line a baking tray with baking paper. Sift the flour and baking powder into a bowl. Mix in the rind, cinnamon and half the walnuts.
2 Cream the butter and sugar in another bowl with electric beaters until pale and fluffy. Mix the oil and orange juice in a jug and add a little at a time to the butter and sugar mixture, whisking constantly.
3 Mix the flour in two batches into the butter mixture, then bring the dough together with your hands. Shape tablespoons of dough into balls and place on the tray. Flatten slightly and bake for 20–25 minutes, until golden. Cool on the tray.
4 Make the syrup by mixing all the ingredients with 1/4 cup (60 ml/2 fl oz) water and the remaining walnuts in a small saucepan. Bring to the boil over medium heat until the sugar dissolves, then reduce the heat to low and simmer for 10 minutes. The syrup will thicken.
5 Using a slotted spoon, dip a few biscuits at a time in the hot syrup. Use another spoon to baste them, then transfer to a plate.

GALATOBOUREKO

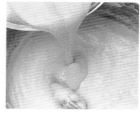

Gradually mix the beaten egg into the mixture.

Use a sharp knife to trim the pastry.

OPPOSITE PAGE:
Galatoboureko (top);
Melomakarona

TSOUREKI TOU PASKA
(Easter bread)

Preparation time: 1 hour
 + 1 hour 40 minutes rising
Total cooking time: 45 minutes
Makes 1 loaf

☆☆

7 g (1/4 oz) sachet dried yeast
1/2 cup (125 ml/4 fl oz) milk
60 g (2 oz) butter
1/4 cup (60 g/2 oz) caster sugar
1 teaspoon grated orange rind
3 cups (375 g/12 oz) white bread flour
1 teaspoon ground anise
1 egg, lightly beaten

TOPPING

1 egg, lightly beaten
1 tablespoon milk
1 tablespoon sesame seeds
1 tablespoon chopped slivered
  almonds
1 tablespoon caster sugar
dyed eggs, optional (see Note)

ABOVE: Tsoureki tou paska

1 Place the yeast and 2 tablespoons warm water in a small bowl and stir well. Leave in a warm, draught-free place for 10 minutes, or until bubbles appear on the surface. The mixture should be frothy and slightly increased in volume. If your yeast doesn't foam it is dead, so you will have to discard it and start again.
2 Combine the milk, butter, sugar, orange rind and 1/2 teaspoon salt in a small saucepan. Heat until the butter has melted and the milk is just warm. Sift 2 1/2 cups (310 g/10 oz) of the flour and the ground anise into a large bowl. Make a well in the centre, add the yeast and the milk mixtures, then the egg. Gradually beat into the flour for 1 minute, or until a smooth dough forms.
3 Turn out onto a lightly floured surface. Knead for 10 minutes, incorporating the remaining flour, or until the dough is smooth and elastic. Place in an oiled bowl and brush the surface with oil. Cover with plastic wrap and leave in a warm place for 1 hour, or until well risen.
4 Lightly grease a baking tray. Punch down the dough and knead for 1 minute. Divide the dough into three equal pieces. Roll each portion into a sausage 35 cm (14 inches) long. Plait the strands and fold the ends under. Place on the tray, brush with the combined egg and milk, then sprinkle with sesame seeds, almonds and sugar (if using dyed eggs, add them at this stage).

Cover with lightly oiled plastic wrap and set aside in a warm place for 40 minutes, or until well risen.

5 Preheat the oven to moderate 180°C (350°F/ Gas 4). Bake for 30–40 minutes, or until cooked. It should sound hollow when tapped.
NOTE: Powdered red dye is available from Greek food stores and includes instructions on how to dye the eggs.

HALVAS FOURNO
(Semolina cake)

Preparation time: 20 minutes
Total cooking time: 1 hour
Serves 6–8

☆

SYRUP
2¹/2 cups (625 g/1 lb 5 oz) sugar
2 tablespoons lemon juice

125 g (4 oz) unsalted butter
³/4 cup (185 g/6 oz) caster sugar
2 teaspoons finely grated lemon rind
3 eggs

1¹/2 cups (185 g/6 oz) semolina
1 cup (125 g/4 oz) self-raising flour
¹/2 cup (125 ml/4 fl oz) milk
¹/2 cup (80 g/2³/4 oz) blanched almonds, toasted and finely chopped
blanched flaked almonds, to decorate

1 Preheat the oven to warm 170°C (325°F/ Gas 3). Grease a 30 x 20 cm (12 x 8 inch) cake tin.
2 In a saucepan, dissolve the sugar in 3 cups (750 ml/24 fl oz) water over high heat, add the lemon juice and bring to the boil. Reduce the heat to medium and simmer for 20 minutes. Remove from the heat and leave until cool.
3 While the syrup is cooking, cream the butter, sugar and lemon rind with electric beaters until light and fluffy. Add the eggs one at a time, beating well after each addition.
4 Sift together the semolina and flour and fold into butter mixture alternately with the milk. Mix in the chopped almonds, then spread the mixture into the tin and arrange rows of flaked almonds on top. Bake for 35–40 minutes, or until the cake is golden and shrinks slightly from the sides of the tin. Prick the surface with a fine skewer, then pour the cooled syrup over the hot cake. When the cake is cool, cut it into squares or diamonds.

GREEK SWEETS
Fruit, rather than dessert is usually served at the end of a Greek meal. The enormous collection of sweet pastries, biscuits and sweetmeats are instead eaten in the late afternoon, or for supper, before bed. They are a measure of hospitality as well as the cook's skill. Many such as the Tsoureki tou paska (Easter bread), are associated with festive holidays. Greek halva differs from that in Middle Eastern countries, where it is a confection made from ground sesame seeds and honey.

LEFT: Halvas fourno

TURKEY

Turkish cuisine takes its place alongside French as one of the foremost in the world. It owes this enviable reputation to the culinary expertise developed in the grand houses and palaces centuries ago. Here, a large number of chefs specialized in their own particular type of cooking and their skills were honed and passed down from generation to generation. Lamb is the basic meat and shish kebab and lamb pilaf are famous worldwide. Vegetables are very prominent in the cuisine and in some areas there is also abundant seafood. Staples are yoghurt and many breads, including pide and lavash. Coffee plays an important role in the culture, and coffee houses are a popular meeting place.

HUMMUS
(Chickpea dip)

Preparation time: 20 minutes + overnight soaking
Total cooking time: 1 hour 15 minutes
Makes 3 cups

1 cup (220 g/6½ oz) dried chickpeas
2 tablespoons tahini
4 cloves garlic, crushed
2 teaspoons ground cumin
⅓ cup (80 ml/2¾ fl oz) lemon juice
3 tablespoons olive oil
large pinch of cayenne pepper
extra lemon juice, optional
extra virgin olive oil, to garnish
paprika, to garnish
chopped fresh flat-leaf parsley, to garnish

1 Put the chickpeas in a bowl, add 1 litre water, then soak overnight. Drain and place in a large saucepan with 2 litres water, or enough to cover the chickpeas by 5 cm (2 inches). Bring to the boil, then reduce the heat and simmer for 1 hour 15 minutes, or until the chickpeas are very tender. Skim any scum from the surface. Drain well, reserving the cooking liquid and leave until cool enough to handle. Pick through for any loose skins and discard them.
2 Combine the chickpeas, tahini, garlic, cumin, lemon juice, olive oil, cayenne pepper and 1½ teaspoons salt in a food processor until thick and smooth. With the motor running, gradually add enough of the reserved cooking liquid, about ¾ cup (185 ml/6 fl oz), to form a smooth creamy purée. Season with salt or some extra lemon juice.
3 Spread onto flat bowls or plates, drizzle with the extra virgin olive oil, sprinkle with paprika and scatter parsley over the top. Delicious served with warm pita bread or pide.

WALNUT TARATOOR

Preparation time: 5 minutes
Total cooking time: Nil
Serves 8

☆

250 g (8 oz) shelled walnuts
1 cup (80 g/2¾ oz) soft white breadcrumbs
3 cloves garlic
¼ cup (60 ml/2 fl oz) white wine vinegar
1 cup (250 ml/8 fl oz) olive oil
chopped fresh parsley, to garnish

1 Finely chop the walnuts in a blender or food processor. Set aside ½ teaspoon of the walnuts for a garnish. Add the breadcrumbs, garlic, vinegar and 3 tablespoons water to the rest and blend well.
2 With the motor running, gradually add the olive oil in a thin steady stream until smooth. Add a little more water if the sauce appears to be too thick. Season to taste, then transfer to a serving bowl and refrigerate.
3 Combine the reserved walnuts and parsley and sprinkle on top before serving.
NOTE: This is suitable for serving with seafood, salads, fried vegetables or bread. It can be made with almonds, hazelnuts or pine nuts instead of the walnuts. Lemon juice can be used as a substitute for the vinegar.

BELOW: Hummus

BOREK

(Turkish filo parcels)

Preparation time: 1 hour
Total cooking time: 20 minutes
Makes 24

☆☆

400 g (13 oz) feta
2 eggs, lightly beaten
3/4 cup (25 g/3/4 oz) chopped fresh flat-leaf
  parsley
375 g (12 oz) filo pastry
1/3 cup (80 ml/23/4 fl oz) good-quality olive oil

1 Preheat the oven to moderate 180°C (350°F/ Gas 4). Lightly grease a baking tray. Crumble the feta into a large bowl using a fork or your fingers. Mix in the eggs and parsley and season with freshly ground black pepper.

2 Cover the filo pastry with a damp tea towel so it doesn't dry out. Remove one sheet at a time. Brushing each sheet lightly with olive oil, layer 4 sheets on top of one another. Cut the pastry into four 7 cm (23/4 inch) strips.

3 Place 2 rounded teaspoons of the feta mixture in one corner of each strip and fold diagonally, creating a triangle pillow. Place on the baking tray, seam-side-down, and brush with olive oil. Repeat with the remaining pastry and filling to make 24 parcels. Bake for 20 minutes, or until golden. Serve these as part of a large meze plate.
NOTE: Fillings for borek are versatile and can be adapted to include your favourite cheeses such as haloumi, Gruyère, Cheddar or mozzarella.

CUCUMBER AND YOGHURT SALAD

Unlike the Greek tzatziki, this cucumber and yoghurt salad has only a small amount of garlic and is flavoured with dill instead of mint. It is very popular in Turkey.

Coarsely grate or chop 1 large unpeeled cucumber into a colander, sprinkle with salt and set aside for 15–20 minutes. In a bowl, combine 2 cups (500 g/1 lb) thick, creamy yoghurt with 1 crushed clove of garlic, 2 tablespoons chopped fresh dill and 1 tablespoon of white wine vinegar. Add the cucumber and season with some salt and white pepper, to taste. Cover and refrigerate. If you are making this salad just before serving you don't need to salt the cucumber. Serve drizzled with olive oil.
Serves 6–8.

FETA CHEESE
Feta cheese is traditionally made using sheep or goat's milk but these days milk from cows is more often used. Feta cheese is made in large blocks and cured and stored in brine. It develops a salty rich flavour and quite a crumbly texture.

ABOVE: Borek

BESAN FLOUR

This is made by very finely milling dried chickpeas. It originated in east Indian cuisine and is nutritious and high in protein. It has a fine texture and is a pale, creamy yellow. It is used as an alternative to wheat flour in breads, noodles, dumplings, to thicken soups and sauces and most commonly as a batter for deep-fried foods.

ABOVE: Lubyi bi zayt

LUBYI BI ZAYT

(Green beans with tomato and olive oil)

Preparation time: 10 minutes
Total cooking time: 25 minutes
Serves 4

1/3 cup (80 ml/2³/4 fl oz) olive oil
1 large onion, chopped
3 cloves garlic, finely chopped
400 g (13 oz) can good-quality chopped tomatoes
1/2 teaspoon sugar
750 g (1¹/2 lb) green beans, trimmed
3 tablespoons chopped fresh flat-leaf parsley

1 Heat the olive oil in a large frying pan, add the onion and cook over medium heat for 4–5 minutes, or until softened. Add the garlic and cook for another 30 seconds.
2 Add the tomato, sugar and 1/2 cup (125 ml/4 fl oz) water, then season with salt and freshly ground black pepper. Bring to the boil, then reduce the heat and simmer for 10 minutes, or until reduced slightly.
3 Add the beans and simmer for another 10 minutes, or until the beans are tender and the tomato mixture is pulpy. Stir in the parsley. Check the seasoning, and adjust according to your taste. Serve immediately, as a side dish.

CAULIFLOWER FRITTERS

Preparation time: 10 minutes
    + 30 minutes standing
Total cooking time: 15 minutes
Serves 4–6

600 g (1¹/4 lb) cauliflower
1/2 cup (55 g/2 oz) besan flour
2 teaspoons ground cumin
1 teaspoon ground coriander
1 teaspoon ground turmeric
pinch of cayenne pepper
1 egg, lightly beaten
1 egg yolk
oil, for deep-frying

1 Cut the cauliflower into bite-sized florets. Sift the flour and spices into a bowl, then stir in 1/2 teaspoon salt.
2 Lightly whisk the beaten egg, egg yolk and 1/4 cup (60 ml/2 fl oz) water in a jug. Make a well in the centre of the dry ingredients and pour in the egg mixture, whisking until smooth. Stand for 30 minutes.
3 Fill a deep saucepan one third full of oil and heat to 180°C (350°F), or until a cube of bread dropped into the oil browns in 15 seconds. Dip the florets into the batter, allowing the excess to

drain into the bowl. Deep-fry in batches for 3–4 minutes per batch, or until puffed and browned. Drain, sprinkle with salt and extra cayenne, if desired, and serve hot.

SIGARA BOREGI
(Fried cigar pastries)

Preparation time: 30 minutes
Total cooking time: 20 minutes
Makes 12

☆ ☆

500 g (1 lb) English spinach
1 tablespoon olive oil
4 cloves garlic, crushed
200 g (6¹/₂ oz) French shallots, finely chopped
¹/₂ cup (75 g/2¹/₂ oz) crumbled feta cheese
1 egg, lightly beaten
3 tablespoons chopped fresh flat-leaf parsley
¹/₄ teaspoon finely grated lemon rind
¹/₄ teaspoon paprika
pinch of nutmeg
6 sheets filo pastry
125 g (4 oz) butter, melted
light olive oil, for deep-frying

1 Wash the spinach, leaving a substantial amount of water on the leaves. Place in a large saucepan, cover and briefly cook over low heat until just wilted. Tip the spinach into a colander and press out most of the excess liquid with a wooden spoon. When cool, squeeze dry.

2 Heat the olive oil in a frying pan, add the garlic and shallots and cook for 2 minutes, or until soft but not browned. Transfer to a bowl and add the crumbled feta cheese, egg, parsley, spinach and lemon rind. Season with the paprika, nutmeg and salt and pepper, and mix well.

3 Remove a sheet of filo and cover the rest with a damp tea towel to prevent them drying out. Brush the sheet with melted butter, then fold it in half lengthways. It should measure about 32 x 12 cm (13 x 5 inches). Cut it in half widthways. Brush with butter, place about 1 heaped tablespoon of filling at one end of each and spread it to within 1 cm (¹/₂ inch) of each side. Fold the sides over to cover the ends of the filling, continuing the folds right up the length of the pastry. Brush with melted butter, then roll up tightly. Brush the outside with butter and seal well. Cover with a damp tea towel while you prepare the rest.

4 Heat the light olive oil in a deep frying pan to 180°C (350°F), or until a cube of bread browns in 15 seconds. Deep-fry in small batches until golden. Serve warm or at room temperature.

SIGARA BOREGI

Spread the filling to the edges, leaving a border.

Roll up the pastries tightly to enclose the filling.

LEFT: Sigari boregi

IMAM BAYILDI
Imam bayildi literally translates as 'the priest fainted'. It is possibly the most famous eggplant dish and is eaten all over the Arab world. Much ambiguity surrounds the story behind this dish. Did the priest faint from over-indulging in his sumptuous lunch or from the shock of the quantities of expensive olive oil used in the preparation?

IMAM BAYILDI
(Baked eggplant/aubergine)

Preparation time: 15 minutes
Total cooking time: 1 hour
Serves 4–6

☆ ☆

3/4 cup (185 ml/6 fl oz) olive oil
1 kg (2 lb) elongated eggplants (aubergines), cut in half lengthways
3 onions, thinly sliced
3 cloves garlic, finely chopped
400 g (13 oz) Roma tomatoes, peeled and chopped, or a 400 g (13 oz) can good-quality chopped tomatoes
2 teaspoons dried oregano
4 tablespoons chopped fresh flat-leaf parsley
1/4 cup (35 g/1 1/4 oz) currants
1/4 teaspoon ground cinnamon
2 tablespoons lemon juice
pinch of sugar
1/2 cup (125 ml/4 fl oz) tomato juice

1 Preheat the oven to moderate 180° (350°F/Gas 4). Heat half the olive oil in a large heavy-based frying pan and cook the eggplants on all sides for about 8–10 minutes, until the cut sides are golden. Remove from the pan and scoop out some of the flesh, leaving the skins intact and some flesh lining the skins. Finely chop the scooped-out flesh and set aside.

2 Heat the remaining olive oil in the same frying pan and cook the onion over medium heat for 8–10 minutes, until transparent. Add the garlic and cook for another minute. Add the tomato, oregano, parsley, currants, cinnamon, reserved eggplant flesh and salt and pepper, to taste.

3 Place the eggplant shells in a large ovenproof dish and fill each with tomato mixture.

4 Mix the lemon juice, sugar, tomato juice and some salt and pour over the eggplant. Cover and bake for 30 minutes, then uncover and cook for another 10 minutes. To serve, place on a serving platter and lightly drizzle with any remaining juice.

NOTE: This delicious dish is best served at room temperature and makes an excellent first course.

RIGHT: Imam bayildi

ZUCCHINI (COURGETTE) PATTIES

Preparation time: 20 minutes
Total cooking time: 15 minutes
Makes 16

☆ ☆

300 g (10 oz) zucchini (courgettes), grated
1 small onion, finely chopped
1/4 cup (30 g/1 oz) self-raising flour
1/3 cup (35 g/1 1/4 oz) grated kefalotyri or
   Parmesan
1 tablespoon chopped fresh mint
2 teaspoons chopped fresh flat-leaf parsley
pinch of ground nutmeg
1/4 cup (25 g/3/4 oz) dry breadcrumbs
1 egg, lightly beaten
olive oil, for shallow-frying

1 Put the zucchini and onion in the centre of a clean tea towel, gather the corners together and twist as tightly as possible to remove all the juices. Combine the zucchini, onion, flour, cheese, mint, parsley, nutmeg, breadcrumbs and egg in a large bowl. Season well with salt and cracked black pepper, then mix with your hands to a stiff mixture that clumps together.

2 Heat the oil in a large frying pan over medium heat. When hot, drop level tablespoons of mixture into the pan and shallow-fry for 2–3 minutes, or until well browned all over. Drain well on crumpled paper towels and serve hot, with lemon wedges, or with Cucumber and yoghurt salad (page 65).

CHICKPEA SALAD WITH CUMIN DRESSING

Soak 1 cup (220 g/7 oz) dried chickpeas in plenty of cold water for 8 hours, or overnight. Drain, place in a large saucepan, cover with water and bring to the boil over high heat. Reduce the heat to low and simmer for 1 1/2 hours, topping up with water to keep the chickpeas covered. Drain and cool. Combine in a large bowl with 3 tablespoons finely chopped fresh flat-leaf parsley, 1 small red onion, finely chopped, 1 clove garlic, finely chopped, 1/4 cup (60 ml/2 fl oz) lemon juice, 2 tablespoons olive oil, 1/2 teaspoon each of ground cumin and salt, a pinch of cayenne pepper and 1/2 teaspoon freshly ground black pepper. Toss well. Serves 6.

ABOVE: Zucchini patties

YOGHURT

Thousands of years ago nomadic Balkan tribesmen accidentally developed yoghurt and it became a way of preserving milk. Today yoghurt is made by introducing non-harmful bacteria to milk, which causes it to ferment and coagulate, resulting in a creamy-textured yoghurt with a slightly sharp flavour.

ABOVE: Yoghurt soup

YOGHURT SOUP

Preparation time: 15 minutes
Total cooking time: 20 minutes
Serves 4–6

☆

1.5 litres vegetable stock
1/3 cup (75 g/2 1/4 oz) short-grain white rice
80 g (2 3/4 oz) butter
50 g (1 3/4 oz) plain flour
250 g (8 oz) natural yoghurt
1 egg yolk
1 tablespoon finely sliced fresh mint
1/4 teaspoon cayenne pepper

1 Put the stock and rice in a saucepan and bring to the boil over high heat. Reduce the heat to medium-low and simmer for 10 minutes, then remove from the heat and set aside.
2 In another saucepan, melt 60 g (2 oz) of the butter over low heat. Stir in the flour and cook for 2–3 minutes, or until pale and foaming. Gradually add the stock and rice mixture, stirring constantly, and cook over medium heat for 2 minutes, or until the mixture thickens slightly. Reduce the heat to low.
3 In a small bowl, whisk together the yoghurt and egg yolk, then gradually pour into the soup, stirring constantly. Remove from the heat and stir in the mint and 1/2 teaspoon salt.
4 Just before serving, melt the remaining butter in a small saucepan over medium heat. Add the cayenne pepper and cook until the mixture is lightly browned. Pour over the soup.

CREAMY RED LENTIL SOUP

Preparation time: 25 minutes
Total cooking time: 1 hour
Serves 6

☆ ☆

CROUTONS
4 thick slices of bread, crusts removed
60 g (2 oz) butter
1 tablespoon oil

1 1/2 teaspoons cumin seeds
3/4 cup (185 g/6 oz) red lentils
80 g (2 3/4 oz) butter
1 large brown onion, diced
1.5 litres chicken or beef stock
2 tablespoons flour
2 egg yolks
3/4 cup (185 ml/6 fl oz) milk

1 For the croutons, cut the bread into 1 cm (1/2 inch) cubes. Heat the butter and oil in a frying pan and when the butter foams, add the bread and cook over medium heat until golden and crisp. Drain on crumpled paper towels.
2 In a small frying pan, dry roast the cumin seeds until they start to pop and become aromatic. Leave to cool, then grind to a fine powder in a mortar and pestle.
3 Rinse the lentils under cold water, then drain.
4 Melt half the butter in a heavy-based saucepan and cook the onion over medium heat for 5–6 minutes, until softened. Add the lentils, cumin and stock and bring to the boil. Cover and simmer for 30–35 minutes, until the lentils are very soft. Leave to cool, then purée in batches in a blender and transfer to a jug or bowl.
5 In a large heavy-based saucepan, melt the remaining butter over low heat. Stir in the flour and cook for 2–3 minutes, or until pale and foaming. Stirring constantly, add the lentil purée gradually, then simmer for 4–5 minutes.
6 In a small bowl, combine the egg yolks and the milk. Whisk a small amount of the soup into the egg mixture and then return it all to the soup, stirring constantly. Be careful not to boil the soup or the egg will curdle. Season with salt and pepper, to taste. Heat the soup to just under boiling and serve with the croutons.

GREEN OLIVE, WALNUT AND POMEGRANATE SALAD

Preparation time: 10 minutes
Total cooking time: Nil
Serves 4

1 cup (100 g/3 1/2 oz) walnut halves
1/2 cup (125 ml/4 fl oz) olive oil
1 1/2 tablespoons pomegranate syrup
1/2 teaspoon chilli flakes
2 cups (350 g/11 oz) green olives, pitted and cut in halves
1 cup (175 g/6 oz) pomegranate seeds
1 large red onion, chopped
1 cup (20 g/3/4 oz) fresh flat-leaf parsley leaves

1 Soak the walnut halves in boiling water for 3–4 minutes, or until the skins peel off readily. Drain, peel and pat dry. Lightly toast under a medium grill and when cool, roughly chop.
2 Combine the olive oil, pomegranate syrup and chilli flakes in a screw top jar and shake well.
3 Place the olives, pomegranate seeds, onion, walnuts and parsley in a bowl and toss. Just before serving, pour the dressing over, season, to taste, and combine well.

POMEGRANATES
These are round fruit with a thin, leathery reddish skin. Each fruit has hundreds of tiny translucent rich red edible seeds. The seeds can be eaten as a fruit, or used as a beautiful garnish for either sweet or savoury dishes. They have a delicious and interesting sweet and tart flavour.

LEFT: Green olive, walnut and pomegranate salad

HUNKAR BEGENDI

Peel the cooled eggplants, ensuring all the skin is removed.

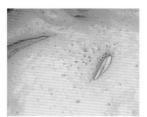

Stir the butter over medium heat until it has a toasty aroma and it darkens slightly.

HUNKAR BEGENDI

(Lamb braise with eggplant cream)

Preparation time: 30 minutes
Total cooking time: 1 hour 45 minutes
Serves 6–8

☆ ☆

2 tablespoons olive oil
1 kg (2 lb) lamb, cut into 2 cm (³/₄ inch) cubes
1 large onion, chopped
1 bay leaf
small pinch of ground cloves
2 cloves garlic, crushed
2 tablespoons tomato paste (tomato purée)
400 g (13 oz) can good-quality chopped tomatoes
1 cup (30 g/1 oz) chopped flat-leaf parsley
3 cups (750 ml/24 fl oz) beef stock
125 g (4 oz) vine-ripened tomatoes, chopped
chopped fresh flat-leaf parsley, to garnish

EGGPLANT CREAM
1 kg (2 lb) eggplants (aubergines)
60 g (2 oz) butter
2¹/₂ tablespoons plain flour
1¹/₄ cups (315 ml/10 fl oz) cream
²/₃ cup (60 g/2 oz) grated kasseri cheese
   (see Note)
large pinch of ground nutmeg

1 Preheat the oven to moderately hot 200°C (400°F/Gas 6). Heat the olive oil in large deep saucepan over high heat and cook the lamb in three batches for 4–5 minutes, or until well browned. Remove the lamb from the pan with a slotted spoon and set aside.
2 Add the onion to the pan, cook for 5 minutes, or until golden, then add the bay leaf, cloves, garlic, tomato paste, tomato, parsley, stock and lamb and stir well. Bring to the boil, then reduce the heat to low, cover and simmer, stirring occasionally for 1¹/₂ hours, or until the lamb is very tender and the sauce is thick. Season.
3 Meanwhile, pierce the eggplants a few times with a fork and, using a long-handled fork, roast them over an open flame (either a gas stovetop or a barbecue) for about 5 minutes, turning occasionally, until blackened and blistered all over. This will give them a good smoky flavour. Place the eggplants in a baking tray and bake for about 30 minutes, or until the eggplants are shrivelled and the flesh is very soft. Transfer to a colander and leave to cool.

4 When cool, peel the eggplants, ensuring all the skin is removed and discarded. Chop the flesh and set aside. Melt the butter in a saucepan over medium heat and add the flour. Stir for 2 minutes, or until it has a toasty aroma and darkens slightly. Gradually pour in the cream, whisking until smooth then add the eggplant and combine. Add the cheese and nutmeg and stir until the cheese has melted. Season.
5 Spread the eggplant cream on a serving plate then place the lamb braise in the centre and sprinkle with the chopped tomato and parsley. Serve immediately.
NOTE: Kasseri cheese, available at specialist delicatessens, is a sheep or goat's milk cheese, often used on top of lamb stews.

SKEWERED SWORDFISH

Preparation time: 15 minutes
   + 3 hours marinating
Total cooking: 10 minutes
Serves 6

☆

MARINADE
¹/₃ cup (80 ml/2³/₄ fl oz) lemon juice
2 tablespoons olive oil
1 small red onion, sliced thinly
1 teaspoon paprika
2 fresh bay leaves, crumpled
10 fresh sage leaves torn

1.5 kg (3 lb) swordfish, cut into 3 cm (1¹/₄ inch)
   cubes

LEMON SAUCE
¹/₄ cup (60 ml/2 fl oz) olive oil
¹/₄ cup (60 ml/2 fl oz) lemon juice
3 tablespoons chopped fresh flat-leaf parsley

1 Combine the marinade ingredients with 1 teaspoon salt and some ground black pepper in a bowl. Add the fish, toss to coat with the marinade, then cover and refrigerate for 3 hours, turning the fish occasionally.
2 Thread the fish onto 6 metal skewers and cook over a hot grill for 5 minutes, turning and brushing with marinade several times.
3 Combine the lemon sauce ingredients in a jar, seal and shake several times. Serve over the fish.
NOTE: You can substitute any firm fish such as blue eye, hake, mahi mahi, or use prawns.

OPPOSITE PAGE:
Hunkar begendi (top);
Skewered swordfish

SHISH KEBABS WITH PEPPERS (CAPSICUMS) AND HERBS

Preparation time: 20 minutes
  + 4 hours marinating
Total cooking time: 5 minutes
Serves 4

1 kg (2 lb) boneless leg of lamb
1 red pepper (capsicum)
1 green pepper (capsicum)
3 red onions
olive oil, for brushing

MARINADE
1 onion, thinly sliced
2 cloves garlic, crushed
1/4 cup (60 ml/2 fl oz) lemon juice
1/3 cup (80 ml/2 3/4 fl oz) olive oil
1 tablespoon chopped fresh thyme
1 tablespoon paprika
1/2 teaspoon chilli flakes
2 teaspoons ground cumin
1/2 cup (15 g/1/2 oz) chopped fresh flat-leaf parsley
1/3 cup (20 g/3/4 oz) chopped fresh mint

1 Trim the sinew and most of the fat from the lamb and cut the meat into 3 cm (1 1/4 inch) cubes.
2 Mix all the ingredients for the marinade in a large bowl. Season well, add the meat and mix well. Cover and refrigerate for 4–6 hours, or overnight.
3 Cut the peppers into 3 cm (1 1/4 inch) squares. Cut each red onion into 6 wedges.
4 Remove the lamb from the marinade and reserve the liquid. Thread the meat onto long skewers, alternating with onion and pepper pieces. Grill the skewers for 5–6 minutes, brushing frequently with the marinade for the first couple of minutes. Serve immediately. These are delicious served with bread or pilaf.

MARINADES
Marinades not only tenderize meats, chicken and fish, but they add flavour and moisture. The length of time needed for the marinade to penetrate will depend on the size of the pieces of meat and the type of meat used. Often the marinade will be used as a basting paste during cooking to add even more flavour.

RIGHT: Shish kebabs with peppers and herbs

CILBIR
(Poached eggs with yoghurt)

Preparation time: 10 minutes
Total cooking time: 20 minutes
Serves 4

60 g (2 oz) butter
1 brown onion, thinly sliced
1 cup (250 g/8 oz) thick natural yoghurt
4 large eggs
1 teaspoon hot paprika

1 Preheat the oven to slow 150°C (300°F/ Gas 2). Melt 20 g (¾ oz) of the butter in a heavy-based frying pan and cook the onion over low heat for 15 minutes, or until golden brown. Remove from the pan and allow to cool slightly. In a small bowl, combine the onion, yoghurt and salt, to taste.

2 Divide the yoghurt mixture among four ovenproof ramekins, each measuring about 7.5 cm (3 inches) in diameter and 4 cm (1½ inches) deep. Place on a tray in the oven to heat gently.

3 Meanwhile, fill a large deep frying pan three-quarters full of water, add a pinch of salt and bring to a gentle simmer. Gently break the eggs one at a time into a small bowl and slide the eggs into the water. Reduce the heat so that the water barely moves. Cook for 2–3 minutes, or until the eggs are just set. Remove with a slotted spoon and pat off any excess water using paper towels. Place an egg in each ramekin and season with salt and pepper.

4 Melt the remaining butter in a small saucepan and add the paprika. Drizzle over the eggs and serve at once.

NOTE: This dish is perfect for a light supper or brunch. Instead of, or as well as, the onions you can use 2 crushed cloves of garlic cooked gently in the butter for 1 minute, or until softened.

PAPRIKA
This spice powder is made by grinding the dried pods of a sweet mild pepper (capsicum), the pimento. Pimentos originated in Turkey, and were taken to Hungary where they were made into paprika. There are several varieties, including sweet, hot and smoked. All lend subtle flavour and can be used either as a seasoning or a garnish.

ABOVE: Cilbir

75

HARICOT BEANS
These are a small white bean usually used in the dried form. They have a mild flavour and are best known as the bean used for baked beans. Like all dried beans, they need to be covered with cold water and soaked overnight, before draining and then cooking until tender.

ABOVE: Braised lamb shanks with haricot beans

BRAISED LAMB SHANKS WITH HARICOT BEANS

Preparation time: 10 minutes + overnight soaking
Total cooking time: 2 hours 15 minutes
Serves 4

☆ ☆

2 cups (400 g/13 oz) dried haricot beans

4 tablespoons oil

4 lamb shanks, trimmed

2 tablespoons butter

2 cloves garlic, crushed

2 brown onions, finely chopped

1 1/2 tablespoons thyme leaves

2 tablespoons tomato paste (tomato purée)

2 x 400 g (13 oz) cans good-quality crushed tomatoes

1 tablespoon paprika

1 dried jalapeño chilli, roughly chopped

1 cup (30 g/1 oz) roughly chopped fresh flat-leaf parsley

1 Put the haricot beans in a bowl, cover well with water and soak overnight.

2 Heat 3 tablespoons of the oil in a large heavy-based frying pan over medium heat and brown the shanks on all sides. Remove and set aside. Drain the fat from the pan.

3 Heat the butter and the remaining oil in the pan and cook the garlic and onion over medium heat for 3–4 minutes, or until softened. Add the thyme, tomato paste, tomato and paprika and simmer for 5 minutes. Add the lamb shanks and 2 cups (500 ml/16 fl oz) hot water. Season well and bring to the boil. Cover the pan, reduce the heat and simmer gently for 30 minutes.

4 Drain the beans and add to the pan with the jalapeño chilli and another 2 cups (500 ml/16 fl oz) of hot water. Bring to the boil again, cover and simmer for another 1–1 1/2 hours or until both the beans and the meat are tender, adding more water, 1/2 cup (125 ml/4 fl oz) at a time, if necessary. Check the seasoning, adjust if necessary, and stir in half the parsley. Serve hot sprinkled with the remaining parsley.

GRILLED LAMB KOFTA

Preparation time: 20 minutes
+ 1 hour soaking
Total cooking time: 10 minutes
Makes 8

400 g (13 oz) lean lamb mince
1 tablespoon chopped fresh
    flat-leaf parsley
1 teaspoon ground cumin
2 tablespoons chopped fresh coriander
pinch of cayenne pepper
2 cloves garlic, crushed
1/2 teaspoon dried mint
3/4 cup (185 g/6 oz) Greek-style
    natural yoghurt
lemon wedges, for serving

1   Soak eight 15 cm (6 inch) wooden skewers in water for 1 hour, or until they sink, to ensure that they don't burn during cooking.
2   Combine the lamb mince, chopped parsley, cumin, coriander, cayenne pepper, half the garlic and 1/2 teaspoon salt in a bowl, and knead the mixture by hand for a few minutes until the mixture is quite smooth and comes away from the side of the bowl.
3   Divide the mixture into 16 portions. Wet your hands with cold water and roll each portion into a ball. Thread 2 balls onto each prepared skewer, moulding each ball into an oval shape about 4–5 cm (1½–2 inches) long.
4   To make the sauce, combine the dried mint, yoghurt and remaining clove of garlic in a bowl. Season with salt and pepper.
5   Heat a lightly oiled barbecue hotplate until hot, or heat a grill to its highest setting. Cook the kofta for about 6 minutes, turning once.
6   Serve the kofta hot with the sauce for dipping and some lemon wedges for sprinkling.

ROASTED RED PEPPERS
(CAPSICUMS)

Cut 8 red peppers (capsicums) into 4 flattish pieces each and carefully remove the seeds and membranes. Arrange in a single layer on a baking tray and cook under a hot grill until the skins are blackened and blistered. Place the peppers in a large bowl, then cover with a plate or plastic wrap and set aside for 10 minutes. Peel away the skins and slice the flesh into 3 cm (1¼ inch) wide strips. Place the strips in a clean bowl. Combine 2 crushed cloves of garlic and 1/3 cup (80 ml/2¾ fl oz) red wine vinegar in a small bowl and season with salt. Pour the dressing over the peppers and gently toss to coat thoroughly. Sprinkle 2 teaspoons of fresh thyme leaves over the top and refrigerate for at least 4 hours. Serve at room temperature. Serves 4–6.

BELOW: Grilled lamb kofta

CERKES TAVUGU
(Circassian chicken)

Preparation time: 25 minutes
Total cooking time: 1 hour
Serves 6

2 teaspoons paprika
1/4 teaspoon cayenne pepper
1 tablespoon walnut oil
4 chicken breasts, on the bone
4 chicken wings
1 large onion, chopped
2 sticks celery, coarsely chopped
1 carrot, chopped
1 bay leaf
4 sprigs fresh parsley
1 sprig fresh thyme
6 peppercorns
1 teaspoon coriander seeds
250 g (8 oz) walnuts, toasted (see Note)
2 slices of white bread, crusts removed
1 tablespoon paprika, extra
4 cloves garlic, crushed

1 Place the paprika and the cayenne pepper in a small dry frying pan and heat over low heat for about 2 minutes, or until aromatic, then add the walnut oil to the pan and set aside until ready to use.

2 Put the chicken in a large saucepan with the onion, celery, carrot, bay leaf, parsley, thyme, peppercorns and coriander seeds. Add 1 litre of water and bring to the boil. Reduce the heat to low and simmer for 15–20 minutes, or until the chicken is tender. Remove from the heat and allow to cool in the stock. Remove the chicken and return the stock to the heat. Simmer it for 20–25 minutes, or until reduced by half. Strain, skim off the fat and reserve the stock. Remove the chicken skin and shred the flesh into bite-sized pieces. Season well and ladle some stock over it to moisten it. Set aside.

3 Reserve a few of the walnuts to use as a garnish and blend the rest in a food processor to form a rough paste. Combine the bread with 1/2 cup (125 ml/4 fl oz) stock, add to the food processor and mix in short bursts for several seconds. Add the extra paprika, the garlic and some salt and pepper and process until smooth. Gradually add 1 cup (250 ml/8 fl oz) warm chicken stock until the mixture is of a smooth pourable consistency, adding a little more stock if necessary.

4 Mix half the sauce with the chicken and place on a serving platter. Pour the rest over to cover, then sprinkle with spiced oil and the remaining walnuts. Serve at room temperature.

NOTE: Californian walnuts are best for this recipe as they are much less bitter than some.

CIRCASSIAN CHICKEN
Circassian chicken comes from the culinary legacy of the Circassian women who were part of the Sultan's harem during the days of the Ottoman Empire. Noted for their gastronomic skills as well as their beauty, the Circassians contributed this dish, which bears their name and has become a classic of Turkish cuisine.

RIGHT: Cerkes tavugu

LAMB PILAF

Preparation time: 25 minutes
  + 1 hour standing
Total cooking time: 40 minutes
Serves 4–6

☆ ☆

1 large eggplant (aubergine), about 500 g (1 lb),
  cut into 1 cm (1/2 inch) cubes

1/2 cup (125 ml/4 fl oz) olive oil

1 large onion, finely chopped

2 teaspoons ground cumin

1 teaspoon ground cinnamon

1 teaspoon ground coriander

300 g (10 oz) long-grain rice

2 cups (500 ml/16 fl oz) chicken or
  vegetable stock

500 g (1 lb) lamb mince

1/2 teaspoon allspice

2 tablespoons olive oil, extra

2 vine-ripened tomatoes, cut into wedges

3 tablespoons toasted pistachios

2 tablespoons currants

2 tablespoons chopped fresh coriander
  leaves, to garnish

1 Place the eggplant in a colander, sprinkle generously with salt and leave for 1 hour. Rinse well and squeeze dry in a clean tea towel. Heat 2 tablespoons oil in a large, deep frying pan with a lid, add the eggplant and cook over medium heat for 8–10 minutes, or until golden and cooked through. Drain on paper towels.

2 Heat the remaining oil, add the onion and cook for 4–5 minutes, or until soft but not brown. Stir in half of each of the cumin, cinnamon and ground coriander. Add the rice and stir to coat, then add the stock, season and bring to the boil. Reduce the heat and simmer, covered, for 15 minutes, adding a little more water if the pilaf starts to dry out.

3 Meanwhile, place the lamb in a bowl with the allspice and the remaining cumin, cinnamon and coriander. Season and mix well. Roll into balls the size of macadamia nuts. Heat the extra oil in the frying pan and cook the meatballs in batches over medium heat for 5 minutes each batch, or until lightly browned and cooked through. Drain on paper towels. Add the tomato to the pan and cook, turning, for 3–5 minutes, or until lightly golden. Remove from the pan.

4 Stir the eggplant, pistachios, currants and meatballs through the rice (this should be quite dry by now). Serve surrounded by the cooked tomato and garnished with the coriander leaves.

PISTACHIOS
These nuts have a hard, pale shell enclosing a green nut which is much prized around the world. As these nuts mature, the shells open slightly, revealing nuts with a delicate flavour. They are eaten roasted and salted, or used in cooking in both sweet and savoury dishes.

ABOVE: Lamb pilaf

TURKISH BREAD

Preparation time: 30 minutes + rising
Total cooking time: 30 minutes
Makes 6

☆ ☆ ☆

2 x 7 g (¹/₄ oz) sachets dry yeast
¹/₂ teaspoon sugar
¹/₂ cup (60 g/2 oz) plain flour
3¹/₂ cups (435 g/14 oz) bread flour
   (see Note)
¹/₄ cup (60 ml/2 fl oz) olive oil
I egg
nigella or sesame seeds, to sprinkle

I Mix the yeast, sugar and ¹/₂ cup (125 ml/ 4 fl oz) warm water in a bowl. Add the plain flour and mix until smooth. Cover with a plate and leave for 30 minutes, or until frothy and trebled in size.
2 Place the bread flour in a large bowl with 1 teaspoon salt. Add the oil, yeast mixture and 270 ml (8¹/₂ fl oz) warm water. Mix to a loose dough, then turn out onto a lightly floured surface and knead for 15 minutes. Add minimal flour as the dough needs to be soft and moist.
3 Shape into a ball and place in a large oiled bowl. Cover with a tea towel and leave in a warm place for 1 hour, or until doubled in size. Punch down once, to expel the air, then divide into 6 portions and shape into smooth balls, kneading as little as possible. Place apart on a tray and place the tray in a plastic bag for 10 minutes.
4 Sprinkle a large baking tray with flour. Roll out two balls of dough, each to a 15 cm (6 inch) circle and place on the baking tray, leaving room for spreading. Cover with a tea towel and set aside for 20 minutes. Preheat the oven to very hot 230°C (450°F/Gas 8) and place another baking tray on the centre rack to heat.
5 Indent the surface of the dough with your finger. Lightly beat the egg with ¹/₄ cup (60 ml/ 2 fl oz) water and brush over the surface, then sprinkle with the seeds. Place the tray on top of the hot tray and bake for 8–10 minutes, or until puffed and golden. Wrap in a clean tea towel to soften the crusts while cooling. Meanwhile, repeat with the remaining dough.
NOTE: Bread flour requires more water so if you have to use all plain flour, start by adding only half the water in step 2, then gradually adding the rest until a loose, soft dough forms. The texture will differ if using all plain flour.

TURKISH PIZZA

Preparation time: 25 minutes + rising
Total cooking time: 45 minutes
Makes 8

☆ ☆ ☆

I teaspoon dried yeast
¹/₂ teaspoon sugar
225 g (7 oz) plain flour
4 tablespoons olive oil
250 g (8 oz) onions, finely chopped
500 g (1 lb) lamb mince
2 cloves garlic
I teaspoon ground cinnamon
I¹/₂ teaspoons ground cumin
¹/₂ teaspoon cayenne pepper
3 tablespoons tomato paste (tomato purée)
400 g (13 oz) can good-quality crushed tomatoes
¹/₃ cup (50 g/1³/₄ oz) pine nuts
3 tablespoons chopped fresh coriander
Greek-style natural yoghurt, for serving

I Mix the yeast, sugar and ¹/₄ cup (60 ml/ 2 fl oz) warm water in a bowl. Leave in a warm place for 20 minutes, or until bubbles appear on the surface. The mixture should be frothy and increased in volume.
2 Sift the flour and 1 teaspoon salt into a bowl, stir in the yeast mixture, 1 tablespoon oil and 100 ml (3 fl oz) warm water. Mix to form a soft dough, then turn onto a floured board and knead for 10 minutes, or until smooth. Place in an oiled bowl, cover and leave in a warm place for 1 hour, or until doubled in size.
3 Heat 2 tablespoons oil in a frying pan over low heat and cook the onion for 5 minutes, or until soft but not golden. Add the lamb and cook for 10 minutes, or until brown. Add the garlic and spices, tomato paste and tomato. Cook for 15 minutes, until quite dry. Add half the pine nuts and 2 tablespoons coriander. Season, then leave to cool. Preheat the oven to hot 210°C (415°F/Gas 6–7). Grease two baking trays.
4 Knock down the dough, then turn out onto a floured surface. Form into 8 portions and roll each into an 18 x 12 cm (7 x 5 inch) oval. Place on the trays. Divide the lamb among them and spread, leaving a small border. Sprinkle with pine nuts. Brush the edges with oil. Roll the uncovered dough over to cover the outer edges of the filling. Pinch the sides together at each end. Brush with oil. Bake for 15 minutes, or until golden. Sprinkle with coriander and serve with yoghurt.

Knock down the dough, then turn onto a floured surface.

Divide the lamb among the ovals of dough and sprinkle pine nuts over the top.

OPPOSITE PAGE: Turkish bread (top); Turkish pizza

2 Place 3 cups (750 ml/24 fl oz) water in a large saucepan, add the sugar and stir over medium heat until the sugar dissolves. Increase the heat and bring to the boil. Stir in the honey, lemon juice, lemon rind and cinnamon stick. Reduce the heat to medium, place the figs in the pan and simmer gently for 30 minutes. Remove with a slotted spoon and place on a large serving dish.

3 Boil the liquid over high heat for about 15–20 minutes, or until thick and syrupy. Remove the cinnamon and rind. Cool the syrup slightly and pour over the figs. Sprinkle with almonds and serve warm or cold with yoghurt.

TURKISH DELIGHT

Preparation time: 10 minutes
Total cooking time: 1 hour
Makes 25 pieces

4 cups (1 kg/2 lb) sugar
1 cup (125 g/4 oz) cornflour
1 teaspoon cream of tartar
2 tablespoons rosewater
red food colouring
1/3 cup (40 g/1 1/4 oz) icing sugar
2 tablespoons cornflour, extra

1 Pour 2 1/2 cups (625 ml/20 fl oz) water into a large, heavy-based saucepan and bring to the boil. Add the sugar and stir until thoroughly dissolved. Remove from the heat.

2 In a large bowl, blend the cornflour and cream of tartar with 1 cup (250 ml/8 fl oz) cold water. Gradually add the blended cornflour to the syrup, then return the saucepan to medium heat and stir until the mixture boils.

3 Reduce the heat and cook very slowly for 45 minutes, stirring often. During this time, the colour will change from cloudy to clear and golden and the mixture will thicken.

4 Add the rosewater and a few drops of food colouring, pour onto a lightly oiled 30 x 20 cm (12 x 8 inch) tray and leave to set. When firm and cool, cut into 2 cm (3/4 inch) squares and toss in the combined icing sugar and extra cornflour.

NOTE: There are many variations you can make to this recipe. For an orange flavour, use 1–2 tablespoons orange blossom water instead of rosewater and use orange food colouring. For almond flavour, add 1/2 cup (80 g/2 3/4 oz) chopped, toasted, unblanched almonds when adding the flavourings and colourings.

FIGS IN HONEY SYRUP

Preparation time: 20 minutes
Total cooking time: 1 hour
Serves 4

100 g (3 1/2 oz) blanched whole almonds
12 whole fresh figs (about 750 g/1 1/2 lb)
1/2 cup (125 g/4 oz) sugar
1/3 cup (115 g/4 oz) honey
2 tablespoons lemon juice
6 cm (2 1/2 inch) sliver of lemon rind
1 cinnamon stick
1 cup (250 g/8 oz) Greek-style natural yoghurt

1 Preheat the oven to moderate 180°C (350°F/ Gas 4). Place the almonds on a baking tray and bake for 5 minutes, or until golden. Leave to cool. Cut the stems off the figs and make a small crossways incision 5 mm (1/4 inch) deep on top of each. Push a blanched almond into the base of each fig. Roughly chop the remaining almonds.

ABOVE: Figs in honey syrup

YOGURT TATLISI
(Yoghurt cake with syrup)

Preparation time: 20 minutes
  + cooling
Total cooking time: 50 minutes
Serves 8–10

185 g (6 oz) unsalted butter, softened
1 cup (250 g/8 oz) caster sugar
5 eggs, separated
1 cup (250 g/8 oz) Greek-style natural
  yoghurt
2 teaspoons grated lemon rind
1/2 teaspoon vanilla essence
21/4 cups (280 g/9 oz) plain flour
1/2 teaspoon bicarbonate of soda
2 teaspoons baking powder
whipped cream, for serving

SYRUP
1 cup (250 g/8 oz) caster sugar
1 cinnamon stick
4 cm (11/2 inch) strip lemon rind
1 tablespoon lemon juice

1 Preheat the oven to moderate 180°C
(350°F/Gas 4) and lightly grease a 20 x 10 cm
(8 x 4 inch) loaf tin.
2 Cream the butter and sugar in a bowl with
electric beaters until light and fluffy. Add the
egg yolks gradually, beating well after each
addition. Stir in the yoghurt, lemon rind
and vanilla essence. Fold in the sifted flour,
bicarbonate of soda and baking powder with
a metal spoon.
3 Whisk the egg whites in a clean, dry bowl
until stiff and gently fold into the mixture.
Spoon into the tin and bake for 50 minutes, or
until a skewer comes out clean when inserted
into the centre of the cake. Cool in the tin for
10 minutes, then turn out onto a wire rack.
4 Meanwhile, for the syrup, place the sugar and
cinnamon stick in a small saucepan with 3/4 cup
(185 ml/6 fl oz) cold water. Stir over medium
heat until the sugar has dissolved. Bring to the
boil, add the lemon rind and juice, then reduce
the heat and simmer for 5–6 minutes. Strain,
then pour the syrup all over the hot cake and
wait for most of it to be absorbed before you
serve the cake. Cut into slices and serve warm
with whipped cream.

ZERDE
(Sweet saffron rice)

Crush 1 teaspoon saffron threads with your
fingers and soak in 2 tablespoons of boiling
water for 30 minutes. Bring 1.25 litres
water to the boil in a large saucepan, then
add 1/2 cup (110 g/31/2 oz) medium-grain
rice. Reduce to a simmer and cook, stirring
occasionally, for 20 minutes. Stir in 1 cup
(250 g/8 oz) caster sugar, 2 tablespoons
rosewater and the saffron with the soaking
liquid and simmer for another 10 minutes.
Add 3 tablespoons toasted pine nuts and
3 tablespoons pistachios, chopped, and
simmer for another 10 minutes. The
mixture should be thick and soupy. If it is
too thick, add a little more water. Serve
either hot or cold (it will thicken as it
cools). Garnish as you prefer, with things
such as pomegranate seeds or pistachios.
Serve with Greek-style natural yoghurt.
This dish is sweet and aromatic. Serves 6.

ABOVE: Yoghurt tatlisi

TURKISH COFFEE
As in many countries around the Mediterranean, coffee in Turkey is prepared in long-handled pots called jezve. It is essential that the coffee is ground to a fine powder just before brewing. Both medium and dark roasts can be used. The addition of a cardamom pod gives a wonderful fragrance to the coffee.

BAKLAVA

Preparation time: 30 minutes + cooling
Total cooking time: 1 hour 15 minutes
Makes 18 pieces

2¼ cups (560 g/1 lb 2 oz) caster sugar
1½ teaspoons grated lemon rind
¼ cup (90 g/3 oz) honey
¼ cup (60 ml/2 fl oz) lemon juice
2 tablespoons orange blossom water
200 g (6½ oz) walnuts, finely chopped
200 g (6½ oz) shelled pistachios, finely chopped
200 g (6½ oz) almonds, finely chopped
2 tablespoons caster sugar, extra
2 teaspoons ground cinnamon
200 g (6½ oz) unsalted butter, melted
375 g (12 oz) ready-made filo pastry

BELOW: Baklava

1 Place the sugar, lemon rind and 1½ cups (375 ml/12 fl oz) water in a saucepan and stir over high heat until the sugar has dissolved, then boil for 5 minutes. Reduce the heat to low and simmer for 5 minutes, or until the syrup has thickened slightly and just coats the back of a spoon. Add the honey, lemon juice and orange blossom water and cook for 2 minutes. Remove from the heat and leave to cool completely.

2 Preheat the oven to warm 170°C (325°F/Gas 3). Combine the nuts, extra sugar and cinnamon in a bowl. Brush the base and sides of a 30 x 27 cm (12 x 11 inch) baking dish or tin with the melted butter. Cover the base with a single layer of filo pastry, brush lightly with the butter, folding in any overhanging edges. Continue layering the filo, brushing each new layer with butter and folding in the edges until 10 sheets have been used. Keep the unused filo under a damp tea towel.

3 Sprinkle half the nut mixture over the pastry and pat down evenly. Repeat the layering and buttering of 5 more filo sheets, sprinkle with the remaining nuts, then continue to layer and butter the remaining sheets, including the top layer. Press down with your hands so the pastry and nuts adhere to each other. Using a large sharp knife, cut into diamond shapes, ensuring you cut through to the bottom layer. Pour any remaining butter evenly over the top and smooth with your hands. Bake for 30 minutes, then lower the temperature to slow 150°C (300°F/Gas 2) and cook for another 30 minutes.

4 Immediately cut through the original diamond markings, then strain the syrup evenly over the top. Cool completely before lifting the diamonds out onto a serving platter.
NOTE: To achieve the right texture, it is important for the baklava to be piping hot and the syrup cold when pouring the syrup.

TURKISH COFFEE

Place 2 tablespoons finely ground coffee beans, 2 teaspoons caster sugar, or to taste, and 1 cracked cardamom pod in a small saucepan with 1 cup (250 ml/8 fl oz) cold water. Stir over medium heat until the coffee starts to rise to the surface. Remove from the heat immediately. Spoon the froth (or the crema) into 2 small cups and return the pan to the heat. When the coffee starts to rise to the top again, remove from the heat and fill the cups. The key sign of a good Turkish coffee is the creamy froth. Serves 2.

SEMOLINA AND NUT DIAMONDS

Preparation time: 30 minutes
  + 30 minutes standing
Total cooking time: 40 minutes
Makes 12

115 g (4 oz) unsalted butter, softened
1/2 cup (125 g/4 oz) caster sugar
1 cup (125 g/4 oz) semolina
1 cup (110 g/3 1/2 oz) ground roasted
  hazelnuts
2 teaspoons baking powder
3 eggs, lightly beaten
1 tablespoon finely grated orange rind
2 tablespoons orange juice
whipped cream or honey-flavoured yoghurt,
  for serving

SYRUP
3 cups (750 g/1 1/2 lb) sugar
4 cinnamon sticks
1 tablespoon thinly julienned orange rind
1/3 cup (80 ml/2 3/4 fl oz) lemon juice
1/2 cup (125 ml/4 fl oz) orange blossom water

TOPPING
1/2 cup (60 g/2 3/4 oz) slivered almonds
1/2 cup (70 g/2 1/4 oz) roasted hazelnuts,
  coarsely chopped

1 Preheat the oven to hot 210°C (415°F/
Gas 6–7). Lightly grease a 23 cm (9 inch) square
baking tin and line the base with baking paper.
Cream the butter and sugar in a medium bowl
until light and fluffy. Stir in the semolina,
ground hazelnuts and baking powder. Add the
eggs, orange rind and juice and fold through
until well combined. Spoon into the tin, smooth
the surface and bake for 20 minutes, or until
golden and just set. Leave in the tin.
2 Meanwhile, for the syrup, place the sugar,
cinnamon sticks and 3 1/3 cups (830 ml/28 fl oz)
water in a saucepan over low heat and stir until
the sugar has dissolved. Increase the heat and
boil rapidly, without stirring, for 5 minutes.
Pour into a heatproof measuring jug then return
half to the saucepan. Boil for 15–20 minutes, or
until thickened and reduced to about 2/3 cup
(170 ml/5 1/2 fl oz). Stir in the orange zest.

3 Add the lemon juice and orange blossom
water to the syrup in the jug and pour it over
the cake in the tin. When absorbed, turn the
cake out onto a large flat plate. Slice into
4 equal strips, then slice each strip diagonally
into 3 diamond-shaped pieces. Discard the end
scraps but keep the pieces touching together.
4 For the topping, combine the almonds and
hazelnuts and scatter over the cake. Pour the
thickened syrup and julienned orange rind over
the nuts and leave to stand for 30 minutes before
serving. Using a cake slice, transfer the diamonds
to individual plates and serve with whipped
cream or honey-flavoured yoghurt.

*ABOVE: Semolina and
nut diamonds*

ITALY

Italians love good food. Friends and family often gather to share a feast. Their cooking is wonderfully uncomplicated and the versatile antipasto spreads have been embraced in many places outside Italy because of their simplicity. Italian cuisine has an interesting history as, traditionally, ingredients and cooking styles varied depending on the region. As recently as the 1950s, this was still the case. However, as people migrated within the country, so did food ideas and this has led to a wonderful mixed cuisine using polenta, risotto, fresh and dried pasta, olive oil, butter, pizza, tomatoes and eggplants (aubergines), as well as citrus, capers, parsley, basil and cheeses including the famous Parmigiano Reggiano.

ZUCCHINI (COURGETTE) FLOWERS
The delicate blossoms of the zucchini are very perishable and are best kept refrigerated on a plate under a moist paper towel. Choose flowers which are fresh and firm and check that they are clean and free of stray insects before use. There are male and female blossoms. The male is attached to the stem while the female blossom is attached to the zucchini.

BEAN AND ROSEMARY DIP

Preparation time: 5 minutes
  + cooling
Total cooking time: 5 minutes
Makes 2 cups

2 x 310 g (10 oz) cans butter
  or cannellini beans
3 tablespoons olive oil
2 cloves garlic, crushed
1 tablespoon finely chopped fresh
  rosemary leaves
1 cup (250 ml/8 fl oz) chicken
  or vegetable stock
2 teaspoons lemon juice

1 Rinse and drain the beans and set aside. Heat the olive oil in a saucepan and cook the garlic and rosemary for 1 minute, or until the garlic is softened. Add the beans and stock and bring to the boil. Reduce the heat and simmer for 3–4 minutes. Allow to cool.
2 Blend or process the mixture in batches until smooth. Add the lemon juice and season, to taste. Serve with bread or grissini. This dip can be kept in the refrigerator in a covered container for several days.

ABOVE: Bean and rosemary dip

STUFFED ZUCCHINI (COURGETTE) FLOWERS

Preparation time: 20 minutes
Total cooking time: 15 minutes
Makes 20

75 g (2¹/2 oz) plain flour
100 g (3¹/2 oz) mozzarella
10 anchovy fillets, cut in half lengthways
10 fresh basil leaves, torn
20 zucchini (courgette) blossoms, stems
  and pistils removed
olive oil, for shallow-frying
2 lemon wedges, for serving

1 In a bowl, combine the flour with about 1 cup (250 ml/8 fl oz) water, enough to obtain a creamy consistency. Add a pinch of salt and mix.
2 Cut the mozzarella into 20 matchsticks and pat dry the anchovies. Insert a piece of mozzarella, half an anchovy fillet and some basil into each zucchini blossom. Press the petals closed.
3 Pour oil into a heavy-based frying pan to a depth of 2.5 cm (1 inch). Heat until a drop of batter sizzles when dropped in the oil.
4 Dip one flower at a time in the batter, shaking off the excess. Cook in batches for 3 minutes, or until crisp and golden. Drain on paper towels. Season and serve immediately with lemon wedges.

BAKED PEPPERS (CAPSICUMS) WITH ANCHOVIES

Preparation time: 15 minutes
Total cooking time: 50 minutes
Serves 6

3 yellow peppers (capsicums)
3 red peppers (capsicums)
2 tablespoons extra virgin olive oil
12 anchovy fillets, halved lengthways
3 cloves garlic, thinly sliced
1/2 cup (25 g/3/4 oz) fresh basil leaves
1 tablespoon baby capers, rinsed
extra virgin olive oil, for serving

1 Preheat the oven to moderate 180°C (350°F/ Gas 4). Cut each pepper in half lengthways, leaving the stems intact. If the peppers are large, quarter them. Remove the seeds and membrane. Drizzle a little of the oil in a baking dish and place the peppers in, skin-side-down. Season with salt and pepper.
2 In each pepper, place a halved anchovy fillet, slivers of garlic and a torn basil leaf. Divide the capers among the peppers. Season with salt and pepper and drizzle with the remaining oil.
3 Cover the dish with foil and bake the peppers for 20 minutes. Remove the foil and cook for another 25–30 minutes, or until the peppers are tender. Drizzle with a little extra virgin olive oil. Scatter the remaining torn basil leaves over the peppers and serve warm or at room temperature.

MOZZARELLA IN CAROZZA
(Mozzarella in carriages/ Cheese sandwiches)

Dip 8 thin slices of crustless day old white bread in 2/3 cup (170 ml/5 1/2 fl oz) milk. Make sandwiches with the bread putting two slices of mozzarella between the bread. Lightly beat 2 eggs and season well with salt and pepper. Dip the sandwiches in the egg, then coat well with fresh breadcrumbs. Heat 1 cup (250 ml/8 fl oz) olive oil in a heavy-based frying pan over medium heat and fry the sandwiches for 2–3 minutes on both sides, or until the sandwiches are golden. Drain on crumpled paper towels and serve with lemon wedges. Makes 4.

MOZZARELLA
At one time, all mozzarella in Italy was made from the prized milk of water buffaloes which gives a creamy, fragrant fresh cheese. These days, however, most mozzarella is made with cow's milk and the resulting texture and taste are slightly different. However, buffalo milk mozzarella is becoming increasingly available in speciality food stores if you want to try it.

LEFT: Baked peppers with anchovies

ARANCINI

When cooking the mince, break up any lumps with a wooden spoon.

Place 2 heaped teaspoons of the filling into the centre of each rice ball.

Enclose the rice around the filling, pressing the rice back into a ball shape.

Roll each ball in flour, then dip in egg before coating in the breadcrumbs.

ARANCINI
(Fried stuffed rice balls)

Preparation time: 30 minutes + 30 minutes
   cooling + 30 minutes refrigeration
Total cooking time: 45 minutes
Makes 12

☆ ☆

2¼ cups (500 g/1 lb) short-grain
   white rice
¼ teaspoon saffron threads
2 eggs, beaten
1 cup (100 g/3½ oz) freshly grated Parmesan
plain flour, for coating
2 eggs, beaten, extra
1 cup (100 g/3½ oz) dry breadcrumbs
oil, for deep-frying

FILLING
1 tablespoon olive oil
1 small onion, finely chopped
150 g (5 oz) pork and veal mince
   or beef mince
2/3 cup (170 ml/5½ fl oz) white wine
1 tablespoon tomato paste (tomato purée)
2 teaspoons fresh thyme leaves

1 Bring 1 litre water to the boil in a large saucepan and add the rice and saffron threads. Bring slowly back to the boil, then reduce the heat and simmer. Cover and cook over low heat for 20 minutes, or until tender. Transfer to a large bowl and cool to room temperature. Stir in the egg and grated Parmesan.

2 For the filling, heat the oil in a small frying pan over medium heat. Add the onion and cook for 2–3 minutes, or until soft. Add the mince and cook for 2 minutes, or until it changes colour, pressing out any lumps. Add the wine and tomato paste. Reduce the heat and simmer for 3–4 minutes, or until the wine has evaporated. Stir in the thyme and set aside to cool.

3 With wet hands, divide the rice mixture into 12 balls. Flatten each slightly, make an indent in the centre of each and place 2 heaped teaspoons of the filling into each ball. Close the rice around the filling.

4 Roll each ball in the flour, dip in the extra egg, then roll in the breadcrumbs. Refrigerate for 30 minutes.

5 Fill a deep heavy-based saucepan one third full of oil and heat to 180°C (350°F), or until a cube of bread dropped into the oil browns in 15 seconds. Deep-fry the balls in four batches for 2–3 minutes each, or until golden brown. Drain on crumpled paper towels. Serve warm or at room temperature.

RIGHT: Arancini

FRITTATA DI ASPARAGI ALLA MENTA

(Asparagus and mint frittata)

Preparation time: 10 minutes
Total cooking time: 20 minutes
Serves 4

6 eggs
1/3 cup (35 g/1 1/2 oz) grated Pecorino
  or Parmesan
1/4 cup (5 g/1/4 oz) fresh mint leaves,
  finely shredded
200 g (6 1/2 oz) baby asparagus spears
2 tablespoons extra virgin olive oil

1 Put the eggs in a large bowl, beat well, then stir in the cheese and mint and set aside.
2 Trim the woody part off the asparagus, then cut the asparagus on the diagonal into 5 cm (2 inch) pieces. Heat the oil in a 20 cm (8 inch) frying pan that has a heatproof handle. Add the asparagus and cook for 4–5 minutes, until tender and bright green. Season with salt and pepper, then reduce the heat to low.
3 Pour the egg mixture over the asparagus and cook for 8–10 minutes. During cooking, use a spatula to gently pull the sides of the frittata away from the sides of the pan and tip the pan slightly so the egg runs underneath the frittata.
4 When the mixture is nearly set but still slightly runny on top, place the pan under a low grill for 1–2 minutes, until the top is set and just browned. Serve warm or at room temperature.

FIGS AND PROSCIUTTO

Using 6 ripe, unblemished figs, with good colouring, make a deep cross on the top of each with a small, sharp knife, opening each fig up without breaking it into two pieces. Wrap a thin slice of prosciutto loosely around each. Secure with a toothpick. Serves 6.

ASPARAGUS
When buying fresh asparagus make sure that the tips of the spears are tightly closed and the stalk is firm and green with no tinges of yellow. Not all asparagus needs to be peeled, especially if thin, but if the stems are thick and woody, they should be trimmed and the bottom third of the stems peeled using a vegetable peeler. There is also a white asparagus, which takes longer to cook, and a purple variety called *viola*.

ABOVE: Frittata di asparagi alla menta

PANCETTA

Coming from the Italian word *pancia* which means belly, pancetta is exactly the same cut of meat as bacon but it is not smoked. There are two types of pancetta: *pancetta stesa,* a flat type which is cured for about three weeks and then hung to air and dry for up to four months, and *pancetta arrotolata,* which is rolled into a salami-like shape. In the Italian kitchen, pancetta stesa is used to flavour sauces, stews and pastas, and the rolled pancetta is mainly used as part of an antipasto platter.

ABOVE: Stuffed sardines

STUFFED SARDINES

Preparation time: 20 minutes
Total cooking time: 25 minutes
Serves 4–6

☆ ☆

1 kg (2 lb) butterflied fresh sardines
1/4 cup (60 ml/2 fl oz) olive oil
1/2 cup (40 g/1 1/4 oz) soft white breadcrumbs
1/4 cup (40 g/1 1/4 oz) sultanas
1/4 cup (40 g/1 1/4 oz) pine nuts, toasted
20 g (3/4 oz) can anchovies, drained, mashed
1 tablespoon finely chopped fresh flat-leaf parsley
2 spring onions, finely chopped

1 Preheat the oven to moderately hot 200°C (400°F/Gas 6). Open out each sardine and place skin-side-up on a chopping board.
2 Heat half the oil in a frying pan, add the breadcrumbs and cook over medium heat, stirring until light golden. Drain on paper towels.
3 Put half the fried breadcrumbs in a bowl and stir in the sultanas, pine nuts, anchovies, parsley and spring onion. Season with salt and pepper, to taste. Spoon about 2 teaspoons of the mixture into each prepared sardine, then carefully fold up to enclose the stuffing.

4 Place the stuffed sardines in a single layer in a well-greased baking dish. Sprinkle any remaining stuffing over the top of the sardines, with the cooked breadcrumbs. Drizzle with the remaining olive oil and bake for 15–20 minutes.

FRIED STUFFED OLIVES

Preparation time: 45 minutes
Total cooking time: 1 hour 15 minutes
Serves 6–8 as part of an antipasto platter

☆ ☆ ☆

1 tablespoon olive oil
100 g (3 1/2 oz) pork and veal mince
60 g (2 oz) pancetta, chopped
3 cloves garlic, crushed
1/2 tablespoon chopped fresh flat-leaf parsley
pinch of cayenne pepper
1/2 cup (125 ml/4 fl oz) dry white wine
1 cup (500 ml/16 fl oz) chicken stock
1/3 cup (25 g/3/4 oz) fresh white breadcrumbs
1 egg yolk
2 tablespoons grated provolone
1 kg (2 lb) extra jumbo green olives, such as Gordal, pitted

½ cup (60 g/2 oz) plain flour
1 egg, beaten
1 cup (100 g/3½ oz) dry breadcrumbs
oil, for deep-frying

1 Heat the oil in a frying pan over low heat and add the mince, pancetta, garlic and parsley. Cook, stirring, until the pork changes colour. Add the cayenne and season with salt and black pepper. Increase the heat to high, pour in the wine and cook until almost evaporated. Add the stock, reduce the heat and simmer for 45 minutes, by which time the liquid should have evaporated. If not, increase the heat and reduce it until dry.
2 Pass the meat mixture through a fine mincer, or process in a food processor until as smooth as possible. Stir in the breadcrumbs, egg yolk and provolone. Using a pastry bag fitted with a small round nozzle, pipe the filling into the olives. Roll in the flour and shake off any excess. Roll in the beaten egg, then the breadcrumbs.
3 Fill a deep heavy-based saucepan one third full of oil and heat to 180°C (350°F), or until a cube of bread dropped into the oil browns in 15 seconds. Fry the olives in batches until golden. Drain on paper towels before serving.

INSALATA CAPRESE
(Tomato and bocconcini salad)

Preparation time: 10 minutes
Total cooking time: Nil
Serves 4

3 large vine-ripened tomatoes
250 g (8 oz) bocconcini
12 fresh basil leaves
¼ cup (60 ml/2 fl oz) extra virgin olive oil
4 fresh basil leaves, roughly torn, extra

1 Slice the tomato into twelve 1 cm (½ inch) slices. Slice the bocconcini into 24 slices the same thickness as the tomato.
2 Arrange the tomato slices on a serving plate, alternating them with 2 slices of bocconcini and placing a basil leaf between the bocconcini slices.
3 Drizzle with the olive oil, sprinkle with the torn basil and season well with salt and freshly ground black pepper.
NOTE: You could use whole cherry tomatoes and toss them with the bocconcini and basil.

TOMATO AND BOCCONCINI SALAD
This is a very popular summer salad in Italy. It is delicious made with buffalo mozzarella if you can find it. We've used bocconcini in this recipe as it is more readily available than very fresh mozzarella.

LEFT: Insalata caprese

OLIVE CROSTINI

Preparation time; 10 minutes
Total cooking time: 5 minutes
Serves 4

150 g (5 oz) pitted Kalamata olives
4 anchovy fillets
2 tablespoons baby capers
1 clove garlic
2 tablespoons chopped fresh basil
1/4 cup (60 ml/2 fl oz) olive oil
1 baguette, cut into 12 slices

1   Preheat the oven to moderately hot 190°C (375°F/Gas 5). Combine all the ingredients except the bread in a food processor and process in short bursts until all the ingredients are finely chopped but not smooth. Season, to taste. Bake the bread on a baking tray for 2–3 minutes on each side, or until golden. Spread with the paste.

CHICKEN LIVER CROSTINI

Preparation time: 15 minutes
Total cooking time: 20 minutes
Serves 4

1 baguette, cut into 12 slices
1/3 cup (80 ml/2³/4 fl oz) extra virgin olive oil
220 g (7 oz) chicken livers, trimmed
2 button mushrooms, sliced
4 fresh sage leaves
2 cloves garlic, crushed
pinch of nutmeg
1/2 cup (125 ml/4 fl oz) Madeira
1 anchovy fillet
1/2 tablespoon capers
1 egg yolk

1   Preheat the oven to moderately hot 190°C (375°F/Gas 5). Use half the oil to brush both sides of the bread, then bake on a baking tray for 5 minutes, or until golden on both sides. Cool.
2   Heat the remaining oil in a heavy-based frying pan and add the livers, mushrooms and sage. Cook for 5 minutes, stirring often, or until the livers change colour. Add the garlic and nutmeg and season. Cook for 1 minute, add the Madeira

and cook until it has evaporated. Transfer to a food processor. Add the anchovy and capers and process until smooth. Add the egg yolk, blend, then taste for seasoning. Spread on the toasts.

TOMATO AND BASIL CROSTINI

Preparation time: 10 minutes
Total cooking time: 5 minutes
Serves 4

4 vine-ripened tomatoes, roughly chopped
1/2 cup (15 g/¹/2 oz) fresh basil leaves, torn
2 tablespoons extra virgin olive oil
1 baguette, cut into 12 slices
1 large clove garlic

1   Preheat the oven to moderately hot 190°C (375°F/Gas 5). Gently squeeze any excess juice from the tomatoes, or drain them in a sieve. Combine the tomato, basil and oil in a small bowl and season well with salt and pepper.
2   Bake the bread on a baking tray until golden. While hot, rub one side of each slice with the garlic, then top with the tomato mixture. Serve.

NAPOLETANA CROSTINI

Preparation time: 10 minutes
Total cooking time: 15 minutes
Serves 4

100 g (3¹/2 oz) unsalted butter, softened
1 baguette, cut into 12 slices
6 bocconcini, each cut into quarters
12 anchovy fillets, cut in half lengthways
2 vine-ripened tomatoes, peeled, cut into
   wedges and deseeded
1 teaspoon dried oregano

1   Preheat the oven to moderate 180°C (350°/ Gas 4). Brush a baking tray with melted butter.
2   Butter each bread slice thickly on one side only and top each with 2 slices of bocconcini. Lay 2 anchovy halves and a piece of tomato over the cheese on each. Season with oregano and salt and freshly ground pepper and bake on the tray for 12–15 minutes. Brush the tomatoes with a little of the butter left on the tray and serve.

CAPERS
The immature, small flower buds of a Mediterranean plant, capers are preserved in vinegar, brine or salt. The highest grade capers are Lilliput which, as their name suggests, are the smallest, picked from the hardest buds. Tiny capers are slightly larger, but also of high quality. Caper aficionados swear by salted, rather than brined capers as they retain their distinct taste and texture. All capers, however they are preserved, should be rinsed and drained before using. Caperberries are the pollinated fruit of the caper bush and are sold with the stalk attached and preserved in brine.

OPPOSITE PAGE, FROM LEFT: Chicken liver crostini; Napoletana crostini; Olive crostini; Tomato and basil crostini

ANTIPASTO

WHAT IS ANTIPASTO?

Antipasto, probably the most modern aspect of the Italian table, means 'before the meal'. The variety and combinations of these small tasty, aromatic dishes are endless. Antipasti are still not usually part of the main family meal of the day, but a formal Italian dinner, particularly in wealthy households or at restaurants and weddings, usually begins with antipasti.

There are no hard and fast rules when it comes to the type of food but many of the dishes take advantage of fresh local ingredients. They can be served as starters, snacks, or together as a meal in themselves. While on one occasion chargrilled vegetables may be part of the antipasto table, on another they may be the *contorno*, a side dish of vegetables served with or after the main meal. This flexibility and the fact that antipasti generally require advance preparation makes them a perfect option when entertaining. You can mix and match to make an impressive banquet, a meal for two or a simple snack.

Antipasto dishes can range from a plate of sliced, cured meats, especially prosciutto and salamis, with fresh fruits in season such as figs or melons, to a warm frittata, a simple salad of tuna and beans or a plate of fried whitebait. Good-quality ingredients such as grilled marinated vegetables, fresh cheeses and marinated olives can be used to supplement home-made dishes.

All of the dishes on pages 88 to 103 are classic antipasti recipes. It is easy to adjust the quantities to suit your needs.

Although we have presented the following recipes in the book as main course side vegetables, they also make perfect choices for the antipasto table:
Fennel fritters (page 124), Carciofi alla Romana (page 127), Sautéed silverbeet (Swiss chard) (page 129) and Green beans with garlic breadcrumbs (page 121).

The most important thing to remember when putting together a selection of antipasti is to use fresh seasonal produce. For example, to make the most of vine-ripened tomatoes, a typical summer selection might include Insalata caprese (page 93), Panzanella (page 103), or Tomato and basil crostini (page 95). A winter selection might include such dishes as Bean and rosemary dip (page 88), Arancini (page 90) or Sauteed silverbeet (Swiss chard) (page 129). If you are including foods such as meats from the delicatessen, buy from a reliable supplier that has a good turnover.

Perhaps the most important ingredient on the antipasto table is olive oil. A drizzle of fruity extra virgin olive oil can transform even the most simple ingredient into a dish. Don't be tempted to compromise on the quality of the oil because although they are significantly more expensive than regular olive oils, the difference is enormous. If you use extra virgin olive oil only for dressing or drizzling over breads, and not for cooking, you will find that it goes a long way. Drizzle your good-quality extra virgin olive oil over a slice of rustic bread that has been rubbed with a piece of garlic and you have a simple yet flavoursome bruschetta. A plate of boiled vegetables such as globe artichokes becomes a meal when served with extra virgin olive oil, sea salt and cracked pepper.

The secret of all Italian cooking lies in the quality of the ingredients, not in the complexity of the dish. Antipasti dishes reflect this only too well and are a perfect opportunity to make the most of the best, fresh seasonal produce with little fuss.

FROM BACK LEFT: Stuffed zucchini flowers (page 88); Platter of meats, cheeses, olives, chargilled vegetables, artichokes; Stuffed sardines (page 92); Tomato and basil crostini (page 95)

97

BALSAMIC VINEGAR
This centuries-old speciality is produced in the province of Modena, just north of Bologna in Italy. It is made from boiled-down must, which is the concentrated sweet juice of white grapes. True balsamic vinegar is aged for decades in a succession of barrels, each made from a different wood to produce a syrupy sweet-and-sour liquid. Labelled *aceto balsamico tradizionale di Modena* and originally made only by wealthy families who could afford to wait for their vinegar to mature, much of what is available today is a far cry from the real thing and is consequently sold without the traditional label. True balsamic is used sparingly and in cooking should be put in at the very end so the aromas are present in the final dish.

ROASTED BALSAMIC ONIONS

Preparation time: 15 minutes
  + overnight refrigeration
Total cooking time: 1 hour 30 minutes
Serves 8 (as part of an antipasto platter)

1 kg (2 lb) pickling onions, unpeeled
  (see Note)
3/4 cup (185 ml/6 fl oz) balsamic vinegar
2 tablespoons soft brown sugar
3/4 cup (185 ml/6 fl oz) olive oil

1 Preheat the oven to warm 160°C (315°F/ Gas 2–3). Bake the onions in a baking dish for 1½ hours. When cool enough to handle, trim the stems from the onions and peel away the skin (the outer part of the root should come away but the onions will remain intact). Rinse a 1 litre wide-necked jar with boiling water and dry in a warm oven (do not dry with a tea towel). Add the onions to the jar.
2 Combine the vinegar and sugar in a small screw top jar and stir to dissolve the sugar. Add the oil, seal the jar and shake the jar vigorously until the mixture is combined.
3 Pour the vinegar mixture over the onions, seal, and turn upside-down to coat. Marinate overnight in the refrigerator, turning occasionally. Return to room temperature and shake to combine the dressing before serving.
NOTE: Pickling onions are very small. The ideal size is around 35 g (1¼ oz) each. Sizes will probably range from 20 g (3/4 oz) up to 40 g (1¼ oz). The cooking time given is suitable for this range and there is no need to cook the larger ones for any longer. The marinating time given is a minimum time and the onions can be marinated for up to three days in the refrigerator. The marinade may separate after a few hours, which is fine — simply stir occasionally.

SHAVED FENNEL SALAD

Trim two round fennel bulbs by cutting off the tops where they meet the bulb. Reserve any of the small green fronds and discard the tops. Remove any tough outer parts of the bulb that are bruised or discoloured. Slice off 3 mm (1/8 inch) from the end and slice the bulb horizontally into paper-thin rings. Soak the slices in 2 changes of cold water for 5 minutes, then drain well and pat dry with a paper towel or clean tea towel. Toss in a serving bowl with enough extra virgin olive oil to coat well. Season with salt and freshly ground black pepper. Serves 4.

RIGHT: Roasted balsamic onions

INSALATA DI FRUTTI DI MARE
(Seafood salad)

Preparation time: 45 minutes
  + 40 minutes marinating
Total cooking time: 25 minutes
Serves 4

☆ ☆

500 g (1 lb) small squid
1 kg (2 lb) large clams
1 kg (2 lb) mussels
5 tablespoons chopped fresh flat-leaf parsley
  (reserve the stalks)
500 g (1 lb) raw medium prawns, peeled,
  deveined, tails intact
2 tablespoons lemon juice
1/3 cup (80 ml/2¾ fl oz) olive oil
1 clove garlic, crushed

1 Grasp each squid body in one hand and the head and tentacles in the other. Pull to separate. Cut the tentacles from each head below the eyes. Discard the heads. Push out the beaks and discard. Pull the quill from inside each body and discard. Under cold running water, pull away the skin (the flaps can be used). Rinse, then slice into 7 mm (¼ inch) rings.

2 Scrub the clams and mussels with a stiff brush and remove the hairy beards. Discard any that are cracked or don't close when tapped. Rinse under cold water. Fill a wide shallow pan with 1 cm (½ inch) water, add the parsley stalks, cover the pan and bring the water to simmering point. Add the clams and mussels in batches, being careful not to overcrowd the pan. Cover and steam over high heat for 2–3 minutes, or until the shells begin to open. Remove with a slotted spoon and place in a colander over a bowl. Return any drained juices to the pan before cooking the next batch. Continue until all the clams and mussels are cooked. Reserve the cooking liquid. Allow the clams and mussels to cool before removing them from the shells. Discard any unopened ones.

3 Add 1 litre water to the pan with the cooking liquid. Bring to the boil, then add the prawns and cook for 3–4 minutes, or until the water returns to the boil. Remove with a slotted spoon and drain in a colander. Add the squid and cook for 30–40 seconds, until the flesh becomes white and opaque. Remove immediately and drain.

4 Whisk the lemon juice, oil and garlic in a bowl, then season. Pour over the seafood with 4 tablespoons parsley, then toss. Adjust the seasoning if necessary. Marinate for 30–40 minutes to allow the flavours to develop. Sprinkle with parsley. Serve with crusty bread.

MUSSELS
Mussels attach themselves to rocks or, in the case of farmed mussels, to bags or ropes, with the tough brown fibres known as the 'beard'. Farmed mussels take up to two years to mature. When buying mussels, avoid any that have broken shells. Use soon after purchasing, or keep in a very cool place in a small amount of water, covered with a damp hessian bag. Do not use any mussels that are already open. When mussels are cooked, the shells should open. If they don't open after 3–5 minutes cooking, they should be thrown away.

ABOVE: Insalata di frutti di mare

WHITEBAIT

These tiny fish are the young of herrings and sprats. They are most plentiful in spring and summer, but also available all year round. Eaten whole, they are usually deep-fried or used in fritters or patties. They can be kept in the refrigerator, in a covered container that allows them to drain, for up to two days. Before tossing in flour to fry, drain the fish well and pat dry, otherwise the flour will form clumps of dough. Any other small fish can be cooked in the same manner as whitebait.

FRIED WHITEBAIT

Preparation time: 10 minutes
Total cooking time: 10 minutes
Serves 6

☆ ☆

1/3 cup (40 g/1 1/4 oz) plain flour
1/4 cup (30 g/1 oz) cornflour
500 g (1 lb) whitebait
2 teaspoons finely chopped fresh flat-leaf
    parsley
oil, for deep-frying
1 lemon, cut into wedges, for serving

1   Combine the sifted flours and parsley in a bowl and season well with salt and cracked black pepper. Fill a deep, heavy-based pan one third full of oil and heat until a cube of bread dropped into the oil browns in 15 seconds. Toss a third of the whitebait in the flour mixture, shake off the excess flour, and deep-fry for 1 1/2 minutes, or until pale and crisp. Drain well on crumpled paper towels. Repeat with the remaining whitebait, cooking in two batches.
2   Reheat the oil and fry the whitebait a second time in three batches for 1 minute each batch, or until lightly browned. Drain on paper towels and serve hot with lemon wedges.

ABOVE: Fried whitebait

SAUTEED MUSHROOMS WITH GARLIC

Wipe any dirt off 750 g (1 1/2 lb) mushroom (field, Swiss brown or any wild mushroom) caps. Trim the stems and thinly slice the mushrooms, keeping the stems and caps intact. Heat 1/3 cup (80 ml/2 3/4 fl oz) extra virgin olive oil in a large heavy-based frying pan and cook 2 teaspoons crushed garlic over low heat until it colours lightly but does not brown. Add 1 teaspoon chopped fresh thyme and the mushrooms and toss. Increase the heat, season and cook for 10 minutes, or until the mushrooms have soaked up all the oil and softened. Reduce the heat to low and cook, stirring with a wooden spoon, until the mushrooms release their juices. Return the heat to high and cook for 4–5 minutes, or until the juices have evaporated. Adjust the seasoning, add 3 tablespoons chopped fresh flat-leaf parsley and combine. Serve warm or at room temperature as part of an antipasto with bruschetta. Serves 4–6.

TUNA AND CANNELLINI BEAN SALAD

Preparation time: 25 minutes
Total cooking time: 5 minutes
Serves 4–6

400 g (13 oz) tuna steaks
1 tablespoon olive oil
1 small red onion, thinly sliced
1 ripe tomato, seeded and chopped
1 small red pepper (capsicum), thinly sliced
2 x 400 g (13 oz) cans cannellini beans
2 cloves garlic, crushed
1 teaspoon chopped fresh thyme
4 tablespoons chopped fresh flat-leaf parsley
1 1/2 tablespoons lemon juice
1/3 cup (80 ml/2 3/4 floz) extra virgin olive oil
1 teaspoon honey
100 g (3 1/2 oz) rocket (arugula)
1 teaspoon lemon zest

1 Heat the grill or barbecue. Place the tuna steaks on a plate, brush with the oil and sprinkle with cracked black pepper on both sides. Cover with plastic wrap and refrigerate until needed.
2 Combine the onion, tomato and red pepper in a large bowl. Rinse the cannellini beans under cold running water for 30 seconds, drain and add to the bowl with the garlic, thyme and 3 tablespoons of the parsley.
3 Place the lemon juice, oil and honey in a small saucepan, bring to the boil, then reduce the heat to low and simmer, stirring, for 1 minute, or until the honey dissolves. Remove from the heat.
4 Sear the tuna for 1 minute on each side. The meat should still be pink in the middle. Slice into 3 cm (1 1/4 inch) cubes and combine with the salad. Pour on the warm dressing and toss well.
5 Place the rocket on a large platter. Top with the salad, season and garnish with the lemon zest and remaining parsley. Serve immediately.
NOTE: Good-quality canned tuna is a delicious substitute for the fresh tuna in this recipe. Drain well before using.

TUNA
Fresh tuna has a dark meaty flesh that is delicious raw or cooked. The superior taste of the red flesh indicates that the fish was caught by hand, killed and bled quickly. On the other hand if tuna has a muddy-brown flesh, it usually indicates that the fish was caught by net and probably drowned. The fishing industry in Sicily is one of the most important in the south of Italy. The preserving of tuna is an enormous industry and good-quality canned tuna which still retains its meaty, firm texture is much sought after.

LEFT: Tuna and cannellini bean salad

BAKED EGGPLANT (AUBERGINE) WITH TOMATO AND MOZZARELLA

Preparation time: 20 minutes
Total cooking time: 40 minutes
Serves 6

6 large slender eggplants (aubergines), cut in half lengthways, leaving stems attached
5 tablespoons olive oil
2 onions, finely chopped
2 cloves garlic, crushed
400 g (13 oz) can good-quality chopped tomatoes
1 tablespoon tomato paste (tomato purée)
3 tablespoons chopped fresh flat-leaf parsley
1 tablespoon chopped fresh oregano
125 g (4 oz) mozzarella, grated

1 Preheat the oven to moderate 180°C (350°F/ Gas 4). Score the eggplant flesh by cutting a criss-cross pattern with a sharp knife, being careful not to cut through the skin. Heat 2 tablespoons oil in a large frying pan, add 3 eggplants and cook for 2–3 minutes each side, or until the flesh is soft. Remove. Repeat with another 2 tablespoons oil and the remaining eggplants. Cool slightly and scoop out the flesh, leaving a 2 mm (1/8 inch) border. Finely chop the flesh and reserve the shells.

2 In the same pan, heat the remaining oil and cook the onion over medium heat for 5 minutes. Add the garlic and cook for 30 seconds, then add the tomato, tomato paste, herbs and eggplant flesh, and cook, stirring occasionally, over low heat for 8–10 minutes, or until the sauce is thick and pulpy. Season well.

3 Arrange the eggplant shells in a lightly greased baking dish and spoon in the tomato filling. Sprinkle with mozzarella and bake for 5–10 minutes, or until the cheese has melted.

HERB BAKED RICOTTA

Preparation time: 25 minutes
  + overnight refrigeration
Total cooking time: 30 minutes
Serves 6–8

1 kg (2 lb) wedge full-fat ricotta (see Note)
2 tablespoons fresh thyme leaves
2 tablespoons chopped fresh rosemary
2 tablespoons chopped fresh oregano
1/4 cup (15 g/1/2 oz) chopped fresh parsley
1/4 cup (15 g/1/2 oz) chopped fresh chives
2 cloves garlic, crushed
1/2 cup (125 ml/4 fl oz) olive oil

1 Pat the ricotta dry with paper towels and place in a baking dish.

2 Mix the herbs, garlic, oil and 2 teaspoons of cracked pepper in a bowl. Spoon onto the ricotta, pressing with the back of a spoon. Cover and refrigerate overnight.

3 Preheat the oven to moderate 180°C (350°F/ Gas 4). Bake for 30 minutes, or until the ricotta is golden. Delicious served with crusty bread.
NOTE: If you can't buy a wedge of ricotta, drain the wet ricotta in a colander overnight over a large bowl. Spread half the herb mixture in a 1.25 litre loaf tin, then spoon the ricotta in and spread with the remaining herbs before baking.

BELOW: Baked eggplant with tomato and mozzarella

PANZANELLA

Preparation time: 30 minutes
  + 15 minutes standing
Total cooking time: 5 minutes
Serves 6–8

☆

1 small red onion, thinly sliced
250 g (8 oz) stale bread such as ciabatta, crusts removed
4 ripe tomatoes
6 anchovy fillets, finely chopped
1 small clove garlic, crushed
1 tablespoon baby capers, chopped
2 tablespoons red wine vinegar
1/2 cup (125 ml/4 fl oz) extra virgin olive oil
2 small Lebanese cucumbers, peeled and sliced
1 cup (30 g/1 oz) fresh basil leaves, torn

1   In a small bowl, cover the onion with cold water and leave for 5 minutes. Squeeze the rings in your hand, closing tightly and letting go and repeating that process about five times. This removes the acid from the onion. Repeat the whole process twice more, using fresh water each time.

2   Tear the bread into rough 3 cm (1 1/4 inch) squares and toast lightly under a grill for 4 minutes, or until bread is crisp but not browned. Allow to cool. Set aside.

3   Score a cross in the base of each tomato and soak in boiling water for 10 seconds. Plunge into cold water and peel away from the cross. Cut each tomato in half and scoop out the seeds with a teaspoon. Roughly chop two of the tomatoes and purée the other two.

4   Combine the anchovies, garlic and capers in a screw top jar. Add the vinegar and olive oil, screw the lid on tightly and shake well. Season, then transfer to a large bowl and add the bread, onion, puréed and chopped tomato, cucumber and basil. Toss well and season, to taste. Leave to stand for at least 15 minutes to allow the flavours to develop. Serve at room temperature.

ANCHOVIES

In Italy, the preserved anchovies used in cooking are usually those preserved in salt. They are whole and much larger than the fillets preserved in oil, and have a far superior flavour and texture. All the recipes in this book, however, call for those preserved in oil because they are much more readily available outside Italy. If using salt-preserved anchovies, wash the salt off under running water and remove the fillets from the bone using your fingers. Remember that the salted anchovies are usually up to four times larger than those preserved in oil so you should adjust the recipe accordingly.

ABOVE: Panzanella

103

MINESTRONE
Because not all the ingredients for minestrone go into the saucepan at the same time, you can reduce the preparation time by peeling and cutting up one vegetable while another is cooking. It is not even necessary to make minestrone entirely from scratch on the same day you plan to serve it because, like most vegetable soups, the flavour improves with standing.

MINESTRONE WITH PESTO

Preparation time: 25 minutes + overnight soaking
Total cooking time: 2 hours
Serves 6

☆ ☆

125 g (4 oz) dried borlotti beans
1/4 cup (60 ml/2 fl oz) olive oil
1 large onion, finely chopped
2 cloves garlic, crushed
60 g (3 oz) pancetta, finely chopped
1 stick celery, halved lengthways, then cut
   into 1 cm (1/2 inch) slices
1 carrot, halved lengthways, then cut into
   1 cm (1/2 inch) slices
1 potato, diced
2 teaspoons tomato paste (tomato purée)
400 g (13 oz) can good-quality crushed tomatoes
6 fresh basil leaves, roughly torn
2 litres chicken or vegetable stock
2 thin zucchini (courgettes), cut into
   1.5 cm (5/8 inch) slices
3/4 cup (115 g/4 oz) shelled fresh peas
60 g (2 oz) green beans, cut into short lengths
80 g (2 3/4 oz) silverbeet (Swiss chard) leaves,
   shredded
3 tablespoons chopped fresh flat-leaf parsley
75 g (2 1/2 oz) ditalini or other small pasta

PESTO
1 cup (30 g/1 oz) fresh basil leaves
20 g (3/4 oz) lightly toasted pine nuts
2 cloves garlic
100 ml (3 1/2 fl oz) olive oil
1/4 cup (25 g/3/4 oz) grated Parmesan

1 Soak the borlotti beans in plenty of cold water overnight. Drain and rinse thoroughly under cold water.
2 Heat the oil in a large deep saucepan, add the onion, garlic and pancetta and cook over low heat, stirring occasionally, for 8–10 minutes, until softened.
3 Add the celery, carrot and potato to the saucepan and cook for 5 minutes. Stir in the tomato paste, tomato, basil and drained borlotti beans. Season, to taste, with freshly ground black pepper. Add the stock and bring slowly to the boil. Cover and simmer, stirring occasionally, for 1 hour 30 minutes.
4 Add the remaining vegetables, parsley and the pasta. Simmer for 8–10 minutes, or until the vegetables and pasta are *al dente*. Check for seasoning and adjust if necessary.
5 For the pesto, combine the fresh basil, pine nuts and garlic with a pinch of salt in a food processor. Process until finely chopped. With the motor running, slowing add the olive oil. Transfer to a bowl and stir in the Parmesan and ground black pepper, to taste. Spoon on top of the soup.

ABOVE: Minestrone
with pesto

PAPPA AL POMADORO
(Tomato bread soup)

Preparation time: 25 minutes
Total cooking time: 25 minutes
Serves 4

☆

750 g (1 ½ lb) vine-ripened tomatoes
1 loaf (450 g/14 oz) day-old crusty Italian bread
1 tablespoon olive oil
3 cloves garlic, crushed
1 tablespoon tomato paste (tomato purée)
1.25 litres hot vegetable stock or water
⅓ cup (20 g/¾ oz) torn fresh basil leaves
2–3 tablespoons extra virgin olive oil
extra virgin olive oil, extra, for serving

1 Score a cross in the base of each tomato. Place the tomatoes in a bowl of boiling water for 10 seconds, then plunge into cold water and peel the skin away from the cross. Cut the tomatoes in half and scoop out the seeds with a teaspoon. Roughly chop the tomato flesh.
2 Discard most of the crust from the bread and tear the bread into 3 cm (1¼ inch) pieces.

3 Heat the oil in a large saucepan. Add the garlic, tomato and tomato paste, then reduce the heat and simmer, stirring occasionally, for 10–15 minutes, or until reduced. Add the stock and bring to the boil, stirring for 2–3 minutes. Reduce the heat to medium, add the bread pieces and cook, stirring, for 5 minutes, or until the bread softens and absorbs most of the liquid. Add more stock or water if the soup is too thick. Remove the saucepan from the heat.
4 Stir in the basil leaves and extra virgin olive oil, and leave for 5 minutes so the flavours have time to develop. Serve drizzled with a little extra virgin olive oil.

ROCKET (ARUGULA) AND PECORINO SALAD

In a large bowl, combine 3 tablespoons extra virgin olive oil with 2 tablespoons lemon juice and salt and pepper. Add 150 g (5 oz) washed rocket (arugula) leaves and toss lightly to coat. Place in a serving dish. Using a vegetable peeler, shave thin curls of pecorino (or Parmesan) over the salad. Adjust the seasoning and serve. Serves 4.

SALAD PREPARATION
It is important to shake washed salad leaves thoroughly, otherwise the water will dilute the dressing and won't coat the leaves. If you do not have a salad spinner, wrap the leaves in a large tea towel, gather all four corners of the towel in one hand and shake the towel several times over the sink. Traditionally, the simple Italian dressings of olive oil, vinegar or lemon juice, salt and pepper are not mixed in advance. Instead, they are drizzled separately on the salad at the table, then lightly tossed.

LEFT: Pappa al pomadoro

MAKING PASTA

FRESH OR DRIED?

Fresh pasta, unlike dried, has eggs added to the dough and a softer wheat flour is used rather than the hard durum wheat semolina that gives dried pasta its *al dente* texture. Fresh pasta is ideal for lasagne sheets, pasta lengths and filled pastas.

BEFORE YOU START

Making pasta isn't difficult but there are a few tips that will help. A well-ventilated kitchen and good-quality ingredients brought to room temperature are a good starting point. A large work area with a hard, even surface, ideally wood or marble, dusted with flour, makes the process easier. Kneading is critical as it works the flour's gluten content, resulting in a firm yet tender dough. This is especially important if you are rolling and cutting the dough by hand, as the more elastic the dough, the easier it will be to roll. The dough should be kneaded until pliable, gradually adding small amounts of flour if it is too soft or sticky. Rolling is equally important as it makes the pasta more porous, enabling it to absorb a maximum amount of sauce, while the thinness ensures it is tender after cooking.

BASIC PLAIN PASTA DOUGH

To make enough to serve six as a first course or four as a main course, you will need 300 g (10 oz) of plain flour, 3 large (60 g/2 oz) eggs, 30 ml (1 fl oz) of olive oil and a pinch of salt.

1 Mound the flour on a work surface or in a large bowl and make a well in the centre. Break the eggs into the well and add the oil and a large pinch of salt. Using a fork, begin to whisk the eggs and oil together, incorporating a little of the flour as you go. Gradually blend the flour with the eggs, working from the centre out.

2 Knead the dough on a lightly floured surface for 6 minutes, or until you have a soft, smooth elastic dough which is dry to touch. If it is sticky, knead in a little flour. Cover with plastic wrap and allow to rest for 30 minutes.

ROLLING BY HAND

1 Divide the dough into four even portions and cover with a cloth. Lightly flour a large work surface and using a floured long rolling pin, roll out one portion from the centre to the edge. Continue, always rolling from in front of you outwards. Rotate the dough often.

2 When a well-shaped circle has formed, fold the dough in half and roll it out again. Continue this process seven or eight times to make a smooth circle of pasta about 5 mm (1/4 inch) thick. Roll this sheet quickly and smoothly to a thickness of 2.5 mm (1/8 inch).

3 As each sheet is done, transfer it to a dry tea towel. Keep the pasta sheets covered if making filled pasta, or leave uncovered to dry slightly if cutting the pasta sheets into lengths or shapes.

4 To make lasagne sheets, cut the pasta into the required sizes.

5 For cutting lengths such as fettucine, roll each pasta sheet up like a swiss roll, then cut into uniform lengths with a long, sharp knife. Allow the lengths to dry in a single layer on a tea towel for a maximum of 10 minutes or hang on broom handles between two chairs.

6 To make farfalle (bow-ties), roll pasta sheets to a thickness of 2.5 mm (1/8 inch). Using a zigzag pastry wheel against a ruler, cut 2.5 x 5.5 cm (1 x 2 1/4 inch) rectangles and pinch the centres together to form bow-tie shapes. Lay them on a tea towel to dry for 10–12 minutes.

7 To make ravioli, follow the recipe on page 112.

USING A MACHINE

1 Divide the pasta dough into four even portions. Keep the unworked portions covered so they don't dry out. Take one portion and flatten it with a rolling pin, forming rectangles roughly the same width as the machine. Lightly dust the dough and the pasta machine rollers with flour.

2 With the machine rollers set to the widest setting, crank the dough through the machine two or three times. Fold the dough into thirds, turn it by 90 degrees and feed it through again, repeating this process eight to ten times, until the pasta dough is smooth and elastic and has a velvety appearance.

3 Reduce the roller width by one setting and pass the dough through. Repeat this process with the roller setting one notch closer each time until the dough is rolled to the required thickness. If using the cutting attachment on the machine, pass the lengths through immediately after rolling, then allow them to dry for 10 minutes. Cover them if they are to be filled.

LINGUINE PESTO

Preparation time: 15 minutes
Total cooking time: 15 minutes
Serves 4–6

2 cups (100 g/3½ oz) fresh basil leaves
2 cloves garlic, crushed
¼ cup (40 g/1¼ oz) pine nuts, toasted
¾ cup (185 ml/6 fl oz) olive oil
½ cup (50 g/1¾ oz) grated Parmesan
500 g (1 lb) linguine
shaved or grated Parmesan, extra, for serving

1 Finely chop the basil, garlic and pine nuts together in a food processor. With the motor running, add the oil in a steady stream until mixed to a smooth paste. Transfer to a bowl, stir in the Parmesan and season, to taste.
2 Cook the pasta in a large saucepan of rapidly boiling salted water until *al dente*. Drain and return to the pan. Toss enough of the pesto through the pasta to coat it well. Serve sprinkled with Parmesan.
NOTE: Refrigerate any leftover pesto in an airtight jar for up to a week. Cover the surface with a layer of oil. Freeze for up to a month.

ORECCHIETTE WITH BROCCOLI

Preparation time: 5 minutes
Total cooking time: 15 minutes
Serves 6

750 g (1½ lb) broccoli, cut into florets
450 g (14 oz) orecchiette
¼ cup (60 ml/2 fl oz) extra virgin olive oil
8 anchovy fillets
½ teaspoon dried chilli flakes
⅓ cup (30 g/1 oz) grated Pecorino or Parmesan

1 Blanch the broccoli in a large saucepan of boiling salted water for 5 minutes, or until just tender. Remove with a slotted spoon, drain well and return the water to the boil. Cook the pasta in the boiling water until *al dente*, then drain well and return to the pan.
2 Meanwhile, heat the oil in a heavy-based frying pan and cook the anchovies over very low heat for 1 minute. Add the chilli flakes and broccoli. Increase the heat to medium and cook, stirring, for 5 minutes, or until the broccoli is well-coated and beginning to break apart. Season. Add to the pasta, add the cheese and toss.

PESTO
This famous Italian sauce goes especially well with pasta or fish. It requires a little patience when adding the oil which must be drizzled very slowly and gradually into the basil and pine nut mixture. Always stir in the cheese last, whether making the pesto in a food processor or by the traditional method using a mortar and pestle. Pesto should always be used raw at room temperature and never warmed up.

RIGHT: Linguine pesto

PENNE ALLA NAPOLITANA

Preparation time: 20 minutes
Total cooking time: 25 minutes
Serves 4–6

2 tablespoons olive oil
1 onion, finely chopped
2–3 cloves garlic, finely chopped
1 small carrot, finely diced
1 celery stick, finely diced
2 x 400 g (13 oz) cans peeled, chopped
   tomatoes, or 1 kg (2 lb) ripe tomatoes,
   peeled and chopped
1 tablespoon tomato paste (tomato purée)
1/4 cup (15 g/1/2 oz) shredded fresh basil leaves
500 g (1 lb) penne
Parmesan, for serving

1 Heat the oil in a large frying pan, add the onion and garlic and cook for 2 minutes, or until golden. Add the carrot and celery and cook for another 2 minutes.
2 Add the tomato and tomato paste. Simmer for 20 minutes, or until the sauce thickens, stirring occasionally. Stir in the shredded basil and season, to taste, with salt and freshly ground black pepper.
3 While the sauce is cooking, cook the pasta in a large saucepan of rapidly boiling salted water until *al dente*. Drain well and return to the pan. Add the sauce to the pasta and mix well. This dish is delicious served with freshly grated or shaved Parmesan.

BUCATINI AMATRICIANA

Place 1 finely chopped onion in a heavy-based frying pan with 2 tablespoons olive oil and cook over medium heat until golden. Add 150 g (5 oz) chopped pancetta to the pan and stir for 1 minute. Add a 400 g (13 oz) can crushed tomatoes, salt and pepper and 1/2 teaspoon chilli flakes. Simmer for 20–25 minutes. Meanwhile, cook 450 g (14 oz) bucatini in a large pan of boiling water until *al dente*. Drain and add to the sauce with 3 tablespoons of freshly grated Parmesan. Toss well and serve immediately. Serves 4.

TOMATOES
Unless tomatoes have been allowed to ripen on the vine, they are, more often than not, tasteless and watery and impart very little to cooking apart from acid. Outside the summer months, most tomatoes available to the consumer are very poor in quality. For this reason it is important to consider the season when planning a meal which calls for fresh tomatoes. If you are unable to get good-quality fresh tomatoes, it is better to use canned tomatoes, preferably whole peeled Roma tomatoes from Italy.

*ABOVE: Penne
alla Napolitana*

PUTTANESCA

The name puttanesca is a derivation of the word *puttana* which in Italian means whore. There are many stories surrounding this dish but according to one story, the name comes from the fact that the intense flavours of the sauce were like a siren call to the men who visited such 'ladies of pleasure'. Another story claims that the dish got its name because these wayward women were forbidden to shop for groceries during regular hours like the gentile ladies and were left to rely upon the pantry staples such as olives, capers and anchovies.

ABOVE: Spaghetti puttanesca

SPAGHETTI PUTTANESCA

Preparation time: 15 minutes
Total cooking time: 20 minutes
Serves 6

1/3 cup (80 ml/2³/4 fl oz) olive oil
2 onions, finely chopped
3 cloves garlic, finely chopped
1/2 teaspoon chilli flakes
6 large ripe tomatoes, diced
4 tablespoons capers, rinsed
8 anchovies in oil, drained, chopped
150 g (5 oz) Kalamata olives
3 tablespoons chopped fresh
    flat-leaf parsley
375 g (12 oz) spaghetti

1 Heat the olive oil in a saucepan, add the onion and cook over medium heat for 5 minutes. Add the garlic and chilli flakes to the saucepan and cook for 30 seconds. Add the tomato, capers and anchovies. Simmer over low heat for 10–15 minutes, or until the sauce is thick and pulpy. Stir the olives and parsley through the sauce.

2 While the sauce is cooking, cook the spaghetti in a large saucepan of rapidly boiling salted water until *al dente*. Drain and return to the pan.
3 Add the sauce to the pasta and stir it through. Season with salt and freshly ground black pepper, to taste, and serve immediately.

SPAGHETTINI WITH GARLIC AND CHILLI

Cook 500 g (1 lb) spaghettini in a large saucepan of rapidly boiling salted water until *al dente*. Drain and return to the pan. Meanwhile, heat 1/2 cup (125 ml/4 fl oz) of extra virgin olive oil in a large frying pan. Add 2–3 finely chopped cloves of garlic and 1–2 seeded, finely chopped, fresh red chillies, and cook over very low heat for 2–3 minutes, or until the garlic is golden. Take care not to burn the garlic or chillies as this will make the sauce bitter. Toss 3 tablespoons chopped fresh flat-leaf parsley and the warmed oil, garlic and chilli mixture through the pasta. Season with salt and freshly ground black pepper. Serve with grated Parmesan. Serves 4–6.

SPAGHETTI WITH SARDINES, FENNEL AND TOMATO

Preparation time: 30 minutes
Total cooking time: 45 minutes
Serves 4–6

3 Roma tomatoes, peeled, seeded and chopped
1/3 cup (80 ml/2 3/4 fl oz) olive oil
3 cloves garlic, crushed
1 cup (80 g/2 3/4 oz) fresh white breadcrumbs
1 red onion, thinly sliced
1 fennel bulb, quartered and thinly sliced
1/4 cup (40 g/1 1/4 oz) raisins
1/4 cup (40 g/1 1/4 oz) pine nuts, toasted
4 anchovy fillets, chopped
1/2 cup (125 ml/4 fl oz) white wine
1 tablespoon tomato paste (tomato purée)
4 tablespoons finely chopped fresh
    flat-leaf parsley
350 g (11 oz) butterflied sardine fillets
500 g (1 lb) spaghetti

1 Score a cross in the base of each tomato. Place the tomatoes in a bowl of boiling water for 10 seconds, then plunge into cold water and peel the skin away from the cross. Cut the tomatoes in half and scoop out the seeds with a teaspoon. Roughly chop the tomato flesh.

2 Heat 1 tablespoon of the oil in a large frying pan over medium heat. Add 1 clove of the garlic and the breadcrumbs and stir for about 5 minutes, until golden and crisp. Transfer to a plate.

3 Heat the remaining oil in the same pan and cook the onion, fennel and remaining garlic for 8 minutes, or until soft. Add the tomato, raisins, pine nuts and anchovies and cook for another 3 minutes. Add the wine, tomato paste and 1/2 cup (125 ml/4 fl oz) water. Simmer for 10 minutes, or until the mixture thickens slightly. Stir in the parsley and set aside.

4 Pat the sardines dry with paper towels. Cook the sardines in batches in a lightly greased frying pan over medium heat for 1 minute, or until cooked through. Take care not to overcook or they will break up. Set aside.

5 Cook the pasta in a large saucepan of rapidly boiling salted water until *al dente*. Drain and return to the pan.

6 Stir the sauce through the pasta until the pasta is well coated and the sauce evenly distributed. Add the sardines and half the breadcrumbs and toss gently. Sprinkle the remaining breadcrumbs over the top and serve immediately.

SARDINES
These small fish have an oily, soft flesh with a fine texture. The backbone is easy to remove and the small remaining bones are edible. Sardines are sold whole, butterflied and filleted. They have a strong distinctive flavour and are suitable for baking, grilling, pan-frying and barbecuing.

LEFT: Spaghetti with sardines, fennel and tomato

HERB-FILLED RAVIOLI WITH SAGE BUTTER

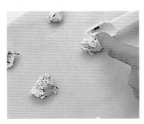

Place heaped teaspoons of filling at intervals along the pasta sheets.

Use a pastry wheel or sharp knife to cut the ravioli.

HERB-FILLED RAVIOLI WITH SAGE BUTTER

Preparation time: 1 hour
+ 30 minutes standing
Total cooking time: 10 minutes
Serves 4

☆☆☆

PASTA
300 g (10 oz) plain flour

3 eggs, beaten

3 tablespoons oil

1 cup (250 g/8 oz) ricotta

2 tablespoons grated Parmesan, plus extra, shaved, to garnish

2 teaspoons chopped fresh chives

1 tablespoon chopped flat-leaf parsley

2 teaspoons chopped fresh basil

1 teaspoon chopped fresh thyme

SAGE BUTTER
200 g (6¹/2 oz) butter

12 fresh sage leaves

1 Sift the flour into a bowl and make a well in the centre. Gradually mix in the eggs and oil.

Turn out onto a lightly floured surface and knead for 6 minutes, or until smooth. Cover with plastic wrap and leave for 30 minutes.

2 Mix the ricotta, Parmesan and herbs. Season.

3 Follow the pasta rolling instructions on page 107 to make 4 sheets of pasta, two slightly larger than the others. Cover with a tea towel.

4 Spread 1 of the smaller sheets out on a work surface and place heaped teaspoons of filling at 5 cm (2 inch) intervals. Brush a little water between the filling along the cutting lines. Place a larger sheet on top and firmly press the sheets together along the cutting lines. Cut the ravioli with a pastry wheel or knife and transfer to a lightly floured baking tray. Repeat with the remaining dough and filling.

5 For the sage butter, melt the butter over low heat in a small heavy-based saucepan, without stirring or shaking. Carefully pour the clear butter into another container and discard the remaining white sediment. Return the clarified butter to a clean pan and heat gently over medium heat. Add the sage leaves and cook until crisp but not brown. Remove and drain on paper towels. Reserve the warm butter.

6 Cook the ravioli in batches in a large pan of salted simmering water for 5–6 minutes, or until tender. Top with warm sage butter and leaves and garnish with shaved Parmesan.

NOTE: Don't cook the ravioli in rapidly boiling water or the squares will split and lose the filling.

RIGHT: Herb-filled ravioli with sage butter

BASIL
Perhaps one of the most useful tips for cooking with basil is the fact that the less it cooks the better. So when adding basil to a pasta sauce it is best to add it at the last moment when it is being tossed with the pasta. Occasionally however, one might cook basil in a soup or stew in order that the flavour marries with the other ingredients but if in doubt, add it at the last moment. Use only the freshest basil, never blackened or drooping leaves. Unless the recipe calls for julienned basil, it is preferable to tear the basil leaves with your hands rather than cut them with a knife which tends to bruise the basil and cause it to go brown.

BUCATINI ALLA NORMA

Preparation time: 15 minutes
Total cooking time: 40 minutes
Serves 4–6

3/4 cup (185 ml/6 fl oz) olive oil
1 brown onion, finely chopped
2 cloves garlic, crushed
2 x 400 g (13 oz) cans crushed good-quality
  tomatoes
1 large eggplant (aubergine), about 500 g (1 lb)
1/2 cup (30 g/1 oz) fresh basil leaves, torn
400 g (13 oz) bucatini
1/2 cup (60 g/2 oz) ricotta salata (see Note),
  crumbled
1/2 cup (50 g/1 3/4 oz) grated Pecorino or
  Parmesan
1 tablespoon extra virgin olive oil

1 Heat 2 tablespoons of the oil in a heavy-based frying pan and cook the onion over moderate heat for 5 minutes, or until softened. Add the garlic to the pan and cook for another 30 seconds. Add the tomato and salt and pepper, to taste, and reduce the heat. Cook for 20–25 minutes, or until the sauce has thickened and reduced.
2 While the sauce is cooking, cut the eggplant lengthways into 5 mm (1/4 inch) thick slices. Heat the remaining olive oil in a large heavy-based frying pan. When the oil is hot but not smoking, add the eggplant slices a few at a time and cook for 3–5 minutes, or until lightly browned on both sides. Remove from the pan and drain well on crumpled paper towels.
3 Cut each slice of eggplant into 3 pieces and add to the tomato sauce with the torn basil. Stir and keep warm over very low heat.
4 Cook the bucatini in a large saucepan of rapidly boiling, salted water until al dente. Drain well and add to the tomato sauce with half each of the ricotta and pecorino. Toss well and serve immediately sprinkled with the remaining cheeses. Drizzle with the extra virgin olive oil.
NOTE: Ricotta salata is a lightly salted, pressed ricotta. If unavailable, use a mild feta.

ABOVE: Bucatini alla Norma

CRESPELLE RIPIENE

Swirl the batter quickly in the pan so it covers the base.

Spoon the tomato sauce over the crepes.

OPPOSITE PAGE:
Crespelle ripiene (top);
Gnocchi Romana

CRESPELLE RIPIENE
(Stuffed crepes)

Preparation time: 25 minutes + 30 minutes resting
Total cooking time: 1 hour 10 minutes
Makes about 12

CREPES
1 1/3 cups (165 g/5 1/2 oz) plain flour
2 cups (500 ml/16 fl oz) milk
3 eggs, lightly beaten
30 g (1 oz) butter, melted

TOMATO SAUCE
2 tablespoons oil
1 clove garlic, crushed
400 g (13 oz) can crushed good-quality
   tomatoes
3 tablespoons chopped fresh flat-leaf parsley

CHEESE FILLING
400 g (13 oz) ricotta, crumbled
100 g (3 1/2 oz) mozzarella, grated
1/4 cup (25 g/3/4 oz) freshly grated Parmesan
pinch of freshly grated nutmeg
3 tablespoons chopped fresh flat-leaf parsley

2 tablespoons extra virgin olive oil, to drizzle
1/4 cup (25 g/3/4 oz) freshly grated Parmesan

1   For the crepes, sift the flour and 1/2 teaspoon salt into a bowl. Make a well in the flour and add the milk gradually, stirring constantly until the mixture is smooth. Add the eggs, one at a time, beating well until smooth. Cover and set aside for 30 minutes.
2   Meanwhile, to make the tomato sauce, heat the oil in a heavy-based frying pan and add the garlic. Cook for 30 seconds over low heat until just golden, then add the tomatoes and 1/2 cup (125 ml/4 fl oz) water and season well. Simmer over low heat for 30 minutes, or until the sauce has reduced and thickened. Stir in the parsley.
3   Heat a crepe or non-stick frying pan and brush lightly with melted butter. Pour 1/4 cup (60 ml/2 fl oz) of batter into the pan, swirling quickly to thinly cover the base. Cook for 1 minute, or until the underside is golden. Turn and cook the other side until golden. Transfer to a plate and continue with the remaining batter, stacking the crepes as you go.

4   Preheat the oven to moderately hot 200°C (400°F/Gas 6) and lightly grease a shallow baking dish with butter or oil.
5   For the filling, mix all the ingredients and season well.
6   To assemble, spread 1 heaped tablespoon of filling over each crepe, leaving a 1 cm (1/2 inch) border. Fold the crepe in half and then in quarters. Place in the baking dish, so that they overlap but are not crowded. Spoon the tomato sauce over the crepes, sprinkle with Parmesan and drizzle with the oil. Bake for 20 minutes, or until heated.
NOTE: The crepes can be made up to 3 days in advance but must be refrigerated with greaseproof paper to separate them.

GNOCCHI ROMANA

Preparation time: 20 minutes
   + 1 hour refrigeration
Total cooking time: 40 minutes
Serves 4

3 cups (750 ml/24 fl oz) milk
1/2 teaspoon ground nutmeg
2/3 cup (85 g/3 oz) semolina
1 egg, beaten
1 1/2 cups (150 g/5 oz) freshly grated Parmesan
40 g (1 1/4 oz) butter, melted
1/3 cup (80 ml/2 3/4 fl oz) cream
1/2 cup (75 g/2 1/2 oz) freshly grated mozzarella

1   Line a deep swiss roll tin with baking paper. Combine the milk, half the nutmeg, and salt and freshly ground black pepper in a saucepan. Bring to the boil, reduce the heat and gradually stir in the semolina. Cook, stirring frequently, for 5–10 minutes, or until the semolina is very stiff.
2   Remove the pan from the heat, add the egg and 1 cup of the Parmesan. Stir to combine and then spread the mixture in the tin. Refrigerate for 1 hour, or until the mixture is firm.
3   Preheat the oven to moderate 180°C (350°F/Gas 4). Cut the semolina into rounds using a floured 4 cm (1 1/2 inch) cutter and arrange in a greased shallow ovenproof dish.
4   Pour the butter over the top, followed by the cream. Combine the remaining grated Parmesan with the mozzarella and sprinkle on the rounds. Sprinkle with the remaining nutmeg. Bake for 20–25 minutes, or until the mixture is golden and warmed through.

SEAFOOD RISOTTO

Add the prawns to the pan and cook them until pink.

Gradually stir in the hot liquid until it is all absorbed.

SEAFOOD RISOTTO

Preparation time: 25 minutes
Total cooking time: 45 minutes
Serves 4

☆☆

2 ripe tomatoes

500 g (1 lb) black mussels

1¼ cups (315 ml/10 fl oz) white wine

1.25 litres fish stock

pinch of saffron threads

2 tablespoons olive oil

30 g (1 oz) butter

500 g (1 lb) raw prawns, peeled and deveined

225 g (7 oz) squid hoods, sliced into thin rings

200 g (6½ oz) scallops

3 cloves garlic, crushed

1 onion, finely chopped

2 cups (370 g/12 oz) risotto rice (arborio, vialone nano or carnaroli)

2 tablespoons chopped fresh parsley

1 Score a cross in the base of each tomato. Place in a bowl of boiling water for 10 seconds, then plunge into cold water and peel the skin away from the cross. Chop the tomato flesh.
2 Scrub the mussels with a stiff brush and remove the hairy beards. Discard any broken mussels or any that do not close when tapped.

Pour the wine into a large saucepan and bring to the boil. Add the mussels and cook, covered, over medium heat for 3–5 minutes, or until the mussels open. Discard any that do not open. Strain, reserving the liquid. Remove the mussels from their shells.
3 Combine the mussel liquid, stock and saffron in a saucepan, cover and keep at a low simmer.
4 Heat the oil and butter in a large saucepan over medium heat. Add the prawns and cook until pink. Remove. Add the squid and scallops and cook for about 1–2 minutes, until white. Remove. Add the garlic and onion and cook for 3 minutes, or until golden. Add the rice and stir until coated.
5 Add ½ cup (125 ml/4 fl oz) of the hot liquid, stirring constantly until it is all absorbed. Continue adding liquid, ½ cup (125 ml/4 fl oz) at a time, stirring constantly, for 25 minutes, or until the liquid is absorbed. Stir in the tomato, seafood and parsley and heat through. Season, to taste.
NOTE: You can use almost any combination of seafood for this risotto. Try using small pieces of firm, white fish, clams or octopus.

ABOVE: Seafood risotto

MUSHROOM RISOTTO

Preparation time: 10 minutes
+ 30 minutes soaking
Total cooking time: 1 hour
Serves 4–6

☆ ☆

20 g (³/₄ oz) dried porcini mushrooms
1 litre chicken or vegetable stock
2 tablespoons olive oil
100 g (3¹/₂ oz) butter, chopped
650 g (1 lb 5 oz) small cap or Swiss brown
    mushrooms, stems trimmed, sliced
3 cloves garlic, crushed
¹/₃ cup (80 ml/2³/₄ fl oz) dry white
    vermouth
1 onion, finely chopped
2 cups (440 g/14 oz) risotto rice
    (arborio, vialone nano or carnaroli)
1¹/₂ cups (150 g/5 oz) grated Parmesan

1 Soak the porcini mushrooms in 2 cups (500 ml/16 fl oz) warm water for 30 minutes. Drain, retaining the liquid. Chop them and pour the liquid through a fine sieve lined with a paper towel.

2 Put the stock and the mushroom liquid together in a saucepan, bring to the boil, then reduce the heat, cover and keep at a low simmer.

3 Heat half the oil and 40 g (1¹/₄ oz) of the butter in a large frying pan over high heat. Add all the mushrooms and the garlic to the pan and cook, stirring, for 10 minutes, or until soft and all the mushroom juices have been released. Reduce the heat to low and cook for another 5 minutes, or until all the juices have evaporated. Increase the heat, add the vermouth and cook for 2–3 minutes, until evaporated. Set aside.

4 Heat the remaining olive oil and 20 g (³/₄ oz) butter in a large saucepan over medium heat. Add the onion and cook for 10 minutes, or until soft. Add the rice and stir for 1–2 minutes, or until well coated. Add ¹/₂ cup (125 ml/4 fl oz) stock to the pan and stir constantly over medium heat until all the liquid is absorbed. Continue adding more stock, ¹/₂ cup (125 ml/4 fl oz) at a time, stirring constantly for 20–25 minutes, or until tender and creamy.

5 Remove from the heat and stir in the mushrooms, Parmesan and the remaining butter. Season, to taste, with salt and freshly ground black pepper.

NOTE: It is important to make sure that the porcini mushrooms are soaked for at least 30 minutes in warm water and that the soaking liquid is passed through a fine sieve lined with a paper towel to ensure that all the grit has been removed. If stored in a tightly sealed container, porcini mushrooms will keep indefinitely.

RISOTTO
A common misconception surrounding risotto is that it should be eaten piping hot, straight from the stove. However, unlike pasta, risotto benefits from resting on your plate for a minute or so to allow the flavours to settle and the steam to disperse. Italians often spread the risotto on their plate from the centre out and then eat from the rim to the centre.

LEFT: Mushroom risotto

MAKING PIZZA

Pizza has transcended its rustic origins in Naples to become an international symbol of Italian food. It usually combines three to five ingredients so the character and flavour of each shines through. This is evident in the Margherita, a trio of tomato, cheese and basil, representing the colours of the Italian flag; the Romana, which is little more than the addition of oregano and anchovies to the Margherita; and the Marinara, which despite its name, traditionally does not include seafood, but consists of a tomato sauce flavoured with garlic, olive oil and oregano.

The following hints will help when making pizza. The base is a flat form of bread so use good-quality bread flour. To prevent sticking, brush the pan with oil and sprinke it with polenta before using. Distribute toppings evenly on the base so that when cooked, each bite effectively combines the chosen flavours. Leave a 3 cm (1¼ inch) border when assembling the topping so that it doesn't drizzle onto the pizza pan.

PIZZA MARGHERITA

For a medium pizza, you will need 225 g (7 oz) white bread flour, 1 teaspoon sugar, 7 g (¾ oz) sachet dry yeast, 2 tablespoons olive oil, 90 ml (3 fl oz) milk, 1 crushed clove garlic, a 425 g (14 oz) can crushed tomatoes, 1 bay leaf, 1 teaspoon chopped fresh thyme, 6 chopped fresh basil leaves, 150 g (5 oz) thinly sliced bocconcini and some extra olive oil, to drizzle.

1 Place the flour, sugar, yeast and ½ teaspoon salt in a large bowl. Stir half the olive oil with the milk and ⅓ cup (80 ml/2¾ fl oz) warm water and add to the bowl. Stir with a wooden spoon.

2 Place on a lightly floured work surface and knead for 5 minutes, or until soft and smooth. Lightly oil a bowl, add the dough and turn to coat in the oil. Leave in a warm place for 1 hour, or until doubled in size. Preheat the oven to hot 210°C (415°F/Gas 6–7).

3 Heat the remaining oil in a saucepan over medium heat, add the garlic and stir for 30 seconds. Add the tomato, bay leaf, thyme and basil and simmer, stirring occasionally, for 20–25 minutes, or until thick. Cool, then remove the bay leaf.

4 Place the dough on a floured work surface, punch down to expel the air and knead for 5 minutes. Shape into a neat ball and roll to 28–30 cm (11–12 inch) diameter. Oil a pizza tray the size of the dough. Sprinkle the tray with polenta and place the dough on it. Spread the sauce over the dough, leaving a 3 cm (1¼ inch) border. Arrange the bocconcini over the top and drizzle with olive oil. Bake for 15 minutes, or until crisp and bubbling.

THICK BASE

To make a thick base for a medium pizza, you will need a 7 g (¾ oz) sachet dried yeast, ½ teaspoon each of salt and sugar, 2½ cups (310 g/10 oz) plain white bread flour, 2 tablespoons olive oil, 2 teaspoons semolina or polenta and 1 quantity cooled tomato sauce, as described above.

1 Combine the yeast, salt, sugar and water in a bowl. Cover with plastic wrap and leave in a warm place for 10 minutes, or until frothy. If the yeast doesn't froth, it is dead and you will have to start again. Sift the flour into a large bowl. Make a well in the centre, add the yeast mixture and mix to a firm dough. Preheat the oven to hot 210°C (415°F/Gas 6–7).

2 Place on a lightly floured work surface and knead for 5 minutes, or until smooth and elastic. Roll out to 35 cm (14 inch) diameter. Oil a 30 cm (12 inch) pizza tray, sprinkle with polenta and place the dough on the tray, tucking in the edges to form a rim. Spread the sauce over the dough, leaving a 3 cm (1¼ inch) border. Arrange toppings of your choice over the sauce, drizzle with olive oil and bake for 25 minutes, or until the crust is golden.

TOPPINGS

The combinations of cheeses, seafood, antipasto vegetables, cured meats, onions, olives and herbs are endless. Instead of a tomato base, the following pizzas are brushed with olive oil and scattered with mozzarella or Parmesan, then seasoned with salt and pepper before topping.

PROSCIUTTO E RUCOLA: Layer thinly shaved slices of prosciutto on top. When cooked, scatter with rocket and drizzle with extra virgin olive oil.

QUATTRO FORMAGGIO: This 'four cheeses' pizza generally combines grated mozzarella, Parmesan, fontina, Gorgonzola or Pecorino.

PIZZA RUSTICA

Fold the beaten egg whites through the ricotta mixture.

Spread the filling evenly over the pastry base, then smooth the surface with the back of a spoon.

PIZZA RUSTICA

Preparation time: 35 minutes + 30 minutes
  refrigeration + 20 minutes standing
Total cooking time: 50 minutes
Serves 6

☆ ☆ ☆

PASTRY
3 cups (375 g/12 oz) plain flour
1 teaspoon icing sugar
155 g (5 oz) butter, chilled and chopped
1 egg
1 egg yolk
2 tablespoons iced water

FILLING
2 cups (500 g/1 lb) ricotta
6 eggs, separated
100 g (3½ oz) lean bacon, cut into small strips
75 g (2½ oz) thickly sliced Milano salami, cut
  into 5 mm (¼ inch) cubes
100 g (3½ oz) mozzarella, grated
100 g (3½ oz) smoked mozzarella or other
  naturally smoked cheese, cut into
    1 cm (½ inch) cubes
¼ cup (25 g/¾ oz) freshly grated Parmesan
1 tablespoon chopped fresh flat-leaf parsley
½ teaspoon chopped fresh oregano
pinch of nutmeg
1 egg beaten with 1 tablespoon cold water,
  for glazing

1   For the pastry, sift the flour, icing sugar and 1 teaspoon salt into a bowl. Rub in the butter with your fingertips until the mixture resembles fine breadcrumbs. Add the egg and yolk and the water, ½ teaspoon at a time, cutting in with a flat-bladed knife, to form a dough. Turn out onto a lightly floured surface and gather together into a smooth ball. Cover with plastic wrap and refrigerate for 30 minutes.

2   Preheat the oven to moderately hot 190°C (375°F/Gas 5) and place a baking tray on the centre shelf. Grease a pie dish with a 23 cm (9 inch) base, 25 cm (10 inch) top, 4 cm (1½ inches) deep.

3   For the filling, place the ricotta in a large bowl and beat until smooth. Gradually add the egg yolks, beating well after each addition. Add the bacon, salami, mozzarella cheeses, Parmesan, parsley, oregano and nutmeg. Season well. Beat the egg whites in a large bowl until stiff and fold through the ricotta mixture.

RIGHT: Pizza rustica

4 Divide the pastry into two portions, one slightly larger than the other. Roll out the larger portion on a lightly floured surface to a size big enough to fit the base and sides of the dish. Line the dish. Roll out the second pastry portion to the same thickness for the pie lid. Spread the filling over the base and smooth the surface. Brush the pastry edges with the egg glaze and position the lid on top. Press the edges together firmly then trim with a sharp knife. Press a fluted pattern around the rim with your fingers to further seal in the filling. Brush the surface well with the egg glaze then prick the surface all over with a fork.

5 Place the pie dish on the heated tray and bake for 45–50 minutes, until the pastry is golden and the filling is set. Loosely cover the top with foil if it browns too quickly. Set aside for 20 minutes before serving.

FEGATO GARBO E DOLCE
(Sweet and sour liver)

Preparation time: 10 minutes
Total cooking time: 10 minutes
Serves 4

40 g (1¼ oz) butter

⅓ cup (80 ml/2¾ fl oz) olive oil

600 g (1¼ lb) calves' livers, cut into long thin slices

1 cup (80 g/2¾ oz) fresh white breadcrumbs

1 tablespoon sugar

2 cloves garlic, crushed

¼ cup (60 ml/2 fl oz) red wine vinegar

1 tablespoon chopped fresh flat-leaf parsley

1 Heat the butter and half the oil in a heavy-based frying pan over medium heat. Coat the liver in breadcrumbs, pressing them on firmly with your hands. Shake off the excess and place in the pan when the butter begins to foam. Cook on each side for 1 minute, or until the crust is brown and crisp. Remove from the pan and keep warm.

2 Add the remaining oil to the frying pan and cook the sugar and garlic over low heat until golden. Add the vinegar and cook for 30 seconds, or until almost evaporated. Add the parsley and pour over the liver. Serve hot or at room temperature.

GREEN BEANS WITH GARLIC BREADCRUMBS

Cook 600 g (1¼ lb) trimmed baby green beans, in a large saucepan of boiling salted water until tender but still firm. Drain and refresh under cold running water. Drain again and pat dry with paper towels. Heat ¼ cup (60 ml/2 fl oz) olive oil in a heavy-based frying pan and cook 4 whole, peeled garlic cloves until golden brown. Remove and discard. Add ½ cup (40 g/1¼ oz) fresh breadcrumbs to the oil and cook over low heat, stirring constantly for 3–4 minutes, or until the crumbs are brown and crunchy. Add the beans and 2 tablespoons chopped fresh flat-leaf parsley to the pan, then season, to taste, with salt and freshly ground black pepper. Stir to mix with the breadcrumbs and warm the beans. Can be served warm or at room temperature. Serves 4.

ABOVE: Fegato garbo e dolce

CACCIATORA

Cacciatora means 'in the style of the hunter'. Like many dishes throughout Italy, there are countless variations, with each region adding its own twist to the dish. Generally, the dish consists of a chicken or rabbit fricassee with tomato, onion and other vegetables.

ABOVE: Chicken cacciatora

CHICKEN CACCIATORA

Preparation time: 15 minutes
Total cooking time: 1 hour
Serves 4

☆

1/4 cup (60 ml/2 fl oz) olive oil

1 large onion, finely chopped

3 cloves garlic, crushed

150 g (5 oz) pancetta, finely chopped

125 g (4 oz) button mushrooms, thickly sliced

1 large chicken (at least 1.6 kg/3 1/4 lb), cut into 8 pieces

1/3 cup (80 ml/2 3/4 fl oz) dry vermouth or dry white wine

2 x 400 g (13 oz) cans chopped good-quality tomatoes

1/4 teaspoon soft brown sugar

1/4 teaspoon cayenne pepper

1 sprig of fresh oregano

1 sprig of fresh thyme

1 bay leaf

1 Heat half the olive oil in a large heatproof casserole dish. Add the onion and garlic and cook for 6–8 minutes over low heat, stirring, until the onion is golden. Add the pancetta and mushrooms, increase the heat and cook, stirring, for 4–5 minutes. Transfer to a bowl.

2 Add the remaining oil to the casserole dish and brown the chicken pieces, a few at a time, over medium heat. Season with salt and black pepper as they brown. Spoon off the excess fat and return all the chicken to the casserole dish. Increase the heat, add the vermouth to the dish and cook until the liquid has almost evaporated.

3 Add the chopped tomato, brown sugar, cayenne pepper, oregano, thyme and bay leaf, and stir in 1/3 cup (80 ml/2 3/4 fl oz) water to the dish. Bring to the boil, then stir in the reserved onion mixture. Reduce the heat, cover and simmer for 25 minutes, or until the chicken is tender but not falling off the bone.

4 If the liquid is too thin, remove the chicken from the casserole dish, increase the heat and boil until the liquid has thickened. Discard the sprigs of herbs and adjust the seasoning. Can be garnished with fresh oregano or thyme sprigs and served with steamed rice.

GRILLED SQUID WITH SALSA VERDE

Preparation time: 10 minutes
+ 30 minutes marinating
Total cooking time: 10 minutes
Serves 6

1 kg (2 lb) squid
1 cup (250 ml/8 fl oz) olive oil
2 tablespoons lemon juice
2 cloves garlic, crushed
2 tablespoons chopped fresh oregano
2 tablespoons chopped fresh flat-leaf parsley,
    for serving
6 lemon wedges, for serving

SALSA VERDE
4 anchovy fillets, drained
1 tablespoon capers
1 clove garlic, crushed
1/4 cup (7 g/1/4 oz) chopped flat-leaf parsley
1/4 cup (7 g/1/4 oz) fresh basil leaves
1/4 cup (7 g/1/4 oz) fresh mint leaves
2 teaspoons red wine vinegar
3 tablespoons extra virgin olive oil
1 teaspoon Dijon mustard

1   To clean the squid, hold onto the hood and gently pull the tentacles away from the head. Cut out the beak and discard with any intestines still attached to the tentacles. Rinse the tentacles in cold running water, then dry and cut into 5 cm (2 inch) lengths. Place them in a bowl. Clean out the hood cavity and remove the transparent quill. Under cold running water, pull away the skin, rinse and dry well. Cut into 1 cm (1/2 inch) rings and place in the bowl with the tentacles. Add the oil, lemon juice, garlic and oregano to the bowl, and toss to coat the squid. Leave to marinate for 30 minutes.
2   For the salsa verde, put the anchovies, capers garlic, parsley, basil and mint in a food processor and chop in short bursts until roughly blended. Transfer to a bowl and stir in the vinegar. Slowly mix in the oil, then the mustard. Season.
3   Heat a barbecue or grill until hot. Drain the squid rings and cook them in batches for 1–2 minutes each side.
4   Sprinkle the squid rings with salt, pepper and the fresh parsley and serve with the salsa verde and lemon wedges.

SEMI-DRIED ROMA TOMATOES

Preheat the oven to warm 160°C (315°F/Gas 2–3). Cut 16 Roma tomatoes into quarters lengthways and lay them skin-side-down on a wire rack in a baking dish. Stir together in a small bowl 1 teaspoon each of salt and cracked black pepper and 3 tablespoons fresh thyme, chopped. Sprinkle the mixture over the tomatoes. Bake for 2½ hours, checking occasionally to make sure the tomatoes don't burn. Put them in a bowl and toss with 2 tablespoons olive oil. Leave to cool before transferring to an airtight container. Refrigerate for 24 hours before using. Semi-dried tomatoes should be eaten within 3–4 days. Fills a 500 ml (16 fl oz) jar.

BELOW: Grilled squid with salsa verde

FENNEL FRITTERS

Preparation time: 15 minutes
Total cooking time: 20 minutes
Serves 4

☆

1 kg (2 lb) fennel bulbs
1/3 cup (30 g/1 oz) grated Pecorino
1 cup (80 g/2³/4 oz) fresh breadcrumbs
1/2 cup (60 g/2 oz) plain flour
3 eggs, lightly beaten
olive oil, for shallow-frying
lemon wedges, for serving

1 Remove the tough outer leaves from the fennel, then trim the base and small stalks. Slice the fennel lengthways into 5 mm (1/4 inch) widths and blanch in boiling salted water for 3 minutes, or until tender. Drain and pat dry. Leave to cool.
2 Mix together the cheese and breadcrumbs and season with salt and pepper.
3 Coat the fennel in flour, shake off the excess and dip in beaten egg. Coat in the crumb and cheese mix. Heat the oil in large heavy-based frying pan until the oil beings to sizzle. Fry the fennel in batches, being careful not to overcrowd the pan, for 2–3 minutes per side, until golden

brown and crisp. Drain on paper towels, season and serve immediately with the lemon wedges.
NOTE: Use the rounder, male fennel bulbs, rather than the flatter female bulbs, as they have more flavour.

SALTIMBOCCA
(Veal escalopes with prosciutto)

Preparation time: 15 minutes
Total cooking time: 20 minutes
Serves 4

☆

4 thin veal steaks
2 cloves garlic, crushed
4 slices prosciutto
4 fresh sage leaves
30 g (1 oz) butter
2/3 cup (170 ml/5¹/2 fl oz) Marsala

1 Trim the meat of excess fat and sinew and flatten each steak to 5 mm (1/4 inch) thick. Nick the edges to prevent curling and pat the meat dry with paper towels. Combine the garlic with 1/4 teaspoon salt and 1/2 teaspoon ground black

MARSALA
This fortified wine comes from a small town of the same name in Sicily. Made from local grapes, Marsalas can range from the very dry to the very sweet. While the dry Marsala is used more frequently in the kitchen and also drunk as an aperitif, sweet marsala is used for sweet dishes such as the famous Zabaglione (page 140) and is also drunk as a dessert wine. There are also special Marsala blends with added ingredients such as cream, eggs and almonds.

RIGHT: Fennel fritters

pepper and rub some of the mixture over one side of each veal steak. Place a slice of prosciutto on each and top with a sage leaf. The prosciutto should cover the veal completely but not overlap.
2 Melt the butter in a large heavy-based frying pan, add the veal, prosciutto-side-up, and cook over moderate heat for 5 minutes, or until the underside is golden brown. Do not turn the veal. Add the Marsala, without wetting the top of the veal. Reduce the heat and simmer very slowly for 10 minutes. Transfer the veal to warm serving plates. Boil the sauce for 2–3 minutes, or until syrupy, then spoon it over the veal.

FRITTO MISTO DI MARE
(Fried seafood salad)

Preparation time: 15 minutes
Total cooking time: 10 minutes
Serves 4

☆☆

2 cuttlefish hoods
8 red mullet fillets
¹/₂ teaspoon paprika
75 g (2¹/₂ oz) plain flour

12 raw medium prawns, peeled, deveined, tails intact
good-quality olive oil, for deep-frying
lemons wedges, for serving
fresh flat-leaf parsley, to garnish

1 Preheat the oven to slow 150°C (300°F/ Gas 2). Line a large baking tray with baking paper. Place the cuttlefish bone-side-down on a board and, using a sharp knife, gently cut lengthways through the body. Open out, remove the cuttlebone and then gently remove the insides. Cut the flesh in half. Under cold running water, pull the skin away. Cut the cuttlefish and mullet into even-sized pieces. Season well. Mix the paprika and flour together in a bowl, add the seafood, including the prawns, and toss to coat. Remove any excess flour.
2 Fill a deep heavy-based saucepan one third full of oil and heat to 190°C (375°F), or until a cube of bread dropped into the oil browns in 10 seconds. Add the seafood in batches and cook for 1–2 minutes each batch, or until crisp and golden. Keep warm in the oven.
3 Place the seafood on a serving platter. Sprinkle with extra salt and serve with lemon wedges. Garnish with parsley.

CUTTLEFISH
Cuttlefish belong to the *cephalopod* family (molluscs without shells) along with squid, calamari and octopus. Almost all cephalopods rely upon a brownish or black blanket of ink to hide from their predators. This ink is used by many Mediterranean countries to colour and flavour pasta and seafood stews. Some insist that only the ink of the cuttlefish should be used to cook with as it is sweeter than other varieties, but many cooks also use squid ink. Small cuttlefish are usually very tender but the larger varieties are similar to octopus in that they need special treatment to tenderize them prior to cooking.

ABOVE: Fritto misto di mare

½ cup (15 g/½ oz) finely chopped fresh
flat-leaf parsley
1 tablespoon balsamic vinegar
¼ cup (25 g/¾ oz) grated Parmesan, extra

1   Grease a 20 cm (8 inch) square shallow cake
tin. Place the stock and a pinch of salt in a large
saucepan and bring to the boil. Add the polenta
in a steady stream, stirring constantly. Reduce
the heat and simmer, stirring frequently, for
15–20 minutes. Remove from the heat and stir
in the butter and Parmesan. Spread the mixture
into the tin and refrigerate for 20 minutes.
2   Soak the porcini mushrooms in ½ cup
(125 ml/4 fl oz) boiling water for 10 minutes,
or until softened, then drain, reserving ⅓ cup
(80 ml/2¾ fl oz) liquid.
3   Wipe the other mushrooms with a damp
cloth. Thickly slice the Swiss brown mushrooms,
and coarsely chop the field mushrooms. Heat
⅓ cup (80 ml/2¾ fl oz) oil in a large frying pan,
add the mushrooms, including the porcini
mushrooms, cook for 4–5 minutes, then remove
from the pan. Heat the remaining oil in the pan
and cook the onion and garlic over medium heat
for 2–3 minutes, or until transparent.
4   Add the reserved soaking liquid, bay leaf,
thyme and oregano to the pan, season and cook
for 2 minutes. Return the mushrooms to the pan,
add the parsley and vinegar and cook over
medium heat for 1 minute, or until nearly dry.
Remove the bay leaf and check the seasoning.
5   Sprinkle the extra Parmesan over the polenta
and heat under a medium grill for 10 minutes, or
until lightly browned and the cheese has melted.
Cut into four 10 cm (4 inch) squares.
6   Place a polenta square in the centre of each
serving plate and top with the mushroom
mixture. Garnish with black pepper.

POLENTA SQUARES WITH MUSHROOM RAGU

Preparation time: 25 minutes + refrigeration
Total cooking time: 25 minutes
Serves 4

☆

2 cups (500 ml/16 fl oz) vegetable stock or water
1 cup (150 g/5 oz) polenta
20 g (¾ oz) butter
¾ cup (75 g/2½ oz) grated Parmesan
5 g (¼ oz) dried porcini mushrooms
200 g (6½ oz) Swiss brown mushrooms
300 g (10 oz) field mushrooms
½ cup (125 ml/4 fl oz) olive oil
1 onion, finely chopped
3 cloves garlic, finely chopped
1 fresh bay leaf
2 teaspoons finely chopped fresh thyme
2 teaspoons finely chopped fresh oregano

*ABOVE: Polenta squares
with mushroom ragu*

PORK CHOPS IN MARSALA

Pat dry 4 pork loin chops, about 2.5 cm
(1 inch) thick, and season well. Heat
2 tablespoons olive oil in a heavy-based
frying pan over medium heat and cook the
chops on both sides for 5 minutes each side,
or until brown and cooked. Add ½ cup
(125 ml/4 fl oz) Marsala, 2 teaspoons grated
orange rind and ¼ cup (60 ml/2 fl oz)
orange juice and cook for 4–5 minutes, or
until the sauce has reduced and thickened.
Add 3 tablespoons chopped fresh flat-leaf
parsley and serve. Serves 4.

CARCIOFI ALLA ROMANA
(Roman-style artichokes)

Preparation time: 25 minutes
Total cooking time: 1 hour 30 minutes
Serves 4 as an entrée or as part of an
  antipasto platter

☆ ☆

4 globe artichokes
3 tablespoons lemon juice
1 tablespoon toasted fresh breadcrumbs
1 large clove garlic, crushed
3 tablespoons finely chopped fresh parsley
3 tablespoons finely chopped fresh mint
1 1/2 tablespoons olive oil
1/4 cup (60 ml/2 fl oz) dry white wine

1 Preheat the oven to moderately hot 190°C
(375°F/Gas 5). Add the lemon juice to a large
bowl of cold water. Remove the tough outer
leaves from the artichokes and trim the stalks
to 5 cm (2 inches) long. Peel the stalks with a
potato peeler. Slice off the top quarter of each
artichoke with a sharp knife to give a level
surface. Gently open out the leaves and scrape
out the hairy choke, using a teaspoon or a small
sharp knife. Drop each artichoke into the lemon
water as you go.
2 Combine the breadcrumbs, garlic, parsley,
mint and olive oil in a bowl and season well.
Fill the centre of each artichoke with the
mixture, pressing it in well. Close the leaves
as tightly as possible to prevent the filling from
falling out.
3 Arrange the artichokes with the stalks up in
a deep ovenproof casserole just large enough
to fit them so they are tightly packed. Sprinkle
with salt and pour in the wine. Cover with a lid,
or a double sheet of kitchen foil secured tightly
at the edges. Bake for about 1 1/2 hours, until
very tender. Serve hot as a first course or
side vegetable, or at room temperature
as an antipasto.
NOTE: Check the artichokes halfway through
cooking and, if necessary, add a little water to
prevent them from burning.

ARTICHOKES
This is the common name
given to three unrelated
plants, Jerusalem artichokes,
Chinese artichokes and
globe artichokes. However,
the latter is the only one
considered to be a true
artichoke. Globe artichokes
are a member of the thistle
family and are natives of the
Mediterranean region.
When buying artichokes,
make sure the centres are
well closed and avoid any
that are heavily browned as
they are beyond their
prime. Artichokes are best
used on the day of
purchase but can be stored
in a plastic bag in the fridge
for up to three days. An
interesting fact about
artichokes is that they
sweeten the flavour of the
next thing that you eat. This
is due to the presence of
the chemical cynarin and
has a most marked effect
upon the taste of wine,
making it taste quite
unpleasant. This reaction is
much less pronounced in
artichokes that have been
crumbed or fried. Jerusalem
artichokes are neither from
Jerusalem nor artichokes,
but a variety of sunflower,
whose name derives from
'girasole' the Italian word
for sunflower.

LEFT: Carciofi alla Romana

ABBACCHIO
(Roman lamb)

Preparation time: 15 minutes
Total cooking time: 1 hour 20 minutes
Serves 4–6

1/4 cup (60 ml/2 fl oz) olive oil
1 kg (2 lb) spring lamb, cut into 2 cm
   (3/4 inch) cubes
2 cloves garlic, crushed
6 fresh sage leaves
1 sprig fresh rosemary
1 tablespoon flour
1/2 cup (125 ml/4 fl oz) white wine vinegar
6 anchovy fillets

1 Heat the oil in a heavy-based frying pan and
cook the meat in batches over medium heat for
3–4 minutes, until browned on all sides.
2 Return all the meat to the pan and add the
garlic, sage and rosemary. Season with salt and
pepper, combine well and cook for 1 minute.
3 Dust the meat with the flour using a fine
sieve, then cook for another minute. Add the
vinegar and simmer for 30 seconds, then add
1 cup (250 ml/8 fl oz) water. Bring to a gentle
simmer, lower the heat and cover, leaving the
lid partially askew. Cook for 50–60 minutes,
or until the meat is tender, stirring occasionally
and adding a little more water if necessary.
4 When the lamb is almost cooked, mash
the anchovies in a mortar and pestle with
1 tablespoon of the cooking liquid, until
a paste is formed. Add to the lamb and cook,
uncovered, for another 2 minutes. Delicious
served with Rosemary potatoes.
NOTES: This dish is best served immediately but
can be prepared in advance up to the end of
Step 3. The anchovies should be added at the
last moment or they overpower the delicate
flavour of the lamb.

    The secret of success for this famous recipe
depends very much on the quality of lamb used.
Ideally, the lamb should be just one month old
and entirely milk-fed, but anything no older
than a spring lamb will still give tender results.

ROSEMARY POTATOES

Preparation time: 5 minutes
Total cooking time: 1 hour
Serves 6

1/2 cup (125 ml/4 fl oz) extra virgin olive oil
2 x 12 cm (5 inch) sprigs of fresh rosemary
8 cloves garlic, unpeeled
1.5 kg (3 lb) floury potatoes, cut into
   4 cm (1 1/2 inch) cubes
sea salt, to taste

1 Preheat the oven to moderate 180°C (350°F/
Gas 4). Pour the oil into a large baking dish, add
the rosemary, garlic and potato and toss to coat.
2 Bake on the centre rack for 30 minutes. Turn
the potatoes and sprinkle with sea salt. Bake for
another 30 minutes, or until the potatoes are
crisp and golden. Serve warm.

SAUTEED SILVERBEET
(SWISS CHARD)

Preparation time: 15 minutes
Total cooking time: 10 minutes
Serves 4–6

1 kg (2 lb) silverbeet (Swiss chard)
2 tablespoons olive oil
3 cloves garlic, sliced thinly
extra virgin olive oil, for serving

1 Trim the leaves from the stalks of the silverbeet
and rinse them in cold water. Blanch the leaves
in a large saucepan of boiling, salted water for
1–2 minutes, or until tender but still firm. Drain
well in a colander. Lay out on a tea towel or tray
to cool, then, using your hands, gently wring out
the excess water from the leaves.
2 Heat the oil in a heavy-based frying pan and
cook the garlic over low heat until just starting
to turn golden. Add the silverbeet, season with
salt and pepper and cook over medium heat for
3–4 minutes, or until warmed through. Transfer
to a serving plate and drizzle with extra virgin
olive oil. Serve warm or at room temperature.
NOTE: This is delicious eaten warm with meats
or fish, or at room temperature with bruschetta,
as part of an antipasto platter.

POTATO VARIETIES
The increasing variety of
potatoes available can
sometimes make it
overwhelming when
deciding which one to
choose. Basically, potatoes
can be floury or waxy but
some of the newer breeds
are all-purpose and are
difficult to categorise. Floury
potatoes are low in
moisture and sugar and
high in starch which makes
them perfect for baking,
mashing or frying but
because of their low sugar
content they will collapse
when boiled. Examples of
floury potatoes are spunta,
russet (Idaho) and King
Edward. Waxy potatoes on
the other hand are high in
moisture and low in starch,
so hold their shape and
texture during boiling. They
are not suitable for mashing
or making chips. Examples
of waxy potatoes are bintje,
kipfler, jersey royal and pink
fir apple. Good 'all round'
potatoes include desiree,
pontiac and sebago.

*OPPOSITE PAGE, FROM
TOP: Sautéed silverbeet;
Rosemary potatoes;
Abbacchio*

129

PARMESAN

Parmesan is a hard, crumbly cheese made from skimmed or partially skimmed cow's milk. The most superior Parmesan is Parmigiano Reggiano, produced in the Parma and Reggio provinces of Northern Italy using techniques that are seven centuries old. The name is stringently protected by law. Parmigiano Reggiano is aged for up to 4 years and is unrivalled in flavour and texture. Parmigiano Grana is, as its name implies, a grainy cheese and is suitable for grating or serving as a table cheese. Buy Parmesan in a wedge or if possible, ask that it be cut from the wheel. Grate it as you need it because when cut, the cheese becomes dry and the flavour is altered. For this reason, never buy pre-grated cheese as it bears little resemblance in flavour and texture to the real thing. Select Parmesan with the rind still attached and with no evidence of whitening at the rim. To store, wrap tightly in greaseproof paper, then in heavy-duty aluminium foil.

RIGHT: Parmesan and rosemary crusted veal chops

PARMESAN AND ROSEMARY CRUSTED VEAL CHOPS

Preparation time: 15 minutes
Total cooking time: 15 minutes
Serves 4

☆

4 veal chops
150 g (5 oz) fresh white breadcrumbs
75 g (2$^{1}/_{2}$ oz) grated Parmesan
1 tablespoon fresh rosemary, finely chopped
2 eggs, lightly beaten, seasoned
3 tablespoons olive oil
60 g (2 oz) butter
4 cloves garlic

1   Trim the chops of excess fat and sinew and flatten to 1 cm ($^{1}/_{2}$ inch) thickness. Pat the meat dry with paper towels. Combine the breadcrumbs, Parmesan and rosemary in a shallow bowl.
2   Dip each chop in the beaten egg, draining off the excess. Press both sides of the chops firmly in the crumbs.
3   Heat the oil and butter in a heavy-based frying pan over low heat, add the garlic and cook until golden. Discard the garlic.

4   Increase the heat to medium, add the chops to the pan and cook for 4–5 minutes on each side, depending on the thickness of the chops, until golden and crisp. Transfer to a warm serving dish and season with salt and pepper.

SALSA ROSSA

This is usually paired with Salsa verde when served with boiled meats but is also delicious with breaded meats such as the veal chops on this page.
Slice 3 large red peppers (capsicums) in half lengthways. Remove the membrane and seeds and slice them into 1 cm ($^{1}/_{2}$ inch) wide strips. Heat $^{1}/_{4}$ cup (60 ml/2 fl oz) olive oil in a heavy-based frying pan and cook 3 large finely sliced onions over medium heat until soft but not browned. Add the peppers and cook until both the vegetables are very soft and the bulk has been reduced by half. Add $^{1}/_{4}$ teaspoon chilli flakes, 400 g (13 oz) can tomatoes and season with salt. Simmer the sauce for another 25 minutes, or until the sauce has thickened and the oil has separated from the tomatoes. Check the seasoning and adjust if necessary. Serve warm. Serves 4.

CAPONATA WITH TUNA

Preparation time: 25 minutes
+ 1 hour standing + cooling
Total cooking time: 45 minutes
Serves 6

CAPONATA
500 g (1 lb) ripe tomatoes
750 g (1¹/₂ lb) eggplant (aubergine),
   cut into 1 cm (¹/₂ inch) cubes
¹/₂ cup (125 ml/4 fl oz) olive oil
1 onion, chopped
3 stalks celery, chopped
2 tablespoons capers
¹/₂ cup (125 g/4 oz) green olives, pitted
1 tablespoon sugar
¹/₂ cup (125 ml/4 fl oz) red wine vinegar

6 x 200 g (6¹/₂ oz) tuna steaks
olive oil, for brushing

1 Score a cross in the base of each tomato. Place the tomatoes into a bowl of boiling water for 10 seconds, then plunge into cold water and peel the skin away from the cross. Cut the tomato into 1 cm (¹/₂ inch) cubes.
2 Sprinkle the eggplant with salt and leave in a colander for 1 hour. Rinse under cold water and pat dry. Heat 2 tablespoons oil in a frying pan over medium heat and cook half the eggplant for 4–5 minutes, or until golden and soft. Remove from the pan and drain on crumpled paper towels. Repeat with 2 tablespoons oil and the remaining eggplant.
3 Heat the remaining olive oil in the same pan, add the onion and celery, and cook for 5–6 minutes, or until softened. Reduce the heat to low, add the tomato and simmer for 15 minutes, stirring occasionally. Stir in the capers, olives, sugar and vinegar, season and continue to simmer, stirring occasionally, for 10 minutes, or until slightly reduced. Stir in the eggplant. Remove from the heat and cool to room temperature.
4 Heat a chargrill plate and brush lightly with olive oil. Cook the tuna for 2–3 minutes each side, or to your liking. Serve with the caponata.

BAKED RADICCHIO

Preheat the oven to moderate 180°C (350°F/Gas 4). Remove the outer leaves of 1 kg (2 lb) of radicchio and split the heads into 4 wedges. Heat 2 tablespoons olive oil in a flameproof casserole dish large enough to fit all the radicchio in a single layer. Add 100 g (3¹/₂ oz) thinly sliced bacon and cook over medium heat until the fat has just melted but the meat is not crisp. Add the radicchio and turn it over to coat it well. Bake, covered, for 25–30 minutes, until tender when pierced with a knife, turning the radicchio occasionally. Season and transfer to a warm dish with all the liquid. Serve immediately. Serves 4.

ABOVE: Caponata with tuna

ROSEMARY

The Latin name for rosemary is *Rosmarinus officinalis* meaning 'dew of the sea', a reference probably to the fact that it grows near the sea. Dating back to Roman times, rosemary was used as much for its medicinal properties as for its aromatic flavour. It is a herb which should be used with discretion, as its distinctive flavour can easily overpower others. Rosemary is one of the most commonly used herbs in Italy, along with parsley, and is usually associated with roasts. If possible, use only fresh rosemary, snipping the tips off the younger, more fragrant branches.

ABOVE: Roasted rosemary chicken

ROASTED ROSEMARY CHICKEN

Preparation time: 15 minutes
  + 10 minutes standing
Total cooking time: 1 hour
Serves 4

1.5–1.8 kg (3 lb–3lb 10 oz) chicken
6 large sprigs fresh rosemary
4 cloves garlic
3 tablespoons olive oil

1 Preheat the oven to hot 220°C (425°F/Gas 7). Wipe the chicken inside and out and pat dry with paper towels. Season the chicken cavity and place 4 rosemary sprigs and the garlic cloves inside.
2 Rub the outside of the chicken with 1 tablespoon of the oil, season and place the chicken on its side in a roasting tin. Put the remaining rosemary sprigs in the tin and drizzle the remaining oil around the tin.
3 Place the tin on the middle shelf in the oven. After 20 minutes, turn the chicken onto the other side, baste with the juices and cook for another 20 minutes. Turn the chicken breast-side-up, baste again and cook for another 15 minutes, or until the juices between the body and thigh run clear when pierced with a knife. Transfer the chicken to a warm serving dish and set aside for at least 10 minutes before carving.
4 Meanwhile, pour most of the fat from the roasting tin and return the tin to the stovetop over high heat. Add 2 tablespoons water and, using a wooden spoon, scrape the base of the pan to loosen the residue. Check the seasoning and pour over the chicken to serve.

MARJORAM SALMORIGLIO

This simple dressing is used widely in Sicily to accompany grilled fish or other seafood. Using a mortar and pestle, pound 2 tablespoons fresh marjoram. Transfer to a bowl and gradually add 1/2 cup (125 ml/ 4 fl oz) extra virgin olive oil and 1 tablespoon lemon juice. Season. Thyme or oregano can be used instead of marjoram. Serves 4.

MUSSELS IN TOMATO AND HERB SAUCE

Preparation time: 30 minutes
Total cooking time: 40 minutes
Serves 4

 ☆ ☆

TOMATO AND HERB SAUCE
1/3 cup (80 ml/2 3/4 fl oz) olive oil
3 cloves garlic, finely chopped
1/4 teaspoon dried chilli flakes
2 x 400 g (13 oz) cans crushed
    good-quality tomatoes
pinch of caster sugar, or to taste

8 slices crusty Italian bread
4 tablespoons olive oil
2 large cloves garlic, halved
1 kg (2 lb) black mussels
1 red onion, finely chopped
6 sprigs of fresh flat-leaf parsley
2 sprigs of fresh thyme
2 sprigs of fresh oregano
1 cup (250 ml/8 fl oz) white wine
chopped fresh flat-leaf parsley, extra,
    to garnish
fresh thyme leaves, extra, to garnish
chopped fresh oregano leaves, extra,
    to garnish

1 Preheat the oven to warm 160°C (315°F/ Gas 2–3). To make the tomato and herb sauce, heat the oil in a saucepan, add the garlic and chilli flakes, and cook over low heat for 30 seconds without browning. Add the tomato, sugar and 1/3 cup (80 ml/2 3/4 fl oz) water. Season well and simmer, stirring often, for 15 minutes, or until the sauce has thickened and reduced.

2 Lightly brush the bread with olive oil using half the oil. Place the bread in a single layer on a baking tray and bake for 10 minutes, or until crisp and golden. While still warm, rub one side of each slice with garlic.

3 Meanwhile, scrub the mussels with a stiff brush and pull out the hairy beards. Discard any broken mussels or those that don't close when tapped on a bench. Rinse well.

4 Heat the remaining olive oil in a large saucepan, add the onion and cook for 3 minutes, or until softened but not browned. Add the parsley, thyme, oregano sprigs and wine to the saucepan. Bring to the boil, then reduce the heat and simmer for 5 minutes.

5 Add the mussels to the pan, stir to coat in the onion and wine mixture, and cook, covered, over high heat for 3–4 minutes. Gently shake the pan often, to move the mussels around. Remove the mussels as they open. Discard any unopened mussels.

6 Strain the wine mixture into the tomato sauce, discarding the onion and herbs. Check the sauce for seasoning and adjust if necessary. Add the mussels and toss well to coat in the mixture. Pile into a serving bowl and garnish with the extra parsley, thyme and oregano. Arrange the bread around the bowl and serve.

NOTES: You can keep mussels (uncleaned) for a day or two longer in a bucket of cold, salted water.

Clams can be prepared in the same way as the mussels and used as a substitute in this recipe.

BELOW: Mussels in tomato and herb sauce

INVOLTINI OF
SWORDFISH

Roll out the swordfish
between two pieces of
plastic wrap.

Roll up the fish pieces and
filling to form neat parcels.

Thread the rolls, bay leaves,
lemon peel and onion onto
skewers.

INVOLTINI OF SWORDFISH

Preparation time: 35 minutes
Total cooking time: 10 minutes
Serves 4

☆

1 kg (2 lb) swordfish, skin removed, cut
    into four 4 x 5 cm (1 1/2 inch) pieces
3 lemons
1/3 cup (80 ml/2 3/4 fl oz) olive oil
1 small onion, chopped
3 cloves garlic, chopped
2 tablespoons chopped capers
2 tablespoons finely chopped pitted
    Kalamata olives
1/3 cup (35 g/1 1/4 oz) grated Parmesan
1 1/2 cups (120 g/4 oz) soft white breadcrumbs
2 tablespoons chopped fresh flat-leaf parsley
1 egg, lightly beaten
24 fresh bay leaves
2 small white onions, quartered and
    separated into pieces
lemon wedges, to serve

1 Cut each swordfish piece horizontally into
4 slices to give you 16 slices altogether. Place
each piece between two pieces of plastic wrap
and roll gently with a rolling pin to flatten the
fish without tearing it. Cut each piece in half to
give 32 pieces altogether.
2 Thinly peel the rind from the lemons with a
vegetable peeler and cut the rind into 24 even
pieces. Squeeze the lemons to give 1/4 cup
(60 ml/2 fl oz) juice.
3 Heat 2 tablespoons olive oil, add the onion
and garlic, and cook for 2 minutes. Place in
a bowl with the capers, olives, Parmesan,
breadcrumbs and parsley. Season, add the
egg and mix to bind.
4 Divide the stuffing among the fish pieces and,
with oiled hands, roll up the fish to form neat
parcels. Thread 4 rolls onto each of 8 skewers,
alternating with the bay leaves, lemon peel
and onion.
5 Mix the remaining oil with the lemon juice.
Barbecue or grill the skewers for 3–4 minutes
each side, basting with the oil and lemon
mixture. Serve with lemon wedges.
NOTES: To prevent wooden skewers from
burning during cooking, soak them in cold water
for 20 minutes before using.

RIGHT: Involtini of swordfish

RABBIT WITH ROSEMARY AND WHITE WINE

Preparation time: 25 minutes
Total cooking time: 2 hours
Serves 4

1 large rabbit, weighing at least 1.6 kg (3 1/4 lb)
1/4 cup (30 g/1 oz) seasoned flour
1/4 cup (60 ml/2 fl oz) olive oil
2 onions, thinly sliced
1 large sprig of rosemary
1 small sprig of fresh sage
2 cloves garlic, crushed
2 cups (500 ml/16 fl oz) dry white wine
400 g (13 oz) can chopped good-quality
   tomatoes
good pinch of cayenne pepper
1/2 cup (125 ml/4 fl oz) chicken stock
12 small black olives such as Niçoise
   or Ligurian, optional
3 small sprigs of rosemary, extra

1 Cut the rabbit into large pieces and dredge the pieces in the flour. Heat the oil in a large heavy-based saucepan over moderate heat. Brown the rabbit pieces on all sides, then remove from the saucepan.
2 Reduce the heat and add the onion, rosemary and sage to the saucepan. Cook gently for 10 minutes, then stir in the garlic and return the rabbit to the saucepan.
3 Increase the heat to high, add the wine to the pan and cook for 1 minute. Stir in the tomato, the cayenne and half the stock. Reduce the heat, cover and simmer over low heat for about 1 1/2 hours, until the rabbit is tender. Halfway through cooking, check the sauce and if it seems too dry, add 1/4 cup (60 ml/2 fl oz) water.
4 Discard the herb sprigs. If necessary, thicken the sauce by transferring the rabbit to a serving plate and cooking the sauce, uncovered, over high heat for about 5 minutes. Check the seasoning and adjust if necessary. Pour over the rabbit and garnish with the olives and extra rosemary. Polenta makes an excellent accompaniment to this dish.

RABBIT
There are two types of rabbit, domestic and wild, with the latter being the more flavoursome because it feeds on wild herbs, bay leaves and juniper berries. The quality of the domestic rabbit depends upon its feed, breeding and age but in general they are plumper than their wild counterparts. Ideally a rabbit should weigh between 1 and 1.25 kilos (2 and 2 1/2 pounds) and have light-coloured flesh. These are the most tender and can be cooked in any manner suitable for young chicken. Older or wild rabbits benefit from longer, more moist cooking methods such as braising.

ABOVE: Rabbit with rosemary and white wine

OLIVE OIL

Like wine, the flavour, colour and taste of olive oil varies according to the type of fruit used and the climate, soil and area of cultivation. The type and ripeness of the olive influences the colour of the oil, so green olives give grassy, green oils, while ripe black olives produce rich yellow oils. Less ripe olives produce a rich, green oil which pales after three months and is considered superior. However, riper olives yield more oil. Some olive trees are grown to produce olives for eating and some for oil — they are not harvested from the same trees.

Unique among oils due to its great diversity, olive oil connoisseurs identify four categories along the taste spectrum.

Fine, gentle-flavoured oil with a hint of olive taste is considered light; delicate, buttery-flavoured oil is mild; oils with a stronger, more distinct olive taste are semi–fruity; and the fully fledged, strongest olive-flavoured oils are regarded as fruity or peppery. Although it is generally thought that you can determine an oil's taste by its colour, this isn't always the case. Changes in the growing conditions, as well as the oils used in various blends, can influence the colour and flavour.

WHAT DOES THE LABEL MEAN?

Olive oils can be divided into four major groups, which are distinguished by their level of acidity.

Extra virgin olive oil is the highest quality oil, made from the first pressing of olives, with the lowest acidity level at less than 1%. It has an intense, fruity flavour. It can only be extracted mechanically or manually cold pressed, without using heat or chemicals, so the oil is not altered.

Virgin olive oil has a good flavour and is treated and extracted in the same way as extra virgin. However, it has an acidity level of less than 2%.

Olive oil once known as pure olive oil, is a blend of unrefined virgin olive oil and refined virgin olive oil which has an acidity level of less than 3.3%. The use of heat to aid extraction contributes to the higher level of acidity.

Light olive oil is made from the filtered combination of refined olive oil with very small amounts of virgin olive oil. Despite popular belief, it is not light in kilojoules as it has exactly the same amount as other oils. It is lighter than other olive oils in texture and taste, making it ideal for baking. Filtration leads to a higher smoke point so it is also suitable for deep-frying.

Olive oil infused with Mediterranean flavours such as lemon, basil, garlic, rosemary, truffle, tarragon and cepe are becoming more readily available. The better-quality infused oils are made by pressing the flavouring with the olives to simultaneously extract both of their essential oils. Otherwise, the essential oil is extracted separately and infused into the olive oil, often with some of the flavouring ingredient put in the bottle.

WHICH TYPE TO USE?

Undoubtedly the best oil to use when preparing Mediterranean food, olive oil's diversity lends itself to most cooking methods and many dishes, including salad dressings, pasta making and baking. Contrary to common wisdom, olive oil is also excellent for frying as it reaches high temperatures without breaking down and forms a seal around the food, minimising fat absorption and giving the food an even, golden glow.

While there are some classic rules, such as using olive oil for general cooking purposes and extra virgin olive oil for making salad dressings and drizzling on food such as pasta before serving, the choice of the type of oil is equally a matter of personal taste.

There are now so many olive oils on the market, it is often difficult to choose which ones to buy. This can only be decided by trying varieties from different countries and regions to find those that you prefer.

Like all oils, olive oil should be stored in a cool, dark place. It can be kept for up to six months when opened and up to two years unopened. Unlike wine, olive oils do not improve with age. Some boutique oils, however, only last for three months. Do not store olive oil in the fridge because it will solidify, and never keep it near the stove. If the olive oil container is left open, the exposure to air will oxidise the oil and cause it to turn rancid.

FROM LEFT: Extra virgin olive oil; Virgin olive oil; Olive oil; Light olive oil

OLIVE BREAD

Preparation time: 30 minutes
  + 2 hours 30 minutes rising
Total cooking time: 35 minutes
Makes 1 loaf

☆☆

3 cups (375 g/12 oz) plain flour
7 g (3/4 oz) sachet dry yeast
2 teaspoons sugar
2 tablespoons olive oil
110 g (3 1/2 oz) Kalamata olives, pitted, halved
2 teaspoons plain flour, extra, to coat
1 small sprig of fresh oregano, leaves removed
  and torn into small pieces, optional
olive oil, to glaze

ABOVE: Olive bread

1 Place a third of the flour in a large bowl and stir in 1 teaspoon salt. Place the yeast, sugar and 1 cup (250 ml/8 fl oz) warm water in a small bowl and stir well. Set aside in a warm, draught-free place for 10 minutes, or until bubbles appear on the surface. The mixture should be frothy and slightly increased in volume. If your yeast doesn't foam, it is dead and you will have to start again.

2 Add the yeast mixture to the flour and salt mixture in the bowl and stir to make a thin, lumpy paste. Cover with a tea towel and set aside in a warm, draught-free place for 45 minutes, or until doubled in size.

3 Stir in the remaining flour and the oil and 1/2 cup (125 ml/4 fl oz) warm water. Mix with a wooden spoon until a rough dough forms. Transfer to a lightly floured work surface and knead for 10–12 minutes, incorporating as little extra flour as possible to keep the dough soft and moist, but not sticky. Form into a ball. Oil a clean large bowl and roll the dough around in it to lightly coat in the oil. Cut a cross on top, cover the bowl with a tea towel and set aside in a warm place for 1 hour, or until doubled in size.

4 Lightly grease a baking tray and dust with flour. Punch down the dough on a lightly floured surface. Roll out to 30 x 25 x 1 cm (12 x 10 x 1/2 inch). Squeeze any excess liquid from the olives and toss to coat in the extra flour. Scatter over the dough and top with the oregano. Roll up tightly lengthways, pressing firmly to expel any air pockets as you roll. Press the ends together to form an oval loaf 25 cm (10 inches) long. Transfer to the prepared tray, join-side-down. Make 3 shallow diagonal slashes across the top. Slide the tray into a large plastic bag and leave in a warm place for 45 minutes, or until doubled in bulk.

5 Preheat the oven to hot 220°C (425°F/Gas 7). Brush the top of the loaf with olive oil and bake for 30 minutes. Reduce the heat to moderate 180°C (350°F/Gas 4) and bake for another 5 minutes. Cool on a wire rack. Serve warm or cold.

NOTE: Instead of the oregano you can use 2 teaspoons of finely chopped rosemary. Fold it through the dough and sprinkle whole leaves on the top after brushing with olive oil.

FOCACCIA
(Italian flatbread)

Preparation time: 30 minutes
   + 3 hours 30 minutes rising
Total cooking time: 20 minutes per loaf
Makes two loaves

1/2 teaspoon caster sugar
7 g (3/4 oz) sachet dry yeast
1 kg (2 lb) bread flour
1/4 cup (60 ml/2 fl oz) olive oil

1 Put the sugar, yeast and 2 tablespoons warm water in a small bowl, mix well and leave in a warm, draught-free place for 10 minutes, or until bubbles appear on the surface. The mixture should be frothy and slightly increased in volume. If your yeast doesn't foam it is dead and you will have to start again.

2 Place the flour and 2 teaspoons salt in a large bowl and mix well. Add 2 tablespoons of the olive oil, the yeast mixture and 3 cups (750 ml/ 24 fl oz) warm water. Mix with a wooden spoon until the mixture comes together in a loose dough, then turn out onto a lightly floured surface. Start kneading to form a soft, moist, but non-sticky dough, adding a little extra flour or warm water as needed. Knead for 8 minutes, or until smooth, or until the impression made by a finger springs straight back out.

3 Lightly oil a large bowl. Place the dough in the bowl and roll around to coat. Cut a cross on top with a sharp knife. Cover the bowl with a clean tea towel and leave in a dry, warm place for 1 hour 30 minutes, or until doubled in size.

4 Punch down the dough on a lightly floured surface and divide in half. One or both portions can be frozen at this point. Roll one portion out to 28 x 20 cm (11 x 8 inches). Use the heels of your hands to work from the middle outwards and shape to measure 38 x 28 cm (15 x 11 inches).

5 Lightly oil a baking tray and dust with flour. Place the dough in the centre and slide the tray inside a large plastic bag. Leave in a dry, warm place for 2 hours, or until doubled in size.

6 Preheat the oven to hot 220°C (425°F/ Gas 7). Brush the surface of the dough with some of the remaining olive oil and bake for 20 minutes, or until golden. Transfer to a wire rack to cool. Allow plenty of air to circulate under the loaf to keep the crust crisp. Repeat with the remaining dough. Best eaten within 6 hours of baking.

NOTES: When bread flour is unavailable and plain flour must be used, start by adding 1 cup (250 ml/8 fl oz) of the water in step 2, then gradually adding more to give a soft but non-sticky dough. Plain flour requires less water in a dough, and will give a denser textured bread.

For a simple variation, try the simple toppings given below. Add them when the dough has risen a second time.

Brush the top with olive oil, scatter 200 g (6½ oz) green olives over the dough and press them down firmly. Sprinkle with sea salt and rosemary sprigs and bake.

Brush the top with olive oil, scatter 100 g (3½ oz) diced pancetta over the dough and press it down firmly. Sprinkle with 2 tablespoons grated Parmesan and bake.

BELOW: Focaccia

STRAWBERRIES WITH BALSAMIC VINEGAR

Preparation time: 10 minutes
    + 1 hour marinating
Total cooking time: Nil
Serves 4

750 g (1 1/2 lb) ripe small strawberries
1/4 cup (60 g/2 oz) caster sugar
2 tablespoons good-quality balsamic vinegar
1/2 cup (125 g/4 oz) mascarpone, to serve

1 Wipe the strawberries with a clean damp cloth and hull them. Halve large strawberries.
2 Place the strawberries in a glass bowl, sprinkle the sugar evenly over the top and toss gently to coat. Leave for 30 minutes to macerate. Sprinkle the vinegar over the strawberries, toss and refrigerate for 30 minutes.
3 Spoon the strawberries into four glasses, drizzle with the syrup and top with a dollop of mascarpone.

ZABAGLIONE

Preparation time: 5 minutes
Total cooking time: 10 minutes
Serves 4

4 egg yolks
1/3 cup (90 g/3 oz) caster sugar
1/3 cup (80 ml/2 3/4 fl oz) Marsala

1 Combine all the ingredients in a large heatproof bowl set over a pan of barely simmering water. Make sure the bowl does not touch the water. Whisk with a balloon whisk or electric beaters for 5 minutes, or until the mixture is smooth and foamy and has tripled in volume. Do not stop whisking and do not allow the bowl to become too hot or the eggs will scramble. The final result will be creamy, pale and mousse-like.
2 Pour the zabaglione into four glasses and serve immediately.
NOTE: Sometimes zabaglione is served chilled. If you want to do this, cover the glasses with plastic wrap and refrigerate for at least 1 hour. You must make sure the zabaglione is properly cooked or it may separate when left to stand.

ZABAGLIONE
Zabaglione is a custard traditionally made in a copper bowl. Usually it is served as soon as it is made, although sometimes it is chilled for several hours before serving. It is also delicious poured over fruit in a gratin dish and browned under the grill. It can be made using sweet Madeira or dessert wine.

RIGHT: Strawberries with balsamic vinegar

CASSATA ALLA
SICILIANA

Arrange the pieces of
sponge cake around the
base and side of the bowl.

Spoon the ricotta mixture
into the cake-lined bowl.

Top with a layer of sponge
cake, press down firmly and
neaten any edges.

CASSATA ALLA SICILIANA

Preparation time: 25 minutes
 + overnight refrigeration
Total cooking time: 2 minutes
Serves 6

☆☆

60 g (2 oz) blanched almonds, halved
650 g (1 lb 5 oz) fresh ricotta (see Note)
1/2 cup (80 g/2 3/4 oz) icing sugar
1 1/2 teaspoons vanilla essence
2 teaspoons finely grated lemon rind
60 g (2 oz) cedro, chopped (see Note)
60 g (2 oz) glacé orange, chopped
60 g (2 oz) red glacé cherries,
    halved
30 g (1 oz) shelled pistachios
375 g (12 oz) ready-made round sponge
    cake, unfilled
1/2 cup (125 ml/4 fl oz) Madeira
6 blanched almonds, extra
red glacé cherries, extra, halved
icing sugar, for dusting
sweetened whipped cream, to serve

1 Place the almonds in a small frying pan
and dry-fry, tossing, over medium heat for
2 minutes, or until just starting to change colour.
Remove and cool.
2 Press the ricotta through a sieve over a bowl.
Stir in the icing sugar, vanilla, lemon rind,
cedro, glacé orange, glacé cherries, almonds and
pistachios. Mix together well.
3 Grease a 1.5 litre pudding basin. Cut the cake
horizontally into 1 cm (1/2 inch) thick slices. Set
aside 1 round and cut the remaining rounds into
wedges, trimming the base to make triangles.
Lightly sprinkle the cut side of the triangles with
Madeira and arrange around the base and side of
the bowl, cut-side-down, trimming if necessary
to fit. Spoon the ricotta mixture into the centre.
Top with a layer of sponge cake. Press down
firmly and neaten the rough edges, if necessary.
Refrigerate overnight.
4 Carefully unmould onto a serving plate.
Arrange the extra almonds and cherries on top
and dust with icing sugar just before serving.
Serve with the cream, which can be piped in
patterns over the cassata for a true Sicilian look.
NOTES: Fresh ricotta from delicatessens is best as
it can be successfully moulded.
    If cedro is not available, you can use glacé
citrus instead.

ABOVE: Cassata alla Siciliana

141

ALMOND SEMIFREDDO

Place the amaretti biscuits in a plastic bag and crush them with a rolling pin.

Beat the egg yolks and sugar together with electric beaters.

Carefully spoon the mixture into the lined loaf tin.

ABOVE: Almond semifreddo

ALMOND SEMIFREDDO

Preparation time: 30 minutes + 4 hours freezing
Total cooking time: 10 minutes
Serves 8–10

☆

1 1/4 cups (315 ml/10 fl oz) cream
4 eggs, room temperature, separated
2/3 cup (85 g/3 oz) icing sugar
1/4 cup (60 ml/2 fl oz) amaretto
1/2 cup (80 g/2 3/4 oz) toasted almonds, chopped
8 amaretti biscuits, crushed
fresh fruit or extra amaretto, for serving

1 Whip the cream until firm peaks form, then cover and refrigerate. Line a 10 x 21 cm (4 x 8 1/2 inch) loaf tin with plastic wrap so that it overhangs the two long sides.
2 Beat the egg yolks and icing sugar in a large bowl until pale and creamy. Whisk the egg whites in a separate bowl until firm peaks form. Stir the amaretto, almonds and amaretti biscuits into the egg yolk mixture, then carefully fold in the chilled cream and the egg whites until well combined. Carefully pour or spoon into the lined loaf tin and cover with the overhanging plastic. Freeze for 4 hours, or until frozen but not rock hard. Serve slices with fresh fruit or a sprinkling of amaretto. The semifreddo can also be frozen in individual moulds or serving dishes.
NOTE: Semifreddo means semi frozen, so if you leave it in the freezer overnight, place it in the refrigerator for 30 minutes before serving.

ZUPPA INGLESE

Preparation time: 25 minutes
   + 3 hours refrigeration
Total cooking time: 5 minutes
Serves 6

☆

2 cups (500 ml/16 fl oz) milk
1 vanilla bean, split lengthways
4 egg yolks
1/2 cup (125 g/4 oz) caster sugar
2 tablespoons plain flour
300 g (10 oz) Madeira cake, cut into
   1 cm (1/2 inch) slices
1/3 cup (80 ml/2 3/4 fl oz) rum
30 g (1 oz) chocolate, grated or shaved
50 g (1 3/4 oz) flaked almonds, toasted

1 Heat the milk and vanilla bean in a saucepan over low heat until bubbles appear around the edge of the pan.

2 Whisk the egg yolks, sugar and flour together in a bowl until thick and pale.

3 Discard the vanilla bean and whisk the warm milk slowly into the egg mixture, then blend well. Return to a clean pan and stir over medium heat until the custard boils and thickens. Allow to cool slightly.

4 Line the base of a 1.5 litre serving dish with one-third of the cake slices and brush well with the rum combined with 1 tablespoon water. Spread one-third of the custard over the cake, top with cake slices and brush with rum mixture. Repeat this process, finishing with a layer of custard. Cover and refrigerate for 3 hours. Sprinkle with chocolate and almonds just before serving.

PESCHE RIPIENE
(Stuffed peaches)

Preparation time: 15 minutes
Total cooking time: 25 minutes
Serves 6

6 ripe peaches
60 g (2 oz) amaretti biscuits, crushed
1 egg yolk
2 tablespoons caster sugar
20 g (¾ oz) almond meal
1 tablespoon amaretto
¼ cup (60 ml/2 fl oz) white wine
1 teaspoon caster sugar, extra
20 g (¾ oz) unsalted butter

1 Preheat the oven to moderate 180°C (350°/Gas 4) and lightly grease a 30 x 25 cm (12 x 10 inch) ovenproof dish with butter.

2 Cut each peach in half and carefully remove the stones. Scoop a little of the pulp out from each and combine in a small bowl with the crushed biscuits, egg yolk, caster sugar, almond meal and amaretto.

3 Spoon some of the mixture into each peach and place them cut-side-up in the dish. Sprinkle with the white wine and the extra sugar. Place a dot of butter on the top of each and bake for 20–25 minutes, until golden.

NOTE: When they are in season, you can also use ripe apricots or nectarines for this recipe.

MACERATED ORANGES

Cut a thin slice off the top and bottom of 4 oranges. Using a small sharp knife, slice off the skin and pith, removing as much pith as possible. Slice down the side of a segment between the flesh and the membrane. Repeat on the other side and lift the segment out. Do this over a bowl to catch the juice. Repeat with all the segments. Squeeze out any juice remaining in the membranes. Place the segments on a shallow dish and sprinkle with 1 teaspoon grated lemon rind, 3 tablespoons caster sugar and 1 tablespoon lemon juice. Toss carefully. Cover and refrigerate for at least 4 hours. Toss again. Serve chilled. For a variation, add 2 tablespoons Cointreau or Maraschino just before serving. Serves 4.

BELOW: Pesche ripiene

SICILIAN CANNOLI

Knead the dough until it is quite smooth.

Fold the squares of dough over the tube, moisten the overlap with water and press the dough together.

OPPOSITE PAGE:
Sicilian cannoli (top);
Sicilian rice fritters

SICILIAN CANNOLI

Preparation time: 30 minutes
  + 30 minutes refrigeration
Total cooking time: 5 minutes
Makes 12

☆ ☆ ☆

FILLING
500 g (1 lb) ricotta
1 teaspoon orange flower water
1/2 cup (100 g/3 oz) cedro, diced
60 g (2 oz) bittersweet chocolate,
  coarsely grated or chopped
1 tablespoon grated orange rind
1/2 cup (60 g/2 oz) icing sugar

300 g (10 oz) plain flour
1 tablespoon caster sugar
1 teaspoon ground cinnamon
40 g (1 1/4 oz) unsalted butter
3 tablespoons Marsala
vegetable oil, for deep-frying
icing sugar, for dusting

1   For the filling, combine all the ingredients in a bowl and mix. Add 2–3 tablespoons water and mix well to form a dough. Cover with plastic wrap and refrigerate.
2   Combine the flour, sugar and cinnamon in a bowl, rub in the butter and add the Marsala. Mix until the dough comes together in a loose clump, then knead on a lightly floured surface for 4–5 minutes, or until smooth. Wrap in plastic wrap and refrigerate for at least 30 minutes.
3   Cut the dough in half and roll each portion on a lightly floured surface into a thin sheet about 5 mm (1/4 inch) thick. Cut each dough half into six 9 cm (3 1/2 inch) squares. Place a metal tube (see Note) diagonally across the middle of each square. Fold the sides over the tube, moistening the overlap with water, then press together.
4   Heat the oil in a large deep frying pan to 180°C (350°F), or until a cube of bread dropped into the oil browns in 15 seconds. Drop one or two tubes at a time into the hot oil. Fry gently until golden brown and crisp. Remove from the oil, gently remove the moulds and drain on crumpled paper towels. When they are cool, fill a piping bag with the ricotta mixture and fill the shells. Dust with icing sugar and serve.
NOTE: Cannoli tubes are available at kitchenware shops. You can also use 2 cm (3/4 inch) diameter wooden dowels cut into 12 cm (5 inch) lengths.

SICILIAN RICE FRITTERS

Preparation time: 20 minutes + 1 hour standing
Total cooking time: 25 minutes
Makes 8

☆ ☆

1/2 cup (110 g/3 1/2 oz) arborio rice
1 1/3 cups (330 ml/11 fl oz) milk
2 teaspoons unsalted butter
1 tablespoon caster sugar
1 vanilla bean, scraped
1 teaspoon dried yeast
2 tablespoons cedro, finely chopped
2 teaspoons grated lemon rind
vegetable oil, for deep-frying
flour, for rolling
2 tablespoons fragrant honey

1   Combine the rice, milk, butter, sugar, vanilla bean and scraped seeds, and a pinch of salt in a heavy-based saucepan. Bring to the boil over medium heat, then reduce the heat to very low, cover and cook for 15–18 minutes, or until most of the liquid has been absorbed. Remove from the heat, cover and set aside.
2   Dissolve the yeast in 2 tablespoons tepid water and allow to stand for 5 minutes, or until frothy. If your yeast doesn't foam, it is dead and you will have to start again.
3   Discard the vanilla bean. Add the yeast, cedro and lemon rind to the rice, mix well, cover and let stand for 1 hour.
4   Fill a deep-fryer or heavy-based saucepan one third full of oil and heat to 180°C (350°F), or until a spoonful of the batter dropped into the oil browns in 15 seconds.
5   Shape the rice into croquettes about 2.5 x 8 cm (1 x 3 inches) and roll them in flour. Deep-fry for 5–6 minutes, or until golden brown on all sides. Remove with a slotted spoon and drain on crumpled paper towels. Drizzle with honey and serve immediately.

PANETTONE

When the yeast mixture has been standing for 15 minutes, it should have bubbles on the surface.

Knead the dough until it is smooth and elastic.

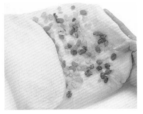

Spread half the fruit over the rectangle of dough and fold the dough over it from the sides.

Use a sharp knife to make a deep cross shape in the top of the dough.

PANETTONE

Preparation time: 40 minutes
+ 3 hours 45 minutes rising
Total cooking time: 50 minutes
Makes 1

☆☆☆

1/2 cup (95 g/3 oz) candied mixed peel

1/2 cup (80 g/2³/4 oz) sultanas

1 teaspoon grated lemon rind

1 teaspoon grated orange rind

1 tablespoon brandy or rum

7 g (1/4 oz) sachet dried yeast

220 ml (7 fl oz) warm milk

1/4 cup (60 g/2 oz) caster sugar

3¹/4 cups (400 g/13 oz) white bread flour

2 eggs

1 teaspoon vanilla essence

150 g (5 oz) unsalted butter, softened

20 g (1/2 oz) unsalted butter, melted, to glaze

1 Put the peel, sultanas and grated rind in a small bowl. Add the brandy, mix well and set aside.

2 Put the yeast, warm milk and 1 teaspoon sugar in a small bowl and leave in a warm place for 10–15 minutes, or until foamy. If your yeast doesn't rise, it is dead and you will have to start again. Sift 200 g (6¹/2 oz) flour and 1/2 teaspoon salt into a large bowl, make a well in the centre and add the yeast mixture. Mix together with a large metal spoon to form a soft dough. Cover the bowl and leave to 'sponge' and rise in a warm place for 45 minutes, or until frothy and risen.

3 Add the eggs, vanilla and remaining sugar and mix. Add the butter and stir until well combined. Stir in the remaining flour and mix well. Knead well on a floured surface until the dough is smooth and elastic. You may need to add up to 1/2 cup (60 g/2 oz) flour to the dough as you knead. Place the dough in a lightly greased bowl, cover with plastic wrap and leave in a warm place for 1¹/2–2 hours, or until doubled.

4 Lightly grease a 15 cm (6 inch) round cake tin and line the base and side with a double thickness of baking paper, ensuring the collar extends above the rim of the tin by 10 cm (4 inches).

5 Knock back the dough and turn out onto a floured work surface. Roll into a 30 x 20 cm (12 x 8 inch) rectangle. Drain the fruit mixture and spread half the fruit over the surface of the dough. Fold over the short edges like an envelope to cover the fruit. Roll again and repeat the process to incorporate all the fruit. Gently knead the dough for 2–3 minutes and shape into a neat ball. Place in the tin, brush

RIGHT: Panettone

with the melted butter, then slash a cross on the top with a sharp knife and leave to rise again in a warm place for 45 minutes, or until doubled.
6 Preheat the oven to moderately hot 190°C (375°F/Gas 5). Bake for 50 minutes, or until golden brown and a skewer inserted into the centre comes out clean. Leave in the tin for 5 minutes, then transfer to a wire rack to cool.

ESPRESSO GRANITA

Dissolve 2 tablespoons caster sugar in 2 cups (500 ml/16 fl oz) hot espresso coffee and stir thoroughly until dissolved. Pour into a shallow metal container or tray and cool completely. Freeze for 30 minutes, then scrape with a fork to distribute the ice crystals evenly. Freeze again for 30 minutes. Using a fork, scrape the granita into fine crystals and return to the freezer for 1 hour before serving. Spoon into glasses and top with a dollop of lightly whipped cream. This granita is very hard when frozen, so use a shallow tray and break the granita up when partially frozen. It is difficult to break up if made in a deep container. Serves 6.

LEMON GRANITA

Preparation time: 15 minutes
  + 2 hours freezing
Total cooking time: 5 minutes
Serves 4–6

1 1/4 cups (275 ml) lemon juice
1 tablespoon grated lemon rind
200 g (6 1/2 oz) caster sugar

1 Place the lemon juice, rind and sugar in a small saucepan and stir over low heat for 5 minutes, or until the sugar is dissolved. Allow to cool.
2 Add 2 cups (500 ml/16 fl oz) water to the lemon mixture and mix well. Pour into a shallow 30 x 20 cm (12 x 8 inch) metal container or tray and cool completely. Freeze for 30 minutes, then scrape with a fork to distribute the ice crystals evenly. Return to the freezer for 30 minutes.
3 Using a fork, scrape the granita into fine crystals and return to the freezer for 1 hour before serving. Spoon into chilled glasses and serve immediately.

ABOVE: Lemon granita

BISCOTTI
Meaning 'twice cooked', biscotti originally referred to ships' biscuits, which were very dry, rock-hard little slabs of cooked flour and water paste made to last indefinitely for the long voyages in old sailing ships. The biscuits were so hard that they had to be soaked before eating and only weevils and sea water could destroy them. Nowadays, biscotti generally refers to the sweet Italian biscuits which are first shaped into a loaf and baked, then thinly sliced and baked again. The result is a very crunchy biscuit that is perfect for dipping into coffee or a sweet dessert wine.

ABOVE: Biscotti

BISCOTTI

Preparation time: 25 minutes
Total cooking time: 50 minutes
Makes 45

☆ ☆

2 cups (250 g/8 oz) plain flour
1 teaspoon baking powder
1 cup (250 g/8 oz) caster sugar
3 eggs
1 egg yolk
1 teaspoon vanilla essence
1 teaspoon grated orange rind
3/4 cup (110 g/3 1/2 oz) pistachio nuts

1 Preheat the oven to moderate 180°C (350°F/ Gas 4). Line two baking trays with baking paper and lightly dust with flour.
2 Sift the flour and baking powder into a large bowl. Add the sugar and mix well. Make a well in the centre and add 2 whole eggs, the egg yolk, vanilla essence and orange rind. Using a large metal spoon, stir until just combined. Mix in the pistachios. Knead for 2–3 minutes on a lightly floured surface. The dough will be stiff at first. Sprinkle a little water onto the dough.

Divide the mixture into two portions and roll each into a log about 25 cm (10 inches) long and 8 cm (3 inches) wide. Slightly flatten the tops.
3 Place the logs on the trays, allowing room for spreading. Beat the remaining egg and brush over the logs to glaze. Bake for 35 minutes, then remove from the oven.
4 Reduce the oven to slow 150°C (300°F/ Gas 2). Allow the logs to cool slightly and cut each into 5 mm (1/4 inch) slices. Place flat-side-down on the trays and bake for 8 minutes. Turn the biscuits over and cook for another 8 minutes, or until slightly coloured and crisp and dry. Transfer to a wire rack to cool completely. Store in an airtight container.

CHIMNEYSWEEP'S GELATO

This simple yet unexpectedly wonderful dessert can be made using home-made gelato, or equally well using a premium-quality bought vanilla ice cream. For each portion of vanilla gelato or ice cream, sprinkle 1 teaspoon of finely ground espresso coffee over the top. Pour on 1 tablespoon of whisky or bourbon and serve immediately.

HONEY AND PINE NUT TART

Preparation time: 25 minutes
  + 15 minutes refrigeration
Total cooking time: 1 hour
Serves 6

PASTRY

2 cups (250 g/8 oz) plain flour

1½ tablespoons icing sugar

115 g (4 oz) chilled unsalted butter,
  chopped

1 egg, lightly beaten

1½ cups (235 g/7½ oz) pine nuts

½ cup (175 g/6 oz) honey

115 g (4 oz) unsalted butter, softened

½ cup (125 g/4 oz) caster sugar

3 eggs, lightly beaten

¼ teaspoon vanilla essence

1 tablespoon almond liqueur

1 teaspoon finely grated lemon rind

1 tablespoon lemon juice

icing sugar, for dusting

crème fraîche or mascarpone, to serve

1 Preheat the oven to moderately hot 190°C
(375°F/Gas 5) and place a baking tray on the
middle shelf. Lightly grease a 23 cm (9 inch),
3.5 cm (1½ inch) deep loose-based tart tin. To
make the pastry, sift the flour and icing sugar
into a large bowl and add the butter. Rub the
butter into the flour with your fingertips until
it resembles fine breadcrumbs. Make a well in
the centre and add the egg and 2 tablespoons
cold water. Mix with a flat-bladed knife, using
a cutting action, until the mixture comes
together in beads.

2 Gather the dough together and lift out onto
a lightly floured work surface. Press together
into a ball, roll out to a circle 3 mm (⅛ inch)
thick and invert into the tin. Use a small ball of
pastry to press the pastry into the tin, allowing
any excess to hang over the sides. Roll a rolling
pin over the tin, cutting off any excess pastry.
Prick the base all over with a fork and chill
for 15 minutes. Roll out the pastry scraps and
cut out 3 leaves for decoration. Cover and
refrigerate for 15 minutes.

3 Line the pastry with baking paper and fill
with baking beads or uncooked rice. Bake on
the heated tray for 10 minutes, then remove the
tart tin, leaving the tray in the oven. Reduce the
oven to moderate 180°C (350°F/Gas 4).

4 To make the filling, spread the pine nuts on a
baking tray and roast in the oven for 3 minutes,
or until golden. Heat the honey in a small
saucepan until runny, then allow to cool. Cream
the butter and sugar in a bowl until smooth and
pale. Gradually add the eggs, beating well after
each addition. Mix in the honey, vanilla,
liqueur, lemon rind and juice and a pinch of salt.
Stir in the pine nuts, spoon into the pastry case
and smooth the surface. Arrange the reserved
pastry leaves in the centre.

5 Place the tin on the hot tray and bake for
40 minutes, or until golden and set. Cover the
top with foil after 25 minutes. Serve warm or
at room temperature, dusted with icing sugar.
Serve with crème fraîche or mascarpone.

BELOW: Honey and pine nut tart

FRANCE

Think of France and you immediately think of food and wine. French cooking is famous for its simplicity — a few herbs, a little wine and some garlic are used in subtle ways to flavour meat, chicken or seafood which are cooked to perfection. Accompanying sauces, another feature of French cuisine, are often strongly flavoured as with the garlicky aïoli. Long, slow cooking is often utilized to produce melt-in-the-mouth dishes such as Chicken with forty cloves of garlic. Olives, olive oil, eggplants (aubergines), zucchini (courgettes) and tomatoes fresh from the vine are very popular in the Provençal region. French desserts, many of which are based on pears, cherries, figs and apricots, are renowned.

TAPENADE

TAPENADE
(Provençal olive, anchovy and caper paste)

Preparation time: 10 minutes
Total cooking time: Nil
Makes 1 1/2 cups

☆

400 g (13 oz) Kalamata olives, pitted
2 cloves garlic, crushed
2 anchovy fillets in oil, drained
2 tablespoons capers in brine, rinsed,
    squeezed dry
2 teaspoons chopped fresh thyme
2 teaspoons Dijon mustard
1 tablespoon lemon juice
1/4 cup (60 ml/2 fl oz) olive oil
1 tablespoon brandy, optional

1   Process all the ingredients together in a
food processor until they form a smooth
consistency. Season with freshly ground black
pepper. Spoon into a sterilized, warm jar
(see Note), seal and refrigerate for up to
2 weeks.
NOTES: To prepare a sterilized storage jar,
preheat the oven to very slow 120°C (250°F/
Gas 1/2). Wash the jar and lid in hot soapy water
and rinse with hot water. Put the jar in the oven
for 20 minutes, or until fully dry. Do not dry
with a tea towel.

If refrigerated, the olive oil may solidify,
making it white. This will not affect the flavour
of the dish. Bring to room temperature before
serving and the oil will return to a liquid state.

BAGNA CAUDA

Preparation time: 5 minutes
Total cooking time: 8 minutes
Makes about 1 cup

☆

1 1/4 cups (315 ml/10 fl oz) cream
45 g (1 1/2 oz) can anchovy fillets, drained
10 g (1/4 oz) butter
2 cloves garlic, crushed

1   Bring the cream slowly to the boil in a small
heavy-based saucepan. Boil for 8 minutes,
stirring frequently and taking care that the cream
doesn't boil over. This cooking time reduces and
thickens the cream.
2   Meanwhile, finely chop the anchovies. Melt
the butter in a small saucepan, add the anchovies
and garlic and cook, stirring, over low heat for
1 minute without allowing to brown.
3   Pour in the cream and mix thoroughly, then
add salt and pepper, to taste, if necessary. Pour
into a serving bowl. Serve warm as a dipping
sauce, with vegetable crudités. The mixture
will thicken on standing.

TAPENADE
This Provençal paste takes
its name from the 'tapeno',
or capers, which are its
key ingredient. Although
only invented in Marseilles
in the nineteenth century,
this timeless liaison
between anchovies,
olives and capers quickly
established itself as
a classic appetizer. It is
delicious served with
fresh or toasted bread and
makes an excellent stuffing
for hard-boiled eggs.

RIGHT: Tapenade

AIOLI WITH CRUDITES
(Garlic mayonnaise with blanched vegetables)

Preparation time: 15 minutes
Total cooking time: 1 minute
Serves 4

☆

Aïoli

4 garlic cloves, crushed

2 egg yolks

1¼ cups (315 ml/10 fl oz) light olive or
   vegetable oil

1 tablespoon lemon juice

pinch of ground white pepper

12 asparagus spears, trimmed

12 radishes, trimmed

½ telegraph cucumber, deseeded, halved
   lengthways and cut into batons

1 head of witloof, leaves separated

1 For the aïoli, place the garlic, egg yolks and a
pinch of salt in a food processor and process for
10 seconds. With the motor running, add the
oil in a thin, slow stream. The mixture will
start to thicken. When this happens you can
add the oil a little faster. Process until all the
oil is incorporated and the mayonnaise is thick
and creamy. Stir in the lemon juice and pepper.
2 Bring a saucepan of water to the boil, add
the asparagus and cook for 1 minute. Remove
and plunge into a bowl of iced water.
3 Arrange the asparagus, radish, cucumber and
witloof decoratively on a platter and place the
aïoli in a bowl on the platter. The aïoli can also
be used as a sandwich spread or as a sauce for
chicken or fish.
NOTE: It is important that all the ingredients are
at room temperature when making this recipe.
Should the mayonnaise start to curdle, beat in
1–2 teaspoons boiling water. If this fails, put
another egg yolk in a clean bowl and very
slowly whisk into the curdled mixture, one
drop at a time, then continue as above.
   Many other vegetables, including green
beans, baby carrots, broccoli and cauliflower
florets, sliced peppers (capsicums) and cherry
tomatoes are suitable for making crudités.
Choose vegetables in season when they are
at their best.

AIOLI
Referred to as 'the butter
of Provence', aïoli holds
such an important place
in the region's cuisine that
local villagers honour it in
annual festivals, or 'fête de
la grande aïoli'. It is the
name of both the garlic
mayonnaise and the
Provençal feast where
it accompanies cooked
and raw vegetables, salt
cod, seafood and snails.
Aïoli is the traditional
and indispensable
accompaniment to
bourride, the French
Riviera's fish soup.

ABOVE: Aïoli with crudités

SALAD NICOISE

This dish literally has dozens of interpretations, although the most traditional is not instantly recognised. It does not contain modern additions such as cooked ingredients, except hard boiled eggs. Ingredients depend on what is seasonally available, although the staples are black olives such as Niçoise, anchovy fillets, tomatoes and garlic. Tuna often makes an appearance.

ABOVE: Salad Niçoise

SALAD NICOISE

Preparation time: 30 minutes
Total cooking time: 15 minutes
Serves 4

☆

3 eggs
2 vine-ripened tomatoes
175 g (6 oz) baby green beans, trimmed
1/2 cup (125 ml/4 fl oz) olive oil
2 tablespoons white wine vinegar
1 large clove garlic, halved
325 g (11 oz) iceberg lettuce heart, cut into
 8 wedges
1 small red pepper (capsicum), seeded and
 sliced thinly
1 Lebanese cucumber, cut into thin 5 cm
 (2 inch) lengths
1 stick celery, cut into thin 5 cm (2 inch)
 lengths
1/4 large red onion, thinly sliced
2 x 185 g (6 oz) cans tuna, drained, broken
 into chunks
12 Kalamata olives
45 g (1 1/2 oz) can anchovy fillets, drained
2 teaspoons baby capers
12 small fresh basil leaves

1 Place the eggs in a saucepan of cold water. Bring to the boil, then reduce the heat and simmer for 10 minutes. Stir during the first few minutes to centre the yolks. Cool under cold water, then peel and cut into quarters. Meanwhile, score a cross in the base of each tomato and place in a bowl of boiling water for 10 seconds. Plunge into cold water and peel away from the cross. Cut each tomato into eight.
2 Cook the beans in a saucepan of boiling water for 2 minutes, rinse under cold water, then drain.
3 For the dressing, place the oil and vinegar in a jar and shake to combine.
4 Rub the garlic over the base and sides of a platter. Arrange the lettuce over the base. Layer the egg, tomato, beans, red pepper, cucumber and celery over the lettuce. Scatter the onion and tuna over them, then the olives, anchovies, capers and basil. Drizzle with dressing and serve.

ANCHOVY BUTTER

Mash 50 g (1 3/4 oz) drained anchovies in a mortar and pestle. Cream 125 g (4 oz) softened unsalted butter until smooth. Gradually beat in the anchovies, then mix in 1 teaspoon lemon juice, or to taste, a few drops at a time. Season with ground black pepper. You can also stir in 1 tablespoon chopped mixed fresh thyme and parsley. Serve with grilled fish or beef. Serves 4–6.

POTATO AND ANCHOVY SALAD

Preparation time: 20 minutes
Total cooking time: 25 minutes
Serves 6

1 kg (2 lb) waxy potatoes (such as pink
    fir apple, binji, kipfler), unpeeled
1/4 cup (60 ml/2 fl oz) dry white wine
1 tablespoon cider vinegar
1/4 cup (60 ml/2 fl oz) olive oil
4 spring onions, finely chopped
35 g (1 1/4 oz) drained anchovy fillets
1 tablespoon chopped parsley
1 tablespoon chopped fresh chives

1   Cook the potatoes in their skins in boiling
salted water for about 20 minutes, until just
tender. Drain and then peel away the skins while
the potatoes are still hot. Cut into 1 cm (1/2 inch)
thick slices.
2   Place the wine, vinegar, olive oil and spring
onion in a large heavy-based frying pan over
low heat and add the potato slices. Shake the
pan to coat the potatoes, then reheat gently.
3   When hot, remove from the heat and season,
to taste. Coarsely chop half the anchovies and
toss them through the potatoes with the parsley
and chives. Transfer to a platter and put the
remaining anchovies on top. Serve warm or at
room temperature.

FRESH BEETROOT AND GOAT'S CHEESE SALAD

Preparation time: 20 minutes
Total cooking time: 30 minutes
Serves 4

1 kg (2 lb) fresh beetroot (4 bulbs with leaves)
200 g (6 1/2 oz) green beans
1 tablespoon red wine vinegar
2 tablespoons extra virgin olive oil
1 clove garlic, crushed
1 tablespoon drained capers, coarsely chopped
100 g (3 1/2 oz) goat's cheese

1   Trim the leaves from the beetroot. Scrub the
bulbs and wash the leaves well. Add the whole

bulbs to a large saucepan of salted water, bring
to the boil, then reduce the heat and simmer,
covered, for 30 minutes, or until tender when
pierced with the point of a knife.
2   Meanwhile, bring a saucepan of water to
the boil, add the beans and cook for 3 minutes,
or until just tender. Remove with a slotted
spoon and plunge into a bowl of cold water.
Drain well. Add the beetroot leaves to the same
saucepan of water and cook for 3–5 minutes,
or until the leaves and stems are tender. Drain,
plunge into a bowl of cold water, then drain well.
3   Drain and cool the beetroots, then peel the
skins off and cut the bulbs into thin wedges.
4   For the dressing, put the red wine vinegar,
oil, garlic, capers, 1/2 teaspoon each of salt and
pepper in a screw top jar and shake.
5   To serve, divide the beans, beetroot leaves
and bulbs among four serving plates. Crumble
goat's cheese over the top of each and drizzle
with dressing. Delicious served with fresh
crusty bread.

*BELOW: Fresh beetroot
and goat's cheese salad*

PAN BAGNAT

Preparation time: 15 minutes
  + 1 hour standing
Total cooking time: Nil
Serves 4

☆

4 crusty bread rolls, or 1 French
  baguette sliced into 4 chunks
1 clove garlic
1/4 cup (60 ml/2 fl oz) olive oil
1 tablespoon red wine vinegar
3 tablespoons fresh basil leaves, torn
2 tomatoes, sliced
2 hard-boiled eggs, sliced
75 g (2 1/2 oz) can tuna
8 anchovy fillets
1 small cucumber, sliced.
1/2 green pepper (capsicum),
  thinly sliced
1 French shallot, thinly sliced

1 Slice the bread rolls in half and remove some of the soft centre from the tops. Cut the garlic clove in half and rub the insides of the rolls with the cut sides. Sprinkle both sides of the bread with olive oil, vinegar, salt and pepper.
2 Place all the salad ingredients on the base of the rolls, cover with the other half and wrap each sandwich in foil. Press firmly with a light weight and stand in a cool place for 1 hour before serving.

BRANDADE DE MORUE

Preparation time: 25 minutes + 24 hours soaking
Total cooking time: 45 minutes
Serves 6 as first course

☆ ☆

450 g (14 oz) salt cod (this is the dried weight
  and is about half a cod)
200 g (6 1/2 oz) floury potatoes (such as russet,
  spunta, pontiac), cut in 3 cm (1 1/4 inch) chunks
150 ml (5 fl oz) olive oil
1 cup (250 ml/8 fl oz) milk
4 garlic cloves, crushed
2 tablespoons lemon juice
olive oil, extra to drizzle

1 Place the salt cod in a large bowl, cover with cold water and soak for 24 hours, changing the water frequently. Drain the cod and place in a large saucepan of clean water. Bring to the boil over moderate heat, reduce the heat and simmer for 30 minutes. Drain, then cool for 15 minutes.
2 Meanwhile, cook the potatoes in a saucepan of boiling salted water for 12–15 minutes, until tender. Drain and keep warm.
3 Remove the skin from the fish and break the flesh into large flaky pieces, discarding any bones. Place the flesh in a food processor. Using two separate saucepans, gently warm the oil in one, and the milk and garlic in another.
4 Start the food processor and with the motor running, alternatively add small amounts of the milk and oil until you have a thick wet paste-like mixture. Add the potato and process this in short bursts until combined. Be careful not to overwork the mixture once the potato has been added. Transfer to a bowl and add the lemon juice gradually, to taste, and plenty of freshly ground black pepper. Gently lighten the mixture a little by fluffing it up with a fork. Drizzle with olive oil before serving. Serve warm or cold with fried bread.

BELOW: Pan bagnat

FRISEE (CURLY ENDIVE) AND GARLIC CROUTON SALAD

Preparation time: 20 minutes
Total cooking time: 10 minutes
Serves 4–6

VINAIGRETTE
1 French shallot, finely chopped
1 tablespoon Dijon mustard
1/4 cup (60 ml/2 fl oz) tarragon vinegar
2/3 cup (170 ml/5 1/2 fl oz) extra virgin olive oil

1 tablespoon olive oil
250 g (8 oz) speck, rind removed, cut into
   5 mm x 2 cm (1/4 x 3/4 inch) pieces
1/2 medium bread stick, sliced
4 whole cloves garlic
1 baby frisee (curly endive), washed and dried
1/2 cup (100 g/3 1/2 oz) walnuts, toasted

1   For the vinaigrette, whisk together in a bowl the shallot, mustard and vinegar. Slowly add the oil, whisking constantly until thickened. Set aside.

2   Heat the oil in a large frying pan, add the speck, bread and garlic cloves and cook over medium–high heat for 5–8 minutes, until the bread and speck are both crisp. Remove the garlic from the pan.

3   Place the frisee, bread, speck, walnuts and vinaigrette in a large bowl. Toss together well and serve.

ANCHOIADE

This classic Provençal sauce is often served as a dip for crudités or toasts.

Place 75 ml (2 1/2 fl oz) olive oil in a small saucepan with 150 g (5 oz) anchovy fillets and cook over very low heat for 10 minutes, or until the anchovies have 'melted'. Remove from the heat and allow to cool. Mash the anchovies into a paste and then add 2 crushed cloves of garlic, 2 tablespoons of red wine vinegar and 1 tablespoon of Dijon mustard and combine well. Add 50 ml (2 fl oz) olive oil in a slow steady stream, whisking constantly. Check the seasoning and serve with crudités or toasts. Makes about 1 cup.

ABOVE: Frisee and garlic crouton salad

DRESSINGS AND SAUCES

The sauces and dressings from Provençe are different from those in other regions in France in that they are not based on butter, cream and flour but on vegetables, herbs and oil. This reflects one of the most important elements in Provençal cuisine — the notion that the natural flavours of the food be allowed to shine and not be masked by heavy, rich sauces. There are many variations on those below.

BASIC VINAIGRETTE
Dissolve a pinch of salt in 2 tablespoons of red wine vinegar and very slowly beat in 6 tablespoons of extra virgin olive oil. Season with pepper and stir. To vary this recipe you can add any of the following:

1 clove crushed garlic, 1 teaspoon Dijon mustard, 2 tablespoons chopped fresh chives, parsley or mint. You can use lemon juice or any type of wine vinegar instead of the red wine vinegar.

CLASSIC MAYONNAISE
Home-made mayonnaise is very good and easy to prepare. Whether making it by hand or in a food processor, all the ingredients should be at room temperature and the oil must be added very slowly. To make a simple mayonnaise, beat 2 egg yolks and 1 teaspoon of Dijon mustard with a whisk for 1 minute. Slowly add 1¾ cups (450 ml/14 fl oz) olive oil

in a thin stream while continuing to beat. When the mayonnaise begins to thicken, you can add the oil more rapidly, still beating well after each addition. When all the oil has been added, beat in 2 tablespoons lemon juice and some salt and pepper. If the mayonnaise separates, place a fresh yolk in a clean bowl and start adding the curdled mixture very slowly, whisking continuously until the mixture is silky and firm. Makes 1¾ cups (450 ml/14 fl oz). This recipe can be varied as follows:

For a herb mayonnaise, stir in 3 tablespoons chopped fresh herbs such as chives, parsley, basil, chervil or tarragon.

For a remoulade sauce, stir in 2 tablespoons

each of capers and chopped gherkins, 2 teaspoons Dijon mustard, 2 finely chopped French shallots, 3 anchovy fillets, 1 tablespoon chopped fresh tarragon and 2 tablespoons chopped fresh flat-leaf parsley.

FRESH TOMATO DRESSING

Peel, seed and finely dice 900 g (1 lb 13 oz) ripe tomatoes. Place in a bowl and mix with 1 tablespoon each of chopped fresh basil and flat-leaf parsley, 2 finely chopped French shallots and 3 tablespoons extra virgin olive oil. Season and stir well to combine. Serve at room temperature. Makes 625 ml (20 fl oz).

SAUCE VIERGE

This raw tomato sauce is excellent with grilled tuna and swordfish. In a bowl, combine 700 g (1 lb 7 oz) peeled, seeded and chopped tomatoes, 2/3 cup (170 ml/ 5 fl oz) extra virgin olive oil, 3 tablespoons lemon juice, 2 cloves crushed garlic and salt and pepper. Set aside for 2 hours. Just before serving, stir in 6 pitted, finely chopped black olives and 1 tablespoon each of finely chopped fresh chives, parsley and tarragon. Makes 1 3/4 cups (450 ml/15 fl oz).

SAUCE VERTE

This sauce is delicious on poached or grilled fish and cold meats. It will keep, refrigerated, covered, for up to 3 days. Blanch and drain 280 g (9 oz) English spinach and when cool enough to handle, squeeze with your hands to remove excess moisture. Alternatively, you can use 140 g (4 1/2 oz) frozen spinach, thawed and drained well. Put in a blender or food processor. Add 1 slice of bread that has been moistened with a little water, 1 chopped hard-boiled egg, 6 anchovy fillets, 2 tablespoons red wine vinegar and 1/2 cup (125 ml/4 fl oz) olive oil. Process until smooth. Stir in 1 tablespoon finely chopped cornichons and 1 teaspoon finely chopped capers. Season, to taste. Makes 220 ml (7 fl oz).

SAUCE RAVIGOTE

This sauce teams well with cold chicken, turkey, prawns or vegetables. Dissolve a pinch of salt in 2 tablespoons red wine vinegar. Stir in 6 tablespoons olive oil, 3 tablespoons chopped fresh parsley, tarragon or chives, 1 small finely chopped onion, 2 tablespoons finely chopped gherkins or cornichons and 2 tablespoons capers. Season, to taste. Makes 3/4 cup (185 ml/6 fl oz).

FROM LEFT: Sauce ravigote; Basic vinaigrette; Classic mayonnaise; Fresh tomato dressing; Sauce verte; Sauce vierge

159

1 Preheat the oven to moderately hot 200°C (400°F/Gas 6). Trim the fronds from the fennel and reserve. Remove the stalks and cut a slice off the base of each fennel about 5 mm (¼ inch) thick. Slice each fennel into 6 wedges, place in a baking dish and drizzle with 3 tablespoons olive oil. Season well. Bake for 40–45 minutes, or until the fennel is tender and slightly caramelized. Turn once or twice during cooking. Allow to cool.

2 Cut a thin slice off the top and bottom of each orange. Using a small sharp knife, slice the skin and pith off the oranges. Remove as much pith as possible. Slice down the side of a segment between the flesh and the membrane. Repeat with the other side and lift the segment out. Do this over a bowl to catch the juices. Repeat with all the segments on both. Squeeze out any juice remaining in the membranes.

3 Whisk the remaining oil into the orange juice and the lemon juice until emulsified. Season well. Combine the orange segments, onion and olives in a bowl, pour on half the dressing and add half the mint. Mix well. Transfer to a serving dish. Top with the roasted fennel, drizzle with the remaining dressing, and scatter the parsley and remaining mint over the top. Chop the reserved fronds and sprinkle over the salad.

SNAILS WITH GARLIC AND HERB BUTTER

Preparation time: 15 minutes
Total cooking time: 5 minutes
Serves 6

400 g (13 oz) can snails
125 g (4 oz) butter, softened
4 cloves garlic, crushed
2 tablespoons chopped fresh flat-leaf parsley
2 teaspoons chopped fresh chives
3 dozen snail shells (see Note)
¼ cup (20 g/¾ oz) fresh white breadcrumbs
French bread, for serving

1 Preheat the oven to moderately hot 200°C (400°F/Gas 6). Rinse the snails under cold water. Drain well and set aside.

2 In a small bowl, combine the butter, garlic, parsley and chives until smooth. Season with salt and black pepper.

3 Place a small amount of the butter and a snail in each shell. Seal the shells with the remaining butter and sprinkle with breadcrumbs.

ROASTED FENNEL AND ORANGE SALAD

Preparation time: 30 minutes
Total cooking time: 45 minutes
Serves 4

8 baby fennel bulbs
5 tablespoons olive oil
2 oranges
1 tablespoon lemon juice
1 red onion, halved and thinly sliced
100 g (3½ oz) Kalamata olives
2 tablespoons roughly chopped fresh mint
1 tablespoon roughly chopped fresh flat-leaf parsley

ABOVE: Roasted fennel and orange salad

4 Place the snails on a baking tray with the open end of the snail facing up so that the butter will not run out of the shell. Bake for 5–6 minutes, or until the butter is bubbling and the breadcrumbs are lightly browned. Serve with crusty French bread.
NOTE: Escargot (snail) shells are available from speciality food stores. If unavailable, use small ovenproof ramekins instead.

GOAT'S CHEESE GALETTE

Preparation time: 20 minutes + refrigeration
Total cooking time: 1 hour 15 minutes
Serves 6

PASTRY

1 cup (125 g/4 oz) plain flour
1/4 cup (60 ml/2 fl oz) olive oil
3–4 tablespoons chilled water

FILLING

1 tablespoon olive oil
2 onions, thinly sliced
1 teaspoon fresh thyme leaves
125 g (4 oz) ricotta
100 g (3 1/2 oz) goat's cheese
2 tablespoons pitted Niçoise olives
1 egg, lightly beaten
1/4 cup (60 ml/2 fl oz) cream

1 For the pastry, sift the flour and a pinch of salt into a large bowl and make a well. Add the olive oil and mix with a flat-bladed knife until crumbly. Gradually add the water until the mixture comes together. Remove and pat together to form a disc. Refrigerate for 30 minutes.
2 For the filling, heat the olive oil in a frying pan. Add the onion, cover and cook over low heat for 30 minutes. Season and stir in half the thyme. Cool slightly.
3 Preheat the oven to moderate 180° C (350°F/ Gas 4). Lightly flour the work bench and roll out the pastry to a 30 cm (12 inch) circle. Evenly spread the onion over the pastry leaving a 2 cm (3/4 inch) border. Sprinkle the ricotta and the goat's cheese evenly over the onion. Place the olives over the cheeses, then sprinkle with the remaining thyme. Fold the pastry border in to the edge of the filling, gently pleating as you go.
4 Combine the egg and cream in a small jug, then carefully pour over the filling. Bake on a heated baking tray on the lower half of the oven for 45 minutes, or until the pastry is golden. Serve warm or at room temperature.

GOAT'S CHEESE
Commonly called chevre, the French word for goat, goat's cheeses are prized for their distinct tart, nutty flavours, ranging from strong to mild, depending on the altitude and locality of the milk and ripeness of the cheese.

BELOW: Goat's cheese galette

PISSALADIERE

Preparation time: 30 minutes
+ 15 minutes standing
+ 1 hour 30 minutes rising
Total cooking time: 1 hour 25 minutes
Serves 4–6

☆ ☆

7 g (¼ oz) sachet dry yeast
1½ cups (185 g/6 oz) plain flour
1 egg, beaten
1 tablespoon olive oil

FILLING

¼ cup (60 ml/2 fl oz) olive oil
2 cloves garlic
1 sprig of fresh thyme
4 large onions, thinly sliced
pinch of ground nutmeg
30 g (1 oz) drained anchovy fillets,
  halved lengthways
16 pitted black olives

BELOW: Pissaladière

1 Place the yeast in a small bowl with 2 tablespoons lukewarm water. Leave in a warm, draught-free place for 15 minutes, or until foamy. If your yeast doesn't froth, it is dead and you will have to start again.
2 Sift the flour and ¼ teaspoon salt into a large bowl, make a well in the centre and add the yeast mixture, egg, oil and 2 tablespoons warm water. Bring the ingredients together with a wooden spoon and when clumped together, transfer to a lightly floured surface. Knead to a soft, pliable dough, adding a little more water or flour as needed. Continue kneading for 6–8 minutes, or until smooth and elastic. Lightly oil a clean large bowl and place the dough in it. Roll the dough around to coat with oil, cover the bowl with a dry tea towel and place in a warm place for 1 hour, or until doubled in size.
3 For the filling, heat the oil in a large, heavy-based frying pan, add the garlic, thyme and onion and cook, stirring occasionally, over very low heat for 1 hour, or until the onion is soft and buttery but not brown. Discard the garlic and thyme, add the nutmeg and season well.
4 Brush a 30 cm (12 inch) pizza tray with oil. Punch down the dough and lightly knead into a ball. Roll out to a 30 cm (12 inch) circle and place on the oiled tray. Spread the onions over the surface leaving a 1 cm (½ inch) border. Make a diamond cross-hatch pattern on top with the anchovies. Intersperse with the olives. Slide the tray into a large plastic bag and leave to rise again for 30 minutes. Preheat the oven to moderately hot 200°C (400°F/Gas 6).
5 Bake for 20–25 minutes, or until the dough is cooked and golden. Reduce the heat to 190°C (375°F/Gas 5) if the crust starts to overbrown towards the end of baking. Cut into wedges for serving.

PANISSES

(Chickpea chips)

Preparation time: 20 minutes + cooling
Total cooking time: 30 minutes
Serves 6

☆

170 g (5½ oz) chickpea flour
1½ tablespoons olive oil
vegetable oil, for frying

1 Spray six saucers with cooking oil spray. Place the flour in a bowl and stir in 2¾ cups (685 ml/22 fl oz) cold water. Whisk with a wire

Cook and stir the mixture until it goes lumpy and starts to pull away from the sides of the pan.

Divide the mixture among the saucers and spread to an even thickness.

whisk for about 2 minutes, or until smooth. Stir in the olive oil and season, to taste, with salt and finely ground black pepper.

2 Pour into a heavy-based saucepan and cook over low heat for about 8 minutes, stirring constantly, until thickened. Cook and stir until the mixture goes lumpy and starts to pull away from the sides of the pan, about 10–12 minutes. Remove from the heat and beat until smooth. Working quickly before the mixture sets, distribute among the saucers and spread to an even thickness. Allow to cool and set.

3 Preheat the oven to very slow 120°C (250°F/ Gas ½). Remove the mixture from the saucers and cut into sticks 5 cm (2 inches) long and 2 cm (¾ inch) wide. Pour vegetable oil into a large heavy-based saucepan to a depth of about 2.5 cm (1 inch). Heat to very hot and fry the sticks in batches until crisp and golden, about 2 minutes on each side. Remove with a slotted spoon and drain on crumpled paper towels. Transfer cooked batches to trays and keep warm in the oven while the rest are being fried. Serve hot, sprinkled with salt and freshly ground black pepper and perhaps some grated Parmesan. NOTE: For a sweet snack, sprinkle with sugar while still hot.

CHICKPEA FLOUR PANCAKES

Preparation time: 5 minutes
Total cooking time: 25 minutes
Serves 4–6

☆

125 g (4 oz) chickpea flour
1 tablespoon olive oil

1 Preheat the oven to very hot 230°C (450°F/ Gas 8) and oil a 30 cm (12 inch) pizza tray. Put the chickpea flour and ½ teaspoon salt in a bowl and gradually stir in 1 cup (250 ml/8 fl oz) water. Whisk until smooth, then add the oil. Transfer to a heavy-based saucepan and cook, stirring over low heat for 4 minutes, or until the mixture thickens to the consistency of hot custard. If the mixture starts to form small lumps, remove from the heat and beat well.

2 Pour half into the centre of the pizza tray. Tip the tray from side to side so that the batter spreads out evenly and thinly, not quite reaching the edges of the tray. If a few lumps have formed, strain onto the tray. Bake until golden, 8–10 minutes. It should be crisp on the edges, but soft and pancake-like inside. Make a second pancake with the remaining batter. Sprinkle with black pepper. Serve hot, cut into wedges.

ABOVE: Panisses

BOURRIDE
While there are numerous versions of this French Riviera classic, with Provençe and Languedoc claiming it as their own, the one defining characteristic of all bourride is the addition of aïoli, as this gives it the customary smooth texture, pale yellow colour and hearty garlic flavour.

ABOVE: Bourride

BOURRIDE
(Garlic seafood soup)

Preparation time: 25 minutes
Total cooking time: 1 hour 10 minutes
Serves 8

☆ ☆

1 tablespoon butter
1 tablespoon olive oil
4 slices good white bread, trimmed of crusts and cut into 1.5 cm (^{5}/8 inch) cubes
2 kg (4 lb) white-fleshed whole fish (preferably three varieties, in any proportion, such as bass, whiting, cod, flounder)
1 quantity aïoli (see page 153)
3 egg yolks

STOCK
^{1}/3 cup (80 ml/2^3/4 fl oz) olive oil
1 large onion, chopped
1 carrot, sliced
1 leek, white part only, chopped
1^2/3 cups (410 ml/13 fl oz) dry white wine
1 teaspoon dried fennel seed
2 cloves garlic, bruised
2 bay leaves
1 large strip orange peel
2 sprigs of fresh thyme

1   Heat the butter and oil in a heavy-based frying pan. When the butter begins to foam, add the bread cubes and cook for 5 minutes, or until golden. Drain on crumpled paper towels.
2   Fillet the fish (or ask your fishmonger to do it), reserving the heads and bones for the stock.
3   For the stock, heat the olive oil in large saucepan or stockpot and add the onion, carrot and leek. Cook over low heat for 12–15 minutes, until the vegetables are soft. Add the fish heads and bones, wine, fennel seed, garlic, bay leaves, orange peel, thyme, black pepper and ^{1}/2 teaspoon salt. Cover with 2 litres water. Bring to the boil and skim off the froth. Reduce the heat and simmer for 30 minutes. Strain into a pot, crushing the

bones well to release as much flavour as possible. Return to the stove.

4 Cut the fish fillets into large pieces about 9 cm (3½ inches) long. Add them to the stock and slowly bring to simmering point, putting the heavier pieces in first and adding the more delicate pieces later. Poach for 6–8 minutes, until the flesh starts to become translucent and begins to flake easily. Transfer the fish pieces to a serving platter and moisten with a little stock. Cover with foil and keep warm in a low oven.

5 Place 8 tablespoons of the aïoli in a large bowl and slowly add the egg yolks, stirring constantly. Ladle a little stock into the aïoli mixture, blend well and return slowly to the rest of the stock and cook over very low heat. Stir continuously with a wooden spoon for 8–10 minutes, or until the soup has thickened and coats the back of a spoon. Do not boil or the mixture will curdle.

6 Serve the croutons in the soup and the fish and the remaining aïoli separately.

SOUPE AU PISTOU
(Vegetable soup with basil sauce)

Preparation time: 45 minutes
Total cooking time: 35 minutes
Serves 8

3 stalks fresh flat-leaf parsley
1 large sprig of fresh rosemary
1 large sprig of fresh thyme
1 large sprig of fresh marjoram
¼ cup (60 ml/2 fl oz) olive oil
2 onions, thinly sliced
1 leek, thinly sliced
1 bay leaf
375 g (12 oz) pumpkin, cut into small pieces
250 g (8 oz) potato, cut into small pieces
1 carrot, cut in half lengthways and
　thinly sliced
2 litres vegetable stock or water
½ cup (90 g/3 oz) fresh or frozen
　broad beans
½ cup (80 g/2¾ oz) fresh or frozen peas
2 small zucchinis (courgettes), finely chopped
2 ripe tomatoes, peeled and roughly chopped
½ cup (60 g/2 oz) short macaroni or shell pasta

PISTOU
½ cup (25 g/¾ oz) fresh basil leaves
2 large cloves garlic, crushed
⅓ cup (35 g/1¼ oz) grated Parmesan
⅓ cup (80 ml/2¾ fl oz) olive oil

1 Tie the parsley, rosemary, thyme and marjoram together with string. Heat the oil in a heavy-based saucepan and add onion and leek. Cook over low heat for 10 minutes, or until soft.

2 Add the herb bunch, bay leaf, pumpkin, potato, carrot, 1 teaspoon salt and the stock. Cover and simmer 10 minutes, or until vegetables are almost tender.

3 Add the broad beans, peas, zucchini, tomato and pasta. Cover and cook for 15 minutes, or until the vegetables are very tender and the pasta is cooked. Add more water if necessary. Remove the herbs, including the bay leaf.

4 For the pistou, finely chop the basil and garlic in a food processor. Pour in the oil gradually, processing until smooth. Stir in the Parmesan and ½ teaspoon freshly ground black pepper and serve spooned over the soup.

NOTE: The flavour of this soup improves if refrigerated overnight, then gently reheated.

BELOW: Soup au pistou

BOUILLABAISSE WITH
ROUILLE

Cook the firmer-fleshed fish
pieces slightly longer than
the more delicate pieces.

Rub the halved garlic cloves
over the toasted bread.

BOUILLABAISSE WITH ROUILLE

Preparation time: 35 minutes soaking
Total cooking time: 1 hour 10 minutes
Serves 6

☆ ☆

500 g (1 lb) ripe tomatoes
3 tablespoons olive oil
1 large onion, chopped
2 leeks, sliced
4 cloves garlic, crushed
1–2 tablespoons tomato paste (tomato purée)
6 sprigs fresh flat-leaf parsley
2 fresh bay leaves
2 sprigs of fresh thyme
1 sprig of fresh fennel
2 pinches of saffron threads
2 kg (4 lb) fish trimmings (such as heads, bones, shellfish remains, etc.)
1 tablespoon Pernod or Ricard
4 potatoes, cut into 1.5 cm (5/8 inch) slices
1.5 kg (3 lb) mixed fish fillets and steaks (such as rascasse, snapper, red fish, blue eye and bream), cut into large chunks (see Note)
2 tablespoons chopped fresh flat-leaf parsley

TOASTS

12 slices of baguette
2 large cloves garlic, sliced in half

ROUILLE

3 slices white bread, crusts removed
1 red pepper (capsicum), seeded, cut into quarters
1 small red chilli, seeded, chopped
3 cloves garlic, crushed
1 tablespoon shredded fresh basil
1/3 cup (80 ml/2 3/4 fl oz) olive oil

1   Score a cross in the base of each tomato and place the tomatoes in boiling water for 10 seconds, then plunge into cold water and peel away from the cross. Roughly chop the flesh.
2   Heat the oil in a large saucepan over medium heat, add the onion and leek and cook for 5 minutes without browning. Add the garlic, tomato and 1 tablespoon tomato paste, reduce the heat and simmer for 5 minutes. Stir in 2 litres cold water, then add the parsley, bay leaves, thyme, fennel, saffron and fish trimmings. Bring to the boil, then reduce the heat and simmer for 30 minutes. Strain into a large saucepan, pressing the juices out of the ingredients.

*RIGHT: Bouillabaisse
with rouille*

3 Reserve ¼ cup (60 ml/2 fl oz) stock. Add the Pernod to the saucepan and stir in extra tomato paste if needed to enrich the colour. Season, then bring to the boil and add the potato. Reduce the heat and simmer for 5 minutes.

4 Add the firmer-fleshed fish to the saucepan and cook for 2–3 minutes, then add the more delicate pieces of fish and cook for 5 minutes, or until cooked.

5 Toast the bread until golden on both sides. While warm, rub the surfaces with the garlic.

6 For the rouille, soak the bread in cold water for 5 minutes. Cook the pepper pieces, skin-side-up, under a hot grill until the skin blackens and blisters. Cool in a plastic bag, then peel. Roughly chop the flesh. Squeeze the bread dry and place in a the food processor with the pepper, chilli, garlic and basil. Process to a smooth paste. With the motor running, gradually add the oil until the consistency resembles mayonnaise. Thin with 1–2 tablespoons of the stock. Season, to taste. To serve, place 2 pieces of toast in each soup bowl. Spoon in the soup and fish. Sprinkle with parsley. Serve the rouille on the side.

NOTE: Use at least four different fish with a range of textures and flavours. Shellfish such as lobster, crab, scallops or mussels can be used.

RABBIT CASSEROLE WITH MUSTARD SAUCE

Preparation time: 30 minutes
Total cooking time: 2 hours
Serves 4–6

☆☆☆

2 rabbits (800 g/1 lb 10 oz each)

2 tablespoons olive oil

2 onions, sliced

4 rashers bacon, cut into 3 cm (1¼ inch) pieces

2 tablespoons plain flour

1½ cups (375 ml/12 fl oz) chicken stock

½ cup (125 ml/4 fl oz) white wine

1 teaspoon fresh thyme leaves

½ cup (125 ml/4 fl oz) cream

2 tablespoons Dijon mustard

fresh sprigs of thyme, extra, to garnish

1 Preheat the oven to moderate 180°C (350°F/ Gas 4). Remove any fat from the rabbits and wash the rabbits under cold water. Pat dry with paper towels. Cut along both sides of the backbones with kitchen scissors and discard. Cut each rabbit into eight even-sized pieces and pat dry again.

2 Heat half the oil in a 2.5 litre flameproof casserole dish. Brown the rabbit in batches, adding oil when necessary, then remove from the dish.

3 Add the onion and bacon to the casserole, and cook, stirring, for 5 minutes, or until lightly browned. Sprinkle the flour into the pan and mix. Stir with a wooden spoon to scrape the sediment from the base. Add the stock and wine, and stir until the sauce comes to the boil. Return the rabbit to the casserole dish and add the thyme.

4 Cover and bake for 1¼–1½ hours, or until the rabbit is tender and the sauce has thickened. Stir in the combined cream and mustard. Garnish with thyme sprigs. Delicious with steamed vegetables.

ABOVE: Rabbit casserole with mustard sauce

OPPOSITE PAGE,
CLOCKWISE FROM BACK:
Provençal roast tomatoes;
Rack of lamb with herb crust;
Provençal potato galette;
Jus (in bowl)

PROVENCAL ROAST TOMATOES

Preparation time: 10 minutes
Total cooking time: 40 minutes
Makes 4

60 g (2 oz) fresh breadcrumbs
2 tablespoons chopped fresh flat-leaf parsley
2 tablespoons chopped fresh basil
1 tablespoon chopped fresh oregano
4 large vine-ripened tomatoes,
4–6 cloves garlic, finely chopped
2 tablespoons olive oil

1   Preheat the oven to moderate 180°C (350°F/
Gas 4). Combine the breadcrumbs and herbs in
a bowl and season with salt and pepper.
2   Halve each tomato horizontally and scoop out
the core and seeds with a teaspoon.
3   Sprinkle garlic into each tomato, then top
with the breadcrumb mixture. Drizzle with olive
oil and bake for 40 minutes, or until soft.

PROVENCAL POTATO GALETTE

Preparation time: 10 minutes
Total cooking time: 1 hour 10 minutes
Serves 4–6

1 tablespoon olive oil
225 g (7 oz) streaky bacon, finely chopped
2 brown onions, thinly sliced
2 teaspoons chopped fresh thyme
500 g (1 lb) potatoes such as desiree, pontiac
    or King Edward, thinly sliced
30 g (1 oz) butter

1   Preheat the oven to moderate 180°C (350°F/
Gas 4). Heat the oil in a frying pan and fry
the bacon over medium heat until starting to
brown. Add the onion and thyme and cook for
3–4 minutes, until softened. Transfer to a large
bowl, add the potato, season with salt and
pepper and toss well.
2   Transfer the mixture to an 18 cm (7 inch)
round cake tin and press down well. Dot with
the butter. Place a piece of doubled baking paper
over the top and place a weight, such as a

ramekin or a smaller cake tin, over the paper.
Bake for 40 minutes. Remove the weight and
the paper and cook for another 20–25 minutes,
or until the potato is tender and lightly golden.
Leave to rest for 10 minutes. Run a knife around
the edge of the tin and turn out the galette.

RACK OF LAMB WITH HERB CRUST

Preparation time: 25 minutes
Total cooking time: 25 minutes
Serves 4

2 x 6–chop racks of lamb trimmed and bones
    cleaned (ask your butcher to do this)
1 tablespoon oil
1 cup (80 g/2¾ oz) fresh breadcrumbs
3 cloves garlic
3 tablespoons finely chopped fresh flat-leaf
    parsley
1/2 tablespoon fresh thyme leaves
1/2 teaspoon finely grated lemon rind
60 g (2 oz) butter, softened
1 cup (250 ml/8 fl oz) beef stock
1 clove garlic, extra, finely chopped
1 sprig of fresh thyme

1   Preheat the oven to very hot 250°C (500°F/
Gas 10). Score the fat on racks in a diamond
pattern. Rub the rack with a little of the oil and
season with salt and pepper.
2   Heat the oil in a frying pan over high heat,
add the lamb and brown for 4–5 minutes.
Remove and set aside. Do not wash the pan
as you will need it later.
3   In a large bowl, mix the breadcrumbs, garlic,
parsley, thyme and lemon rind. Season, then mix
in the butter to form a paste.
4   Firmly press a layer of breadcrumb mixture
over the fat on the racks, leaving the bones and
base clean. Bake in a baking dish for 12 minutes
for medium-rare. Rest the lamb while you make
the jus.
5   To make a jus, add the beef stock, extra garlic
and thyme sprig to the roasting pan juices,
scraping the pan. Return this liquid to the
original frying pan and simmer over high heat
for 5–8 minutes, until the sauce is reduced.
Strain and serve on the side.

FISH COOKED IN PAPER

Put a teaspoon of butter and 3 slices of lemon over the leek and spring onion.

Fold the paper into a parcel around the fish, tucking the ends under.

FISH COOKED IN PAPER

Preparation time: 20 minutes
Total cooking time: 20 minutes
Serves 4

☆

4 skinless fish fillets, 200 g/6 1/2 oz each
    (e.g. John dory, orange roughy, snapper, bream)
1 leek, white part only, julienned
4 spring onions, julienned
30 g (1 oz) butter, softened
1 lemon, cut into 12 very thin slices
2–3 tablespoons lemon juice

1   Preheat the oven to moderate 180°C (350°F/ Gas 4). Place each fish fillet in the centre of a piece of baking paper large enough to enclose the fish. Season lightly.
2   Scatter with the leek and spring onion. Top each with a teaspoon of butter and 3 slices of lemon. Sprinkle with the extra lemon juice. Bring the paper together and fold over several times. Fold the ends under. Bake on a baking tray for 20 minutes (the steam will make the paper puff up). Check to see that the fish is cooked (it should be white and flake easily when tested with a fork) and then serve. Serve as parcels or lift the fish out and pour the juices over.

ABOVE: Fish cooked in paper

POACHED SALMON

Preparation time: 40 minutes
Total cooking time: 1 hour
Serves 8–10

☆ ☆

2 litres good-quality white wine
1/4 cup (60 ml/2 fl oz) white wine vinegar
2 onions
10 whole cloves
4 carrots, chopped
1 lemon, cut into quarters
2 bay leaves
1 teaspoon whole black peppercorns
4 sprigs fresh parsley
2.5 kg (5 lb) Atlantic salmon, cleaned
    and scaled
watercress and lemon slices, to garnish

DILL MAYONNAISE

1 egg, at room temperature
1 egg yolk, at room temperature, extra
1 tablespoon lemon juice
1 teaspoon white wine vinegar
1 1/2 cups (375 ml/12 fl oz) light olive oil
1 tablespoon chopped fresh dill

1 Put the wine, wine vinegar and 2.5 litres water in a large heavy-based pan. Stud the onions with the cloves. Add to the pan with the carrot, lemon, bay leaves, peppercorns and parsley. Bring to the boil, reduce the heat and simmer for 30–35 minutes. Cool. Strain into a fish kettle that will hold the salmon.

2 Place the whole fish in the fish kettle and cover. Bring to the boil, reduce the heat and poach gently for 10–15 minutes, until the fish flakes when tested in the thickest part. Remove from the heat and cool the fish in the liquid.

3 Process the egg, extra yolk, juice and vinegar in a food processor for 10 seconds, or until blended. With the motor running, add the oil in a thin, steady stream, blending until all the oil is added and the mayonnaise is thick and creamy. Transfer to a bowl and stir in the dill, and salt and pepper, to taste.

4 Remove the fish from the liquid, place on a work surface or serving platter and peel back the skin. Garnish with watercress and lemon slices and serve with the dill mayonnaise.

and simmer for several minutes until reduced slightly, then add the tomato. Season with salt and pepper and cook, stirring occasionally, for 20 minutes, or until thick and pulpy. Preheat the oven to moderate 180°F (350°F/Gas 4).

3 Heat the butter and remaining oil in a frying pan over high heat until foamy. Cook half the scallops for 1–2 minutes each side, or until lightly golden and cooked to your liking. Remove and repeat with the remaining scallops. Set aside.

4 Add the garlic to the hot scallop pan and stir for 1 minute. Remove from the heat and stir in the parsley, thyme and breadcrumbs.

5 To serve, warm the shells on a baking tray in the oven. Place a small amount of tomato mixture on each shell, top with a scallop and sprinkle with breadcrumb and parsley mixture.
NOTE: If the shells are not available, simply serve the scallops on a small plate. Place them on a bed of the tomato mixture and top with the breadcrumb mixture.

BELOW: Scallops Provençale

SCALLOPS PROVENCALE

Preparation time: 20 minutes
Total cooking time: 30 minutes
Serves 4 as a starter

600 g (1 ¼ lb) ripe tomatoes
3 tablespoons olive oil
1 onion, finely chopped
4 French shallots, finely chopped
¼ cup (60 ml/2 fl oz) dry white wine
60 g (2 oz) butter
20 fresh scallops, cleaned and dried, with shells
4 cloves garlic, crushed
2 tablespoons finely chopped fresh parsley
½ teaspoon fresh thyme leaves
2 tablespoons fresh breadcrumbs

1 Score a cross in the base of each tomato. Place the tomatoes in boiling water for 10 seconds, then plunge into cold water and peel. Cut each tomato in half and scoop out the seeds with a teaspoon and discard them. Finely dice the tomato flesh.

2 Heat 2 tablespoons of the oil in a frying pan over medium heat until hot, add the onion and shallots, then reduce the heat to low and cook slowly for 5 minutes, or until soft. Add the wine

Duck is available whole (head off or on), portioned, fresh and frozen. When selecting a fresh duck, look for those that have an adequate layer of fat beneath the skin of the breast and have pearly, creamy white skin. If you are not intending to cook the fresh duck within two or three days of purchasing, it is preferable to buy a properly blast-frozen duck than to place a fresh duck in a domestic freezer where it may take days to freeze solid and will progressively deteriorate. Always thaw frozen ducks or other poultry in the refrigerator, uncovered and placed on paper towels. It is not advisable to cook partially frozen poultry, because while the outside may appear crisp and browned, the interior temperature may not have reached a level whereby dangerous bacteria are killed.

ROAST DUCK WITH OLIVES

Preparation time: 30 minutes
Total cooking time: 1 hour 30 minutes
Serves 4

☆☆

SAUCE
1 tablespoon olive oil
1 onion, chopped
1 garlic clove, crushed
2 ripe Roma tomatoes, peeled and chopped
1 cup (250 ml/8 fl oz) Riesling
2 teaspoons fresh thyme leaves
1 bay leaf
24 Niçoise olives, pitted

STUFFING
1/3 cup (60 g/2 oz) medium-grain rice, cooked
1 garlic clove, crushed
100 g (4 oz) frozen chopped spinach, defrosted
2 duck's livers (about 100 g/3 1/2 oz), chopped
1 egg, lightly beaten
1 teaspoon fresh thyme leaves
1.8 kg (4 lb) duck
2 bay leaves

1 Preheat the oven to moderately hot 200°C (400°F/Gas 6). For the sauce, heat the oil in a frying pan, add the onion and cook for 5 minutes, or until transparent. Add the garlic, tomato, wine, herbs and some seasoning. Cook for 5 minutes, then add the olives before removing from the heat.

2 For the stuffing, thoroughly mix all the ingredients in a bowl and season well. Before stuffing the duck, rinse out the cavity with cold water and pat dry inside and out with paper towels. Put the bay leaves in the cavity, then spoon in the stuffing.

3 Tuck the wings under the duck, then close the flaps of fat over the parson's nose and secure with a skewer or toothpick. Place in a deep baking dish and rub 1 teaspoon salt into the skin. Prick the skin all over with a skewer.

4 Roast on the top shelf for 35–40 minutes, then carefully pour off the excess fat. Roast for another 35–40 minutes. To check that the duck is cooked, gently pull away one leg from the side. The flesh should be pale brown with no blood in the juices. Remove, then carve, serving a spoonful of the stuffing next to the duck and topping with the sauce.

RIGHT: Roast duck with olives

LAMB AND ARTICHOKE FRICASSEE

Preparation time: 50 minutes
Total cooking time: 1 hour 50 minutes
Serves 8

☆ ☆

6 fresh globe artichokes
1/4 cup (60 ml/2 fl oz) lemon juice
2 large, ripe tomatoes
1/3 cup (80 ml/2 3/4 fl oz) olive oil
2 kg (4 lb) diced lamb
750 g (1 1/2 lb) brown onions, thinly sliced
1 tablespoon plain flour
2 cloves garlic, crushed
3/4 cup (185 m/l6 fl oz) white wine
1 1/3 cups (350 ml/11 fl oz) chicken stock
1 bouquet garni
chopped fresh flat-leaf parsley, to garnish
lemon wedges, for serving

1   To prepare the globe artichokes, bring a large saucepan of water to the boil and add the lemon juice. Trim the stems from the artichokes and remove the tough outer leaves. Cut off the hard tips of the remaining leaves using scissors. Blanch the artichokes for 5 minutes. Remove and turn upside-down to drain. When cool enough to handle, use a small spoon to remove the choke from the centre of each. Scrape the bases well to remove all the membrane. Cut the artichokes into quarters and set aside.

2   Score a cross in the base of each tomato and place in a bowl of boiling water for 10 seconds. Plunge into cold water and peel away from the cross. Cut each tomato in half and scoop out the seeds with a teaspoon. Chop the tomatoes.

3   Heat half the oil in a deep heatproof casserole and fry batches of the lamb until golden. Add the remaining oil and cook the onion for about 8 minutes, until soft and caramelized. Add the flour and cook for 1 minute. Add the garlic, tomato, wine and chicken stock. Return the lamb to the pan add the bouquet garni and simmer, covered, for 1 hour.

4   Place the artichokes in the casserole and simmer, uncovered, for another 15 minutes. Remove the meat and artichokes with a slotted spoon and place in a serving dish. Keep warm. Discard the bouquet garni. Cook the sauce over high heat until it thickens. Pour the sauce over the lamb and garnish with parsley. Serve with lemon wedges.

NOTE: If fresh artichokes are not available, you can use 1 cup (270 g/9 oz) marinated artichokes. Drain them well and pat dry with paper towels.

BOUQUET GARNI
This is a small bundle of herbs used to flavour casseroles, soups and fricassees. It usually includes a few stalks of parsley, a sprig of thyme and a bay leaf. The herbs can be tied together with string or in a knot of muslin. Other herbs can be added if you feel they are appropriate to the dish you are making. Ready-made bouquet garni are also available.

ABOVE: Lamb and artichoke fricassee

¹/₄ teaspoon cayenne pepper

2 teaspoons chopped fresh thyme

2 bay leaves

I tablespoon red wine vinegar

I teaspoon caster sugar

3 tablespoons shredded fresh basil

I Score a cross in the base of each tomato. Place in a bowl of boiling water for 10 seconds, then plunge into cold water and peel away from the cross. Roughly chop the flesh.

2 Heat 2 tablespoons of the oil in a large saucepan, add the eggplant and cook over medium heat for 4–5 minutes, or until softened but not browned. Remove. Add another 2 tablespoons oil to the pan, add the zucchini and cook for 3–4 minutes, or until softened. Remove. Add the green pepper, cook for 2 minutes and remove.

3 Heat the remaining oil, add the onion and cook for 2–3 minutes, or until softened. Add the garlic, cayenne, thyme and bay leaves, and cook, stirring, for 1 minute. Return the eggplant, zucchini and pepper to the pan and add the tomato, vinegar and sugar. Simmer for 20 minutes, stirring occasionally. Stir in the basil and season with salt and black pepper. Serve hot or at room temperature.

NOTE: You can serve ratatouille as a vegetable on the side or as a starter with bread.

RATATOUILLE
(French vegetable stew)

Preparation time: 25 minutes
Total cooking time: 40 minutes
Serves 4–6

6 vine-ripened tomatoes

5 tablespoons olive oil

500 g (I lb) eggplants (aubergines), cut
   into 2 cm (³/4 inch) cubes

375 g (12 oz) zucchini (courgettes), cut
   into 2 cm (³/4 inch) slices

I green pepper (capsicum), seeded, cut
   into 2 cm (³/4 inch) squares

I red onion, cut into 2 cm (³/4 inch) wedges

3 cloves garlic, finely chopped

ABOVE: Ratatouille

ASPARAGUS VINAIGRETTE

To make the vinaigrette, combine ¹/2 tablespoon Dijon mustard, 2 tablespoons sherry vinegar, ¹/3 cup (80 ml/2³/4 fl oz) good-quality olive oil and ¹/2 teaspoon finely chopped chives in a small jug. Cook 24 asparagus spears, woody ends trimmed, in a large saucepan of boiling salted water over medium heat for 8–10 minutes, until tender. While the asparagus is cooking, heat 3 tablespoons olive oil in a medium frying pan, add 2 whole peeled cloves garlic and cook over low heat until the cloves are golden. Discard the garlic. Add 1 cup (80 g/2³/4 oz) fresh breadcrumbs and increase the heat to medium. Cook until the breadcrumbs are crisp and golden. Season and drain on paper towels. Drain the asparagus and place on a platter. Drizzle with the vinaigrette and sprinkle with breadcrumbs. Serves 4.

BEEF PROVENCALE

Preparation time: 20 minutes
  + overnight refrigeration
Total cooking time: 2 hours 25 minutes
Serves 6

1.5 kg (3 lb) chuck steak, cut into
  3 cm (1¼ inch) cubes
2 tablespoons olive oil
1 small onion, sliced
1½ cups (375 ml/12 fl oz) red wine
2 tablespoons chopped fresh flat-leaf parsley
1 tablespoon chopped fresh rosemary
1 tablespoon chopped fresh thyme
2 fresh bay leaves
250 g (8 oz) speck, rind removed, cut into
  1 x 2 cm (½ x ¾ inch) pieces
400 g (13 oz) can crushed good-quality tomatoes
1 cup (250 ml/8 fl oz) beef stock
500 g (1 lb) baby carrots
⅓ cup (45 g/1½ oz) pitted Niçoise olives

1 In a bowl, combine the cubed beef with 1 tablespoon of the oil, the onion, 1 cup (250 ml/8 fl oz) of wine and half the herbs. Cover with plastic wrap and marinate in the refrigerator overnight.

2 Drain the beef, reserving the marinade. Heat the remaining oil in a large heavy-based saucepan and brown the beef and onion in batches. Remove from the pan.

3 Add the speck to the saucepan and cook for 3–5 minutes, until crisp. Return the beef to the pan with the remaining wine and marinade and cook, scraping the residue from the base of the pan for 2 minutes, or until the wine has slightly reduced. Add the tomato and stock and bring the boil. Reduce the heat and add the remaining herbs. Season well, cover and simmer for 1½ hours.

4 Add the carrots and olives to the saucepan and cook, uncovered, for another 30 minutes, or until the meat and the carrots are tender. Before serving, check the seasoning and adjust if necessary.

NICOISE OLIVES
Niçoise olives are small and ripe, ranging in colour from purple to brown to black. Cured in brine and often packed in olive oil, they are an integral ingredient in Provençal cuisine, where they are eaten as a table olive and also added to beef stews, poultry stuffing, savoury tarts and as an addition to Niçoise salad.

LEFT: Beef Provençale

175

POTATO AND OIL PUREE

Preparation time: 5 minutes
Total cooking time: 20 minutes
Serves 4

1 kg (2 lb) floury potatoes (such as russet,
   spunta and pontiac), cut into large chunks
200 ml (6/2 fl oz) stock (choose according to
   the dish the potatoes will be served with)
2 garlic cloves, peeled and bruised
2 sprigs of fresh thyme
150 ml (5 fl oz) extra-virgin olive oil

1 Cook the potatoes in boiling salted water
until tender but still firm. While the potatoes are
cooking, heat the stock in a small saucepan with
the garlic and thyme. Bring to simmering point,
then remove from the heat and allow to infuse.
2 Drain the potatoes well and pass them
through a mouli or mash with a potato masher.
Strain the stock, return to the saucepan, add the
olive oil and reheat gently. Place the potato
purée in a bowl and add the stock in a thin
steady stream, stirring continuously with a flat
wooden spoon. Season with salt and pepper,
then beat well until the purée is smooth.

CHICKEN WITH FORTY CLOVES OF GARLIC

Preparation time: 20 minutes
Total cooking time: 1 hour 45 minutes
Serves 4

10 g (1/4 oz) butter
1 tablespoon olive oil
1 large (No. 20) free-range chicken
40 cloves garlic, unpeeled (see Note)
2 tablespoons chopped fresh rosemary
2 sprigs fresh thyme
275 ml (9 fl oz) dry white wine
150 ml (5 fl oz) chicken stock
225 g (7 oz) plain flour

1 Preheat the oven to 180°C (350°F/Gas 4).
You will need a 4.5 litre lidded casserole dish.
2 Melt the butter and oil in the casserole and
brown the chicken over medium heat until

golden all over. Remove the chicken and add
the garlic cloves, rosemary and thyme and cook
together for 1 minute. Return the chicken to the
dish and add the wine and chicken stock. Bring
to a simmer, basting the chicken with the sauce.
3 Place the flour in a bowl and add up to
150 ml (5 fl oz) water to form a firm pliable
paste. Divide into four and roll into cylinder
shapes. Place around the rim of the casserole.
Replace the lid, pressing down well to form
a seal. Bake for 1 1/4 hours. Remove the lid by
cracking the paste. Return the chicken to the
oven to brown for 15 minutes, then transfer to
a plate. Reduce the juices to 1 cup (250 ml/
8 fl oz) over medium heat. Carve the chicken,
pierce the garlic skins and squeeze the garlic
flesh onto the chicken. Serve with the jus.
NOTE: Don't be alarmed by the amount of garlic
in this recipe. The garlic becomes soft and
creamy when cooked in this way.

LENTILS IN RED WINE

Preparation time: 20 minutes
Total cooking time: 1 hour 15 minutes
Serves 4–6

2 tablespoons olive oil
1 stick celery, finely diced
1 large carrot, finely diced
1 large onion, finely diced
2 cloves garlic, crushed
2 tablespoons tomato paste (tomato purée)
1 1/2 cups (280 g/9 oz) lentils de puy
1 cup (250 ml/8 fl oz) red wine
1 cup (250 ml/8 fl oz) beef stock
1 fresh bay leaf, crushed
5 sprigs of fresh thyme
3 tablespoons chopped fresh flat-leaf parsley

1 Heat the olive oil in a large heavy-based
saucepan. Add the celery, carrot and onion and
cook over medium-low heat for 10 minutes.
Add the garlic and cook for another 2 minutes.
2 Add the tomato paste and cook over low heat
for 5 minutes. Stir in the lentils, then add the wine
and cook over medium heat for 3–5 minutes,
until slightly reduced. Add the stock and 1 1/2 cups
(375 ml/12 fl oz) water, bring to the boil, then
reduce the heat and add the herbs. Season and
simmer for 45–50 minutes, until the liquid is
absorbed and the lentils are cooked.

LENTILS DE PUY
The most prized of all
lentils come from the
French village of Le Puy.
The advantage of using
these small, dark green
lentils is that they hold their
shape and texture when
cooked, and have a deeper,
richer flavour. Unlike other
pulses, it is not necessary to
soak lentils de puy before
cooking. In fact it is
advisable not to do so as
they can ferment and start
to sprout.

*OPPOSITE PAGE, FROM
TOP: Potato and oil purée;
Lentils in red wine; Chicken
with forty cloves of garlic*

SAGE
Once believed to enhance longevity and give wisdom, this strongly flavoured, fragrant herb is commonly paired with pork, chicken and veal in southern French cuisine as it was traditionally used to counteract rich, oily meats. Use sage, especially in its dried form, with discretion, as a heavy hand will cause its pungent flavour to overpower rather than complement that of the food with which it is being cooked.

PORK WITH SAGE AND CAPERS

Preparation time: 25 minutes
Total cooking time 1 hour 15 minutes
Serves 4

☆☆

1/4 cup (60 ml/2 fl oz) extra virgin olive oil
25 g (3/4 oz) unsalted butter
1 onion, finely chopped
100 g (3 1/2 oz) fresh white breadcrumbs
2 teaspoons chopped fresh sage
1 tablespoon chopped fresh flat-leaf parsley
2 teaspoons grated lemon zest
2 1/2 tablespoons salted baby capers, rinsed and drained
1 egg
2 large pork fillets (about 500 g/1 lb each)
8 large thin slices of streaky bacon or prosciutto
2 teaspoons plain flour
100 ml (3 1/2 fl oz) dry vermouth
1 1/4 cups (315 ml/10 fl oz) chicken or vegetable stock
8 whole sage leaves, extra, to garnish

1 Preheat the oven to warm 170°C (325°F/ Gas 3). Heat 1 tablespoon of the oil and the butter in a frying pan, add the onion and cook for 5 minutes, or until lightly golden.
2 Place the breadcrumbs, chopped sage, parsley, lemon zest, 1/2 tablespoon capers and the cooked onion in a bowl. Add the egg and season well.
3 Split each pork fillet in half lengthways and open out. Spread the stuffing down the length of one and cover with the other fillet.
4 Stretch the bacon or prosciutto with the back of a knife and wrap each piece slightly overlapping around the pork to form a neat parcel. Tie with string at intervals.
5 Place the pork in a baking dish and drizzle with 1 tablespoon oil. Bake for 1 hour. To test if the meat is cooked, insert a skewer in the thickest part. The juices should run clear. Remove the meat from the tin, cover with foil and leave to rest. Place the baking dish on the stovetop, add the flour and stir in well. Add the vermouth and allow to bubble for 1 minute. Add the stock and stir while cooking to remove all the lumps. Simmer for 5 minutes. Add the remaining capers to the sauce.
6 In a small saucepan, heat the remaining oil and when very hot, fry the whole sage leaves until crisp. Drain on crumpled paper towels.
7 Slice the pork into 1 cm (1/2 inch) slices. Spoon a little sauce over the pork and serve each portion with fried sage leaves on top.

RIGHT: Pork with sage and capers

VEGETABLE TIAN

Preparation time: 40 minutes
Total cooking time: 1 hour 20 minutes
Serves 6–8

1 kg (2 lb) red peppers (capsicums)
1/2 cup (125 ml/4 fl oz) olive oil
800 g (1 lb 10 oz) silverbeet (Swiss chard), stalks removed and coarsely shredded
2 tablespoons pine nuts
ground nutmeg, to taste
1 onion, chopped
2 cloves garlic
2 teaspoons chopped thyme
750 g (1 1/2 lb) tomatoes, peeled, seeded, diced
1 large eggplant (aubergine), cut into 1 cm (1/2 inch) rounds
5 small zucchini (courgettes) (about 500 g/1 lb), thinly sliced diagonally
3 ripe tomatoes, cut into 1 cm (1/2 inch) slices
1 tablespoon fresh breadcrumbs
30 g (1 oz) Parmesan, grated
30 g (1 oz) butter

1 Preheat the oven to moderately hot 200°C (400°F/Gas 6). Preheat the grill to high.

2 Remove the seeds and membrane from the peppers and grill until black and blistered. Cool in a plastic bag, then peel and cut into 8 x 3 cm (3 x 1 inch) slices. Place in a lightly greased 25 x 20 x 5 cm (10 x 8 x 2 inch) ovenproof dish and season lightly.

3 Heat 2 tablespoons of the olive oil in a heavy-based frying pan and cook the silverbeet over medium heat for 8–10 minutes, or until softened. Add the pine nuts and season, to taste, with salt, pepper and nutmeg. Place the silverbeet over the pepper slices.

4 Heat another tablespoon of olive oil in a heavy-based frying pan. Add the onion and cook over medium heat for 7–8 minutes, or until soft and golden. Add the garlic and thyme, cook for 1 minute, then add the diced tomato and bring to the boil. Reduce the heat and simmer for 10 minutes. Spread the sauce evenly over the silverbeet.

5 Heat the remaining olive oil in a heavy-based frying pan and fry the eggplant slices over high heat for 8–10 minutes, or until golden on both sides. Drain on paper towels and place in a single layer over the tomato sauce. Season lightly.

6 Arrange the zucchini and tomato slices in alternating layers over the eggplant. Sprinkle the breadcrumbs and Parmesan over the top and then dot with the butter. Bake for 25–30 minutes or until golden. Serve warm or at room temperature.

TIAN
Tian is the name for a glazed earthenware dish which is used for baking. Now, tian has also come to mean the recipe itself.

ABOVE: Vegetable tian

POULPE PROVENCAL

Using a small knife, carefully cut between the head and tentacles of the octopus, just below the eyes.

Grasp the body of the octopus and push the beak out and up through the centre of the tentacles with your finger.

To clean the octopus head, carefully slit through one side, avoiding the ink sac, and scrape out any gut from inside.

When you have slit the head open, rinse under running water to remove any remaining gut.

ABOVE: Poulpe Provençal

POULPE PROVENCAL
(Octopus braised in tomato and wine)

Preparation time: 25 minutes
Total cooking time: 1 hour 30 minutes
Serves 6

☆ ☆

500 g (1 lb) ripe tomatoes
1 kg (2 lb) baby octopus
1/4 cup (60 ml/2 fl oz) olive oil
1 large brown onion, chopped
2 cloves garlic
1 1/3 cups (350 ml/11 fl oz) dry white wine
1/4 teaspoon saffron threads
2 sprigs fresh thyme
2 tablespoons roughly chopped fresh
    flat-leaf parsley

1 Score a cross in the base of each tomato. Place the tomatoes in a bowl of boiling water for 10 seconds, then plunge into cold water and peel the skin away from the cross. Cut each tomato in half and scoop out the seeds with a teaspoon. Chop the flesh.

2 To clean each octopus, use a small sharp knife and cut each head from the tentacles. Remove the eyes by cutting a round of flesh from the base of each head. To clean the heads, carefully slit them open and remove the gut. Rinse thoroughly. Cut the heads in half. Push out the beaks from the centre of the tentacles from the cut side. Cut the tentacles into sets of four or two, depending on the size of the octopus.

3 Blanch all the octopus in boiling water for 2 minutes then drain and allow to cool slightly. Pat dry with paper towels.

4 Heat the olive oil in heavy-based frying pan and cook the onion for 7–8 minutes over medium heat until lightly golden. Add the octopus and garlic to the pan and cook for another 2–3 minutes. Add the tomato, wine, saffron and thyme. Add just enough water to cover the octopus.

5 Simmer, covered, for 1 hour. Uncover and cook for another 15 minutes, or until the octopus is tender and the sauce has thickened a little. The cooking time will vary quite a bit depending upon the size of the octopus. Season, to taste. Serve hot or at room temperature, sprinkled with chopped parsley.

ZUCCHINI (COURGETTE) OMELETTE

Preparation time: 5 minutes
Total cooking time: 15 minutes
Serves 4

80 g (2¾ oz) butter
400 g (13 oz) zucchini (courgettes), sliced
1 tablespoon finely chopped fresh basil
pinch of ground nutmeg
8 eggs, lightly beaten

1 Melt half the butter in a non-stick 23 cm (9 inch) frying pan. Add the zucchini and cook over moderate heat for about 8 minutes, until lightly golden. Stir in the basil and nutmeg, season with salt and pepper and cook for 30 seconds. Transfer to a bowl and keep warm.
2 Wipe out the pan, return it to the heat and melt the remaining butter. Lightly season the eggs and pour into the pan. Stir gently over high heat. Stop stirring when the mixture begins to set in uniform, fluffy small clumps. Reduce the heat and lift the edges with a fork to prevent it catching. Shake the pan from side to side to prevent the omelette sticking. When it is almost set but still runny on the surface, spread the zucchini down the centre. Using a spatula, fold the omelette over and slide onto a serving plate.

GRILLED FISH WITH FENNEL AND LEMON

Preparation time: 10 minutes
Total cooking time: 10 minutes
Serves 4

4 whole red mullet or bream, scaled and gutted
1 lemon, thinly sliced
1 baby fennel bulb, thinly sliced
1½ tablespoons fennel seeds
¼ cup (60 ml/2 fl oz) lemon juice
⅓ cup (80 ml/2¾ fl oz) olive oil

1 Cut 3 diagonal slashes on both sides of each fish. Place two or three slices of lemon and some slices of fennel bulb in the cavity of each fish. Place the fennel seeds in a mortar and pestle and bruise roughly. Sprinkle both sides of each fish with the cracked fennel seeds and some salt, making sure you rub well into the flesh.
2 Mix the lemon juice and olive oil in a bowl. Heat a chargrill or hotplate and when very hot, add the fish. Drizzle a little of the lemon and oil over each fish. After 5 minutes, turn carefully with tongs, ensuring the filling doesn't fall out, and drizzle with the oil mix. Gently flake a piece of flesh gently with a fork to test whether it is cooked through, then serve with salad.

OMELETTES
Omelettes are a triumph of simple French country cooking. Using the freshest possible eggs, quality butter and uncomplicated flavourings, it is possible to have a satisfying meal in minutes if you follow these tips. Don't overbeat the eggs but stir until just combined. Use simple fillings with flavours and quantities that don't overpower the subtle egg-flavour. Don't overcook the omelette or it will be rubbery.

LEFT: Zucchini omelette

STUFFED MUSHROOMS

Preparation time: 10 minutes
Total cooking time: 25 minutes
Serves 4

8 large cap mushrooms
4 tablespoons olive oil
30 g (1 oz) prosciutto, finely chopped
1 clove garlic crushed
2 tablespoons soft fresh breadcrumbs
30 g (1 oz) grated Parmesan
2 tablespoons chopped fresh flat-leaf parsley

1 Preheat the oven to moderately hot 190°C (375°F/Gas 5). Oil a baking dish. Remove the mushroom stalks and finely chop them.
2 Heat 1 tablespoon oil in a frying pan, add the prosciutto, garlic and mushroom stalks and cook for 5 minutes. Mix in a bowl with the breadcrumbs, Parmesan and parsley.
3 Brush the mushroom caps with 1 tablespoon olive oil and place them gill-side-up on the baking dish. Divide the stuffing among the caps and bake for 20 minutes. Drizzle with the remaining oil and serve hot or warm.

OIGNONS FARCIES
(Stuffed onions)

Preparation time: 30 minutes
Total cooking time: 1 hour 5 minutes
Serves 4

8 brown onions, about 125 g (4 oz) each
6 slices bacon, diced
4 cloves garlic, finely chopped
1 tablespoon cream
1 egg, lightly beaten
1/4 teaspoon ground nutmeg
3 tablespoons chopped fresh flat-leaf parsley
3/4 cup (60 g/2 oz) fresh breadcrumbs
2 tablespoons grated Parmesan
40 g (1 1/4 oz) butter, softened
1 cup (250 ml/8 fl oz) chicken stock

1 Preheat the oven to moderately hot 200°C (400°F/Gas 6). Lightly grease a shallow earthenware dish.
2 Peel the onions, place in a large saucepan or stockpot of boiling water and simmer for 5–6 minutes. Remove the onions and drain well. Cool slightly and, using a small sharp knife, hollow out the centres, leaving a 1 cm (1/2 inch) rim. Reserve 1/2 cup of the onion centres. Season the onions.
3 Meanwhile, cook the bacon in a small frying pan over medium heat until the fat has melted. Chop the reserved onion and add to the pan with the garlic. Cook for 5 minutes, or until lightly golden. Remove from the heat, add the cream, egg, nutmeg, parsley and 1/2 cup (40 g/ 1 1/4 oz) of the crumbs. Season well and mix.
4 Spoon about 1–1 1/2 tablespoons of the filling into the onion shells, piling a little to the top. Combine the remaining breadcrumbs with the Parmesan, sprinkle over the onions and dot with butter. Place in baking dish, and carefully pour stock around the onions. Bake, basting occasionally, for 1 hour, or until the onions are tender.

BELOW: Stuffed mushrooms

GASCONNADE

Preparation time: 25 minutes
Total cooking time: 1 hour 30 minutes
Serves 6

☆ ☆

1 large leg of lamb, about 2.5 kg (5 lb),
   partially boned (see Note)
1 carrot, coarsely chopped
1 stick celery, coarsely chopped
1 large onion, coarsely chopped
1 bay leaf
1 bouquet garni (see page 173)
2 cloves garlic, crushed
6 anchovy fillets, mashed
1/2 tablespoon finely chopped fresh parsley
1/2 tablespoon finely chopped fresh thyme
1/2 tablespoon finely chopped fresh rosemary
3 tablespoons olive oil
25 cloves garlic, unpeeled

1 Preheat the oven to hot 220°C (425°F/Gas 7).
Place the removed lamb bone in a stockpot with
the carrot, celery, onion, bay leaf and bouquet
garni, and add just enough cold water to cover.
Bring to the boil and simmer uncovered for
1 hour. Strain and if necessary simmer until
reduced to 2 cups (500 ml/16 fl oz).

2 Meanwhile, combine the crushed garlic,
anchovies, chopped herbs and olive oil in a small
bowl with some freshly ground black pepper.
Rub the cavity of the lamb with most of the
herb mixture. Roll the meat up and tie securely
with kitchen string. Rub the lamb with the
remaining herb mixture and place in a baking
dish. Bake for 15 minutes, then reduce the
temperature to moderate 180°C (350°F/Gas 4).
Continue baking for about 45 minutes (for
medium-rare), basting with the pan juices
occasionally, until cooked to your liking.

3 Bring a saucepan of water to the boil and add
the garlic cloves. Boil for 5 minutes. Drain and
rinse under cold water. Peel the garlic and purée
the pulp. Put it in the saucepan with the 2 cups
(500 ml/16 fl oz) of stock and bring to the boil.
Simmer for 10 minutes. Transfer the lamb to a
carving tray and keep warm. Spoon off the fat
from the pan juices. Add the garlic stock and
place the dish over high heat. Bring to the boil
and cook until reduced by half. Adjust the
seasoning. Serve the lamb sliced, accompanied
by the sauce.

NOTE: Ask your butcher to partially bone the
leg of lamb, leaving the shank bone in place.
Take home the removed bone to use when
making the stock.

RESTING ROAST LAMB
A perennial French bistro
favourite, roast leg of lamb
has its origins as a one-pot
dish that could be taken to
the village baker to be
cooked in the local baker's
oven. It is important to rest
roast lamb after it is cooked
and before it is carved, as
this ensures that the juices
will permeate the meat
evenly. If cut too early, the
interior will be moist but
the exterior will be dry,
as the juices flow towards
the centre when red meat
is cooked.

ABOVE: Gasconnade

2 Sift the flour and salt into a bowl and make a well in the centre. Add the yeast mixture, olive oil and ³/4 cup (185 ml/6 fl oz) warm water. Mix to a soft dough and gather into a ball with floured hands. Turn out onto a floured surface and knead for 10 minutes, or until smooth.

3 Place in a large, lightly oiled bowl, cover loosely with plastic wrap or a damp tea towel and leave in a warm place for 1 hour, or until doubled in size.

4 Punch down the dough and knead for 1 minute. Divide the mixture into four equal portions. Press each portion into a large, oval shape 1 cm (¹/2 inch) thick and make several cuts on either side of all of them. Lay on large, floured baking trays, cover with plastic wrap and leave to rise for 20 minutes.

5 Preheat the oven to hot 210°C (415°F/ Gas 6–7). Bake the fougasse for 35 minutes, or until crisp. To assist the crust to crispen, after 15 minutes cooking, spray the oven with water. NOTE: Although fougasse is traditionally made as a plain bread, as in the recipe above, these days bakeries often incorporate ingredients such as fresh herbs, olives, chopped ham and anchovies into the dough. You can add your favourite flavouring after you have kneaded the dough for the final time in step 4.

FOUGASSE

Preparation time: 30 minutes
  + 1 hour 20 minutes rising
Total cooking time: 35 minutes
Makes 4

☆ ☆

7 g (¹/4 oz) sachet dried yeast

1 teaspoon sugar

4 cups (500 g/1 lb) white bread flour

2 teaspoons salt

¹/4 cup (60 ml/2 fl oz) olive oil

1 Place the yeast, sugar and ¹/2 cup (125 ml/ 4 fl oz) warm water in a small bowl and stir until dissolved. Leave in a warm, draught-free place for 10 minutes, or until bubbles appear on the surface. The mixture should be frothy and slightly increased in volume. If your yeast doesn't foam it is dead, so you will have to discard it and start again.

ABOVE: Fougasse

GARLIC SOUP

The after-effects of the garlic in this soup are at a minimum because the garlic is boiled. In the Mediterranean, this soup is considered good for the health. Crush the cloves (about 20) from a whole bulb of garlic, using the side of a knife. Discard the skin and place the garlic in a large pan with 2 large sprigs of thyme, 1 litre chicken stock and and 1 cup (250 ml/8 fl oz) water. Bring to the boil, then reduce the heat and simmer, uncovered, for 20 minutes. Strain through a fine sieve into a clean pan. Add ¹/3 cup (80 ml/2³/4 fl oz) cream and reheat gently without allowing to boil. Season, to taste. Preheat the oven to moderate 180°C (350°F/Gas 4). Trim and discard the crusts from 4 thick slices of white bread and cut the bread into bite-sized cubes. Spread on a baking tray and bake for 5–10 minutes, until lightly golden. Distribute among soup bowls, then pour the soup over the bread. Garnish with extra thyme and serve immediately. Serves 4.

WALNUT BREAD

Preparation time: 45 minutes
  + 2 hours 30 minutes rising
Total cooking time: 50 minutes
Makes 1 loaf

☆ ☆

2¹/₂ teaspoons dried yeast
¹/₄ cup (90 g/3 oz) liquid malt
2 tablespoons olive oil
3 cups (300 g/10 oz) walnut halves, lightly
  toasted
4¹/₄ cups (530 g/1 lb 1 oz) white bread flour
1¹/₂ teaspoons salt
1 egg, lightly beaten

1 Grease a baking tray. Place the yeast, liquid malt and 1¹/₃ cups (350 ml/11 fl oz) warm water in a small bowl and stir well. Leave in a warm, draught-free place for 10 minutes, or until bubbles appear on the surface. The mixture should be frothy and slightly increased in volume. If your yeast doesn't foam it is dead, so you will have to discard it and start again. Stir in the oil.

2 Process 2 cups (200 g/6¹/₂ oz) of the walnuts in a food processor to a coarse meal. Combine 4 cups (500 g/1 lb) of the flour and the salt in a large bowl and stir in the walnut meal. Make a well and add the yeast mixture. Mix with a large metal spoon until just combined. Turn out onto a lightly floured surface and knead for 10 minutes, or until smooth, incorporating enough of the remaining flour to keep the dough from sticking—it should be soft and moist, but it won't become very springy. Shape the dough into a ball. Place in a lightly oiled bowl, cover with plastic wrap or a damp tea towel and leave in a warm place for up to 1¹/₂ hours, or until doubled.

3 Punch down the dough and turn out onto a lightly floured surface. With very little kneading, shape the dough into a 25 x 20 cm (10 x 8 inch) rectangle. Spread with the remaining walnuts and roll up firmly from the short end. Place the loaf on the baking tray, cover with plastic wrap or a damp tea towel and leave to rise for 1 hour, or until well risen and doubled in size.

4 Preheat the oven to moderately hot 190°C (375°F /Gas 5). Glaze the loaf with the egg and bake for 45–50 minutes, or until golden and hollow sounding when tapped. Transfer to a wire rack to cool.

NOTE: Use good-quality pale and plump walnuts as cheaper varieties can be bitter.

WALNUTS
Walnuts are thought to have originated in ancient China or Persia. In many countries of the Mediterranean, the word for walnut is also the word for nut. Fresh walnuts in the shell are far superior in taste to those shelled and packaged. When buying walnuts in the shell, choose those free of cracks and holes. Store in a cool dry place for up to three months. Shelled walnuts should be plump and crisp when you buy them. Store in an airtight container in the refrigerator for up to six months.

LEFT: Walnut bread

BEIGNUTS DE FRUITS

Gently fold the beaten egg white into the batter.

When golden, remove the fritters from the oil with a slotted spoon.

LAVENDER ICE CREAM

Preparation time: 15 minutes + freezing
Total cooking time: 15 minutes
Serves 6–8

☆ ☆

8 stems English lavender (or 4–6 if the lavender is in full flower as it has a stronger flavour)
2¹/2 cups (600 ml/20 fl oz) thick (double) cream
I small piece lemon rind
²/3 cup (160 g/5¹/2 oz) sugar
4 egg yolks, lightly whisked

1 Wash and dry the English lavender, then put it in a saucepan with the cream and lemon rind. Heat until almost boiling, then stir in the sugar until dissolved. Strain through a fine sieve, then gradually pour onto the egg yolks in a bowl, return to the pan and stir over low heat until thick enough to coat the back of a spoon — do not boil. Pour into a chilled metal tray to cool, or freeze in an ice cream machine, following the manufacturer's instructions. Freeze until frozen around the edge, but not in the centre.
2 In a food processor or bowl, beat until smooth. Freeze again and repeat this process twice more. Cover with greaseproof paper and freeze.

APRICOT COMPOTE

Preparation time: 15 minutes + cooling
Total cooking time: 30 minutes
Serves 4–6

☆

I orange
I lemon
I small vanilla bean, split
¹/2 cup (125 g/4 oz) sugar
I kg (2 lb) ripe, firm apricots, halved and seeded
I–2 tablespoons caster sugar

1 Peel two strips of rind about 5 cm (2 inches) long from both the orange and lemon. Squeeze all the juice from the orange (about 4 tablespoons) and 1 tablespoon from the lemon.
2 Place 3 cups (750 ml/24 fl oz) water in a saucepan, add the rind, vanilla bean and sugar and bring to the boil. Boil rapidly for 5 minutes.
3 Place the apricots in a wide saucepan and pour the hot syrup over the top. Gently bring to the boil and simmer until the apricots are tender.

This can take from 2–10 minutes, depending on the fruit. Do not damage the apricots by over-cooking. Transfer the apricots to a bowl, using a slotted spoon, and boil the syrup for 10 minutes, or until it thickens. Remove from the heat, allow to cool for 15 minutes, then stir in the juices. Taste for sweetness and add more sugar if necessary. Strain the sauce over the apricots. Serve warm or at room temperature.

BEIGNETS DE FRUITS

Preparation time: 25 minutes + 3 hours resting
Total cooking time: 10 minutes
Serves 4

☆

3 Granny Smith or golden delicious apples
70 g (2¹/4 oz) raisins
3 tablespoons Calvados or rum
I¹/2 tablespoons caster sugar
vegetable oil, for frying
2 tablespoons plain flour, for coating
icing sugar, for dusting

BATTER
I egg, separated
3¹/2 tablespoons warm beer
60 g (2 oz) plain flour
I teaspoon vegetable oil

1 Peel and core the apples and cut into 1 cm (¹/2 inch) cubes. Place in a bowl with the raisins, Calvados and sugar and marinate for 3 hours.
2 For the batter, beat the egg yolk and beer together in a large bowl. Blend in the flour and oil and add a pinch of salt. Stir until smooth. The batter will be very thick at this stage. Cover and leave in a warm place for 1 hour.
3 Pour the oil into a large saucepan to a depth of 10 cm (4 inches) and heat to 170°C (325°F), or until a cube of bread dropped into the oil browns in 20 seconds. Add 1¹/2 tablespoons of the Calvados marinade to the batter and stir until smooth. Whisk the egg white until stiff and gently fold into the batter. Drain the apples and raisins, toss with the flour to coat, then lightly fold them through the batter. Carefully lower heaped tablespoons of batter into the oil in batches and fry for 1–2 minutes, until the fritters are golden on both sides. Remove with a slotted spoon and drain on paper towels. Keep them warm. Dust with icing sugar and serve.

TART AU CITRON

Preparation time: 1 hour + refrigeration
Total cooking time: 1 hour 40 minutes
Serves 6–8

☆ ☆

PASTRY V

1 cup (125 g/4 oz) plain flour
75 g (2¹/2 oz) unsalted butter, softened
1 egg yolk
2 tablespoons icing sugar, sifted

3 eggs
2 egg yolks
³/4 cup (185 g/6 oz) caster sugar
¹/2 cup (125 ml/4 fl oz) cream
³/4 cup (185 ml/6 fl oz) lemon juice
1¹/2 tablespoons finely grated lemon rind
3 small lemons, washed and scrubbed
²/3 cup (160 g/5¹/2 oz) sugar

1 For the pastry, sift the flour and a pinch of salt into a large bowl. Make a well and add the butter, egg yolk and icing sugar. Work together the butter, yolk and sugar with your fingertips, then slowly incorporate the flour. Bring together into a ball—you may need to add a few drops of cold water. Flatten the ball slightly, cover with plastic wrap and refrigerate for 20 minutes.

2 Preheat the oven to moderately hot 200°C (400°F/Gas 6). Lightly grease a shallow loose-based flan tin, about 2 cm (³/4 inch) deep and 21 cm (8¹/2 inches) across the base.

3 Roll out the pastry between two sheets of baking paper until 3 mm (¹/8 inch) thick, to fit the base and side of the tin. Trim the edge. Chill for 10 minutes. Line the pastry with baking paper, fill with baking beads or rice and bake for 10 minutes, or until cooked. Remove the paper and beads and bake for 6–8 minutes, until the pastry looks dry all over. Cool the pastry and reduce the oven to slow 150°C (300°F/Gas 2).

4 Whisk the eggs, yolks and sugar together, add the cream and juice and mix. Strain into a jug and add the rind. Place the flan tin on a baking tray in the centre of the oven and pour in the filling right to the top. Bake for 40 minutes, or until just set—it should wobble in the middle when the tin is tapped. Cool before removing from the tin.

5 Cut the lemons into very thin (about 2 mm/ ¹/8 inch) slices. Blanch in simmering water for 5 minutes. Combine the sugar and 200 ml (6¹/2 fl oz) water in a small frying pan and stir over low heat until the sugar has dissolved. Add the lemon slices and simmer over low heat for 40 minutes, or until the peel is very tender and the pith looks transparent. Lift out of the syrup using a slotted spoon and drain on baking paper. If serving immediately, cover the surface with the lemon. If not, keep the slices covered and decorate the tart when ready to serve. Serve warm or chilled.

TART AU CITRON
Filled, flat, sweet tarts such as Tart au citron are typical of Provençal cooking. Although the filling is much like English lemon curd, it has a distinctly French character due to the addition of cream and the inclusion of whole eggs, not just the yolks.

RIGHT: Tart au citron

TOURTE DE BLETTES
This is one of Nice's most traditional and favoured desserts. The marriage of silverbeet with pine nuts and sultanas points back to the arrival of the Arab spice traders in the Mediterranean circa 827 AD. Although the combination may seem strange at first, you will be pleasantly surprised how complementary the flavours are. It makes a perfect picnic option and can be eaten warm or cold.

TOURTE DE BLETTES
(Apple, silverbeet/Swiss chard and pine nut pie)

Preparation time: 30 minutes
   + 30 minutes refrigeration
Total cooking time: 50 minutes
Serves 6–8

☆ ☆

60 g (2 oz) sultanas

2 tablespoons brandy

400 g (13 oz) plain flour

100 g (3¹/2 oz) icing sugar

250 g (8 oz) unsalted butter, softened
   and chopped

3 eggs

800 g (1 lb 10 oz) silverbeet (Swiss chard),
   stalks removed

100 g (3¹/2 oz) pine nuts, toasted

3 green cooking apples

1 teaspoon grated lemon rind

115 g (4 oz) mild goat's cheese

1 egg yolk, extra, for glazing

icing sugar, extra, for dusting

1 Soak the sultanas in the brandy. Sift the flour and 1 tablespoon icing sugar into a large bowl and rub in the butter with your fingertips until the mixture resembles fine breadcrumbs. Make a well, add 1 egg and mix with a flat-bladed knife, using a cutting action, until the mixture comes together in beads. Add 1 tablespoon water if the mixture is a little dry. Gather together and lift onto a lightly floured work surface. Press into a ball and flatten to a disc. Wrap in plastic wrap and refrigerate for 30 minutes.
2 Preheat the oven to moderate 180°C (350°F/Gas 4). Heat a baking tray in the oven.
3 Wash the silverbeet and pat dry. Place in a food processor with 2 eggs and the remaining icing sugar. Process to chop the silverbeet and combine, but don't overprocess. Transfer to a bowl. Drain the sultanas and add to the bowl with the pine nuts. Season with salt and pepper.
4 Bring the pastry to room temperature, then break into two portions. Roll one half and use to line a 26 cm (10¹/2 inch) loose-based tart tin.
5 Peel the apples, slice thinly and toss with the lemon rind. Place the silverbeet on the pastry and top with the crumbled goat's cheese. Spiral the apples on top, making one or two layers.
6 Roll out the remaining pastry and cover the pie. Trim off the excess pastry and seal the edges with a little water. Crimp the edges.
7 Brush the pie with the egg yolk and bake for 45–50 minutes, until golden. Cool slightly. Dust with icing sugar. Serve warm.

ABOVE: Tourte de blettes

PEARS POACHED IN WINE

Carefully place the pears in the saucepan and stir to gently coat with the wine mixture.

When the pears are cooked, leave them to cool before removing from the saucepan and draining on paper towels.

PEARS POACHED IN WINE

Preparation time: 20 minutes
Total cooking time: 45 minutes
Serves 4

☆

4 firm pears
3 cups (750 ml/24 fl oz) good-quality red wine
3/4 cup (185 g/6 oz) caster sugar
1 cinnamon stick
1/4 cup (60 ml/2 fl oz) orange juice
5 cm (2 inch) piece of orange rind
200 g (6 1/2 oz) mascarpone, for serving

1 Peel the pears, being careful to keep the pears whole with the stalks still attached.
2 Place the wine, sugar, cinnamon stick, orange juice and rind in a saucepan that is large enough for the pears to be able to stand upright. Stir over medium heat until sugar is dissolved. Add the pears to the saucepan and stir gently to coat. The pears should be almost covered with wine mixture. Cover the pan and simmer for 20–25 minutes, or until pears are cooked. Allow to cool in syrup.
3 Remove the pears with a slotted spoon. Bring the liquid to the boil and boil rapidly until about 3/4 cup (185 ml/6 fl oz) of liquid remains. Serve the pears with a little syrup and some mascarpone.

AMANDINE

Preparation time: 25 minutes
Total cooking time: 30 minutes
Serves 4–6

☆ ☆

100 g (3 1/2 oz) hazelnuts
120 g (4 oz) almonds, unblanched (with skins)
1 cup (185 g/6 oz) soft brown sugar
1 2/3 cups (410 g/13 oz) sugar
1/2 cup (175 g/6 oz) honey
1 lemon, halved
115 g (4 oz) unsalted butter

1 Preheat the oven to moderately warm 170°C (325°F/Gas 3). Spread the hazelnuts on a baking tray and roast for about 5 minutes, or until their skins crack. Remove from oven and reduce the temperature to slow 150°C (300°F/Gas 2). Wrap them in a tea towel, rub together to dislodge their skins and allow to cool. Put the skinned nuts into a processor. Place the almonds on the baking tray and bake for 6 minutes, or until browned. Allow to cool, then transfer the almonds to the processor. Chop the nuts until they look like little pebbles (a bit grainier than a coarse meal).
2 Grease a large flat heatproof surface such as marble, stainless steel or a large baking tray. Place 1/2 cup (125 ml4 fl oz) water in a heavy-based

ABOVE: Pears poached in wine

saucepan with the sugars and honey. Bring to the boil, stirring only until the sugars have melted. Remove any seeds visible in the lemon halves and squeeze 2–3 drops of juice into the boiling syrup. Reserve the lemons.

3 Simmer the syrup for 8–10 minutes, or until it reaches 150°C (300°F). Stir in the butter and, when melted, add the nuts. Pour onto the prepared surface and, using the lemon halves as tools, spread and smooth the toffee out to a very thin (5 mm/¼ inch) sheet. Leave to cool and set hard. Crack up into pieces for serving.

NOTE: Amandine can be used as a sprinkling for ice cream, a flavouring for cake fillings and icings, in desserts or sauces, or eaten with coffee.

CHERRY CLAFOUTIS
(French batter pudding)

Preparation time: 15 minutes
Total cooking time: 40 minutes
Serves 6–8

500 g (1 lb) fresh cherries (see Note)
¾ cup (90 g/3 oz) plain flour
2 eggs, lightly beaten
⅓ cup (90 g/3 oz) caster sugar
1 cup (250 ml/8 fl oz) milk
¼ cup (60 ml/2 fl oz) thick cream
60 g (2 oz) unsalted butter, melted
icing sugar, for dusting

1 Preheat the oven to moderate 180°C (350°F/ Gas 4). Lightly grease a 1.5 litre ovenproof dish with melted butter.
2 Pit the cherries and spread into the dish in a single layer.
3 Sift the flour into a bowl, add the eggs and whisk until smooth. Add the sugar, milk, cream and butter, whisking until just combined. Do not overbeat.
4 Pour the batter over the cherries and bake for 30–40 minutes, or until a skewer comes out clean when inserted into the centre. Dust generously with icing sugar before serving. Serve warm, straight from the oven.

NOTE: You can use a 720 g (1½ lb) jar of cherries if fresh ones aren't available. Make sure you drain it thoroughly before using the cherries.

CLAFOUTIS
A clafoutis (pronounced 'clafootee') is a classic French batter pudding traditionally made with cherries. However, other berries such as blueberries, blackberries, raspberries, or small, well-flavoured strawberries can be used instead. A delicious version can be made using slices of peach or pear.

LEFT: Cherry clafoutis

HOT FRUIT SOUFFLE

Preparation time: 15 minutes
Total cooking time: 30 minutes
Serves 4

☆ ☆

unsalted butter, melted, for greasing
caster sugar, for sprinkling
60 g (2 oz) unsalted butter, extra
1/2 cup (60 g/2 oz) plain flour
1 1/2 cups (375 ml/12 fl oz) puréed fruit
   (see Note)
1/4 cup (60 g/2 oz) caster sugar, extra
4 egg whites
icing sugar, to dust

BELOW: Hot fruit soufflé

1 Prepare a 1.25 litre soufflé dish by brushing melted butter evenly and generously over the dish, especially at the rim. Sprinkle with caster sugar, shake to coat evenly, then tip out any excess. Preheat the oven to moderately hot 200°C (400°F/Gas 6) and put a baking tray on the top shelf to heat.

2 Melt the extra butter in a saucepan, add the flour and mix well. Remove from the heat, stir until smooth, then stir in the fruit purée. Return the saucepan to the heat, bring the mixture to the boil and simmer for 2 minutes. Add the extra sugar a little at a time, tasting for sweetness as you go. Add a little extra sugar if necessary. Leave to cool.

3 Whisk the egg whites in a large clean bowl until soft peaks form, add 1 tablespoon to the fruit mixture and mix well. Fold in the remaining whites, being careful not to lose too much volume. Fill the soufflé dish to three-quarters full.

4 Put the soufflé dish on the hot baking tray and bake for 20–25 minutes, until risen well and golden. Serve immediately, dusted with icing sugar.

NOTE: To ensure success when making soufflés, make sure you fold the egg whites into the basic souffle mixture as gently as possible. It is better to leave a few pieces of egg white unmixed than to end up with a flat soufflé.

Suitable fruits to use are those that make a good purée, such as raspberries, strawberries, mangoes, peaches, apricots and passionfruit. Bananas are a little too heavy. You could use apples or plums, or dried fruit, but you'd have to cook them into a purée first.

FIGS POACHED IN RED WINE AND THYME

Soak 375 g (12 oz) dried whole figs in boiling water for 10 minutes, then drain. Put 1 cup (250 ml/8 fl oz) good-quality red wine and 2/3 cup (235 g/7 1/2 oz) honey in a saucepan, warm slightly over low heat, then add the dried figs and 4 sprigs of fresh thyme, tied with string. Cover and simmer for 10 minutes. Uncover and cook for another 10 minutes. Transfer the figs to a bowl and discard the thyme. Bring the syrup to the boil, then boil rapidly for 5–8 minutes, until the syrup is reduced and just coating the back of a spoon. Return the figs to the saucepan, stir to warm through, then allow to cool slightly. Serve warm or at room temperature, with cream. Garnish with extra thyme. Serves 4.

NOUGAT
Said to come from 'nux gatum', Latin for nut cake, the ancient ingredients of nougat are a key to its Mediterranean origins. Honey, almonds and other nuts were originally beaten with egg whites, then sun-dried. Today, the process is much quicker, although the flavourings remain the same.

NOUGAT

Preparation time: 30 minutes
+ 4 hours refrigeration
Total cooking time: 15 minutes
Makes 1 kg (2 lb)

☆ ☆

2 cups (500 g/1 lb) sugar

1 cup (250 ml/8 fl oz) liquid glucose

1/2 cup (175 g/6 oz) honey (preferably blossom honey)

2 egg whites

1 teaspoon vanilla essence

125 g (4 oz) unsalted butter, softened

60 g (2 oz) almonds, unblanched and toasted

100 g (3 1/2 oz) glacé cherries (not imitation)

 Grease a 28 x 18 cm (11 x 7 inch) baking dish and line with baking paper. Place the sugar, glucose, honey, 1/4 cup (60 ml/2 fl oz) water and 1/4 teaspoon salt in a heavy-based saucepan and stir over low heat until dissolved. Bring to the boil and cook at a rolling boil for 8 minutes, or until the mixture forms a hard ball when tested in a small amount of water, or reaches 122°C (225°F) on a sugar thermometer. The correct temperature is very important, otherwise the mixture will not set properly.

2 Beat the egg whites in a bowl with electric beaters until stiff peaks form. Slowly pour a quarter of the syrup onto the egg whites in a thin stream and beat for up to 5 minutes, or until the mixture holds its shape. Place the remaining syrup over the heat and cook for 2 minutes (watch that it doesn't burn), or until a small amount forms brittle threads when dropped in cold water, or reaches 157°C (315°F) on a sugar thermometer. Pour slowly onto the meringue mixture with the beaters running and beat until the mixture is very thick.

3 Add the vanilla and butter and beat for another 5 minutes. Stir in the almonds and cherries using a metal spoon. Turn the mixture into the tin and smooth the top with a palate knife. Refrigerate for at least 4 hours, or until firm. Turn out onto a large chopping board and with a very sharp knife cut into 4 x 2 cm (1 1/2 x 3/4 inch) pieces. Wrap each piece in cellophane and store in the refrigerator.

ABOVE: Nougat

SPAIN

Nothing evokes visions of Spain more than the idea of sitting at a small table at a tapas bar, perhaps out in the warm sunshine, eating delicious, small snacks and sipping a thirst-quenching glass of chilled wine or sherry. In these bars, the Spaniards are able to indulge their passion for seafood as they choose from dishes such as Stuffed mussels, Salt cod fritters or Barbecued prawns. Spanish food embraces a world of brilliant colour which typifies all aspects of the lifestyle. Above all, Spanish food is simple and makes the most of the freshest of ingredients. Chillies, chickpeas, rice, eggs and garlic all feature prominently. Many flavours have been borrowed from South America but Spanish food is not quite as hot and spicy.

EMPANADAS

Empanadas are traditional Spanish and Central American individual pastry turnovers. They usually have a savoury meat and vegetable filling, although they can also be filled with fruit and served as a dessert. They range from tiny, canapé size, to those large enough to feed a family.

ABOVE: Empanadas

EMPANADAS
(Spanish turnovers)

Preparation time: 45 minutes
Total cooking time: 25 minutes
Makes about 15

☆ ☆

2 eggs
40 g (1 1/4 oz) stuffed green olives, chopped
95 g (3 oz) ham, finely chopped
1/4 cup (30 g/1 oz) grated Cheddar
3 sheets ready-rolled puff pastry, thawed
1 egg yolk, lightly beaten

1 Place the eggs in a small saucepan, cover with water and bring to the boil. Boil for 10 minutes, then drain and cool for 5 minutes in cold water. Peel and chop.
2 Preheat the oven to hot 220°C (425°F/Gas 7). Lightly grease two baking trays. Combine the egg, olives, ham and Cheddar in a large bowl.
3 Cut about five 10 cm (4 inch) rounds from each pastry sheet. Spoon a tablespoon of the filling into the centre of each round, fold the pastry over and crimp the edges to seal.
4 Place the pastries on the trays, about 2 cm (3/4 inch) apart. Brush with the egg yolk and

bake in the centre or top half of the oven for 15 minutes, or until well browned and puffed. Swap the trays around after 10 minutes and cover loosely with foil if the empanadas start to brown too much. Serve hot.

GAMBAS AL PIL PIL
(Chilli garlic prawns)

Preparation time: 30 minutes
  + 30 minutes refrigeration
Total cooking time: 10 minutes
Serves 4–6

☆

1 kg (2 lb) medium raw prawns
60 g (2 oz) butter
1/3 cup (80 ml/2 3/4 fl oz) olive oil
3 cloves garlic, roughly chopped
1/4 teaspoon chilli flakes
1/2 teaspoon paprika

1 Peel the prawns, leaving the tails intact. Gently pull out the dark vein from each prawn back, starting at the head end. Mix the prawns with 1/2 teaspoon salt in a large bowl, cover and refrigerate for about 30 minutes.

2 Heat the butter and oil in a flameproof dish over medium heat. When foaming, add the garlic and chilli and stir for 1 minute, or until golden. Add the prawns, cook for 3–6 minutes, or until they change colour, then sprinkle with paprika. Serve hot with bread for dipping.
NOTE: Traditionally, Gambas al pil pil is made and served in small earthenware dishes, with one small dish serving two people. You can make this recipe in two small dishes but remember that it will cook more quickly.

CALAMARES A LA PLANCHA
(Barbecued squid)

Preparation time: 40 minutes + 30 minutes refrigeration
Total cooking time: 15 minutes
Serves 6

 ☆☆

500 g (1 lb) small squid (see Note)

PICADA DRESSING
2 tablespoons extra virgin olive oil
2 tablespoons finely chopped fresh flat-leaf parsley
1 clove garlic, crushed

1 To clean the squid, gently pull the tentacles away from the hood (the intestines should come away at the same time). Remove the intestines from the tentacles by cutting under the eyes, then remove the beak if it remains in the centre of the tentacles by using your fingers to push up the centre. Pull away the soft bone from the hood.
2 Rub the hoods under cold running water. The skin should come away easily. Wash the hoods and tentacles and drain well. Place in a bowl, add ¼ teaspoon salt and mix well. Cover and refrigerate for 30 minutes.
3 Heat a lightly oiled barbecue hotplate or preheat a grill to its highest setting.
4 Close to serving time, whisk the picada dressing ingredients with ¼ teaspoon ground black pepper and some salt in a jug or bowl.
5 Cook the squid hoods in small batches on the barbecue or under the grill for 2–3 minutes, or until the hoods turn white and are tender. Barbecue or grill the squid tentacles, turning to brown them all over, for 1 minute, or until they curl up. Serve hot, drizzled with the dressing.
NOTES: Bottleneck squid is the name given to the small variety of squid used in this recipe. If unavailable, choose the smallest squid you can find. You can also use cuttlefish, octopus, prawns or even chunks of firm white fish fillet.
Make the dressing as close to serving time as possible so the parsley doesn't discolour.

Gently pull the tentacles away from the squid hood.

Cut under the eyes, removing the intestines.

Remove the beak if it remains in the centre of the tentacles.

Pull away the soft bone, rinse the hoods and remove the skin.

LEFT: Calamares la plancha

MARINATED RED PEPPERS (CAPSICUMS)

Preparation time: 20 minutes
+ overnight marinating
Total cooking time: 5 minutes
Serves 6

3 red peppers (capsicums)
3 sprigs of fresh thyme
1 clove garlic, thinly sliced
2 teaspoons coarsely chopped fresh
   flat-leaf parsley
1 bay leaf
1 spring onion, sliced
1 teaspoon paprika
1/4 cup (60 ml/2 fl oz) extra virgin olive oil
2 tablespoons red wine vinegar

1   Preheat the grill. Cut the red peppers into quarters and grill, skin-side-up, until the skin blackens and blisters. Cool in a plastic bag, then peel. Slice thinly, then place in a bowl with the thyme, garlic, parsley, bay leaf and spring onion. Mix well.
2   Whisk together the paprika, oil, vinegar and some salt and pepper. Pour over the red pepper mixture and toss to combine. Cover and refrigerate for at least 3 hours, or preferably overnight. Remove from the refrigerator about 30 minutes before serving.
NOTE: These peppers can be refrigerated for up to 3 days.

TUNA SKEWERS WITH CAPERBERRIES

Soak 8 wooden skewers in cold water for 1 hour to prevent them burning during cooking. Cut 250 g (4 oz) raw tuna into 24 even-sized cubes. Remove the rind from a lemon, avoiding the bitter white pith, and cut the rind into thin strips. Combine the tuna, rind and 1 tablespoon each of lemon juice and olive oil in a bowl. Thread 3 pieces of tuna, 2 caperberries and a green olive, stuffed with anchovy fillet, onto each skewer, alternating each ingredient. Place in a non-metallic dish and pour the marinade over them. Grill under a hot grill for 4 minutes, turning to cook each side, or until done to your liking. Makes 8.

CHICKPEAS WITH CHORIZO SAUSAGE

Preparation time: 15 minutes
+ overnight soaking
Total cooking time: 1 hour 10 minutes
Serves 6

3/4 cup (165 g/5 1/2 oz) dried chickpeas
1 bay leaf
4 cloves
1 cinnamon stick
1 litre chicken stock
2 tablespoons olive oil
1 onion, finely chopped
1 clove garlic, crushed
pinch of dried thyme
375 g (12 oz) chorizo sausages, chopped
1 tablespoon chopped fresh flat-leaf parsley

1   Put the chickpeas in a large bowl, cover well with water and soak overnight. Drain well, then combine in a large saucepan with the bay leaf, cloves, cinnamon stick and stock. Cover well with water, bring to the boil, then reduce the heat and simmer for 1 hour, or until the chickpeas are tender. If they need more time, add a little more water. There should be just a little liquid left in the saucepan. Drain and remove the bay leaf, cloves and cinnamon stick.
2   Heat the oil in a large frying pan, add the onion and cook over medium heat for 3 minutes, or until translucent. Add the garlic and thyme and cook, stirring, for 1 minute. Increase the heat to medium-high, add the chorizo sausage and cook for 3 minutes.
3   Add the chickpeas to the frying pan, mix well, then stir over medium heat until they are heated through. Remove from the heat and mix in the parsley. Taste before seasoning, to taste, with salt and freshly ground black pepper. This dish is equally delicious served hot or at room temperature.

CINNAMON STICKS
Cinnamon sticks are the curled, thin pieces of bark of a tropical evergreen tree. The bark is removed during the rainy season when it is pliable and easy to work with. When it dries, it curls into quills which are then cut to size or ground to a powder. It is a much-prized spice in Spanish cooking, widely used in both sweet and savoury dishes. Cinnamon keeps its flavour best when whole, however if the recipe calls for ground cinnamon, buy a small quantity.

OPPOSITE PAGE:
Marinated red peppers (top);
Chickpeas with chorizo sausage

BARBECUED PRAWNS
WITH ROMESCO SAUCE

Squeeze the garlic and
scrape the tomato flesh
into a blender or processor.

Blend the mixture together
until quite smooth.

BARBECUED PRAWNS
WITH ROMESCO SAUCE

Preparation time: 30 minutes
  + 30 minutes refrigeration
  + 15 minutes cooling
Total cooking time: 25 minutes
Serves 6–8

☆ ☆

30 raw large prawns

ROMESCO SAUCE
4 cloves garlic, unpeeled
1 Roma tomato, halved and seeded
2 long fresh red chillies
1/4 cup (35 g/1 1/4 oz) blanched almonds
60 g (2 oz) sun-dried peppers (capsicums) in oil
1 tablespoon olive oil
1 tablespoon red wine vinegar

1 Peel the prawns, leaving the tails intact.
Gently pull out the dark vein from each
prawn back, starting at the head end. Mix
with 1/4 teaspoon salt and refrigerate for
30 minutes.

2 For the Romesco sauce, preheat the oven
to moderately hot 200°C (400°F/Gas 6).
Wrap the garlic in foil, place on a baking
tray with the tomato and chillies and bake
for 12 minutes. Spread the almonds on the
tray and bake for another 3–5 minutes. Leave
to cool for 15 minutes.
3 Transfer the almonds to a small blender or
food processor and blend until finely ground.
Squeeze the garlic and scrape the tomato flesh
into the blender, discarding the skins. Split the
chillies and remove the seeds. Scrape the flesh
into the blender, discarding the skins. Pat the
peppers dry with paper towels, then chop them
and add to the blender with the oil, vinegar,
some salt and 2 tablespoons water. Blend until
smooth, adding more water, if necessary, to
form a soft dipping consistency. Preheat a grill
or lightly oiled barbecue.
4 Brush the prawns with a little oil and cook
for 3 minutes, or until curled up and changed
colour. Serve with the sauce.
NOTE: Romesco sauce is traditionally served
with seafood. It can be made up to 5 days in
advance and stored in the refrigerator.

*RIGHT: Barbecued prawns
with Romesco sauce*

STUFFED MUSSELS

Preparation time: 40 minutes + cooling
Total cooking time: 20 minutes
Makes 18

18 black mussels
2 teaspoons olive oil
2 spring onions, finely chopped
1 clove garlic, crushed
1 tablespoon tomato paste (tomato purée)
2 teaspoons lemon juice
3 tablespoons chopped fresh flat-leaf parsley
1/3 cup (35 g/1 1/4 oz) dry breadcrumbs
2 eggs, beaten
oil, for deep-frying

WHITE SAUCE
40 g (1 1/4 oz) butter
1/4 cup (30 g/1 oz) plain flour
1/3 cup (80 ml/2 3/4 fl oz) milk

1   Scrub the mussels and remove the hairy beards. Discard any open mussels or those that don't close when tapped on the bench. Bring 1 cup (250 ml/4 fl oz) water to the boil in a saucepan, add the mussels, cover and cook for 3–4 minutes, shaking the pan occasionally, until the mussels have just opened. Remove them as soon as they open or they will be tough. Strain the liquid into a jug until you have 1/3 cup (80 ml/2 3/4 fl oz). Discard any unopened mussels. Remove the other mussels from their shells and discard one half shell from each. Finely chop the mussel meat.
2   Heat the oil in a pan, add the spring onion and cook for 1 minute. Add the garlic and cook for 1 minute. Stir in the mussels, tomato paste, lemon juice, 2 tablespoons of the parsley, salt and pepper, then set aside to cool.
3   For the white sauce, melt the butter in a saucepan over low heat. Stir in the flour and cook for 1 minute, or until pale and foaming. Remove from the heat and gradually whisk in the reserved mussel liquid, milk and some pepper. Return to the heat and boil, stirring, for 1 minute, or until the sauce boils and thickens. Reduce the heat and simmer for 2 minutes. Set aside to cool.
4   Spoon the mussel mixture into the shells. Top each with some of the sauce and smooth the surface, making the mixture heaped.
5   Combine the crumbs and remaining parsley. Dip the mussels in the egg, then press in the crumbs to cover the top. Fill a deep, heavy-based saucepan one third full of oil and heat to 180°C (350°F), or until a cube of bread dropped in the oil browns in 15 seconds. Cook the mussels in batches for 2 minutes each batch. Remove with a slotted spoon and drain well. Serve hot.

PAN CON TOMATE

Slice a baguette diagonally and toast the slices very lightly. Rub them on one side with a cut garlic clove, then with half a tomato, squeezing the juice onto the bread. Season with a little salt and drizzle with extra virgin olive oil. Serve as part of a tapas, or as a simple snack.

ABOVE: Stuffed mussels

CHORIZO

Chorizo is a popular sausage in Spanish cuisine and most regions have their own special variety. They are a pork sausage with a coarse texture, highly seasoned with paprika and garlic, and are either mild or made spicy with the addition of chillies. In Spain they are generally sold cured or smoked, and are indispensable in many traditional recipes. They can also be grilled, then cut into chunks and served as part of a tapas spread.

ALBONDIGAS EN PICANT SALSA DE TOMATE
(Meatballs in spicy tomato sauce)

Preparation time: 40 minutes
  + 30 minutes refrigeration
Total cooking time: 30 minutes
Serves 6

☆ ☆

175 g (6 oz) pork mince
175 g (6 oz) veal mince
3 cloves garlic, crushed
1/3 cup (35 g/1 1/4 oz) dry breadcrumbs
1 teaspoon ground coriander
1 teaspoon ground nutmeg
1 teaspoon ground cumin
pinch of ground cinnamon
1 egg
2 tablespoons olive oil

SPICY TOMATO SAUCE
1 tablespoon olive oil
1 onion, chopped
2 cloves garlic, crushed
1/2 cup (125 ml/4 fl oz) dry white wine
400 g (13 oz) can crushed good-quality
  tomatoes
1 tablespoon tomato paste (tomato purée)
1/2 cup (125 ml/4 fl oz) chicken stock
1/2 teaspoon cayenne pepper
1/2 cup (80 g/2 3/4 oz) frozen peas

1 Combine the minces, garlic, breadcrumbs, spices, egg and some salt and pepper in a bowl. Mix by hand until smooth and leaving the side of the bowl. Refrigerate, covered, for 30 minutes.
2 Roll tablespoons of mixture into balls. Heat 1 tablespoon of the oil in a frying pan and toss half the meatballs over medium-high heat for 2–3 minutes, until browned. Drain on paper towels. Add the remaining oil, if necessary, and brown the rest of the balls. Drain on paper towels.
3 For the sauce, heat the oil in a frying pan over medium heat and cook the onion, stirring occasionally, for 3 minutes, or until transparent. Add the garlic and cook for 1 minute. Increase the heat to high, add the wine and boil for 1 minute. Add the tomato, tomato paste and stock and simmer for 10 minutes. Add the cayenne, peas and meatballs. Simmer for 5–10 minutes, or until the sauce is thick. Serve hot.

CHORIZO EN SIDRA
(Chorizo in cider)

Preparation time: 5 minutes
Total cooking time: 15 minutes
Serves 4

☆ ☆

3 teaspoons olive oil
1 small onion, finely chopped
1 1/2 teaspoons paprika
1/2 cup (125 ml/4 fl oz) dry alcoholic
  apple cider
1/4 cup (60 ml/2 fl oz) chicken stock
1 bay leaf
280 g (9 oz) chorizo, sliced diagonally
2 teaspoons sherry vinegar, or to taste
2 teaspoons chopped fresh flat-leaf parsley

1 Heat the oil in a saucepan over low heat, add the onion and cook for 3 minutes, stirring occasionally, or until soft. Add the paprika and cook for 1 minute.
2 Increase the heat to medium, add the apple cider, stock and bay leaf to the pan and bring to the boil. Reduce the heat and simmer for 5 minutes. Add the sliced chorizo and simmer for 5 minutes, or until the sauce has reduced slightly. Stir in the sherry vinegar and parsley. Serve hot.

SALTED ALMONDS

Preheat the oven to very slow 120°C (250°F/Gas 1/2). In a large bowl, lightly whip an egg white and 1/4 teaspoon sweet paprika with a fork until the mixture starts to froth. Add 500 g (1 lb) blanched almonds and toss to coat evenly. Divide the nuts between two non-stick baking trays. Sprinkle with 1 1/2 tablespoons coarse sea salt grains (not flakes), turning the nuts several times so that the salt adheres to them. Spread over the trays. Bake for 30 minutes, turning the nuts over occasionally to prevent them sticking. Turn off the heat and leave the almonds in the oven for 30 minutes. When completely cooled, store in airtight jars. Serves 6–8.

OPPOSITE PAGE: Albondigas en picant salsa de tomate (top); Chorizo en sidra

BUNUELOS DE
BACALAO

Remove the skin and any
bones from the cooked
salt cod.

Fold the whisked egg white
into the potato and cod
mixture.

Deep-fry the fritters in hot
oil until puffed and golden.

BUNUELOS DE BACALAO
(Salt cod fritters)

Preparation time: 15 minutes + 24 hours soaking
Total cooking time: 1 hour
Makes 35

☆ ☆

500 g (1 lb) salt cod
1 large potato (200 g/6 1/2 oz), unpeeled
2 tablespoons milk
3 tablespoons olive oil
1 small onion, finely chopped
2 cloves garlic, crushed
1/4 cup (30 g/1 oz) self-raising flour
2 eggs, separated
1 tablespoon chopped fresh flat-leaf parsley
olive oil, extra, for deep-frying

1 Soak the cod in cold water for 24 hours,
changing the water regularly to remove as much
salt as possible. Cook the potato in a pan of
boiling water for 20 minutes, or until soft.
When cool, peel and mash with the milk
and 2 tablespoons of the olive oil.
2 Drain the cod, cut into large pieces and place
in a saucepan. Cover with water, bring to the
boil over high heat, then reduce the heat to
medium and cook for 10 minutes, or until soft
and there is a froth on the surface. Drain. When
cool enough to handle, remove the skin and any
bones, then mash well with a fork until flaky.
3 Heat the remaining oil in a small frying pan
and cook the onion over medium heat for
5 minutes, or until softened and starting to
brown. Add the garlic and cook for 1 minute.
Remove from the heat.
4 Combine the potato, cod, onion, flour, egg
yolks and parsley in a bowl and season. Whisk
the egg whites until stiff, then fold into the
mixture. Fill a large heavy-based saucepan one
third full of olive oil and heat to 190°C (375°F),
or until a cube of bread dropped into the oil
browns in 10 seconds. Drop heaped tablespoons
of mixture into the oil and cook for 2 minutes,
or until puffed and golden. Drain and serve.

RINONES AL JEREZ
(Kidneys in sherry)

Preparation time: 15 minutes
Total cooking time: 20 minutes
Serves 4

☆

2 tablespoons olive oil
1 large onion, finely chopped
2 cloves garlic, crushed
1 tablespoon plain flour
1 1/4 cups (315 ml/10 fl oz) chicken stock
1 tablespoon tomato paste (tomato purée)

1 bay leaf

1 kg (2 lb) lambs' kidneys, cut into halves

40 g (1 1/4 oz) butter

150 ml (5 fl oz) dry sherry

1 tablespoon chopped fresh flat-leaf parsley

1 Heat the oil in a frying pan and cook the onion and garlic over moderate heat for about 5 minutes, until the onion softens. Add the flour and cook, stirring, for 1 minute. Add the stock, tomato paste and bay leaf. Bring to the boil and cook, stirring, until thickened. Season with salt and ground black pepper and simmer for 3–4 minutes. Keep warm.

2 Cut out the white cores from the kidneys. Slice each half into three. Melt the butter in a large frying pan and add half the kidneys. Cook over high heat, stirring often, until they brown on all sides. Remove from the pan and cook the rest. Remove, pour the sherry into the pan and cook over high heat, stirring to deglaze, until reduced by half. Return the kidneys to the pan, add the sauce and stir the parsley through. Taste for seasoning and simmer for another 2 minutes before serving. Delicious with rice.

PATATAS BRAVAS
(Crisp potatoes in spicy tomato sauce)

Preparation time: 15 minutes
Total cooking time: 1 hour
Serves 6

☆ ☆

1 kg (2 lb) desiree potatoes

oil, for deep-frying

500 g (1 lb) ripe Roma tomatoes

2 tablespoons olive oil

1/4 red onion, finely chopped

2 cloves garlic, crushed

3 teaspoons paprika

1/4 teaspoon cayenne pepper

1 bay leaf

1 teaspoon sugar

1 tablespoon chopped fresh flat-leaf
   parsley, to garnish

1 Cut the potatoes into 2 cm (3/4 inch) cubes. Rinse, then drain well and pat completely dry. Fill a deepfryer or large heavy-based saucepan one third full of oil and heat to 180°C (350°F), or until a cube of bread dropped into the oil

browns in 15 seconds. Cook the potato in batches for 10 minutes, or until golden. Drain well on paper towels. Do not discard the oil.

2 Score a cross in the base of each tomato. Place in a bowl of boiling water for 10 seconds, then plunge into cold water and peel the skin away from the cross. Chop the flesh.

3 Heat the olive oil in a saucepan over medium heat and cook the onion for 3 minutes, or until softened. Add the garlic, paprika and cayenne, and cook for 1–2 minutes, until fragrant.

4 Add the tomato, bay leaf, sugar and 90 ml (3 fl oz) water, and cook, stirring occasionally, for 20 minutes, or until thick and pulpy. Cool slightly and remove the bay leaf. Blend in a food processor until smooth, adding a little water if necessary. Before serving, return the sauce to the saucepan and simmer over low heat for 2 minutes, or until heated though. Season well.

5 Reheat the oil to 180°C (350°F) and cook the potato again, in batches, for 2 minutes, or until very crisp and golden. Drain on paper towels. This second frying makes the potato extra crispy and stops the sauce soaking in immediately. Place on a platter and cover with sauce. Garnish with parsley and serve.

BELOW: Patatas bravas

CROQUETAS DEL
JAMON Y DE LA SETA

Roll portions of the mixture
into croquette shapes.

Use two forks to lower
each floured croquette into
the beaten egg.

CROQUETAS DEL JAMON Y DE LA SETA

(Ham and mushroom croquettes)

Preparation time: 35 minutes
+ 2 hours cooling
+ 30 minutes refrigeration
Total cooking time: 20 minutes
Makes 18

☆☆

90 g (3 oz) butter
1 small onion, finely chopped
110 g (3 1/2 oz) cap mushrooms, finely chopped
3/4 cup (90 g/3 oz) plain flour
1 cup (250 ml/4 fl oz) milk
3/4 cup (185 ml/6 fl oz) chicken stock
110 g (3 1/2 oz) ham, finely chopped
1/2 cup (60 g/2 oz) plain flour, extra
2 eggs, lightly beaten
1/2 cup (50 g/1 3/4 oz) dry breadcrumbs
oil, for deep-frying

1 Melt the butter in a saucepan over low heat, add the onion and cook for 5 minutes, or until translucent. Add the mushrooms and cook over low heat, stirring occasionally, for 5 minutes. Add the flour and stir over medium-low heat for 1 minute, or until the mixture is dry and crumbly and begins to change colour. Remove from the heat and gradually add the milk, stirring until smooth. Stir in the stock and return to the heat, stirring until the mixture boils and thickens. Stir in the ham and some black pepper, then transfer to a bowl to cool for about 2 hours.

2 Roll 2 tablespoons of mixture at a time into croquette shapes 6 cm (2 1/2 inches) long. Place the extra flour, beaten egg and breadcrumbs in three shallow bowls. Toss the croquettes in the flour, dip in the egg, allowing the excess to drain away, then roll in the breadcrumbs. Place on a baking tray and refrigerate for about 30 minutes.

3 Fill a deep, heavy-based saucepan one third full of oil and heat to 180°C (350°F), or until a cube of bread dropped into the oil browns in 15 seconds. Deep-fry the croquettes, in batches, for 3 minutes, turning, until brown. Drain well.

NOTE: You can vary these croquettes very easily to suit your taste. For example, they are delicious if you replace the ham with finely chopped chicken or flaked cooked fish and add your favourite finely chopped fresh herb.

RIGHT: Croquetas del
jamon y de la seta

GAMBAS AL AJILLO
(Garlic prawns)

Preparation time: 20 minutes
Total cooking time: 15 minutes
Serves 4

☆

1.25 kg (2¹/₂ lb) raw medium prawns
80 g (2³/₄ oz) butter, melted
³/₄ cup (185 ml/6 fl oz) olive oil
8 cloves garlic, crushed
2 spring onions, thinly sliced

1 Preheat the oven to very hot 250°C (500°F/
Gas 10). Peel the prawns, leaving the tails intact.
Pull out the vein from each back, starting at the
head end. Cut a slit down the back of each prawn.
2 Combine the butter and oil and divide among
four 500 ml (16 fl oz) cast iron pots. Divide half
the crushed garlic among the pots.
3 Place the pots on a baking tray and heat in
the oven for 10 minutes, or until the mixture is
bubbling. Remove and divide the prawns and
remaining garlic among the pots. Return to the
oven for 5 minutes, or until the prawns are
cooked. Stir in the spring onion. Season, to
taste. Serve with bread to mop up the juices.
NOTE: Garlic prawns can also be made in a cast
iron frying pan in the oven or on the stovetop.

CHAMPINONES AL AJILLO
(Garlic mushrooms)

Preparation time: 10 minutes
Total cooking time: 15 minutes
Serves 4

☆

6 cloves garlic
1¹/₂ tablespoons lemon juice
650 g (1 lb 5 oz) button mushrooms, sliced
¹/₄ cup (60 ml/2 fl oz) olive oil
¹/₄ small fresh red chilli, finely chopped
2 teaspoons chopped fresh flat-leaf parsley

1 Crush four of the garlic cloves and finely slice
the rest. Sprinkle the lemon juice over the
sliced mushrooms.
2 Heat the oil in a large frying pan and add
the crushed garlic and chopped chilli. Stir over
medium-high heat for 10 seconds, then add the
mushrooms. Season and cook, stirring often, for
8–10 minutes. Stir in the sliced garlic and parsley
and cook for another minute. Serve hot.
NOTE: You can also use field, Swiss brown or
any wild mushrooms for this recipe, but take
care to adjust the cooking times if you use the
more fragile wild mushrooms.

GAMBAS AL AJILLO
In Spain, this is one of
the most popular tapas
dishes served in bars and
restaurants all around
the coastal regions. It is
traditional for them to be
served in the dish that they
have been cooked in, and
this is usually a small cast
iron or glazed terracotta
pot. It is served with crusty
bread so that all the juices
and crispy flavours can be
mopped up and savoured.

ABOVE: Gambas al ajillo

SARDINAS MURCIANA
(Murcia-style sardines)

Preparation time: 20 minutes
Total cooking time: 30 minutes
Serves 6

1 kg (2 lb) ripe tomatoes
24 fresh large sardines, cleaned, with
   backbones, heads and tails removed
2 green peppers (capsicums), cored,
   seeded and cut into thin rings
2 onions, sliced into thin rings
2 potatoes, cut into 5 mm (1/4 inch) slices
2 tablespoons chopped fresh flat-leaf parsley
3 cloves garlic, crushed
1/4 teaspoon saffron threads, lightly toasted
2 tablespoons olive oil
chopped fresh flat-leaf parsley, extra, for
   serving, optional

1 Score a cross in the base of each tomato and plunge in boiling water for 10 seconds. Transfer to cold water and peel away from the cross. Cut each tomato into thin slices.
2 Preheat the oven to moderate 180°C (350°F/ Gas 4). Oil a large shallow earthenware or ceramic baking dish wide enough to hold the length of the sardines. Open out the sardines and lightly sprinkle the insides with salt. Fold them back into their original shape.
3 Cover the base of the prepared dish with a third of the tomatoes. Layer half the sardines on top. Follow with a layer of half the peppers, then half the onion, then half the potatoes. Sprinkle with half the parsley and garlic and season with freshly ground black pepper. Crumble half the saffron over the top.
4 Layer the remaining sardines, a third of the tomatoes and then the other ingredients as before. Finish with the last of the tomatoes. Season well with salt and freshly ground black pepper. Drizzle the oil over the surface and cover with foil. Bake for 30 minutes, or until the potatoes are cooked. Sprinkle with parsley. Spoon off any excess liquid. Serve straight from the dish.
NOTE: The bodies of the sardines should be about 15 cm (6 inches) long.

ESCABECHE
(Pickled fried fish)

Preparation time: 20 minutes
  + overnight refrigeration
Total cooking time: 15 minutes
Serves 4

plain flour, for dusting
500 g (1 lb) skinless fish fillets
   (e.g. red mullet, whiting, redfish, garfish)
5 tablespoons extra virgin olive oil
1 red onion, thinly sliced
2 cloves garlic, thinly sliced
2 sprigs of fresh thyme
1 teaspoon ground cumin
2 spring onions, finely chopped
1/2 teaspoon finely grated orange rind
1/4 cup (60 ml/2 fl oz) orange juice
3/4 cup (185 ml/6 fl oz) white wine
3/4 cup (185 ml/6 fl oz) white wine vinegar
60 g (2 oz) pitted green olives,
   roughly chopped
1/2 teaspoon caster sugar

1 Mix a little salt and pepper into the flour and dust the fish lightly with the flour. Heat 2 tablespoons of the oil in a frying pan over medium heat and add the fish in batches. Cook the fish on both sides until lightly browned and just cooked through (the fish should flake easily when tested with a fork). Remove from the pan and place in a single layer in a large shallow, non-metallic dish.
2 Heat the remaining oil in the same pan, add the onion and garlic and cook, stirring over medium heat for about 5 minutes, or until soft.
3 Add the thyme, cumin and spring onion and stir until fragrant. Add the orange rind, juice, wine, vinegar, olives, sugar and pepper, to taste. Bring to the boil and pour over the fish. Allow to cool in the liquid, or refrigerate overnight. Serve at room temperature.
NOTE: Traditionally, escabeche is made using whole fish. We have used fish fillets which also work well.

OPPOSITE PAGE: Sardinas murciana (top); Escabeche

CLAMS

When buying clams, look for ones with tightly closed shells. Before cooking, they need to be soaked in salted water for at least an hour as this helps them to purge any grit. Clams only require gentle cooking, otherwise they will be tough and chewy. Like other molluscs such as mussels, once cooked, any that haven't opened must be discarded as they were dead before being cooked.

ALMEJAS A LA MARINERA
(Clams in white wine)

Preparation time: 10 minutes
  + 1 hour soaking
Total cooking time: 20 minutes
Serves 4

1 kg (2 lb) clams
2 large, ripe tomatoes
2 tablespoons olive oil
1 small onion, finely chopped
2 cloves garlic, crushed
1 tablespoon chopped fresh flat-leaf parsley
pinch of nutmeg
1/3 cup (80 ml/2³/4 fl oz) dry white wine

1 Soak the clams in salted water for 1 hour to release any grit. Rinse under running water and discard any open clams.
2 Score a cross in the base of each tomato. Place in a bowl of boiling water for 10 seconds, then plunge into cold water and peel away from the cross. Cut the tomatoes in half and scoop out the seeds with a teaspoon. Finely chop the tomatoes.
3 Heat the oil in a large flameproof casserole and cook the onion over low heat for 5 minutes, or until softened. Add the garlic and tomato and cook for 5 minutes. Stir in the parsley and nutmeg and season with salt and pepper. Add 1/3 cup (80 ml/2³/4 fl oz) water.
4 Add the clams and cook over low heat until they open. Discard any that don't open. Add the wine and cook over low heat for 3–4 minutes, until the sauce thickens, gently moving the casserole back and forth a few times, rather than stirring the clams, so that the clams stay in the shells. Serve at once, with bread.
NOTE: You can use clams instead of mussels in this recipe.

ABOVE: Almejas a la marinera

ALCACHOFAS EN AROMATICO VINAIGRETTE
(Artichokes in aromatic vinaigrette)

Preparation time: 20 minutes + cooling
Total cooking time: 20 minutes
Serves 4

2 tablespoons lemon juice

4 large globe artichokes

2 cloves garlic, crushed

1 teaspoon finely chopped fresh oregano

1/2 teaspoon ground cumin

1/2 teaspoon ground coriander

pinch dried chilli flakes

3 teaspoons sherry vinegar

1/4 cup (60 ml/2 fl oz) olive oil

1 Add the lemon juice to a large bowl of cold water. Trim the artichokes, cutting off the stalks to within 5 cm (2 inches) of the base of each artichoke and removing the tough outer leaves. Cut off the top quarter of the leaves from each. Slice each artichoke in half from top to base, or into quarters if large. Remove each small, furry choke with a teaspoon, then place each artichoke in the bowl of acidulated water to prevent it from discolouring while you prepare the rest.

2 Bring a large non-aluminium saucepan of water to the boil, add the artichokes and a teaspoon of salt and simmer for 20 minutes, or until tender. The cooking time will depend on the artichoke size. Test by pressing a skewer into the base. If cooked, the artichoke should be soft and give little resistance. Strain, then place the artichokes on their cut side to drain while cooling.

3 Combine the garlic, oregano, cumin, coriander and chilli flakes in a small bowl. Season with salt and pepper and blend in the vinegar. Beating constantly, slowly pour in the olive oil to form an emulsion. This step can be done in a small food processor.

4 Arrange the artichokes in rows on a serving platter. Pour the vinaigrette over the top and leave to cool completely.

BELOW: Alcachofas en aromatico vinaigrette

SCALLOPS CEVICHE

Pull away the dark vein and white muscle from each scallop.

Stir the scallops to coat in the marinade.

TORTILLA

Preparation time: 25 minutes
Total cooking time: 20 minutes
Serves 6–8

☆☆

500 g (1 lb) potatoes, cut into 1 cm
   (¹/₂ inch) slices
¹/₄ cup (60 ml/2 fl oz) olive oil
1 brown onion, thinly sliced
4 cloves garlic, thinly sliced
2 tablespoons finely chopped fresh flatleaf parsley
6 eggs

1 Place the potato slices in a large pan, cover with cold water and bring to the boil over high heat. Boil for 5 minutes, then drain and set aside.
2 Heat the oil in a deep-sided non-stick frying pan over medium heat. Add the onion and garlic and cook for 5 minutes, or until the onion softens.
3 Add the potato and parsley to the pan and stir to combine. Cook over medium heat for 5 mintues, gently pressing down into the pan.
4 Whisk the eggs with 1 teaspoon each of salt and freshly ground black pepper and pour evenly over the potato. Cover and cook for about 20 minutes, on low–medium heat until the eggs are just set. Slide onto a serving plate or serve directly from the pan.

SCALLOPS CEVICHE

Preparation time: 20 minutes + 2 hours marinating
Total cooking time: Nil
Makes 15

☆☆

15 scallops on the half shell
1 teaspoon finely grated lime rind
¹/₄ cup (60 ml/2 fl oz) lime juice
2 cloves garlic, chopped
2 red chillies, seeded and chopped
1 tablespoon chopped fresh parsley
1 tablespoon olive oil

1 Take the scallops off their half shell. If they need to be cut off the shell, use a small, sharp paring knife to slice the attached part from the shell, being careful to leave as little scallop meat on the shell as possible. Remove the dark vein and white muscle from each and wash the shells.
2 In a non-metallic bowl, mix the lime rind and juice, garlic, chilli, parsley and oil and season with salt and ground black pepper. Add the scallops and stir to coat. Cover with plastic wrap and refrigerate for 2 hours to 'cook' the scallop meat.
3 To serve, slide the scallops onto the half shells and spoon the dressing over them. Serve cold.
NOTE: These scallops will keep for up to 2 days in the dressing.

RIGHT: Tortilla

PIQUANT POTATO SALAD

Preparation time: 10 minutes
Total cooking time: 10 minutes
Serves 4

500 g (1 lb) baby chat potatoes
2 teaspoons chopped fresh dill
2 spring onions, chopped
1 tablespoon capers, coarsely chopped
2 tablespoons extra virgin olive oil
1 1/2 tablespoons lemon juice
1 teaspoon finely grated orange rind

1 Place the potatoes in a large saucepan of salted water and bring to the boil. Cook for 10 minutes, or until tender when pierced with a knife. Drain well.
2 Place the potatoes in a bowl with the dill, onion, capers and some salt and pepper. Mix well to combine. Whisk together the oil, lemon juice and orange rind in a small jug and pour over the hot potatoes. Toss to coat the potatoes and serve warm.
NOTE: Any small, waxy potato works well in this delicious salad. You can choose from those which are readily available such as pink fir, bintje or kipfler.

BROAD BEANS WITH HAM

Preparation time: 10 minutes
Total cooking time: 30 minutes
Serves 4

20 g (3/4 oz) butter
1 onion, chopped
180 g (6 oz) serrano ham, roughly chopped (see Note)
2 cloves garlic, crushed
500 g (1 lb) broad beans, fresh or frozen
1/2 cup (125 ml/4 fl oz) dry white wine
3/4 cup (185 ml/6 fl oz) chicken stock

1 Melt the butter in a large saucepan and add the onion, ham and garlic. Cook over medium heat for 5 minutes, stirring often, until the onion softens.
2 Add the broad beans and wine and cook over high heat until reduced by half. Add the stock, reduce the heat, cover and cook, for 10 minutes. Uncover and simmer for another 10 minutes. Serve hot as a vegetable accompaniment to meat, or warm as a snack with crusty bread.
NOTE: Instead of serrano ham, you can use thickly sliced prosciutto, choosing one which is pink, soft and sweet, not dry and salty.

SERRANO HAM
'Jamon serrano' is the name given to Spanish salt-cured and air-dried ham. The method of production is carefully controlled to ensure a quality product, and is used in many dishes in all regions of Spain, as well as simply served in thick slices, topped with pimento, as a tapas dish. Serrano ham is left to dry for a mininum of twelve months, and the most deliciously flavoured Serrano has been left to mature for eighteen months.

LEFT: Piquant potato salad

ESCALIVADA
(Grilled vegetable salad)

Preparation time: 15 minutes
+ 30 minutes cooling
Total cooking time: 10 minutes
Serves 4

☆

1 red onion
6 small eggplants (aubergines), not pencil
   eggplant, about 16 cm (6½ inches) long
4 red peppers (capsicums)
4 orange peppers (capsicums)
1 tablespoon baby capers
⅓ cup (80 ml/2¾ fl oz) good-quality olive oil
1 tablespoon chopped fresh flat-leaf parsley
2 cloves garlic, finely chopped

1 Without slicing through the base, cut the onion from top to base into 6 sections, leaving it attached at the base. Place on a barbecue, or over an open-flamed grill or gas stovetop, with the eggplants and peppers. Cook over moderate heat for about 10 minutes, turning occasionally, until the eggplants and pepper skins are blackened and blistered. Cool the peppers in a plastic bag for 10 minutes and set the onion and eggplant aside.
2 Dry-fry the capers with a pinch of salt until crisp. Cut the onion into its 6 sections and discard the charred outer skins. Peel the skins off the eggplants and remove the stalk. Cut from top to bottom into slices. Peel the peppers and remove the seeds. Cut into wide slices. Arrange all the vegetables on a large serving platter. Drizzle the olive oil over them and season with salt and pepper. Scatter the parsley, garlic and capers over the top. Serve cold as a salad or warm as an accompaniment to grilled meats.
NOTE: Grilling the vegetables under a griller or roasting them in a hot oven also works, although the dish will lack the characteristic smoky flavour.

ESPARRAGO DE ANDALUCIA
(Andalucian asparagus)

Preparation time: 10 minutes
Total cooking time: 15 minutes
Serves 4

☆

500 g (1 lb) fresh asparagus
¼ cup (60 ml/2 fl oz) extra virgin olive oil
1 thick slice crusty country bread, crusts
   removed and cut into cubes
2–3 cloves garlic
12 blanched almonds
1 teaspoon paprika
1 teaspoon ground cumin
1 tablespoon red wine or sherry vinegar

1 Trim the woody ends from the asparagus.
2 Heat the oil in a heavy-based frying pan and cook the bread, garlic and almonds over medium heat for 2–3 minutes, or until all the ingredients are golden. Using a slotted spoon, transfer to a food processor and add the paprika, cumin, vinegar, salt and pepper and 1 tablespoon water. Process until the mixture forms a coarse meal.
3 Return the frying pan to the heat and add the asparagus with a little extra oil if necessary. Cook over medium heat for 3–5 minutes, then add the bread and almond mixture with 200 ml (6½ fl oz) water. Simmer for 3–4 minutes, or until the asparagus is tender but still firm to the bite and most of the liquid has boiled away. Serve.

BELOW: Escalivada

INSALATA RUSSA
(Russian salad)

Preparation time: 40 minutes
Total cooking time: 40 minutes
Serves 4–6

☆

MAYONNAISE

2 egg yolks

1 teaspoon Dijon mustard

1/2 cup (125 ml/4 fl oz) extra virgin olive oil

2 tablespoons lemon juice

2 small cloves garlic, crushed

3 canned artichoke hearts (about 120 g/4 oz)

3 waxy potatoes such as desiree, unpeeled

100 g (3 1/2 oz) baby green beans, trimmed and
cut into 1 cm (1/2 inch) lengths

1 large carrot, cut into 1 cm (1/2 inch) dice

125 g (4 oz) fresh peas

30 g (1 oz) cornichons, chopped

2 tablespoons baby capers, rinsed

10 black olives cut into 3 slices

4 anchovy fillets, finely chopped

5 whole black olives, to garnish

1 For the mayonnaise, using electric beaters, beat the egg yolks with the mustard and 1/4 teaspoon salt until creamy. Gradually add the oil in a fine stream, beating constantly until all the oil has been added. Add the lemon juice, garlic and 1 teaspoon boiling water and beat for 1 minute until well combined. Season, to taste.

2 Cut each artichoke into quarters. Rinse the potatoes, cover with cold, salted water and bring to a gentle simmer. Cook for 15–20 minutes, or until tender when pierced with a knife. Drain and allow to cool slightly. Peel and set aside. When the potatoes are completely cool, cut into 1 cm (1/2 inch) dice.

3 Blanch the beans in boiling salted water until tender but still firm to the bite. Refresh in cold water, then drain thoroughly. Repeat with the carrot and peas.

4 Set aside a small quantity of each vegetable, including the cornichons, for the garnish and season, to taste. Place the remainder in a bowl with the capers, anchovies and sliced olives. Add the mayonnaise, toss to combine and season, to taste. Arrange on a serving dish and garnish with the reserved vegetables and the whole olives.

NOTE: This Russian salad can be prepared up to 2 days in advance and stored in the refrigerator but should be served at room temperature.

INSALATA RUSSA
Insalata Russa is served in tapas bars all over Spain and is said to date back to the time of the Napoleonic Wars when many French were residing in Spain and brought with them the Russian 'trend' popular in Paris at the time.

BELOW: Insalata Russa

TAPAS

The eating of tapas lies at the heart of Spanish tradition, where friends come together to share bowls of simple yet delicious morsels washed down with a glass of chilled sherry or wine.

ORIGINS OF TAPAS

The word 'tapa' means literally 'lid' in Spanish. This comes from the days when bar owners served their customers a drink with an edible lid placed over the glass to keep out the flies. Cheese and sausage were then added to make it more appealing and encourage trade. From here grew the extraordinary variety of tapas found today in bars all over Spain, ranging from a simple bowl of marinated olives or a plate of sliced Serrano ham, to warm salt cod fritters or bubbling dishes of garlic prawns.

Like many countries in Europe, the food of Spain differs quite significantly from region to region, all responding to different climatic, geographical and historical influences. These regional variations are best characterized by the Spanish saying which refers to both climate and cooking technique: 'In the north you stew, in the central region, you roast, in the east you simmer, and in the south you fry.'

So while tapas bars in the south of Spain take full advantage of not only an abundance of fresh seafood but also the rich history of Arabic influences, further inland towards the north, heartier tapas dishes of pulses and meat provide comfort from often inhospitable weather whilst embracing many influences from northern neighbours.

There are a few dishes, however, that do not have culinary borders and can be

found in tapas bars all over Spain. The most simple of these 'national' favourites is the raw Serrano ham or 'mountain ham'. Similar to prosciutto although with its own distinct flavour, Jamon serrano is very lean and depending on age, even a little tough due to the fact that the pigs are well exercised from roaming in the forest. It is also reputed to be the sweetest ham in the world. The ham is usually served very simply, just sliced and served on a plate with some country-style bread and a glass of wine.

The dishes we have shown on this page are popular tapas fare, but there are many others that are enjoyed in most parts of Spain. These include Escalivada (page 216), Patatas bravas (page 205), Tortilla (page 212) and Cocido madrileno (page 235), a one-pot dish of meats, sausages and vegetables, although each varies from region to region incorporating local flavours and fresh produce.

Like the Italian antipasti, tapas are perfect entertaining options because most of the food can be prepared in advance. Fried dishes are the exception as they should be served straight after cooking. Almost any of the dishes in this chapter can be served as tapas because it is really only the size of the portions which makes them appetizers. However, because tapas are intended to whet the appetite, they tend to be those dishes which are rich in spice, garlic, lemon or vinegar. All the recipes from pages 196 to 217 are classic tapas dishes. However, more substantial dishes such as Salt cod with red peppers (page 227) or Rice with stuffed squid (page 224) also work well as part of a selection for a larger party.

The tiny oval dishes traditionally used in Spain are becoming more readily available from homeware stores. Regular small plates can also be used. As well as Spanish olives, chunks of rustic, country style bread should also accompany every tapas meal. Keep in mind that nearly all the dishes in this chapter can be adapted to suit your needs, whether you are serving two people or twenty.

CLOCKWISE, FROM TOP LEFT: Serrano ham; Chorizo; Bread; Albondigas en picant salsa de tomate (Meatballs in spicy tomato sauce); Olives; Tortilla; Gambas al ajillo (Garlic prawns)

219

GARNISH

¹/₂ Lebanese cucumber, seeded, finely diced

¹/₂ red pepper (capsicum), seeded, finely diced

¹/₂ green pepper (capsicum), seeded, finely diced

¹/₂ red onion, finely diced

¹/₂ ripe tomato, diced

1 Score a cross in the base of each tomato. Place in a bowl of boiling water for 10 seconds, then plunge into cold water and peel away from the cross. Cut the tomatoes in half and scoop out the seeds with a teaspoon. Chop the tomatoes.

2 Soak the bread in cold water for 5 minutes, then squeeze out any excess liquid. Place the bread in a food processor with the tomato, pepper, garlic, chilli, sugar and vinegar, and process until combined and smooth.

3 With the motor running, add the oil to make a smooth creamy mixture. Season, to taste. Refrigerate for at least 2 hours. Add a little extra vinegar, if desired.

4 For the garnish, mix the ingredients in a bowl. Put 2 ice cubes in each bowl of soup and serve the garnish in separate bowls.

AJO BLANCO

(Chilled garlic and almond soup)

Preparation time: 20 minutes + 5 minutes
    soaking + 2 hours refrigeration
Total cooking time: 3 minutes
Serves 4–6

☆

1 loaf (200 g/6¹/₂ oz) day-old white Italian bread,
    crust removed

1 cup (155 g/5 oz) whole blanched almonds

3–4 cloves garlic, chopped

¹/₂ cup (125 ml/4 fl oz) extra virgin olive oil

¹/₃ cup (80 ml/2³/₄ fl oz) sherry or white
    wine vinegar

1¹/₄–1¹/₂ cups (315–375 ml/10–12 oz) vegetable
    stock

2 tablespoons olive oil, extra

75 g (2³/₄ oz) day-old white Italian bread, extra,
    crust removed, cut into 1 cm (¹/₂ inch) cubes

200 g (6¹/₂ oz) small seedless green grapes

1 Soak the bread in cold water for 5 minutes, then squeeze out any excess liquid. Chop the almonds and garlic in a processor until well ground. Add the bread and process until smooth.

RED GAZPACHO

(Cold tomato soup)

Preparation time: 40 minutes + 5 minutes
    soaking + 2 hours refrigeration
Total cooking time: Nil
Serves 4

☆

1 kg (2 lb) vine-ripened tomatoes

2 slices day-old white Italian bread, crust
    removed, broken into pieces

1 red pepper (capsicum), seeded, roughly
    chopped

2 cloves garlic, chopped

1 small fresh green chilli, chopped, optional

1 teaspoon sugar

2 tablespoons red wine vinegar

2 tablespoons extra virgin olive oil

8 ice cubes

ABOVE: Red gazpacho

2 With the motor running, add the oil in a steady slow stream until the mixture is the consistency of thick mayonnaise. Slowly add the sherry and 1¼ cups (315 ml/10 fl oz) of the stock. Blend for 1 minute. Season with salt. Refrigerate for at least 2 hours. The soup thickens on refrigeration so you may need to add stock or water to thin it.

3 When ready to serve, heat the extra oil in a frying pan, add the bread cubes and toss over medium heat for 2–3 minutes, or until golden. Drain on paper towels. Serve the soup very cold. Garnish with the grapes and bread cubes.

ZARZUELA DE PESCADO
(Catalan fish stew)

Preparation time: 30 minutes
Total cooking time: 35 minutes
Serves 6–8

☆ ☆ ☆

300 g (10 oz) red mullet fillets

400 g (13 oz) firm white fish fillets

300 g (10 oz) cleaned calamari

1.5 litres fish stock

⅓ cup (80 ml/2¾ fl oz) olive oil

1 onion, chopped

6 cloves garlic, chopped

1 small fresh red chilli, chopped

1 teaspoon paprika

pinch of saffron threads

150 ml (5 fl oz) white wine

400 g (13 oz) can crushed good-quality tomatoes

16 raw medium prawns, peeled and deveined, tails intact

2 tablespoons brandy

24 black mussels, cleaned

1 tablespoon chopped fresh parsley

PICADA

2 tablespoons olive oil

2 slices day-old bread, cubed

2 cloves garlic

5 blanched almonds, toasted

2 tablespoons fresh flat-leaf parsley, to garnish

1 Cut the fish and calamari into 4 cm (1½ inch) even-sized pieces. Pour the stock into a large saucepan, bring to the boil and boil for 15–20 minutes, or until reduced by half.

2 For the picada, heat the oil in a frying pan, add the bread and stir for 2–3 minutes, or until golden, adding the garlic for the last minute. Process the bread, garlic, almonds and parsley in a food processor and add enough of the stock to make a smooth paste.

3 Heat 2 tablespoons of the oil in a large saucepan, add the onion, garlic, chilli and paprika, and cook, stirring, for 1 minute. Add the saffron, wine, tomato and stock. Bring to the boil, then reduce the heat and simmer.

4 Heat the remaining oil in a frying pan over medium heat and fry the fish and calamari for 3–5 minutes. Remove. Add the prawns, cook for 1 minute and then pour in the brandy. Ignite the brandy and let the flames burn down. Remove from the pan.

5 Add the mussels to the stock and simmer, covered, for 2–3 minutes, or until opened. Discard any that do not open. Add all the seafood and the picada, stirring until the sauce has thickened and the seafood has cooked. Season, to taste. Serve garnished with parsley.

BELOW: Zarzuela de pescado

FISH BAKED IN SALT

Preparation time: 20 minutes
Total cooking time: 30–40 minutes
Serves 4–6

☆☆

1.8 kg (3 lb 10 oz) whole fish (e.g. blue-eye,
   jewfish, sea bass, groper), scaled and cleaned
2 lemons, sliced
4 sprigs of fresh thyme
1 fennel bulb, thinly sliced
3 kg (6 lb) rock salt

1 Preheat the oven to moderately hot 200°C
(400°F/Gas 6). Rinse the fish and pat dry inside
and out with paper towel. Place the lemon,
thyme and fennel inside the cavity.
2 Pack half the salt into a large baking dish and
place the fish on top. Cover with the remaining
salt, pressing down until the salt is packed firmly
around the fish.
3 Bake the fish for 30–40 minutes, or until a
skewer inserted into the centre of the fish comes
out hot. Carefully remove the salt from the top
of the fish to one side of the pan. Peel the skin
away, ensuring that no salt remains on the flesh.
Serve hot or cold with aïoli (see page 153) or
your choice of accompaniment.

BAKING FISH IN A SALT CRUST

A natural companion to
fish, salt has been used
to preserve and flavour
fish since ancient times.
In Spain and Italy, the close
relationship between these
two oceanic ingredients is
celebrated by the use of
vast quantities of salt to
create a fully sealed crust,
in which a whole fish is
baked. The advantages
of this are to seal in all
the moisture and to steam
the fish, without making it
salty. It is imperative that
the salt crust and fish skin
are not pierced during
cooking, as this will make
the fish far too salty.

TXANGURRO

(Stuffed crab)

Preparation time: 30 minutes + 30 minutes
   cooling
Total cooking time: 50 minutes
Serves 4

☆☆

4 live crabs, about 750 g each (see Note)
1/3 cup (80 ml/2 3/4 fl oz) olive oil
1 onion, finely chopped
1 whole clove garlic
1/2 cup (125 ml/4 fl oz) dry white wine
1 cup (250 ml/8 fl oz) puréed tomato
1/4 teaspoon finely chopped tarragon
2 tablespoons dry breadcrumbs
2 tablespoons chopped fresh flat-leaf parsley
40 g (1 1/4 oz) butter, chopped into small pieces

1 Bring a large saucepan of water to the
boil. Add 3 tablespoons of salt and the crabs.
Return to the boil and simmer, uncovered,
for 15 minutes. Remove the crab from the
water and cool for 30 minutes. Extract the
meat from the legs. Open the body without
destroying the upper shell which is needed for
serving, reserving any liquid in a bowl. Take
out the meat and chop finely with the leg meat.

RIGHT: Fish baked in salt

Scoop out all the brown paste from the shells and mix with the chopped meat.

2 Heat the oil in a frying pan and cook the onion and garlic clove for 5–6 minutes, until softened. Stir in the wine and tomato. Simmer for 3–4 minutes then add any reserved crab liquid. Simmer for 3–4 minutes. Add the crab meat and tarragon, and season with salt and ground black pepper. Simmer for about 5 minutes, until thick. Discard the garlic.

3 Preheat the oven to hot 210°C (415°F/ Gas 6–7). Rinse out and dry the crab shells. Divide the crab mixture among them, levelling the surface. Combine the breadcrumbs and parsley and sprinkle over the top. Dot with butter. Bake for 6–8 minutes, until the butter melts and the breadcrumbs brown. Serve hot.
NOTE: The crab traditionally used in txangurro is the centollo or spider crab. Substitute any large-bodied fresh crab, but avoid swimmer or spanner crabs which do not have enough flesh in them.

POLLO A LA CHILINDRON
(Chicken with peppers and olives)

Preparation time: 30 minutes
Total cooking time: 1 hour 10 minutes
Serves 4

6 ripe tomatoes

1.5 kg (3 lb) chicken, cut into 8 portions

3 tablespoons olive oil

2 large red onions, sliced into 5 mm
    (¹/4 inch) slices

2 cloves garlic, crushed

3 red peppers (capsicums), seeded, white pith
    removed, cut into 1 cm (¹/2 inch) strips

60 g (2 oz) thickly sliced prosciutto,
    finely chopped

1 tablespoon chopped fresh thyme

2 teaspoons sweet paprika

8 pitted black olives

8 pitted green olives

1 Score a cross in the base of each tomato. Place in a bowl of boiling water for 10 seconds, then plunge into cold water and peel away from the cross. Cut each tomato in half and scoop out the seeds with a teaspoon. Finely chop the flesh.

2 Pat dry the chicken with paper towel and season well with salt and pepper. Heat the oil in a heavy-based frying pan and cook the chicken a few pieces at a time skin-side-down, over moderate heat for 4–5 minutes, until golden. Turn the chicken over and cook for another 2–3 minutes. Transfer to a plate.

3 Add the onion, garlic, pepper, prosciutto and thyme to the frying pan. Cook over medium heat, stirring frequently for 8–10 minutes, until the vegetables have softened but not browned.

4 Add the tomato and paprika, increase the heat and cook for 10–12 minutes, or until the sauce has thickened and reduced. Return the chicken to the pan and coat well with the sauce. Cover the pan and reduce the heat to low. Simmer the chicken for 25–30 minutes, or until tender. Add the olives and adjust the seasoning, if necessary, before serving.

ABOVE: Pollo a la chilindron

RICE

Rice was introduced into Spain by the Moors in the eighth century, and since then has become an important staple. Far from being considered an accompaniment, rice forms an important base for many traditional dishes, from the famous Paella, to the delicious Rice with stuffed squid. The variety of rice used in Spain is one specially produced to absorb the flavours of the ingredients it is cooked with.

ABOVE: Garlic chicken

GARLIC CHICKEN

Preparation time: 20 minutes
Total cooking time: 35 minutes
Serves 6

☆☆

1 kg (2 lb) chicken thigh fillets
1 tablespoon paprika
2 tablespoons olive oil
8 cloves garlic, unpeeled
1/4 cup (60 ml/2 fl oz) brandy
1/2 cup (125 ml/4 fl oz) chicken stock
1 bay leaf
2 tablespoons chopped fresh flat-leaf parsley

1   Trim any excess fat from the chicken and cut the thighs into thirds. Combine the paprika with some salt and pepper in a bowl, add the chicken and toss to coat.
2   Heat half the oil in a large frying pan over high heat and cook the garlic for 1–2 minutes, until brown. Remove from the pan. Cook the chicken in batches for 5 minutes each batch, or until brown. Return all the chicken to the pan, add the brandy, boil for 30 seconds, then add the stock and bay leaf. Reduce the heat, cover and simmer over low heat for 10 minutes.
3   Meanwhile, place the garlic pulp in a mortar and pestle or small bowl. Add the parsley and pound or mix with a fork to form a paste. Stir into the chicken, cover and cook for 10 minutes, or until tender. Serve hot.

RICE WITH STUFFED SQUID

Preparation time: 40 minutes
Total cooking time: 1 hour 15 minutes
Serves 4

☆☆☆

8 small squid
about 2 teaspoons plain flour

STUFFING
1 small onion
2 tablespoons olive oil
2 tablespoons currants
2 tablespoons pine nuts
4 tablespoons fresh breadcrumbs
1 tablespoon chopped fresh mint
1 tablespoon chopped fresh flat-leaf parsley
1 egg, lightly beaten

SAUCE

1 tablespoon olive oil

1 small onion, finely chopped

1 clove garlic, crushed

1/4 cup (60 ml/2 fl oz) dry white wine

400 g (13 oz) can chopped good-quality
tomatoes

1/2 teaspoon sugar

1 bay leaf

RICE

1.25 litres fish stock

1/4 cup (60 ml/2 fl oz) olive oil

1 onion, finely chopped

3 cloves garlic, crushed

1 1/4 cups (275 g/9 oz) calasparra or
short-grain rice

1/4 teaspoon cayenne pepper

3 teaspoons squid ink, or 4 x 4 g sachets

1/4 cup (60 ml/2 fl oz) dry white wine

3 tablespoons tomato paste (tomato purée)

2 tablespoons chopped fresh flat-leaf parsley

1   To clean the squid, pull each body from the tentacles. Cut off and keep the tentacles as well as the fins from either side of each body sac. If using the ink sacs, extract them and squeeze the ink into a small bowl. Peel the skin from each body sac and dislodge and remove the quills. Rinse under cold water.

2   For the stuffing, chop the tentacles, fins and onion in a processor until fine. Heat the oil in the pan and cook the currants and pine nuts over low heat, stirring until the nuts are lightly browned. Transfer to a bowl with a slotted spoon. Add the onion mixture to the pan and cook gently over low heat for 5 minutes. Add to the bowl and add the breadcrumbs, mint, parsley and egg. Season and mix well. Stuff into the squid bodies. Close the openings and secure with toothpicks. Dust the squid with flour.

3   For the sauce, wipe out the frying pan with paper towels. Heat the oil, add the onion and cook over low heat for 5 minutes, until softened. Stir in the garlic, cook for 30 seconds then add the wine. Cook over high heat for 1 minute, then add the tomato, sugar and bay leaf. Season, reduce the heat and simmer for 5 minutes. Stir in 1/2 cup (125 ml/4 fl oz) water. Place the squid in the pan in a single layer. Simmer, covered, until the squid are tender, about 20 minutes.

4   For the rice, bring the stock to a simmer in a saucepan. Heat the oil in a large saucepan, add the onion and cook over low heat for 5 minutes, until softened. Add the garlic, cook for 15 seconds, then stir in the rice and cayenne. Mix the ink with 4 tablespoons hot stock. Stir into the rice, then add the wine and tomato paste. Stir until the liquid has almost all evaporated, then add 1 cup (250 ml/8 fl oz) hot stock. Simmer until this evaporates, then stir in a cup at a time until the rice is tender and creamy, about 15 minutes. Cover the pan and leave off the heat for 5 minutes. Season well.

5   To serve, spread the rice on a warm platter and stir in the parsley. Arrange the squid on top and spoon on the sauce.

RICE WITH STUFFED SQUID

After cutting away the tentacles, peel the skin from each body sac.

Close each opening and secure with a toothpick.

BELOW: Rice with stuffed squid

SALT COD WITH RED PEPPERS (CAPSICUMS)

Preparation time: 35 minutes
  + 10 minutes cooling + 12 hours soaking
Total cooking time: 25 minutes
Serves 6

400 g (13 oz) dried salt cod or bacalao
1 red pepper (capsicum)
1 tablespoon olive oil
1 small onion, chopped
1 clove garlic, crushed
1/4 teaspoon dried chilli flakes
1 teaspoon paprika
1/4 cup (60 ml/2 fl oz) dry white wine
2 ripe tomatoes, finely chopped
1 tablespoon tomato paste (tomato purée)
1 tablespoon chopped fresh flat-leaf parsley

1 Soak the dried salt cod in plenty of water for 8–12 hours, changing the water five or six times. This will remove excess saltiness. Add the cod to a pan of boiling water and boil for 5 minutes. Drain and leave for 10 minutes, or until cool enough to handle. Remove the skin and flake the fish into large pieces, removing any bones. Place in a bowl.
2 Preheat the grill. Cut the red pepper into quarters and grill, skin-side-up, until the skin blackens and blisters. Place in a plastic bag and leave to cool, then peel away the skin. Slice thinly.
3 Heat the oil in a pan over medium heat, add the onion and cook, stirring occasionally, for 3 minutes, or until transparent. Add the garlic, chilli flakes and paprika and cook for 1 minute. Increase the heat to high, add the white wine and simmer for 30 seconds. Reduce the heat, add the tomato and tomato paste and cook, stirring occasionally, for 5 minutes, or until thick.
4 Add the cod, cover and simmer for about 5 minutes. Gently stir in the sliced pepper and parsley and taste before seasoning with salt. Serve hot.

SPINACH WITH RAISINS AND PINE NUTS

Preparation time: 15 minutes
Total cooking time: 15 minutes
Serves 6

500 g (1 lb) English spinach
2 tablespoons pine nuts
1 tablespoon olive oil
1 small red onion, halved and sliced
1 clove garlic, thinly sliced
2 tablespoons raisins
pinch of ground cinnamon

1 Trim the stalks from the spinach and discard. Wash the leaves and shred them.
2 Put the pine nuts in a frying pan and stir over medium heat for 3 minutes, or until lightly brown. Remove from the pan.
3 Heat the oil in the pan, add the onion and cook over low heat, stirring occasionally, for 10 minutes, or until translucent. Increase the heat to medium, add the garlic and cook for 1 minute. Add the spinach with the water clinging to it, the raisins and cinnamon. Cover and cook for 2 minutes, or until the spinach wilts. Stir in the pine nuts, and season, to taste.
NOTE: Silverbeet (Swiss chard) works equally well in this recipe, although it may take a little longer to cook than spinach.

SANGRIA

This is a refreshing chilled drink to serve on hot summer days.
Put 1 1/2 tablespoons caster sugar and 1 tablespoon each of lemon juice and orange juice into a large jug or bowl and stir until the sugar has dissolved. Add 1 bottle red wine, 2 cups (500 ml/16 fl oz) lemonade and 2 tablespoons each of gin and Vodka. Cut a lemon, an orange and a lime into halves, remove the seeds and slice all the fruit finely. Add the slices to the jug and fill with ice. Stir well. Serves 10.

SALT COD
Salt cod is widely used throughout Spain, and indeed the whole of the Mediterranean. Salting is a simple process in which the fish are gutted and packed flat in salt, later washed, and then dried. The fish are rehydrated in several changes of water and then used for cooking. Salting was one of the earliest forms of preservation and meant that the cod, which was plentiful in the North Atlantic, could be readily and also inexpensively transported. Salt cod has become an important ingredient in traditional cooking.

OPPOSITE PAGE: Spinach with raisins and pine nuts (top left); Salt cod with red peppers

BAKED FISH WITH
PEPPERS, CHILLI AND
POTATOES

Scatter the garlic, parsley,
onion, chilli and peppers on
top of the potatoes.

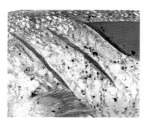

Make 3 or 4 diagonal
slashes on each side of
the fish.

BAKED FISH WITH PEPPERS
(CAPSICUMS), **CHILLI AND
POTATOES**

Preparation time: 30 minutes
+ 2 hours marinating
Total cooking time: 1 hour 35 minutes
Serves 4–6

1.25 kg (2½ lb) whole red bream, red snapper
or porgy, cleaned
1 lemon
3 tablespoons olive oil
800 g (1 lb 10 oz) potatoes, thinly sliced
3 cloves garlic, thinly sliced
3 tablespoons finely chopped parsley
1 small red onion, thinly sliced
1 small dried chilli (guindilla), seeded and
finely chopped
1 red pepper (capsicum), cored, seeded
and cut into thin rings
1 yellow pepper (capsicum), cored, seeded
and cut into thin rings
2 bay leaves
3–4 sprigs of fresh thyme
3 tablespoons dry sherry

1 Cut off and discard the fins from the fish and
place it in a large non-metallic dish. Cut 2 thin
slices from one end of the lemon and reserve.
Squeeze the juice from the rest of the lemon
inside the fish. Add 2 tablespoons oil.
Refrigerate, covered, for 2 hours.

2 Preheat the oven to moderately hot 190°C
(375°F/Gas 5) and lightly oil a shallow
earthenware baking dish large enough to hold
the whole fish. Spread half the potatoes on the
base and scatter the garlic, parsley, onion, chilli
and peppers on top. Season with salt and pepper.
Cover with the rest of the potatoes. Pour in
1/3 cup (80 ml/2¾ fl oz) water and sprinkle the
remaining olive oil over the top. Cover with
foil and bake for 1 hour.

3 Increase the oven temperature to hot 220°C
(425°F/Gas 7). Season the fish inside and out
with salt and pepper and place the bay leaves
and thyme inside the cavity. Make 3–4 diagonal
slashes on each side. Cut the reserved lemon
slices in half and fit these into the slashes on one
side of the fish, to resemble fins. Nestle the fish
into the potatoes with the lemon on top. Bake,
uncovered, for 30 minutes, or until the fish is
cooked through and the surrounding potatoes
are golden and crusty.

4 Pour the dry sherry over the fish and return
to the oven for 3 minutes. Serve straight from
the dish.

*RIGHT: Baked fish with
peppers, chilli and potatoes*

TUMBET
(Vegetable casserole)

Preparation time: 30 minutes
Total cooking time: 1 hour 30 minutes
Serves 6–8

TOMATO SAUCE
1 kg (2 lb) ripe tomatoes
2 tablespoons olive oil
3 cloves garlic, crushed
1 red onion, finely chopped
2 teaspoons fresh thyme, chopped

1 cup (250 ml/8 fl oz) olive oil
500 g (1 lb) waxy potatoes (eg. desiree, kipfler, pontiac), cut into 5 mm (1/4 inch) rounds
500 g (1 lb) eggplants (aubergines), cut into 5 mm (1/4 inch) rounds
500 g (1 lb) green peppers (capsicums), seeded and cut into 3 cm (1 1/4 inch) pieces
1/2 cup (10 g/1/4 oz) fresh flat-leaf parsley, roughly chopped

1 For the tomato sauce, score a cross in the base of each tomato and place in a bowl of boiling water for 10 seconds. Plunge into cold water and peel away from the cross. Cut each tomato in half and scoop out the seeds with a teaspoon. Finely chop the tomatoes. Heat the oil in a heavy-based frying pan and cook the garlic and onion over low heat for 5–6 minutes, or until softened. Add the tomato and the thyme and cook for 20 minutes over medium heat, or until thickened. Season, to taste.

2 While the sauce is cooking, heat the oil in a heavy-based frying pan over low heat and cook the potato in batches until tender but not brown. Remove with a slotted spoon or tongs and place in a heatproof casserole dish measuring about 27 x 21 x 5 cm (10 1/2 x 8 1/2 x 2 inches). Season lightly with salt and pepper.

3 Increase the heat to high and fry the eggplant for 15 minutes, or until golden, turning after about 7 minutes. Drain the slices on paper towels, then place on top of the potatoes. Season lightly. Preheat the oven to moderate 180°C (350°F/Gas 4).

4 Cook the peppers in the same pan until tender but not browned, adding a little more olive oil if needed. Remove with a slotted spoon, drain on paper towels and arrange on the eggplant. Season lightly. Pour the sauce over the top and bake for 20 minutes. Serve warm, sprinkled with parsley, to accompany fish or meat, or at room temperature with aïoli (see page 153).

EGGPLANTS (AUBERGINES)
Eggplants are renowned for their versatility in preparation, as well as for their natural affinity with the robust flavours of Mediterranean cuisine. Choose eggplants that are medium-sized, shiny and firm. The best eggplants have dense, firm and sweet flesh, with small seeds. Eggplants which are old, or simply overmature, will be full of bitter seeds, and will need to be salted for up to an hour before they are used, to remove the unpleasant flavours.

ABOVE: Tumbet

229

PORK SAUSAGES WITH WHITE BEANS

Twist each sausage tightly in opposite directions so that it forms two short fat sausages joined in the middle.

Cook until all the water in the pan has evaporated and the sausages are lightly browned.

PORK SAUSAGES WITH WHITE BEANS

Preparation time: 25 minutes + overnight soaking
Total cooking time: 1 hour 40 minutes
Serves 4

☆ ☆

350 g (11 oz) dried white haricot beans
150 g (5 oz) tocino, speck or pancetta, unsliced
1/2 leek, thinly sliced
2 whole cloves garlic
1 bay leaf
1 small red chilli, split and seeds removed
1 small onion
2 cloves
1 sprig of fresh rosemary
3 sprigs of fresh thyme
1 sprig of fresh parsley
3 tablespoons olive oil
8 pork sausages
1/2 onion, finely chopped
1 green pepper (capsicum), finely chopped
1/2 teaspoon paprika
1/2 cup (125 ml/4 fl oz) puréed tomato
1 teaspoon cider vinegar

ABOVE: Pork sausages with white beans

1   Soak the beans overnight in plenty of cold water. Drain and rinse the beans under cold water. Put them in a large saucepan with the tocino, leek, garlic, bay leaf and chilli. Stud the onion with the cloves and add to the saucepan. Tie the rosemary, thyme and parsley together and add to the saucepan. Pour in 3 cups (750 ml/24 fl oz) cold water and bring to the boil. Add 1 tablespoon oil, reduce the heat and simmer, covered, for about 1 hour, until the beans are tender. When necessary, add a little more boiling water to keep the beans covered.
2   Prick each sausage 5 or 6 times and twist tightly in opposite directions in the middle to give 2 short fat sausages joined in the middle. Put in a single layer in a large frying pan and add enough cold water to reach halfway up their sides. Bring to the boil and simmer, turning two or three times, until all the water has evaporated and the sausages brown lightly in the little fat that is left in the pan. Remove from the pan and cut the short sausages apart. Add the remaining 2 tablespoons oil, the chopped onion and green pepper to the pan and fry over medium heat for 5–6 minutes. Stir in the paprika, cook for 30 seconds then add the puréed tomato. Season, to taste. Cook, stirring, for 1 minute.
3   Remove the tocino, herb sprigs and any loose large pieces of onion from the bean mixture. Leave in any loose leaves from the herbs, and any small pieces of onion. Add the sausages and sauce to the pan and stir the vinegar through. Bring to the boil. Adjust the seasoning.
NOTE: This dish improves if cooked in advance and left for up to 2 days before serving.

PATO CON PERAS
(Duck with pears)

Preparation time: 20 minutes
Total cooking time: 1 hour 40 minutes
Serves 4

☆ ☆

2 tablespoons olive oil

4 duck breasts

2 red onions, finely diced

1 carrot, finely diced

2 teaspoons fresh thyme

1 cup (250 ml/8 fl oz) chicken stock

2 ripe tomatoes, peeled, deseeded
    and diced

4 green, firm pears, peeled, halved and cored
    (leaving the stems intact)

1 cinnamon stick

60 g (2 oz) blanched almonds, toasted, chopped

1 clove garlic

100 ml (3 fl oz) brandy

1 Heat the oil in a heavy-based frying pan and cook the duck, skin-side-down first, over medium heat until brown all over. Remove and set aside, reserving 4 tablespoons of the cooking fat.

2 Return 2 tablespoons of the fat to the pan. Add the onion, carrot and thyme and cook over medium heat for 5 minutes, or until the onion has softened. Add the stock and tomato and bring to the boil. Reduce the heat and simmer for 30 minutes, with the lid slightly askew, or until the sauce has thickened and reduced. Cool slightly, then purée in a food processor until smooth. Return to the pan with the duck. Simmer gently over low heat for 30–40 minutes, or until the duck is tender.

3 While the duck is cooking, place the pears in a saucepan with the cinnamon and just cover with cold water. Bring to the boil, reduce the heat and simmer gently for 5 minutes or until the pears are tender but still firm to the bite. Remove the pears, cover to keep warm and add ½ cup (125 ml/4 fl oz) of the pear poaching liquid to the tomato sauce.

4 Remove the duck from the sauce and keep warm. Grind the almonds, garlic and brandy together in a mortar and pestle or blender to make a smooth paste. Add to the tomato sauce, season, to taste and cook for another 10 minutes.

5 Arrange the duck pieces on a serving plate and pour the sauce over the top. Arrange the warmed pears around the duck and serve.

NOTE: The sauce adds an interesting finish to this Catalan dish, which is traditionally made with goose.

PATO CON PERAS

Put the duck back in the pan with the sauce.

Grind the almonds, garlic and brandy in a mortar and pestle or in a blender.

LEFT: Pato con peras

PREPARING OLIVES

Olives differ in colour at various stages of ripeness. All are inedible straight from the tree and need to be cured, then preserved in oil or brine. Green olives, the youngest, are hard and very bitter, whereas black olives are fully mature and plump. Each requires a different curing process and the resulting textures and flavours vary. Curing olives is simple but takes time and patience.

CURING AND PRESERVING GREEN OLIVES

The first step in curing green olives is to leach out the bitter juices. Crack or split the olives to the stone either with a paring knife or by tapping with a wooden mallet. Put them in a bowl, then cover with cold water. Drain and cover with fresh water every day. Taste after 2 weeks and if still bitter continue soaking and changing the water. It may take up to 4 weeks. The olives can now be preserved in olive oil or in a brine solution and different herbs and aromatics can be added to infuse the olives with flavour.

PRESERVING OLIVES IN OIL

Spread the olives out on paper towels and leave overnight in a warm place to dry. Steep the olives in 2 parts olive oil to 1 part vinegar, seasoning with garlic, mint, peppercorns and salt, to taste. Cover, stirring occasionally, for 3 days. Transfer it all to sterilized glass jars and cover with olive oil. Refrigerate for up to 6 weeks. Serve at room temperature.

PRESERVING OLIVES IN BRINE

Drain and dry the soaked olives. Make a brine solution with 10 parts water to 1 part rock salt (e.g. 10 cups/2.25 litres water to 1 cup/315 g/10 oz rock salt). Bring to the boil and simmer for 5 minutes with bay leaves, citrus zest, peppercorns and herbs. Pack the olives into sterilized glass jars, cover with the brine, seal and cool completely. Store for a week before eating. Use within a month and refrigerate after opening.

CURING AND PRESERVING BLACK OLIVES

A traditional method of curing black olives is simple but may take longer than the green olives to leach out the bitter

juices. Completely cover black olives in cold water, cover and soak for 6 weeks. Replace the water every second day. Drain the olives, then cover with rock salt and set aside for 2 days. Rinse off all the salt and leave to dry thoroughly. As with the green olives, reserve in either olive oil or a brine solution.

ROASTED OLIVES WITH FENNEL AND ORANGE

For 2 cups (350 g/11 oz) olives, sauté 1 finely shaved fennel bulb and 1 teaspoon fennel seeds in olive oil for 10 minutes. Place in a baking dish with the olives, 2 sliced garlic cloves, 1 tablespoon finely grated orange zest and 1/4 cup (60 ml/ 2 fl oz) each of orange juice and red wine vinegar. Bake in a moderate 180°C (350°F/Gas 4) oven for 20 minutes. Season, to taste, drizzle with olive oil and serve warm or at room temperature. Will keep in the fridge for up to 2 weeks.

HERBED OLIVES

Put 250 g (8 oz) each of cracked green and cracked Kalamata olives, 3 sprigs of fresh thyme, 1 tablespoon fresh oregano leaves, 2 bay leaves, 1 teaspoon paprika and 2 teaspoons lemon zest in a bowl and toss. Spoon into a 1 litre sterilized jar and pour in 2 cups (500 ml/16 fl oz) olive oil. Marinate for 1–2 weeks in the fridge. Will keep for up to a month.
NOTE: Cracking olives with a mallet, or cutting to the stone with a paring knife, allows marinade flavours to penetrate into the olives.

MARINATING OLIVES

PRESERVED LEMON AND CHILLI OLIVES

Drain 500 g (1 lb) brined olives, cover with cold water and leave for 1 hour. Drain, add the zest from 1/4 preserved lemon, cut into thin slivers, 2 halved fresh red chillies, 2 bruised cloves of garlic, and 2 teaspoons dried oregano.

Pack into sterilized jars, cover with olive oil, seal, then leave for a week to allow the flavours to infuse. They will keep for up to 4 months in the refrigerator.
NOTE: If stored in oil in the fridge, the oil may solidify. Simply bring back to room temperature before use. When the olives are finished, the oil can be used in dressings, to dip bread in, or to drizzle over grilled fish or chicken.

STERILIZING JARS

To sterilize storage jars, rinse the jar and lid with boiling, soapy water, then place the jars in a warm oven to dry completely.

CLOKWISE, FROM TOP LEFT:
Roasted olives with fennel and orange;
Herbed olives; Preserved lemon and chilli olives

HABAS VERDES EN SALSA DE TOMATE
(Green beans in tomato sauce)

Preparation time: 10 minutes
Total cooking time: 30 minutes
Serves 4

300 g (10 oz) green beans, trimmed
1 tablespoon olive oil
1 onion, finely chopped
2 cloves garlic, finely chopped
1 tablespoon paprika
1/4 teaspoon chilli flakes
1 bay leaf, crushed
400 g (13 oz) can crushed good-quality tomatoes
2 tablespoons chopped fresh flat-leaf parsley

1 Cook the beans in boiling water for 3–5 minutes or until tender. Drain and set aside.
2 Heat the oil in a frying pan. Add the onion and cook over medium heat for 5 minutes, or until soft. Add the garlic and cook for 1 minute. Add the paprika, chilli flakes and bay leaf, cook for 1 minute, then add the tomato. Simmer over medium heat for 15 minutes until reduced and pulpy. Add the beans and parsley and cook for 1 minute, or until warmed through. Season, to taste. Serve warm or at room temperature.

BELOW: Habas verdes en salsa de tomate

COCHIFRITO
(Lamb braise)

Preparation time: 15 minutes
Total cooking time: 2 hours 15 minutes
Serves 4

1/3 cup (80 ml/2³/4 fl oz) olive oil
1 kg (2 lb) lamb shoulder, diced
1 large onion, finely chopped
4 cloves garlic, crushed
2 teaspoons paprika
5 tablespoons lemon juice
2 tablespoons chopped fresh flat-leaf parsley

1 Heat the oil in a large, heavy-based deep frying pan over high heat. Sauté the lamb in two batches for 5 minutes each batch, until well browned. Remove all the lamb from the pan and set aside.
2 Add the onion and cook for 4–5 minutes, or until soft and golden. Add the garlic and paprika and stir for 1 minute. Return the meat to the pan with 4 tablespoons lemon juice and 1.75 litres water and simmer over low heat, stirring occasionally for 2 hours, until the liquid has almost evaporated and the oil starts to reappear. Stir in the remaining lemon juice and the parsley, season to taste, and serve.

Cut the green beans into long slices.

Add the chickpeas, pig's trotter and chorizo to the saucepan.

COCIDO MADRILENO
(Madrileno meat and vegetables)

Preparation time: 25 minutes + overnight soaking
Total cooking time: 2 hours 45 minutes
Serves 6–8

☆☆

1 cup (220 g/7 oz) dried chickpeas

1 kg (2 lb) chicken, trussed

500 g (1 lb) beef brisket, in one piece

250 g (8 oz) piece smoke-cured bacon

125 g (4 oz) tocino, streaky bacon
   or speck

1 pig's trotter

200 g (6¹/₂ oz) chorizo

1 onion, studded with 2 cloves

1 bay leaf

1 morcilla blood sausage (optional)

250 g (8 oz) green beans, sliced lengthways

250 g (8 oz) green cabbage, cut into sections
   through the heart

300 g (10 oz) silverbeet (Swiss chard) leaves,
   rinsed, stalks removed

4 small potatoes

2 leeks, cut into 10 cm (4 inch) lengths

pinch of saffron threads

75 g (2¹/₂ oz) dried rice vermicelli

1 Soak the chickpeas in cold water overnight. Drain and rinse. Tie loosely in a muslin bag.
2 Put 3 litres of cold water in a very large deep saucepan. Add the chicken, beef, bacon and tocino and bring to the boil. Add the chickpeas, pig's trotter and chorizo, return to the boil, then add the onion, bay leaf and ¹/₂ teaspoon salt. Simmer, partially covered, for 2¹/₂ hours.
3 After 2 hours, bring a saucepan of water to the boil, add the morcilla and gently boil for 5 minutes. Drain and set aside. Tie the green beans loosely in a muslin bag. Pour 1 litre of water into a large saucepan and bring to the boil. Add the beans, cabbage, silverbeet, potatoes, leek and saffron with 1 teaspoon of salt. Return to the boil and simmer for 30 minutes.
4 Strain the stock from both the meat and vegetable pans and combine in a large saucepan. Bring to the boil, adjust the seasoning and add the vermicelli. Simmer for 6–7 minutes. Release the chickpeas and pile them in the centre of a large warm platter. Discard the tocino, then slice the meats and sausages. Arrange in groups around the chickpeas at one end of the platter. Release the beans. Arrange the vegetables in groups around the other end. Spoon a little of the simmering broth (minus the vermicelli) over the meat, then pour the rest into a soup tureen. Serve at once. It is traditional to serve the two dishes together, although the broth is eaten first.

ABOVE: Cocido madrileno

STUFFED LEG OF LAMB

Lay the lamb out flat and spoon the filling down the centre.

Spread the seasoned flour all over the lamb.

ABOVE: Stuffed leg of lamb

STUFFED LEG OF LAMB

Preparation time: 25 minutes
Total cooking time: 2 hours 15 minutes
Serves 6–8

 ☆☆

STUFFING

1 thick slice white country-style bread, crusts removed

70 g (2¼ oz) chicken livers, trimmed

60 g (2 oz) tocino or streaky bacon

1 tablespoon dry sherry

1 clove garlic, crushed

1 tablespoon chopped fresh flat-leaf parsley

½ tablespoon chopped fresh chives

1 teaspoon finely chopped fresh rosemary

1 tablespoon capers, finely chopped

1 large leg of lamb (about 3 kg/6 lb), boned (see Note)

1 teaspoon sweet paprika

1 tablespoon plain flour

4 whole cloves garlic, peeled

2 tablespoons olive oil

1½ cups (375 ml/12 fl oz) dry white wine

1 tablespoon lard

½ cup (125 ml/4 fl oz) chicken or vegetable stock

1 To make the stuffing, break the bread into pieces and process with the chicken livers and tocino until medium-fine. Place in a bowl with the sherry, garlic, parsley, chives, rosemary and capers. Season well with salt and freshly ground black pepper and mix well.

2 Preheat the oven to hot 210°C (415°F/ Gas 6–7). Lay the lamb out flat and place the

filling down the centre. Roll the meat up to encase the filling. Tie up tightly with kitchen twine. Combine the paprika and flour with 1/4 teaspoon salt and rub all over the surface of the lamb. Put the garlic in a row in the centre of a baking dish and pour the oil over the top. Place the lamb on the garlic and pour the wine over the top. Spread the lard over the surface.

3 Bake for 20 minutes, then reduce the heat to warm 170°C (325°F/Gas 3). Baste, then bake for another 1 hour 45 minutes, basting frequently, until the lamb is well cooked. Transfer to a carving tray and keep warm. Spoon off excess oil from the pan juices then transfer the contents of the baking dish to a small saucepan; there will be about 1/2 cup (125 ml/4 fl oz). Add the stock and cook over high heat until slightly thickened. Taste for seasoning. Slice the lamb and arrange on a warm serving platter. Pour the sauce over the lamb and serve warm.

NOTE: Have your butcher bone the lamb and flatten out the meat to form a rough rectangle.

CHICKEN AND CHORIZO PAELLA

Preparation time: 30 minutes
Total cooking time: 1 hour
Serves 6

☆☆

1/4 cup (60 ml/2 fl oz) olive oil

1 large red pepper (capsicum), seeded and cut into 5 mm (1/4 inch) strips

600 g (1 1/4 lb) chicken thigh fillets, cut into 3 cm (1 1/4 inch) cubes

200 g (6 1/2 oz) chorizo, cut into 2 cm (3/4 inch) slices

200 g (6 1/2 oz) mushrooms, thinly sliced

3 cloves garlic, crushed

1 tablespoon grated lemon rind

700 g (1 lb 7 oz) ripe tomatoes, roughly chopped

200 g (6 1/2 oz) green beans, cut into 3 cm (1 1/4 inch) lengths

1 tablespoon chopped fresh rosemary

2 tablespoons chopped fresh flat-leaf parsley

1/4 teaspoon saffron threads dissolved in 1/4 cup (60 ml/2 fl oz) hot water

2 cups (440 g/14 oz) short-grain rice

3 cups (750 ml/24 fl oz) hot chicken stock

6 lemon wedges, for serving

1 Heat the olive oil in a paella pan, or in a large, heavy-based, deep frying pan over medium heat. Add the red pepper strips, cook, stirring, for about 6 minutes, or until softened, then remove from the pan.

2 Add the chicken to the pan and cook for 10 minutes, or until brown on all sides. Remove from the pan. Add the chorizo to the pan and cook for 5 minutes, or until golden on all sides. Remove from the pan. Add the mushrooms, garlic and lemon rind to the pan, and cook over medium heat for 5 minutes.

3 Stir in the tomato and pepper, and cook for another 5 minutes, or until the tomato is soft.

4 Add the beans, rosemary, parsley, saffron mixture, rice, chicken and sausage. Stir briefly and add the stock. Do not stir at this point. Reduce the heat and simmer for 30 minutes. Remove from the heat, cover and leave to stand for 10 minutes. Serve with lemon wedges.

NOTE: Paella pans are available from some specialist kitchenware shops.

BELOW: Chicken and chorizo paella

HIGAS RELLENOS

Use a sharp knife to cut the dark chocolate into shards.

Push an almond and a few of the chocolate shards into each slit.

TORTE DE LA ALMENDRA
(Almond torte)

Preparation time: 15 minutes
Total cooking time: 1 hour 20 minutes
Serves 8

☆

450 g (14 oz) blanched whole almonds, lightly toasted
150 g (5 oz) unsalted butter, softened
400 g (13 oz) caster sugar
6 eggs
150 g (5 oz) plain flour
2 teaspoons lemon rind
2 tablespoons lemon juice
icing sugar, to dust

1 Preheat the oven to warm 170°C (325°F/ Gas 3). Lightly grease a 24 cm (9 inch) springform cake tin. Grind the almonds finely in a food processor and set aside.
2 Using electric beaters, cream the butter and sugar in a bowl until light and fluffy. Add the eggs one at a time, beating well after each addition. Using a large metal spoon, fold in the flour, ground almonds and the lemon rind. Stir until just combined and almost smooth.
3 Pour the batter into the prepared tin and bake for 1 hour 20 minutes, or until a skewer inserted in the centre comes out clean. Allow to cool for 5 minutes, then brush the top with lemon juice. Remove to a wire rack and allow to cool completely. Dust with icing sugar in a cross pattern, using a stencil if you wish.

RICOTTA WITH HONEY AND PINE NUTS

Preparation time: 5 minutes
Total cooking time: 2 minutes
Serves 2

☆

300 g (10 oz) ricotta
2 tablespoons honey
pine nuts, toasted, for serving

1 Divide the ricotta between two bowls, drizzle with honey and sprinkle with the pine nuts.
NOTE: This simple dessert is traditionally made with Requeson, a soft, bland cheese.

HIGAS RELLENOS
(Stuffed figs)

Preparation time: 30 minutes + 3 hours soaking
Total cooking time: 30 minutes
Makes 18

☆ ☆

1/2 cup (175 g/6 oz) honey
1/2 cup (125 ml/4 fl oz) sweet dark sherry
1/4 teaspoon ground cinnamon
18 large dried figs
18 whole blanched almonds
100 g (3 1/2 oz) dark chocolate, cut into shards
butter, for greasing
thick (double) cream for serving, optional

1 Combine the honey, sherry, cinnamon and figs with 1 1/2 cups (375 ml/12 fl oz) water in a large saucepan over high heat. Bring to the boil then reduce the heat and simmer for 10 minutes. Remove the pan from the heat and set aside for 3 hours. Remove the figs with a slotted spoon, reserving the liquid.
2 Preheat the oven to moderate 180°C (350°F/ Gas 4). Return the pan of liquid to the stove and boil over high heat for 5 minutes, or until syrupy, then set aside. Snip the stems from the figs with scissors then cut a slit in the top of each fig with small sharp knife. Push an almond and a few shards of chocolate into each slit. Place the figs in a lightly buttered dish and bake for 15 minutes or until the chocolate has melted.
3 Serve three figs per person with a little of the syrup and a dollop of cream.

ALMOND HORCHATA
(Almond milk drink)

This drink is traditionally made with tiger nuts but almonds make a perfect substitute. In a food processor, grind 500 g (1 lb) blanched whole almonds into a coarse meal with 1 litre warm water until you have a very thick paste. Spoon into a large bowl. Cut 1/2 a lemon into slices and add to the paste with 1 cinnamon stick and 2 cups (500 ml/16 fl oz) warm water. Stir well, cover and leave at room temperature for at least 2 hours. Strain the liquid through cheesecloth or muslin, add 2 tablespoons sugar, or to taste, and serve chilled. Serves 4.

OPPOSITE PAGE, FROM TOP: Torte de la almendra; Almond horchata; Higas rellenos

HELADO DE CANELA
(Cinnamon ice cream)

Preparation time: 15 minutes + freezing
Total cooking time: 15 minutes
Serves 6

 ☆ ☆

1 litre milk
2 pieces lemon rind
3 cinnamon sticks
1½ cups (375 g/12 oz) caster sugar
6 egg yolks
1 teaspoon ground cinnamon

1 Put the milk, rind, cinnamon sticks and half the sugar in a saucepan and heat to just below boiling. Set aside for 10 minutes.
2 Using a wire whisk, combine the yolks, remaining sugar and ground cinnamon in bowl until thick and pale. Pour in the milk in a steady stream, whisking constantly.
3 Wash the pan, pour in the mixture and stir over very low heat for 5–10 minutes, until thickened. To test, run a finger through the mixture across the back of a wooden spoon. If it leaves a clear line, the custard is ready. Strain it into a bowl and leave to cool to room temperature. Pour it into a 1.25 litre shallow metal container. Freeze for 2 hours, or until firm.
4 When half frozen around the edges, beat well then freeze again. Repeat the beating and freezing process twice more.

BELOW: Helado de canela

LECHE FRITA
(Fried custard squares)

Preparation time: 20 minutes + 1 hour cooling
Total cooking time: 25 minutes
Serves 4–6

☆

2 cups (500 ml/16 fl oz) milk
1 cinnamon stick
1 piece lemon zest, 5 x 1 cm (2 x ½ inch)
1 vanilla bean, split
140 g (4½ oz) unsalted butter
2 cups (250 g/8 oz) plain flour
⅔ cup (160 g/5½ oz) caster sugar
4 eggs, separated
1¼ cups (125 g/4 oz) dry breadcrumbs
vegetable oil, for frying
4 tablespoons caster sugar, for dusting
1 teaspoon ground cinnamon, for dusting

1 Grease a 27 x 17 cm (11 x 7 inch) slice tin and line the base and two long sides with baking paper. Put the milk, cinnamon stick, lemon zest and scraped vanilla bean in a saucepan and bring to the boil. Turn the heat off.
2 Melt the butter in a large heavy-based saucepan. Stir in 1½ cups (185 g/6 oz) of the flour. The mixture will form a loose clump around your spoon. Stir over low heat for 30 seconds. Stir in the sugar. Gradually strain the milk into the pan, stirring constantly. Beat

until a smooth, glossy mass forms. Remove from the heat and stir in the egg yolks one at a time, beating well after each addition. Spread in the tin, smoothing the surface with your hand. Set aside for about 1 hour, to cool and set.

3 Lightly whisk the egg whites together with a fork. Lift the set custard from the tin and carefully cut into 5 cm (2 inch) squares. Dip in the remaining flour to coat all sides. Dip into the egg whites, then the breadcrumbs. Set aside.

4 Pour the oil in a large frying pan to a depth of 1 cm (½ inch). Heat the oil, add a few squares at a time and cook for about 1 minute per side, until browned. Drain on paper towels and dust all over with the mixed sugar and cinnamon while still hot. Serve hot or cold.

CREMA CATALANA
(Catalan burnt cream)

Preparation time: 15 minutes + overnight refrigeration
Total cooking time: 20 minutes
Serves 6

1 litre milk
1 vanilla bean
1 cinnamon stick
zest of 1 small lemon, sliced into strips
2 strips orange zest, 4 x 2 cm (1½ x ¾ inches)
8 egg yolks
½ cup (125 g/4 oz) caster sugar
4 tablespoons cornflour
3 tablespoons soft brown sugar

1 Place the milk, scraped vanilla bean, cinnamon stick and lemon and orange zests in a saucepan and bring to the boil. Simmer for 5 minutes, then strain and set aside.

2 Whisk the egg yolks with the caster sugar in a bowl for about 5 minutes, until pale and creamy. Add the cornflour and mix well. Slowly add the warm milk mixture to the egg and whisk continuously. Return to the saucepan and cook over low to medium heat, stirring constantly, for 5–10 minutes, or until the mixture is thick and creamy. Do not boil as it will curdle. Pour into six 1-cup (250 ml/8 fl oz) ramekins and refrigerate for 6 hours, or overnight.

3 When ready to serve, sprinkle evenly with brown sugar and grill for 3 minutes, or until it caramelizes.

MEMBRILLO
(Quince paste)

Wash 3 large quinces, place in a saucepan, cover with water and simmer for 30 minutes, or until tender. Drain. Peel and core the quinces then push them through a sieve or potato ricer. Weigh the fruit pulp, place in a heavy-based saucepan and add the same weight of sugar. Cook over low heat, stirring occasionally with a wooden spoon, for 3½–4½ hours, or until very thick. Pour into a shallow 28 x 18 cm (11 x 7 inch) rectangular tin lined with plastic wrap. Allow to cool. Quince paste can be kept for several months in a tightly sealed container. Serve with cheese, or with game such as pheasant.

ABOVE: Crema Catalana

CHURROS

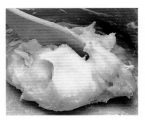

Keep stirring the dough until it forms a ball around the spoon and leaves a coating on the pan.

Fry the lengths of dough until puffed and golden.

CHURROS

Preparation time: 10 minutes
Total cooking time: 25 minutes
Serves 4

☆ ☆

1/2 cup (125 g/4 oz) sugar
1 teaspoon ground nutmeg
30 g (1 oz) butter
150 g (5 oz) plain flour
1/2 teaspoon finely grated orange rind
1/4 teaspoon caster sugar
2 eggs
1 litre vegetable oil, for deep-frying

1 Combine the sugar and nutmeg and spread out on a plate.
2 Place the butter, flour, orange rind, caster sugar, 2/3 cup (170 ml/5 1/2 fl oz) water and a pinch of salt in a heavy-based saucepan. Stir over low heat until the butter softens and forms a dough with the other ingredients. Keep cooking for 2–3 minutes, stirring constantly, until the dough forms a ball around the spoon and leaves a coating on the base of the pan.
3 Transfer the dough to a food processor and, with the motor running, add the eggs. Do not over-process. If the dough is too soft to snip with scissors, return it to the pan and cook, stirring over low heat until it is firmer. Spoon it into a piping bag fitted with a 5 mm (1/4 inch) star nozzle.
4 Heat the oil in a wide saucepan to 180°C (350°F) or when a cube of bread dropped into the oil browns in 15 seconds. Pipe lengths of batter 6–8 cm (2 1/2–3 inches) long into the oil a few at a time. An easy technique is to pipe with one hand and cut the batter off using kitchen scissors in the other hand. Fry for about 3 minutes, until puffed and golden, turning once or twice. Transfer each batch to paper towels to drain. While still hot, toss them in the sugar mixture and serve at once.
NOTE: Churros is a popular breakfast snack in Spain and is usually eaten with hot chocolate (see page 243).

ABOVE: Churros

ANISEED BISCUITS

Preparation time: 15 minutes
Total cooking time: 35 minutes
Makes 16

☆ ☆

3 cups (375 g/12 oz) plain flour
1/2 cup (125 ml/4 fl oz) olive oil
1/2 cup (125 ml/4 fl oz) beer
3 tablespoons anisette liqueur
1/2 cup (125 g/4 oz) caster sugar
1/4 cup (40 g/1 1/4 oz) sesame seeds
2 tablespoons aniseeds

1 Preheat the oven to moderately hot 200°C (400°F/Gas 6). Lightly grease a baking tray and line with baking paper.
2 Sift the flour and 1 teaspoon salt into a large bowl and make a well. Add the oil, beer and anisette and mix with a large metal spoon until the dough comes together. Transfer to a lightly floured surface and knead for 3–4 minutes, or until smooth. Divide the dough into two, then divide each portion into eight. In a small bowl, combine the sugar, sesame seeds and aniseeds.
3 Make a small pile of the seed mix on a work surface and roll out each portion of dough over the mix to a 15 cm (6 inch) round with the seeds embedded underneath. Place the rounds on a baking tray with the seeds on top and cook for 5–6 minutes, until the bases are crisp. Place 10 cm (4 inches) below a grill for about 40 seconds, until the sugar caramelizes and the surface is golden. Transfer to a wire rack to cool.
NOTE: If aniseeds are unavailable, you can use 1 1/2 tablespoons fennel seeds instead.

SPANISH HOT CHOCOLATE

Chocolate a la taza is traditionally used for making this drink because it contains a starch which thickens as it cooks. However, since this is not readily available, you can use cornflour as the thickening agent.
In a small bowl, mix 2 tablespoons cornflour with 2 tablespoons milk to a smooth paste. Place 1 litre milk and 200 g (6 1/2 oz) chopped good-quality dark chocolate in a saucepan and whisk constantly over low heat until just warm. Add 2 tablespoons of the milk to the cornflour paste, then return all the paste to the milk. Whisking constantly, cook the mixture until it just begins to boil. Remove from the heat, add sugar, to taste, and whisk for another minute. Serves 4–6.

ANISEEDS
Aniseeds are the seeds from a bush related to hemlock and are of Middle Eastern origin. They have an intense licorice flavour and are primarily used for making Pernod, ouzo, and Pastis. Used in moderation, they add sweet, interesting undertones to stuffings for fish and are used to flavour breads and cakes. It is best to buy aniseeds in small quantities when needed, as they quickly lose their potency.

LEFT: Aniseed biscuits

NORTH AFRICA

North Africa encompasses perhaps the most exotic parts of the Mediterranean region, covering Morocco, Algeria and Tunisia. Moroccan food is among the most exciting in the world. Great pride is taken in meal preparation. And it's all quite easy thanks to the way Moroccan meals are planned, usually involving one or two tagines, long-simmering stews of meat, chicken or vegetables. Cloves, nutmeg, paprika, saffron, cayenne pepper, cumin, ginger and cinnamon are a major feature in North African cuisine. Also prominent are couscous, citrus, pomegranates, dates, almonds, apricots and chickpeas.

HARISSA

Preparation time: 30 minutes + 1 hour soaking
Total cooking time: Nil
Fills a 600 ml (20 fl oz) jar

☆

125 g (4 oz) dried red chillies, stems removed
1 tablespoon dried mint
1 tablespoon ground coriander
1 tablespoon ground cumin
1 teaspoon ground caraway seeds
10 cloves garlic, chopped
1/2 cup (125 ml/4 fl oz) olive oil

1   Roughly chop the chillies, then cover with boiling water and soak for 1 hour. Drain, place in a food processor and add the mint, spices, garlic, 1 tablespoon of oil and 1/2 teaspoon salt. Process for 20 seconds, scrape down the side of the bowl, then process for another 30 seconds. Add 2 tablespoons oil and process again. Repeat and process until a thick paste forms.
2   Spoon the paste into a clean jar (see Note), cover with a thin layer of olive oil and seal. Label and date.
NOTES: To prepare a storage jar, preheat the oven to very slow 120°C (250°F/Gas 1/2). Wash the jar and lid in hot soapy water and rinse with hot water. Put the jar in the oven for 20 minutes, or until fully dry. Do not dry with a tea towel.

This hot pepper sauce will keep in the fridge for up to six months. It is delicious with tagines and couscous, or can be added to salad dressings, marinades and pasta sauces for extra flavour.

FISH FILLETS WITH HARISSA AND OLIVES

Preparation time: 15 minutes
Total cooking time: 25 minutes
Serves 4

☆

1/3 cup (80 ml/2 3/4 fl oz) olive oil
4 white fish fillets such as cod, snapper or perch
seasoned flour, for dusting
1 brown onion, chopped
2 cloves garlic, crushed
400 g (13 oz) can chopped good-quality tomato
2 teaspoons harissa
2 bay leaves
1 stick cinnamon
1 cup (185 g/6 oz) Kalamata olives
1 tablespoon lemon juice
2 tablespoons chopped fresh flat-leaf parsley

HARISSA
This spicy paste blend is a popular accompaniment for many North African dishes. It is traditionally served with couscous, but is also used as a flavouring in soups, casseroles, tagines and dried bean salads. It can also be mixed with a little olive oil and served with flatbread. Commercial harissa can be purchased from delicatessens.

RIGHT: Harissa

1 Heat half the olive oil in a heavy-based frying pan. Dust the fish fillets with flour and cook over medium heat for 2 minutes on each side, or until golden. Transfer to a plate.

2 Add the remaining olive oil to the pan and cook the onion and garlic for 3–4 minutes, or until softened. Add the chopped tomato, harissa, bay leaves and cinnamon. Cook for 10 minutes, or until the sauce has thickened. Season, to taste, with salt and freshly ground black pepper.

3 Return the fish to the pan, add the olives and cover the fish with the sauce. Remove the bay leaves and cinnamon stick and continue cooking for 2 minutes, or until the fish is tender. Add the lemon juice and parsley and serve.

HAMAD M'RAKAD
(Preserved lemons)

Preparation time: 1 hour
  + 6 weeks standing
Total cooking time: Nil
Fills a 2 litre jar

8–12 small thin-skinned lemons
1 cup (315 g/10 oz) rock salt
2 cups (500 ml/16 fl oz) lemon juice
   (8–10 lemons)
1/2 teaspoon black peppercorns
1 bay leaf
olive oil

1 Scrub the lemons under warm running water with a soft bristle brush to remove the wax coating. Cut into quarters, leaving the base attached at the stem end. Gently open each lemon, remove any visible seeds and pack 1 tablespoon of the salt against the cut edges of each lemon. Push the lemons back into shape and pack tightly into a 2 litre jar that has a clip or tight-fitting lid. Depending on the size of the lemons, you may not need all 12. They should be firmly packed and fill the jar.

2 Add 1 cup (250 ml/8 fl oz) of the lemon juice, the peppercorns, bay leaf and remaining rock salt to the jar. Fill the jar to the top with the remaining lemon juice. Seal and shake to combine all the ingredients. Leave in a cool, dark place for 6 weeks, inverting the jar each week. (In warm weather, store the jar in the refrigerator.) The liquid will be cloudy initially, but will clear by the fourth week.

3 To test if the lemons are preserved, cut through the centre of one of the lemon quarters. If the pith is still white, the lemons aren't ready. In this case, re-seal and leave for another week before testing again. The lemons should be soft-skinned and the pith should be the same colour as the skin.

4 Once the lemons are preserved, cover the brine with a layer of olive oil. Replace the oil each time you remove some of the lemon pieces. Refrigerate after opening.

NOTE: Preserved lemons can be stored for up to 6 months in a cool, dark place. Use preserved lemons to flavour couscous, stuffings, tagines and casseroles. Only the rind is used in cooking. Discard the flesh and bitter pith, rinse and finely slice or chop the rind before adding to the dish.

ABOVE: Hamad m'rakad

1 Sprinkle the eggplant slices with salt and drain in a colander for 30 minutes. Rinse well, squeeze gently and pat dry. Heat about 5 mm (¼ inch) of the oil in a large frying pan and fry the slices in batches over medium heat until golden brown on both sides. Drain on paper towels, then chop finely. Put in a colander until most of the oil has drained off, then transfer to a bowl and add the garlic, paprika, cumin and sugar.

2 Wipe out the pan, add the eggplant mixture and stir constantly over medium heat for 2 minutes. Transfer to a bowl, stir in the lemon juice and season. Serve at room temperature.

PICKLED FRIED FISH

Preparation time: 15 minutes
  + 24 hours marinating
Total cooking time: 15 minutes
Serves 4–6

☆ ☆

½ cup (60 g/2 oz) plain flour
pinch of cayenne pepper
500 g (1 lb) firm white fish such as ling
  or blue eye, cut into 24 strips
½ cup (125 ml/4 fl oz) olive oil
250 g (8 oz) brown onions, thinly sliced
250 g (8 oz) carrots, thinly sliced
8 spring onions, diagonally sliced
12 cloves garlic, chopped
1 tablespoon chopped fresh thyme
2 bay leaves
2 cloves
8 juniper berries
1 teaspoon black peppercorns
1 cup (250 ml/8 fl oz) white wine vinegar
1 cup (250 ml/8 fl oz) white wine
2 tablespoons chopped fresh flat-leaf parsley

1 Season the flour with the cayenne pepper and salt. Pat the fish dry with paper towels, coat each piece in the flour and shake off any excess.

2 Heat 2 tablespoons oil in a large frying pan and cook the fish in batches until golden brown. Don't overcook the fish or it will break up when the marinade is poured over it. Place the fish in a non-metallic dish.

3 Clean the frying pan, heat 3 tablespoons oil and sauté the onion, carrot and spring onion for 5 minutes, or until soft but not brown. Add the garlic, herbs and spices, wine vinegar, wine and

ALGERIAN EGGPLANT
(AUBERGINE) JAM

Preparation time: 10 minutes
  + 30 minutes salting
Total cooking time: 20 minutes
Serves 6–8

☆

2 eggplants (aubergines), about
  400 g (13 oz), cut into 1 cm (½ inch) slices
olive oil, for frying
2 garlic cloves, crushed
1 teaspoon sweet paprika
1½ teaspoons ground cumin
½ teaspoon sugar
1 tablespoon lemon juice

ABOVE: Algerian eggplant jam (top); Pickled fried fish

TUNISIAN CARROT SALAD

Preparation time: 10 minutes
Total cooking time: 10 minutes
Serves 6

500 g (1 lb) carrots, thinly sliced
3 tablespoons finely chopped fresh
  flat-leaf parsley
1 teaspoon ground cumin
1/3 cup (80 ml/2³/4 fl oz) olive oil
1/4 cup (60 ml/2 fl oz) red wine vinegar
2 cloves garlic, crushed
1/4 to 1/2 teaspoon harissa (see page 246)
12 black olives
2 hard-boiled eggs, quartered

1 Bring 2 cups (500 ml/16 fl oz) water to the
boil in a saucepan. Add the carrot and cook until
tender. Drain and transfer to a bowl. Add the
parsley, cumin, olive oil, vinegar and garlic.
Season with harissa and salt and pepper. Stir well.
2 To serve, place the carrots in a serving dish
and garnish with the olives and eggs.
NOTE: If the carrots are not sweet, you can add
a little honey to the dressing.

CUCUMBER, FETA, MINT AND DILL SALAD

Preparation time: 15 minutes
Total cooking time: Nil
Serves 4

120 g (4 oz) feta cheese
4 Lebanese cucumbers
1 small red onion, thinly sliced
1¹/2 tablespoons finely chopped fresh dill
1 tablespoon dried mint
3 tablespoons olive oil
1¹/2 tablespoons lemon juice

1 Crumble the feta into 1 cm (1/2 inch) pieces
and place in a large bowl. Peel and seed the
cucumbers and cut into 1 cm (1/2 inch) dice.
Add to the bowl along with the onion and dill.
2 Grind the mint in a mortar and pestle, or
force through a sieve, until powdered. Combine
with the oil and juice, then season with salt and
black pepper. Pour over the salad and toss well.

TUNISIAN BRIK

Preparation time: 30 minutes
Total cooking time: 20 minutes
Serves 2

☆☆

30 g (1 oz) butter
1 small onion, finely chopped
200 g (6¹/2 oz) can tuna in oil, drained
1 tablespoon tiny capers, rinsed and chopped
2 tablespoons finely chopped fresh
  flat-leaf parsley
2 tablespoons grated Parmesan
6 sheets filo pastry
30 g (1 oz) butter, melted
2 small eggs

1 Preheat the oven to moderately hot 200°C
(400°F/Gas 6). Melt the butter in a small frying
pan and cook the onion over low heat for
5 minutes, or until soft but not brown. Combine
the onion, tuna, capers, parsley and Parmesan
in a bowl. Season with salt and black pepper.
2 Cut the filo pastry sheets in half widthways.
Layer 4 of the half sheets together, brushing each
with melted butter. Keep the remaining pastry
covered with a damp tea towel. Spoon half the
tuna mixture onto one end of the buttered
pastry, leaving a border. Make a well in the
centre of the mixture and break an egg into
the well, being careful to leave it whole. Season
with salt and freshly ground black pepper.
3 Layer 2 more sheets of filo together, brushing
with melted butter, and place on top of the tuna
and egg. Fold in the pastry sides, then roll into
a firm parcel, keeping the egg whole. Place on
a lightly greased baking tray and brush with
melted butter. Repeat with the remaining
pastry, filling and egg. Bake for 15 minutes,
or until the pastry is golden brown. Serve
warm or at room temperature.
NOTE: The yolk is still soft after 15 minutes.
If you prefer a firmer egg, bake for a little
longer. In Tunisia, almost anything goes inside
a brik. Tuna and anchovies are especially
popular. Instead of filo pastry, you can use
large spring roll wrappers, then deep-fry the
briks in hot oil.

TUNISIAN BRIK

Crack an egg into the
centre of the tuna mixture.

Lay another two sheets of
filo over the tuna and egg
and fold in the sides.

Gently roll up the pastry
into a firm package, keeping
the egg intact.

*OPPOSITE PAGE, FROM
TOP: Tunisian carrot salad;
Cucumber, feta, mint and
dill salad; Tunisian brik*

SALATET ADS
(Lentil salad)

Preparation time: 15 minutes
  + 30 minutes standing
Total cooking time: 30 minutes
Serves 4–6

1 small onion
2 cloves
1½ cups (300 g/10 oz) puy lentils (see Note)
1 strip lemon rind
2 cloves garlic, peeled
1 fresh bay leaf
2 teaspoons ground cumin
2 tablespoons red wine vinegar
¼ cup (60 ml/2 fl oz) olive oil
1 tablespoon lemon juice
2 tablespoons finely chopped fresh mint leaves
3 spring onions, finely chopped

1 Stud the onion with the cloves and place in a saucepan with the lentils, rind, garlic, bay leaf, 1 teaspoon cumin and 3½ cups (875 ml/28 fl oz) water. Bring to the boil and simmer gently over medium heat for 25–30 minutes, or until the lentils are tender. Drain off any excess liquid and discard the onion, rind and bay leaf. Reserve the garlic and finely chop.
2 Whisk together the vinegar, oil, juice, garlic and remaining cumin. Stir the dressing through the lentils with the mint and spring onion. Season well, then leave for 30 minutes to allow the flavours to develop. Serve at room temperature.
NOTE: Puy lentils are small green lentils, available from gourmet food stores.

CHORBA BIL HOUT
(Fish soup)

Preparation time: 30 minutes
Total cooking time: 30 minutes
Serves 6

2 red peppers (capsicums)
1 long fresh red chilli
2 tablespoons extra virgin olive oil
1 brown onion, finely chopped
1 tablespoon tomato paste (tomato purée)
2–3 teaspoons harissa (see page 246)
4 cloves garlic, finely chopped
2 teaspoons ground cumin
3 cups (750 ml/24 fl oz) fish stock
400 g (13 oz) can crushed good-quality tomatoes
750 g (1½ lb) firm white fish such as blue eye or ling, cut into 2 cm (¾ inch) squares
2 bay leaves
2 tablespoons chopped fresh coriander
6 thick slices of baguette
1 clove garlic, extra, cut in half

RED WINE VINEGAR
'Vinaigre' the French word for vinegar literally means sour wine. Red wine vinegar is produced by allowing fresh wine to ferment slowly. As it ages, usually in oak barrels, the flavours mature to produce a powerful and delicious vinegar. Today, most vinegar has a bacteria added to protect it from undesirable micro-organisms and yeasts which may cause it to spoil.

RIGHT: Salatet ads

Remove the stones from
the dates and slice the
dates thinly.

Separate the oranges into
sections and remove all the
surrounding membrane.

1 Cut the peppers into quarters and remove the
membrane and seeds. Cut the chilli in half and
remove the seeds. Grill both until the skin is
blackened and blistered. Cool in a plastic bag,
then peel and cut into thin strips.

2 Heat the oil in a large saucepan and cook the
onion for 5 minutes, or until softened. Add the
tomato paste, harissa, garlic, cumin and 1/2 cup
(4 fl oz) water, then stir to combine. Add the
fish stock, tomato and 2 cups (500 ml/16 fl oz)
water. Bring to the boil, then reduce the heat
and add the fish and bay leaves. Simmer for
7–8 minutes, until the fish is just done. Remove
the fish with a slotted spoon and place on a
plate. Discard the bay leaves. When the soup
has cooled slightly, add half the fresh coriander
and purée in a blender until smooth. Season
with salt and pepper.

3 Return the soup to the pan, add the fish and
the pepper and chilli strips and simmer gently
while you prepare the toasts.

4 Toast the bread and, while still warm, rub
with the cut garlic. Place a piece in shallow
rimmed soup bowls and pile several pieces of
fish on top of each. Ladle the soup over the top,
distributing the pepper around. Garnish with
the remaining coriander. Can be served with
lemon wedges on the side.

ORANGE AND DATE SALAD

Preparation time: 30 minutes + refrigeration
Total cooking time: Nil
Serves 4–6

6 navel oranges
2 teaspoons orange blossom water
8 dates, pitted and thinly sliced lengthways
90 g (3 oz) slivered almonds, lightly toasted
1 tablespoon shredded fresh mint
1/4 teaspoon ras el hanout (see page 261)
   or cinnamon

1 Peel the oranges, removing all the pith.
Section them by cutting away all the membranes
from the flesh. Place the segments in a bowl and
squeeze the juice from the remainder of the
orange over them. Add the orange blossom
water and stir gently to combine. Cover with
plastic wrap and refrigerate until chilled.

2 Place the segments and the juice on a large
flat dish and scatter the dates and almonds over
the top. Sprinkle the mint and ras el hanout
over the orange segments. Serve chilled.

*ABOVE: Orange and
date salad*

253

1 litre beef stock

3 x 300 g (10 oz) cans chickpeas, rinsed and drained

800 g (1 lb 10 oz) can diced good-quality tomatoes

1/2 cup (30 g/1 oz) finely chopped fresh coriander

fresh coriander leaves, extra, to garnish

small black olives, for serving

1 Heat the oil in a large heavy-based saucepan or stockpot, add the onion and garlic and cook for 5 minutes, or until softened. Add the meat, in batches, and cook over high heat until the meat is browned on all sides. Return all the meat to the pan.

2 Add the spices and bay leaf to the pan and cook until fragrant. Add the tomato paste and cook for about 2 minutes, stirring constantly. Add the stock to the pan, stir well and bring to the boil.

3 Add the chickpeas, tomato and chopped coriander to the pan. Stir, then bring to the boil. Reduce the heat and simmer for 2 hours, or until the meat is tender. Stir occassionally. Season, to taste.

4 Serve garnished with coriander leaves and small black olives. Can be served with toasted pitta bread drizzled with a little extra virgin olive oil.

MELOKHIA SOUP

Preparation time: 20 minutes
Total cooking time: 35 minutes
Serves 4

2 silverbeet (Swiss chard) leaves, stalks discarded

1.25 litres chicken stock

1 onion, halved

6 cracked cardamom pods

400 g (13 oz) packet frozen shredded melokhia leaves (see Glossary and Note), or 1 cup (30 g/1 oz) dried leaves, crumbled

2 tablespoons ghee

4 cloves garlic, crushed

1 teaspoon ground coriander

pinch of chilli powder

DRESSING

1 small onion, finely chopped

2 tablespoons lemon juice

HARIRA

(Chickpea, lamb and coriander soup)

Preparation time: 15 minutes
Total cooking time: 2 hours 25 minutes
Serves 4

2 tablespoons olive oil

2 small brown onions, chopped

2 large cloves garlic, crushed

500 g (1 lb) lamb shoulder steaks, trimmed of excess fat and sinew, cut into small chunks

1 1/2 teaspoons ground cumin

2 teaspoons paprika

1/2 teaspoon ground cloves

1 bay leaf

2 tablespoons tomato paste (tomato purée)

ABOVE: Harira

254

1 Finely chop the silverbeet leaves. Put the stock, onion and cardamom pods in a large saucepan, bring to the boil and boil for 12–15 minutes, until the stock reduces to about 1 litre. Remove the onion and cardamom with a slotted spoon. Add the silverbeet and melokhia leaves to the pan. Bring to the boil, reduce the heat and simmer, uncovered, for 10 minutes.

2 Meanwhile, heat the ghee in a small saucepan and add the garlic and 1/4 teaspoon salt. Cook over low heat, stirring constantly, until the garlic is golden. Remove from the heat and stir in the coriander and chilli.

3 For the dressing, combine the onion and lemon juice in a small serving bowl.

4 Stir the garlic mixture into the soup and simmer for 2 minutes. Serve accompanied by the dressing to be added according to taste.
NOTE: If you are using frozen cooked leaves, you will notice they appear to be mixed with egg white—don't try to rinse this off. Cooked melokhia leaves have a viscous consistency similar to okra and this is what gives the soup its characteristic texture.

1 If using wooden skewers, soak them for about 30 minutes to prevent them from burning during cooking.

2 Place the tuna in a shallow non-metallic dish. Combine the oil, cumin and lemon rind and pour over the tuna. Toss to coat, then cover and marinate in the refrigerator for 10 minutes.

3 Meanwhile, for the chermoula, place the coriander, cumin, paprika and cayenne pepper in a small frying pan and cook over medium heat for 30 seconds, or until fragrant. Combine with the remaining chermoula ingredients and set aside.

4 Thread the tuna onto the skewers. Lightly oil a chargrill or barbecue and cook the skewers for 1 minute on each side for rare or 2 minutes for medium. Serve the skewers on a bed of couscous with the chermoula drizzled over the tuna.

BELOW: Tuna skewers with Moroccan spices and chermoula

TUNA SKEWERS WITH MOROCCAN SPICES AND CHERMOULA

Preparation time: 20 minutes
+ 10 minutes marinating
Total cooking time: 5 minutes
Serves 4

☆

800 g (1 lb 10 oz) tuna steaks, cut into 3 cm
(1 1/4 inch) cubes
2 tablespoons olive oil
1/2 teaspoon ground cumin
2 teaspoons finely grated lemon rind

CHERMOULA
1/2 teaspoon ground coriander
3 teaspoons ground cumin
2 teaspoons paprika
pinch of cayenne pepper
4 garlic cloves, crushed
1/2 cup (15 g/1/2 oz) chopped fresh flat-leaf
parsley
1/2 cup (25 g/3/4 oz) chopped fresh coriander
1/3 cup (80 ml/2 3/4 fl oz) lemon juice
1/2 cup (125 ml/4 fl oz) olive oil

KEFTA GHAN' MI BEL'
(Lamb kefta)

Preparation time: 30 minutes
Total cooking time: 40 minutes
Serves 4

1 kg (2 lb) lamb mince
1 onion, finely chopped
2 cloves garlic, finely chopped
2 tablespoons finely chopped fresh
    flat-leaf parsley
2 tablespoons finely chopped fresh
    coriander leaves
1/2 teaspoon cayenne pepper
1/2 teaspoon ground allspice
1/2 teaspoon ground ginger
1/2 teaspoon ground cardamom
1 teaspoon ground cumin
1 teaspoon paprika

SAUCE

2 tablespoons olive oil
1 onion, finely chopped
2 cloves garlic, finely chopped
2 teaspoons ground cumin
1/2 teaspoon ground cinnamon
1 teaspoon paprika
2 x 400 g (13 oz) cans chopped good-quality
    tomatoes
2 teaspoons harissa (see page 246)
4 tablespoons chopped fresh coriander leaves

1 Preheat the oven to moderate 180°C (350°F/
Gas 4). Lightly grease two baking trays. Place the
lamb, onion, garlic, herbs and spices in a bowl
and mix well. Season with salt and pepper. Roll
tablespoons of mixture into balls and place on
the trays. Bake for 20 minutes, or until browned.
2 Meanwhile, for the sauce, heat the oil in a
large saucepan, add the onion and cook over
medium heat for 5 minutes, or until soft. Add
the garlic, cumin, cinnamon and paprika, and
cook for 1 minute, or until fragrant. Stir in the
tomato and harissa, and bring to the boil. Reduce
the heat and simmer for 20 minutes. Add the
meatballs and simmer for 10 minutes, or until
cooked. Stir in the coriander, season and serve.

SAFFRON RICE

Preparation time: 5 minutes + 30 minutes standing
Total cooking time: 15 minutes
Serves 6

500 g (1 lb) long-grain rice
1/2 teaspoon saffron threads, crushed
2 tablespoons olive oil
20 g (3/4 oz) butter
60 g (2 oz) shelled pistachio nuts, coarsely
    chopped, to garnish, optional

1 Wash the rice in a sieve until the water runs
clear, then drain well.
2 Bring 900 ml (28 fl oz) water to the boil and
add the saffron. Allow to infuse for 20 minutes.
3 Heat the oil in a heavy-based saucepan and
add the rice, stirring well so that all the rice is
coated evenly in the oil. Add the saffron water
and 1/4 teaspoon of salt and stir well. Bring to the
boil and boil for 1 minute. Cover with a tight-
fitting lid, then reduce the heat to as low as

BELOW: Kefta Ghan' mi bel'

possible and cook for 10–12 minutes, until all the water has been absorbed. Steam tunnels will form holes on the surface. Turn off the heat, then leave the pan covered for at least 10 minutes. Add the butter and fluff lightly with a fork. Garnish with pistachios and serve.
NOTE: Because saffron is the main flavour in this recipe, it is important to use real saffron threads.

TROUT STUFFED WITH DATES

Preparation time: 30 minutes
Total cooking time: 20 minutes
Serves 4

4 medium-sized trout
3/4 cup (140 g/4 1/2 oz) chopped dates
1/4 cup (45 g/1 1/2 oz) cooked rice
1 onion, finely chopped
4 tablespoons chopped fresh coriander leaves
1/4 teaspoon ground ginger
1/4 teaspoon ground cinnamon
1/3 cup (50 g/1 3/4 oz) roughly chopped blanched almonds
40 g (1 1/2 oz) butter, softened
cinnamon, for dusting

1 Preheat the oven to moderate 180°C (350°F/Gas 4). Rinse the trout under cold running water and pat dry with paper towels. Season lightly with salt and pepper.
2 Combine the dates, rice, half the onion, the coriander, ginger, cinnamon, almonds and half the butter in a bowl. Season well with salt and pepper.
3 Spoon the stuffing into the fish cavities and place each fish on a well-greased double sheet of foil. Brush the fish with the remaining butter, season with salt and pepper and divide the remaining onion among the four parcels. Wrap the fish neatly and seal the edges of the foil. Place the parcels on a large baking tray and bake for 15–20 minutes, or until cooked to your liking. Serve dusted with cinnamon.

ABOVE: Trout stuffed with dates

257

VEGETABLE COUSCOUS

Add the pumpkin, cauliflower and zucchini to the pan and cook for 10 minutes.

Add the remaining oil and butter to the couscous and fluff it up with a fork.

OPPOSITE PAGE, FROM TOP: Vegetable couscous; Lamb tagine with quince

VEGETABLE COUSCOUS

Preparation time: 40 minutes
Total cooking time: 30 minutes
Serves 4–6

3 tablespoons olive oil
2 small onions, thinly sliced
1 teaspoon turmeric
1/2 teaspoon chilli powder
2 teaspoons grated fresh ginger
1 cinnamon stick
2 carrots, thickly sliced
2 parsnips, thickly sliced
1 1/2 cups (375 ml/12 fl oz) vegetable stock
315 g (10 oz) pumpkin, cut into small cubes
250 g (8 oz) cauliflower, cut into small florets
2 zucchini (courgettes), cut into thick slices
425 g (13 1/2 oz) can chickpeas, drained
pinch of saffron threads
2 tablespoons chopped fresh coriander
2 tablespoons chopped fresh flat-leaf parsley
1 1/4 cups (230 g/7 1/2 oz) instant couscous
1 cup (250 ml/8 oz) boiling water
30 g (1 oz) butter

1 Heat 2 tablespoons of the oil in a large saucepan. Add the onion and cook over medium heat for 5 minutes, or until the onion is soft, stirring occasionally. Add the turmeric, chilli powder and ginger and cook, stirring, for another minute.
2 Add the cinnamon stick, carrot, parsnip and stock to the pan and stir to combine. Cover and bring to the boil. Reduce the heat and simmer for 5 minutes, or until the vegetables are almost tender.
3 Add the pumpkin, cauliflower and zucchini and simmer for another 10 minutes. Stir in the chickpeas, saffron, coriander and parsley and simmer, uncovered, for 5 minutes. Remove the cinnamon stick.
4 Place the couscous in a bowl and add the boiling water. Cover, allow to stand for 5 minutes, then add the remaining oil and butter and fluff with a fork. Place a bed of couscous on each serving plate and top with the vegetables.
NOTE: Almost any seasonal vegetables can be used in this recipe. Potato, orange sweet potato, green beans, baby onions, or red or green peppers (capsicums) are all suitable.

LAMB TAGINE WITH QUINCE

Preparation time: 20 minutes
Total cooking time: 1 hour 40 minutes
Serves 4–6

1.5 kg (3 lb) lamb shoulder, cut into 3 cm (1 1/4 inch) pieces
2 large onions, diced
1/2 teaspoon ground ginger
1/2 teaspoon cayenne pepper
1/4 teaspoon pulverised saffron threads
1 teaspoon ground coriander
1 cinnamon stick
1/2 cup (25 g/3/4 oz) roughly chopped fresh coriander
40 g (1 1/4 oz) butter
500 g (1 lb) quinces, peeled, cored and quartered
100 g (3 1/2 oz) dried apricots
fresh coriander sprigs, extra, to garnish

1 Place the lamb in a heavy-based, flameproof casserole dish and add half the onion, the ginger, cayenne pepper, saffron, ground coriander, cinnamon stick, fresh coriander and some salt and pepper. Cover with cold water and bring to the boil over medium heat. Lower the heat and simmer, partly covered, for 1 1/2 hours, or until the lamb is tender.
2 While the lamb is cooking, melt the butter in a heavy-based frying pan and cook the remaining onion and the quinces for 15 minutes over medium heat, or until lightly golden.
3 When the lamb has been cooking for 1 hour, add the quinces and apricots.
4 Taste the sauce and adjust the seasoning if necessary. Transfer to a warm serving dish and sprinkle with coriander sprigs. Delicious served with couscous or rice.
NOTE: The word 'tagine' not only refers to the classic stews of Morocco but also the special, often beautifully decorated, earthenware dish, with its distinctive pointed top, in which the stews are cooked. Although these vessels are becoming more readily available in kitchenware stores, a heavy-based casserole with a tight-fitting lid is a perfect substitute.

1 Crush the coriander seeds in a mortar and pestle. Transfer to a bowl, add the cracked black pepper and the pork and toss to coat. Cover and refrigerate overnight.

2 Add the flour to the pork and toss. Heat 2 tablespoons oil in a frying pan and cook the pork in batches over high heat for 1–2 minutes, or until brown. Remove from the pan.

3 Heat the remaining oil in the pan, add the onion and cook over medium heat for 2–3 minutes, or until just golden. Return the meat to the pan, add the red wine, stock and sugar. Season, bring to the boil, then reduce the heat and simmer, covered, for 1 hour.

4 Remove the meat. Return the pan to the heat and boil over high heat for 3–5 minutes, or until the sauce is reduced and slightly thickened. Pour over the meat and garnish with coriander sprigs.

BISTEEYA
(Moroccan chicken pie)

Preparation time: 30 minutes
Total cooking time: 1 hour 20 minutes
Serves 6–8

☆ ☆ ☆

200 g (6 1/2 oz) butter
1.5 kg (3 lb) chicken, cut into 4 portions
1 large onion, finely chopped
3 teaspoons ground cinnamon
1 teaspoon ground ginger
2 teaspoons ground cumin
1/4 teaspoon cayenne pepper
1/2 teaspoon ground turmeric
1/2 teaspoon saffron threads soaked in
   2 tablespoons warm water
1/2 cup (125 ml/4 fl oz) chicken stock
4 eggs, lightly beaten
1/2 cup (25 g/3/4 oz) chopped fresh coriander
3 tablespoons chopped fresh flat-leaf parsley
1/3 cup (50 g/1 3/4 oz) chopped almonds
3 tablespoons icing sugar, plus extra,
   for dusting
375 g (12 oz) filo pastry

1 Preheat the oven to moderate 180°C (350°F/ Gas 4). Grease a 30 cm (12 inch) pizza tray.

2 Melt 40 g (1 1/4 oz) of the butter in a large frying pan, add the chicken, onion, 2 teaspoons of the cinnamon, all the other spices and the chicken stock. Season with salt and pepper,

AFELIA
(Cypriot pork and coriander stew)

Preparation time: 15 minutes
   + overnight refrigeration
Total cooking time: 1 hour 20 minutes
Serves 4–6

☆ ☆

1 1/2 tablespoons coriander seeds
1/2 teaspoon cracked black pepper
800 g (1 lb 10 oz) pork fillet, cut into 2 cm
   (3/4 inch) dice
1 tablespoon plain flour
1/4 cup (60 ml/2 fl oz) olive oil
1 large onion, thinly sliced
1 1/2 cups (375 ml/12 fl oz) red wine
1 cup (250 ml/8 fl oz) chicken stock
1 teaspoon sugar
fresh coriander sprigs, to garnish

ABOVE: Afelia

cover and simmer for 30 minutes, or until the chicken is cooked through.

3 Remove the chicken from the sauce. When cool enough to handle, remove the meat from the bones, discard the skin and bones and shred the meat into thin strips.

4 Bring the liquid in the pan to a simmer and add the eggs. Cook the mixture, stirring constantly, until the eggs are cooked and the mixture is quite dry. Add the chicken, chopped coriander and parsley, season well with salt and pepper and mix. Remove from the heat.

5 Bake the almonds on a baking tray until golden brown. Cool slightly, then blend in a food processor or spice grinder with the icing sugar and remaining cinnamon until they resemble coarse crumbs.

6 Melt the remaining butter. Place a sheet of filo on the pizza tray and brush with melted butter. Place another sheet on top in a pinwheel effect and brush with butter. Continue brushing and layering until you have used 8 sheets. Place the chicken mixture on top and sprinkle with the almond mixture.

7 Fold the overlapping filo over the top of the filling. Place a sheet of filo over the top and brush with butter continue to layer buttered filo over the top in the same pinwheel effect until you have used 8 sheets. Tuck the overhanging edges over the pie to form a neat round parcel. Brush well with the remaining butter. Bake the pie for 40–45 minutes until cooked through and golden. Dust with icing sugar before serving.

RAS EL HANOUT

This spice mixture may contain up to twelve spices, each vendor fiercely guarding the secret recipe. It is commonly used in Moroccan cooking.

To make your own mixture, grind 7 g (¼ oz) turmeric, 15 g (½ oz) allspice berries, 30 g (1 oz) black peppercorns, 1½ whole nutmegs, 1 whole clove, 10 cardamom pods, 1 cinnamon stick, 1 teaspoon cayenne pepper and 3 rosebuds in a spice blender until you have a fine mixture, then sieve and store in a tightly sealed jar.

Sprinkle the almond mixture all over the chicken.

Fold the overlapping sheets of filo over the top of the filling.

LEFT: Bisteeya

MECHOUI
(Slow-roasted lamb with cumin and paprika)

Preparation time: 15 minutes
Total cooking time: 3 hours 30 minutes
Serves 6

2.2 kg (4 lb 6¹/₂ oz) leg of lamb

75 g (3 oz) butter, softened at room
   temperature

3 cloves garlic, crushed

2 teaspoons ground cumin

3 teaspoons ground coriander

1 teaspoon paprika

1 tablespoon cumin, extra, for dipping

1 Preheat the oven to hot 220°C (425°F/Gas 7). With a small sharp knife, cut small deep slits in the top and sides of the lamb.
2 Mix the butter, garlic, spices and ¹/₄ teaspoon salt in a bowl until a smooth paste forms.
3 With the back of a spoon rub the paste all over the lamb, then use your fingers to spread the paste and make sure all the lamb is covered.
4 Put the lamb bone-side-down in a deep baking dish and place on the top shelf of the oven. Bake for 10 minutes, then baste and return to the oven. Reduce the temperature to warm 160°C (315°F/Gas 2–3). Bake for 3 hours 20 minutes, basting every 20–30 minutes. Basting makes the lamb tender and flavoursome. Carve the lamb into chunky pieces. Mix the cumin with 1¹/₂ teaspoons salt and serve on the side for dipping.

MECHOUI
Traditionally, mechoui was a dish consisting of an entire lamb roasted in a mud oven that was dug deep in the ground. In many parts of North Africa it is still prepared in this way for family celebrations and on special holy days. Regarded as a national dish, it is often served as the centrepiece of mechoui parties and is also an integral part of the region's street food, where it is accompanied by a mixture of salt and ground cumin.

RIGHT: Mechoui

OKRA WITH CORIANDER AND TOMATO SAUCE

Preparation time: 5 minutes
Total cooking time: 15 minutes
Serves 4–6

1/4 cup (60 ml/2 fl oz) olive oil
1 onion, chopped
2 cloves garlic, crushed
500 g (1 lb) fresh okra (see Note)
400 g (13 oz) can chopped good-quality tomatoes
2 teaspoons sugar
1/4 cup (60 ml/2 fl oz) lemon juice
60 g (2 oz) fresh coriander, finely chopped

1 Heat the oil in a large frying pan, add the onion and cook over medium heat for 5 minutes, or until transparent and golden. Add the garlic and cook for another minute.
2 Add the okra to the pan and cook, stirring, for 4–5 minutes, then add the tomato, sugar and lemon juice, and simmer, stirring occasionally, for 3–4 minutes, or until softened. Stir in the coriander, remove from the heat and serve.
NOTE: If fresh okra is not available, you can use an 800 g (1 lb 10 oz) can instead. Rinse and drain the okra before adding with the coriander.

CHICKEN WITH ALMONDS

Preparation time: 15 minutes
Total cooking time: 1 hour
Serves 6

1.5 kg (3 lb) chicken, quartered
60 g (2 oz) butter
1 onion, chopped
1/2 teaspoon ground ginger
1/2 teaspoon saffron powder or 2 pinches of threads
1/2 teaspoon ground cinnamon
1 tablespoon finely chopped fresh coriander leaves
2 tablespoons oil
125 g (4 oz) blanched almonds
30 g (1 oz) finely chopped fresh flat-leaf parsley

1 Put the chicken in a large saucepan or stockpot. Add the butter, onion, spices, chopped coriander and 1 teaspoon each of salt and pepper. Add 1 1/4 cups (315 ml/10 fl oz) water, cover and cook over low heat for 1 hour. Turn the chicken over occasionally and add water if necessary.
2 Heat the oil in a frying pan over low heat, add the almonds and cook until golden. Remove.
3 Add the parsley to the chicken and cook for 2–3 minutes. Serve sprinkled with the almonds.

OKRA
Okra is a vegetable native to Africa which was introduced to Middle Eastern and Arabian countries by slave traders. When sliced and cooked slowly, the texture becomes sticky and is perfect for thickening and adding body to stews. Okra has become an integral ingredient in many Middle Eastern dishes, the texture melding with tomatoes, garlic, onions, and spices. The sticky texture is minimal if the okra is left whole and cooked simply and quickly.

ABOVE: Okra with coriander and tomato sauce

2 bay leaves

2 chicken livers

3 tablespoons chopped fresh coriander leaves

1 Preheat the oven to moderate 180°C (350°F/ Gas 4). Heat 2 tablespoons oil in a large frying pan, add the chicken and brown on all sides. Place in a deep baking dish.

2 Heat the remaining oil, add the onion and garlic and cook over medium heat for 3–4 minutes, or until softened. Add the stock, ginger, cinnamon, saffron, olives, lemon and bay leaves and pour around the chicken. Bake for 45 minutes, adding a little more water or stock if the sauce gets too dry.

3 Remove the chicken from the dish, cover with foil and leave to rest. Pour the contents of the baking dish into a frying pan, add the chicken livers and mash into the sauce as they cook. Cook for 5–6 minutes, or until the sauce has reduced and thickened. Add the chopped coriander. Cut the chicken into four pieces and serve with the sauce.

SEMIT
(Egyptian sesame bread rings)

Preparation time: 45 minutes + 2 hours rising
Total cooking time: 15 minutes
Makes 20

☆ ☆

7 g (3/4 oz) sachet dried yeast

1 teaspoon sugar

3 cups (375 g/12 oz) plain flour, plus
    up to 1 cup (125 g/4 oz) extra

1/2 cup (125 ml/4 fl oz) milk

1 egg, lightly beaten

1/2 cup (80 g/23/4 oz) sesame seeds

1 Place the yeast, sugar and 1/4 cup (60ml/ 2 fl oz) warm water in a small bowl and stir until dissolved. Leave in a warm place for 10 minutes, or until bubbles appear on the surface. The mixture should be frothy and slightly increased in volume. If your yeast doesn't foam, it is dead and you will have to start again.

2 Sift the 3 cups flour into a bowl and season well with 1 teaspoon salt. Heat the milk and 1/2 cup (125 ml/4 fl oz) water together until tepid. Make a well in the flour and pour in the liquid and the yeast mixture. Mix with a wooden spoon, adding the extra flour a little

CHICKEN WITH PRESERVED LEMON AND OLIVES

Preparation time: 10 minutes
Total cooking time: 1 hour
Serves 4

☆

1/4 cup (60 ml/23/4 fl oz) olive oil

1.6 kg (31/4 lb) free-range chicken

1 onion, chopped

2 cloves garlic, chopped

21/2 cups (600 ml/20 fl oz) chicken stock

1/2 teaspoon ground ginger

11/2 teaspoons ground cinnamon

pinch saffron threads

100 g (31/2 oz) green olives

1/4 preserved lemon (see page 247), pulp
    removed, rind washed and cut into slivers

ABOVE: Chicken with preserved lemon and olives

264

at a time until a soft dough forms. Turn onto a lightly floured board and knead for 10 minutes, or until smooth and elastic. Place in an oiled bowl, cover and leave in a warm, draught-free place for 15 minutes, or until doubled in size.

3 Turn the dough onto a floured board and knock down. Break off pieces the size of an egg and roll each into a rope 1 cm (½ inch) thick and 20 cm (8 inches) long. Form the rope into a ring. Moisten the edges to seal. Continue until you have used all the dough.

4 Preheat the oven to moderately hot 200°C (400°F/Gas 6). Place a baking dish filled with hot water on the bottom of the oven to create steam while cooking the rings.

5 Grease two baking trays and dust with flour. Place the rings on the trays. Brush the surface with the beaten egg and sprinkle with the sesame seeds. Cover the rings with a damp tea towel and leave to rise in a warm place for 30 minutes. Bake the rings for 15 minutes, or until cooked and golden. While still hot, brush the rings with hot water to help create crisp crusts while they are cooling.

MOROCCAN FLATBREAD

Preparation time: 1 hour + 30 minutes rising
Total cooking time: 12 minutes
Makes 16

☆ ☆

2½ cups (375 g/12 oz) wholemeal flour
1 teaspoon caster sugar
7 g (¾ oz) sachet dried yeast
½ teaspoon sweet paprika
⅓ cup (50 g/1¾ oz) cornmeal
1 tablespoon oil
1 egg, lightly beaten
2 tablespoons sesame seeds

1 Preheat the oven to moderate 180°C (350°F/Gas 4). Lightly grease a baking tray. Put ½ cup (75 g/2½ oz) of the flour, the sugar, yeast, 1 teaspoon salt and 1¼ cups (315 ml/ 10 fl oz) tepid water in a bowl and stir until dissolved. Cover and leave in a warm place for 10 minutes, or until bubbles appear. The mixture should be frothy and slightly increased in volume. If your yeast doesn't foam, it is dead and you will have to start again.

2 Sift the paprika, cornmeal and remaining flour into a bowl. Add the oil, then stir in the yeast mixture. Mix to a firm dough and knead until smooth. Cover and leave in a warm, draught-free place for 20 minutes.

3 Divide into 16 portions, roll each into a ball, then flatten into 8 cm (3 inch) rounds. Place on the baking tray, brush with egg and sprinkle with sesame seeds. Cover and set aside for 10 minutes, or until puffed up. Bake for 12 minutes, or until golden.

MOROCCAN MINT TEA

This light sweet tea is often served before, and always after every meal, and is prepared at any hour of the day when friends or guests arrive at a Moroccan home. It is sipped in cafes. Traditionally it is served from a silver teapot into ornately painted glasses.

To make the tea in the traditional manner, heat the teapot and add 1 tablespoon green tea leaves, 30 g (1 oz) sugar and a large handful of fresh spearmint leaves and stalks. Fill with boiling water and brew for at least 5 minutes. Adjust the sweetness if necessary.

BELOW: Moroccan flatbread

SWEET COUSCOUS

Preparation time: 10 minutes + 10 minutes standing
Total cooking time: 5 minutes standing
Serves 4–6

80 g (2³/4 oz) combined pistachio nuts,
    pine nuts and blanched almonds
45 g (1¹/2 oz) dried apricots
¹/2 cup (90 g/3 oz) pitted dried dates
250 g (8 oz) instant couscous
¹/4 cup (60 g/2 oz) caster sugar
1 cup (250 ml/8 fl oz) boiling water
90 g (3 oz) unsalted butter, softened

FOR SERVING
2 tablespoons caster sugar
¹/2 teaspoon ground cinnamon
1¹/2 cups (375 ml/12 fl oz) hot milk

BELOW: Sweet couscous

1 Preheat the oven to warm 160°C (315°F/
Gas 2–3). Spread the nuts on a baking tray and
bake for about 5 minutes, until light golden.
Allow to cool, then chop coarsely and place in
a bowl. Slice the apricots into matchstick-sized
pieces and quarter the dates lengthways. Add
both to the bowl and toss to combine.
2 Put the couscous and sugar in a large bowl
and cover with the boiling water. Stir well, then
add the butter and a pinch of salt. Stir until the
butter melts. Cover with a tea towel and set
aside for 10 minutes. Fluff with a fork, then
toss half the fruit and nut mixture through.
3 To serve, pile the warm couscous in the
centre of a platter. Arrange the remaining nut
mixture around the base. Combine the sugar and
cinnamon in a small bowl and serve separately
for sprinkling. Pass around the hot milk in a jug
for guests to help themselves.
NOTE: This can be made up to 4 days ahead.
Spoon it into an earthenware baking dish, cover
with foil and refrigerate. To reheat, bring to
room temperature, then place in a moderate
180°C (350°F/Gas 4) oven for 20 minutes.

OM ALI
(Nut and filo pudding)

Preparation time: 20 minutes
Total cooking time: 35 minutes
Serves 6

6 sheets filo pastry
3 tablespoons butter, melted
60 g (2 oz) raisins
140 g (4¹/2 oz) mixed nuts, such as pistachios,
    flaked almonds and chopped hazelnuts
1 litre milk
1¹/4 cups (315 ml/10 fl oz) thick (double) cream
¹/3 cup (90 g/3 oz) sugar
1 teaspoon ground cinnamon

1 Preheat the oven to moderately hot 200°C
(400°F/Gas 6).
2 Remove a sheet of filo and cover the rest
with a damp tea towel. Brush the filo sheet
with melted butter and place on a baking tray.
Cover loosely with 2 more buttered sheets.
Repeat with the other 3 sheets on another tray.
Bake for 5 minutes, or until the pastry sheets
are crisp and golden. Reduce the heat to
moderate 180°C (350°F/Gas 4). Crumple the
filo into a 2 litre baking dish, sprinkling some

Roll each portion of dough into a sausage.

Add the cinnamon to the egg yolk and brush over the snake.

of the raisins and nuts over each sheet as you go.

3 Heat the milk, cream and sugar in a heavy-based saucepan over low heat until just below boiling point. Pour over the pastry and bake for 25–30 minutes, or until golden brown. Sprinkle with cinnamon. Serve warm or cold.

ALMOND FILO SNAKE

Preparation time: 30 minutes
Total cooking time: 40 minutes
Serves 8

☆ ☆

²/₃ cup (70 g/2¹/₄ oz) ground almonds

¹/₃ cup (30 g/1 oz) flaked almonds

175 g (6 oz) icing sugar

1 egg, separated

1 teaspoon finely grated lemon rind

¹/₄ teaspoon almond essence

1 tablespoon rosewater

2 tablespoons olive oil

2 tablespoons almond oil

9 sheets filo pastry

pinch of ground cinnamon

icing sugar, extra, to dust

1 Preheat the oven to moderate 180°C (350°F/Gas 4). Lightly grease a 20 cm (8 inch) round springform tin.

2 Place all of the almonds in a bowl with the icing sugar. Put the egg white in a bowl and lightly beat with a fork. Add to the almonds with the lemon rind, essence and rosewater. Mix to a paste.

3 Divide the mixture into 3 and roll each portion into a sausage 45 cm (18 inches) long and 1 cm (¹/₂ inch) thick. If the paste is too sticky to roll, dust the bench with icing sugar.

4 Mix the oils in a bowl. Remove 1 sheet of filo and cover the rest with a damp tea towel to prevent it drying out. Brush the filo sheet with the oils, then cover with 2 more oiled sheets. Place 1 almond 'sausage' along the length of the oiled pastry and roll up to enclose the filling. Form into a coil and sit the coil in the centre of the tin. Use oil to join the other sausages and continue shaping to make a large coil.

5 Add the cinnamon to the egg yolk and brush over the snake. Bake for 30 minutes, then remove the side of the tin and turn the snake over. Bake for another 10 minutes to crisp the base. Dust with icing sugar and serve warm.
NOTE: The snake will keep for up to 3 days but should not be refrigerated.

ABOVE: Almond filo snake

FRIED HONEY CAKES

Mix the dough with a wooden spoon until smooth, but still slightly sticky.

Use a biscuit cutter to cut out round cakes from the dough.

FRIED HONEY CAKES

Preparation time: 20 minutes
  + 1 hour standing
Total cooking time: 20 minutes
Serves 4–6

☆ ☆

3 eggs
1/4 cup (60 ml/2 fl oz) orange juice
1/4 cup (60 ml/2 fl oz) vegetable oil
1 tablespoon grated orange rind
1/4 cup (60 g/2 oz) caster sugar
300 g (10 oz) plain flour
1 teaspoon baking powder
about 4 tablespoons flour, extra,
  for rolling

SYRUP
2 tablespoons lemon juice
275 g (9 oz) sugar
1/3 cup (115 g/4 oz) honey
1 tablespoon grated orange rind
vegetable oil, for deep-frying

1 Whisk the eggs, orange juice and oil together in a large bowl. Add the orange rind and sugar and whisk until frothy. Sift in the flour and baking powder and mix with a wooden spoon until smooth, but still a bit sticky. Cover and set aside for 1 hour.
2 For the syrup, in a saucepan, heat 1 1/4 cups (315 ml/10 fl oz) cold water with the lemon juice and sugar, stirring until the sugar dissolves. Bring to the boil, reduce the heat and simmer for 5 minutes. Add the honey and orange rind and simmer for another 5 minutes. Keep warm.
3 Sprinkle a little of the extra flour onto the dough and transfer it to a lightly floured surface. Work in just enough extra flour to give a dough which doesn't stick to your hands. Roll it out to a thickness of 5 mm (1/4 inch). It will be very elastic, so keep rolling and resting it until it stops shrinking. Using a 5 cm (2 inch) biscuit cutter, cut out round cakes.
4 Heat the oil in a large deep-sided frying pan to 170°C (325°F), or until a cube of bread dropped into the oil browns in 20 seconds. Fry the cakes 3 or 4 at a time until puffed and golden, about 1 minute on each side. Remove with tongs and drain on paper towels.
5 Using tongs, dip each cake into the warm syrup long enough for it to soak in. Transfer to a platter. Serve warm or cold.

ABOVE: Fried honey cakes

BAKED SPICED QUINCE

Preparation time: 25 minutes
Total cooking time: 1 hour
Serves 4–6

☆

4 quinces (see Note)
40 g (1¼ oz) unsalted butter
1 tablespoon rosewater
1¼ cups (310 g/10 oz) sugar
½ teaspoon ground cinnamon
¼ teaspoon cloves
thick natural yoghurt, for serving
honey, for serving
roasted pistachio nuts, for serving

1 Preheat the oven to slow 150°C (300°F/
Gas 2). Lightly grease an ovenproof dish.
2 Peel the quinces, then cut them into quarters,
removing the cores.
3 Place the quinces cut-side-up in the dish,
distribute the butter among the pieces of quince,
then sprinkle with rosewater, sugar and spices.
Cover the dish tightly with foil and bake for
1 hour, or until tender. Serve with the yoghurt,
drizzled with honey and sprinkled with
pistachios.
NOTE: The cooking time will vary depending
on the size of the quinces.

DATE CANDIES

Preparation time: 10 minutes
Total cooking time: 15 minutes
Serves 6–8

☆

1½ cups (150 g/5 oz) walnut halves
2 tablespoons sesame seeds
100 g (3½ oz) ghee
600 g (1¼ lb) pitted dried dates, coarsely
  chopped

1 Preheat the oven to moderate 180°C (350°F/
Gas 4) and line the base and two opposite sides
of an 18 cm (7 inch) square slice tin with baking
paper. Spread the walnuts on a baking tray and
bake for 5 minutes, until lightly toasted. Chop
coarsely. Bake the sesame seeds until golden.
2 Melt the ghee in a large heavy-based
saucepan and cook the dates, covered, over low
heat for about 10 minutes, stirring often, until
the dates soften. Using the back of a spoon
dipped in cold water, spread half in the tin.
Scatter the walnuts on top and press into the
dates. Spread the remaining date mixture over
the walnuts. Smooth the surface with wet fingers
and press down firmly. Sprinkle with the sesame
seeds and press lightly into the dates. When
cool, cut into small diamonds. Serve at the
end of a meal or as a delicious treat.

QUINCES
When cooked slowly,
quinces become a glorious
deep red pink. They are
meltingly tender, sweet and
perfumed, and it is easy
to understand why they
became the symbol of love,
happiness and fertility in
ancient times. They can
be used in the making of
desserts, for adding a
sweetness to savoury
dishes, as well as in pastes
to serve with cheeses, and
jellies to spread on your
breakfast brioche.

LEFT: Date candies

MIDDLE EAST

A history dating back thousands of years has led to an interesting variety in Middle Eastern cuisine developed by a diverse group of peoples. Ingredients commonly used elsewhere along the Mediterranean, such as parsley, mint, citrus, olive oil and cinnamon, are used far more subtly here. Allspice, yoghurt, dried beans, rice and burghul, artichokes, fish, lamb and chicken all come into play. The cooking may seem elaborate but is surprisingly easy. The unique dishes tabbouleh, baba ghannouj and kibbeh are popular in many places besides this area. Some dishes require lengthy cooking but involve little work. Many can be cooked ahead. Meals don't usually include sweets or puddings but these are enjoyed with visitors and at festive occasions.

CHICKPEAS

Legumes such as chickpeas are a key feature of Middle Eastern cuisine. This is due in part to the dietary laws of the region's predominant religion, Islam, as chickpeas can be eaten during times of fasting. A food source since ancient times, they have historically been regarded in literature, songs and proverbs as the food of the poor, and are mentioned in the Bible. An affordable and popular source of protein, there are many regional dishes based on chickpeas, which can be eaten hot as vegetables, cold in salads and dips, or used to add substance and texture to vegetable, meat, rice and pasta dishes. As with other legumes, chickpeas need to be soaked before cooking. They require a large amount of water as they absorb a lot. Some cooks like to remove the skins after cooking. Chickpeas should not be cooked initially with salt as this will toughen them. Soaking and cooking times should be adjusted, depending on the age of the chickpeas, as older ones require longer soaking and cooking.

ABOVE: Falafel

FALAFEL
(Deep-fried chickpea balls)

Preparation time: 20 minutes + 48 hours soaking + 50 minutes standing
Total cooking time: 10 minutes
Makes 30

1 cup (150 g/5 oz) dried split broad beans (see Note)
1 cup (220 g/7 oz) dried chickpeas
1 onion, roughly chopped
6 cloves garlic, roughly chopped
2 teaspoons ground coriander
1 tablespoon ground cumin
1/2 cup (15 g/1/2 oz) chopped fresh flat-leaf parsley
1/4 teaspoon chilli powder
1/2 teaspoon bicarbonate of soda
3 tablespoons chopped fresh coriander leaves
light oil, for deep-frying

1 Place the broad beans in a large bowl, cover well with water and soak for 48 hours. Drain, then rinse several times in fresh water.

2 Place the chickpeas in a large bowl, cover well with water and soak for 12 hours.
3 Drain the broad beans and chickpeas well, then process in a food processor with the onion and garlic until smooth.
4 Add the ground coriander, cumin, parsley, chilli powder, bicarbonate of soda and fresh coriander. Season, to taste, and mix until well combined. Transfer to a large bowl and set aside for 30 minutes.
5 Shape tablespoons of mixture into balls, flatten to 4 cm (1½ inch) rounds, place on a tray and refrigerate for 20 minutes.
6 Fill a deep, heavy-based saucepan one third full of oil and heat to 180°C (350°F), or until a cube of bread dropped in the oil browns in 15 seconds. Cook the felafel in batches for 1–2 minutes, or until golden. Drain on paper towels. Serve hot or cold with hummus, baba ghannouj and pitta bread.
NOTE: Split broad beans, which are already skinned, are available from specialist stores. If whole broad beans are used, they will need to be skinned after soaking. To do this, squeeze each broad bean to allow the skin to pop off, or pierce each skin with your fingernail, then peel it off.

RED PEPPER, WALNUT AND POMEGRANATE DIP

Preparation time: 10 minutes
  + overnight refrigeration
Total cooking time: 15 minutes
Serves 4–6

450 g (14 oz) red peppers (capsicums)
1/2 cup (50 g/1 3/4 oz) walnuts
2 cloves garlic, crushed
1/2 cup (40 g/1 1/4 oz) fresh breadcrumbs
2 small fresh red chillies, seeded, finely chopped
2 tablespoons olive oil
1 teaspoon pomegranate syrup
2 tablespoons lemon juice
1 teaspoon cumin seeds, coarsely ground
1/2 teaspoon crushed red chilli flakes

1 Cut the peppers into large, flat pieces and put skin-side-up under a hot grill until black. Cool in a plastic bag, then peel and process until fine.
2 Chop the walnuts, garlic and breadcrumbs in a food processor until finely ground. Add the peppers, chopped chilli, olive oil, pomegranate syrup and lemon juice and process in short bursts to combine. Transfer to a bowl and stir in the cumin and chilli flakes. Season with salt, then chill overnight to allow the flavours to mellow. Serve at room temperature with flatbread.

TABBOULEH

Preparation time: 20 minutes + 1 hour
  30 minutes soaking + 30 minutes drying
Total cooking time: Nil
Serves 6

3/4 cup (130 g/4 1/2 oz) burghul
3 ripe tomatoes
1 telegraph cucumber
4 spring onions, sliced
4 cups (120 g/4 oz) chopped fresh
  flat-leaf parsley
1/2 cup (25 g/3/4 oz) chopped fresh mint

DRESSING
1/3 cup (80 ml/2 3/4 fl oz) lemon juice
1/4 cup (60 ml/2 fl oz) olive oil
1 tablespoon extra virgin olive oil

1 Place the burghul in a bowl, cover with 2 cups (500 ml/16 fl oz) water and leave for 1 1/2 hours.
2 Cut the tomatoes in half, squeeze gently to remove any excess seeds and cut into 1 cm (1/2 inch) cubes. Cut the cucumber in half lengthways, remove the seeds with a teaspoon and cut the flesh into 1 cm (1/2 inch) cubes.
3 To make the dressing, place the lemon juice and 1 1/2 teaspoons salt in a bowl and whisk until well combined. Season well with freshly ground black pepper and slowly whisk in the olive oil and extra virgin olive oil.
4 Drain the burghul and squeeze out any excess water. Spread the burghul out on a clean tea towel or paper towels and leave to dry for about 30 minutes. Put the burghul in a large salad bowl, add the tomato, cucumber, spring onion, parsley and mint, and toss well to combine. Pour the dressing over the salad and toss until evenly coated.

BELOW: Tabbouleh

273

BAY LEAVES
A feature of Middle Eastern food is the use of aromatics such as bay leaves. Available either fresh or dried, bay leaves come from the native Mediterranean evergreen bay laurel tree. A historical symbol of triumph, honour and celebration, they are an essential ingredient in a bouquet garni and are used to impart their fragrance to vegetable and meat dishes, soups and stews. Be careful not to overuse them as they can make a dish taste bitter.

LABNEH MAKBUR
(Marinated yoghurt cheese balls)

Preparation time: 35 minutes
+ 3 days draining
+ 3 hours refrigeration
Total cooking time: Nil
Makes 18 balls

☆ ☆ ☆

1.5 kg (3 lb) thick natural yoghurt
2 clean 50 cm (20 inch) square muslin squares
2 fresh bay leaves
3 sprigs fresh thyme
2 sprigs fresh oregano
2 cups (500 ml/16 fl oz) good-quality olive oil

1 Place the yoghurt in a bowl with 2 teaspoons salt and mix well. Put the muslin squares one on top of the other and place the yoghurt mixture in the centre. Gather up the corners of the muslin and tie securely with string, suspended over a bowl. Refrigerate and leave to drain for 3 days.
2 Once drained, the yoghurt will have become the texture and consistency of ricotta cheese. Remove from the cloth, and place in a bowl.
3 Roll tablespoons of mixture into balls and place on a large tray. You should have 18 balls. Cover and refrigerate for 3 hours, or until firm.

4 Place the balls in a clean, dry 1 litre glass jar with the bay leaves, fresh thyme and oregano sprigs. Fill the jar with the olive oil. Seal and refrigerate for up to 1 week. Return to room temperature for serving.
NOTE: This dish is traditionally served at breakfast or as an appetizer.

FATAYER SABANIKH
(Spinach pies)

Preparation time: 25 minutes
+ 2 hours rising
Total cooking time: 20 minutes
Makes about 20

☆ ☆

7 g (¼ oz) sachet dried yeast
1 teaspoon sugar
3 cups (375 g/12 oz) flour
½ cup (125 ml/4 fl oz) olive oil
750 g (1½ lb) English spinach, trimmed
1 large onion, finely chopped
1 clove garlic, crushed
½ cup (80 g/2¾ oz) pine nuts, toasted
2 tablespoons lemon juice
1 teaspoon finely grated lemon rind
¼ teaspoon ground nutmeg

RIGHT: Labneh makbur

1 Place the yeast and sugar in a bowl with
¼ cup warm water. Set aside for 10 minutes
until frothy. Sift the flour into a bowl, add
the yeast mixture, 2 tablespoons olive oil
and ¾ cup (185 ml/6 fl oz) warm water. Mix
to form a dough, then turn onto a lightly
floured board and knead for 10 minutes until
smooth and elastic. Place in an oiled bowl and
leave for up to 2 hours in a warm, draught-free
place until doubled in size.

2 Preheat the oven to moderately hot 190°C
(375°F/Gas 5). Grease two large baking trays.
Wash the spinach, leaving a generous amount
of water on the leaves. Place in a saucepan,
cover and cook over high heat until wilted.
Transfer to a colander and squeeze against the
sides to remove the excess water. Chop coarsely.

3 Heat 1 tablespoon oil in a frying pan and
cook the onion and garlic until softened. Place
in a bowl with the spinach, pine nuts, lemon
juice and rind. Season with the nutmeg and
some salt and pepper. Set aside to cool.

4 Turn the dough onto a floured board and
knock down. Divide into balls the size of an egg
and roll each into a 10 cm (4 inch) round. Place
1 tablespoon of the filling in the centre of each
round. Brush the edges of the rounds with
water, then bring up the sides at three points to
form a triangle, pressing the edges together to
seal. Place on the trays, leaving room for the pies
to rise as they cook. Brush them with beaten egg
and bake for 15 minutes until golden. Serve hot.

BABA GHANNOUJ
(Eggplant/aubergine dip)

Preparation time: 20 minutes
  + 30 minutes cooling
Total cooking time: 50 minutes
Makes 1¾ cups

2 large eggplants (aubergines)
3 cloves garlic, crushed
½ teaspoon ground cumin
⅓ cup (80 ml/2¾ fl oz) lemon juice
2 tablespoons tahini
pinch of cayenne pepper
1½ tablespoons olive oil
1 tablespoon chopped fresh flat-leaf parsley
black olives, to garnish

1 Preheat the oven to moderately hot 200°C
(400°F/Gas 6). Prick the eggplants several times
with a fork, then cook over an open flame for
about 5 minutes, until the skin is black and
blistered. Transfer to a baking tin and bake for
40–45 minutes, or until the eggplants are very
soft and wrinkled. Place in a colander over a
bowl to drain off any bitter juices, leaving them
for 30 minutes, or until cool.

2 Carefully peel the skin from the eggplants,
chop the flesh and put it in a food processor
with the garlic, cumin, lemon juice, tahini,
cayenne pepper and olive oil. Process until
smooth and creamy. Alternatively, use a potato
masher or fork. Season with salt and stir in the
parsley. Spread in a flat bowl or on a plate and
garnish with the olives. Serve with flatbread or
pide for dipping.

NOTE: If you prefer, you can bake the eggplant
in a baking tin in a moderately hot (200°C/
400°F/Gas 6) oven for 1 hour, or until very soft.

ABOVE: Baba ghannouj

LAHM BI AJEEN
(Lamb filo fingers)

Preparation time: 25 minutes
Total cooking time: 25 minutes
Makes 12

☆☆

1 tablespoon olive oil

350 g (11 oz) lean lamb mince

1 small onion, finely chopped

2 cloves garlic crushed

1 tablespoon ground cumin

1 teaspoon ground ginger

1 teaspoon paprika

1 teaspoon ground cinnamon

pinch of saffron threads, soaked in
    a little warm water

1 teaspoon harissa (see Glossary page 15)

2 tablespoons chopped fresh coriander

2 tablespoons chopped fresh flat-leaf parsley

3 tablespoons pine nuts, toasted

1 egg

6 sheets filo pastry

60 g (2 oz) butter, melted

1 tablespoon sesame seeds

YOGHURT SAUCE

1 cup (250 g/8 oz) natural yoghurt

2 tablespoons chopped fresh mint

1 clove garlic, crushed

1 Preheat the oven to moderate 180°C (350°F/ Gas 4). Lightly grease a large baking tray.
2 Heat the oil in a large frying pan, add the lamb and cook for 5 minutes, breaking up any lumps with the back of a wooden spoon. Add the onion and garlic and cook for 1 minute. Add the spices, harissa, chopped coriander and parsley and cook for 1 minute, stirring to combine. Transfer to a sieve and drain to remove the fat.
3 Place the mixture in a bowl and allow to cool slightly. Mix in the pine nuts and egg.
4 Place a sheet of filo on the bench with the shortest side facing you. Cover the remaining sheets with a damp tea towel to prevent them from drying out. Cut the sheet of filo into four equal strips lengthways. Brush one of the strips with melted butter and place another on top. Do the same with the other two pieces. Place 1 tablespoon of the lamb mixture on each at the short end of the filo and roll each up, tucking in the ends to hold the mixture in and form each into a cigar shape. Repeat this process until you have used up all the filo and meat mixture.
5 Place the lamb fingers on the baking tray. Brush with any remaining melted butter and sprinkle with sesame seeds. Bake for 15 minutes, or until lightly golden.
6 For the yoghurt sauce, stir all the ingredients together in a small bowl. Serve the filo fingers warm with the sauce on the side.

SLAT AVOCADO VE PRI HADA
(Citrus and avocado salad)

Preparation time: 10 minutes
Total cooking time: Nil
Serves 4

☆

2 ripe avocados, sliced into 1 cm (1/2 inch) slices

2 oranges, segmented, reserving
    1 tablespoon juice

1 grapefruit (preferably pink), segmented

90 g (3 oz) baby rocket leaves

1 teaspoon finely grated orange rind

1 tablespoon orange juice

75 ml (2 1/2 fl oz) extra virgin olive oil

1 tablespoon red wine vinegar

1/2 teaspoon Dijon mustard

1 teaspoon sugar

1 tablespoon chopped fresh mint

1 Place the avocado and citrus fruit in a serving bowl or platter and toss gently with the rocket leaves.
2 In a separate bowl, place the orange rind and juice, oil, vinegar, mustard and sugar. Season with salt and pepper and whisk together. Pour over the salad and cover all the leaves and the fruit. Sprinkle with the chopped mint and serve immediately.

LAHM BI 'AJEEN
These delicate pastries often appear on menus as *Ladies Fingers* or are sometimes called *Sambusik bi Lahm*. Any combination of lamb and pastry or dough is usually called *Lahm bi ajeen* which means literally 'meat with dough'.

OPPOSITE PAGE: Slat avocado ve pri hada (top); Lahm bi ajeen

STUFFED VEGETABLES
Claimed by the Turks
and the Greeks as their
creation, the popularity
of stuffed vegetables
spread throughout the
Mediterranean, appearing
as far back as the time of
the Ottoman Empire and
served at the lavish
banquets of the sultans.
The long and complicated
preparation usually required
of these dishes satisfied
the ostentatious desires
of the rich and powerful,
while the subtle balance
of the vegetables and
their fillings satisfied their
refined palates.

ABOVE: Aroishawki mihshi

AROISHAWKI MIHSHI
(Stuffed artichokes)

Preparation time: 1 hour 30 minutes
Total cooking time: 1 hour 25 minutes
Serves 6

☆☆

1/2 cup (125 ml/4 fl oz) lemon juice
12 globe artichokes
500 g (1 lb) lamb mince
1/2 cup (40 g/1 1/4 oz) fresh breadcrumbs
1 egg, lightly beaten
1 tablespoon chopped fresh thyme
olive oil, for deep-frying
1/2 cup (125 ml/4 fl oz) extra virgin olive oil
1 1/2 cups (375 ml/12 fl oz) chicken stock
1/2 teaspoon ground turmeric
1 bay leaf
40 g (3/4 oz) butter
2 tablespoons plain flour

1 Fill a large bowl with water and add 60 ml (2 fl oz) lemon juice. Peel the outer leaves from the artichokes, trimming the bases and stems to reveal the bases. Cut the tops off to reveal the chokes and remove the chokes. Place the artichokes in the bowl of acidulated water.
2 Place the lamb, breadcrumbs, egg and thyme in a bowl, season and mix well. Pat the artichokes dry with paper towels and fill each with 2 tablespoons of the lamb mixture.
3 Fill a large heavy-based saucepan one-third full of oil and heat to 180°C (350°F), or until a cube of bread browns in 15 seconds. Cook the artichokes in batches for 5 minutes, or until golden brown. Drain.
4 Place the extra virgin olive oil, turmeric, bay leaf, remaining lemon juice and 1 cup (250 ml/8 fl oz) stock in a 1.25 litre casserole dish. Season, then bring to the boil. Add the artichokes, reduce the heat, cover and simmer for 1 hour, or until tender, adding more stock if necessary. Turn the artichokes twice during cooking. Remove the artichokes and keep them warm. Reserve the liquid.
5 Melt the butter in a saucepan, add the flour and stir for 1 minute, or until pale and foamy. Remove from the heat and gradually stir in the reserved liquid. Return to the heat and stir until the sauce boils and thickens, then reduce the heat and simmer for 2 minutes. Serve immediately with the artichokes.

FATTOUSH
(Lebanese toasted bread salad)

Preparation time: 15 minutes
Total cooking time: 10 minutes
Serves 6

2 pitta bread rounds (17 cm/7 inch diameter)
6 cos lettuce leaves, shredded
1 large Lebanese cucumber, cut into 1 cm (1/2 inch) cubes
4 ripe tomatoes, cut into 1 cm (1/2 inch) cubes
8 spring onions, chopped
4 tablespoons chopped fresh flat-leaf parsley
1 tablespoon chopped fresh mint
2 tablespoons chopped fresh coriander

DRESSING
2 cloves garlic, crushed
100 ml (3 1/2 fl oz) extra virgin olive oil
100 ml (3 1/2 fl oz) lemon juice

1 Preheat the oven to moderate 180°C (350°F/ Gas 4). Split the bread into two through the centre and bake on a baking tray for about 8 minutes, or until golden and crisp, turning halfway through. Break into small pieces.
2 For the dressing, whisk all the ingredients together in a bowl until combined.
3 Place the bread pieces and remaining salad ingredients in a bowl and toss. Pour on the dressing and toss well. Season, to taste, with salt and ground black pepper. Serve immediately.

SALATA BALADI
(Arabic fresh vegetable salad)

Preparation time: 10 minutes
Total cooking time: Nil
Serves 4–6

2 tablespoons extra virgin olive oil
2 tablespoons lemon juice
1 cos lettuce, torn into bite sized pieces
3 ripe tomatoes, each cut into 8 pieces
1 green pepper (capsicum), cut into bite-sized pieces
1 telegraph cucumber, seeded and chopped
6 radishes, sliced
1 small salad or red onion, thinly sliced
2 tablespoons chopped fresh flat-leaf parsley
2 tablespoons chopped fresh mint

1 In a bowl, whisk together the olive oil and lemon juice. Season well with salt and pepper.
2 Combine the remaining ingredients in a large serving bowl and toss well. Add the dressing and toss to combine.
NOTE: Salad onions are sweeter than normal onions and are readily available.

RADISHES
The root of a plant belonging to the mustard family, the radish is said to have been part of the rations given to the Egyptian labourers who built the pyramids. Traditionally, the role of the radish was to cleanse the palate and prepare it for other food and drink. Radishes, both the long white ones and round scarlet ones, are popular in a region where vegetables are generally enjoyed both cooked and raw. They are used in Middle Eastern salads for their crisp texture and pungent peppery taste, often contrasted with the softer, juicy texture of oranges. To enhance their crispness, radishes can be soaked in iced water for a few hours before eating.

LEFT: Fattoush

KIBBEH BIL SANIEH
(Layered lamb and burghul)

Preparation time: 30 minutes + 30 minutes
    soaking + 10 minutes cooling
Total cooking time: 50 minutes
Serves 4–6

☆ ☆

2 cups (350 g/11 oz) burghul
400 g (13 oz) lamb mince
1 large onion, finely chopped
1 tablespoon ground cumin
1 teaspoon ground allspice
olive oil, for brushing

FILLING
1 tablespoon olive oil, plus extra for brushing
1 onion, finely chopped
1 teaspoon ground cinnamon
1 tablespoon ground cumin
500 g (1 lb) lamb mince
1/2 cup (80 g/2 3/4 oz) raisins
100 g (3 1/2 oz) pine nuts, toasted

BELOW: Kibbeh bil sanieh

1 Soak the burghul in cold water for 30 minutes, drain and squeeze out excess water. Place the mince, onion, cumin, allspice and some salt and pepper in a food processor, and process until combined. Add the burghul and process to a paste. Refrigerate until needed. Preheat the oven to moderate 180°C (350°F/Gas 4). Lightly grease a 20 x 30 cm (8 x 12 inch) baking dish.

2 For the filling, heat the oil in a large frying pan over medium heat and cook the onion for 5 minutes, or until softened. Add the cinnamon and cumin and stir for 1 minute, or until fragrant. Add the mince, stirring to break up any lumps, and cook for 5 minutes, or until the meat is brown. Stir in the raisins and nuts and season, to taste.

3 Press half the burghul mixture into the base of the tin, smoothing the surface with wet hands. Spread the filling over the top, then cover with the remaining burghul, again smoothing the top.

4 Score a diamond pattern in the top of the mixture with a sharp knife and brush lightly with olive oil. Bake for 35–40 minutes, or until the top is brown and crisp. Cool for 10 minutes before cutting into diamond shapes. Serve with yoghurt and salad.

FISH AND CUMIN KEBABS

Preparation time: 10 minutes + marinating
Total cooking time: 6 minutes
Serves 4

☆ ☆

750 g (1 1/2 lb) firm white fish fillets
2 tablespoons olive oil
1 clove garlic, crushed
3 tablespoons chopped fresh coriander
2 teaspoons ground cumin
1 teaspoon ground pepper

1 Cut the fish fillets into 3 cm (1 1/4 inch) cubes. Thread on oiled skewers and set aside.

2 For the marinade, combine the oil, garlic, coriander, cumin and pepper in a small bowl. Brush the marinade over the fish, cover with plastic wrap and refrigerate for several hours, or overnight, turning occasionally. Drain, reserving the marinade. Season just before cooking.

3 Place the skewers on a hot, lightly oiled grill. Cook for 5–6 minutes, or until tender, turning once and brushing with reserved marinade several times during cooking. Serve with pitta bread and salad.

WARM CHICKPEA AND SILVERBEET (SWISS CHARD) SALAD WITH SUMAC

Preparation time: 30 minutes
  + overnight soaking
Total cooking time: 2 hours
Serves 4

☆ ☆

250 g (8 oz) dried chickpeas
1/2 cup (125 ml/4 fl oz) olive oil
1 onion, cut into thin wedges
2 ripe tomatoes
1 teaspoon sugar
1/4 teaspoon ground cinnamon
2 cloves garlic, chopped
1.5 kg (3 lb) silverbeet (Swiss chard)
3 tablespoons chopped fresh mint
2–3 tablespoons lemon juice
1 1/2 tablespoons ground sumac (see Note
  and Glossary page 15)

1 Place the chickpeas in a large bowl, cover with water and leave to soak overnight. Drain and place in a large saucepan. Cover with water and bring to the boil, then simmer for 1 3/4 hours, or until tender. Drain thoroughly.

2 Heat the oil in a heavy-based frying pan, add the onion and cook over low heat for 5 minutes, or until softened and just starting to brown.

3 Cut the tomatoes in half, scrape out the seeds with a teaspoon and dice the flesh. Add the tomato flesh to the pan with the sugar, cinnamon and garlic, and cook for 2–3 minutes, or until softened.

4 Thoroughly wash the silverbeet and pat dry with paper towels. Trim the stems and finely shred the leaves. Add to the tomato mixture with the chickpeas and cook for 3–4 minutes, or until the silverbeet wilts. Add the mint, lemon juice and sumac, season, and cook for 1 minute. Serve immediately.

NOTE: Sumac is a powder ground from berries that adds flavour and colour to dishes. It is available from Middle Eastern speciality shops.

SILVERBEET
Also known as Swiss chard or chard, silverbeet is a member of the beet family. It is often confused with spinach. Silverbeet has large, crinkled, deep green leaves and silver stems, both of which are edible. The wilted leaves are used in salads, served as a vegetable and mixed with other ingredients like cheese to make a stuffing for savoury pastries and filled pasta. The stems are also delicious braised, boiled, steamed, dressed with olive oil and lemon juice, in béchamel sauce or served au gratin. Choose bunches with firm, inflexible stems and the smallest leaves, as they should be the youngest. Store silverbeet in plastic bags in the refrigerator, only washing immediately before use.

ABOVE: Warm chickpea and silverbeet salad with sumac

ABOVE: Adas bis silq

ADAS BIS SILQ
(Lentil and silverbeet/Swiss chard soup)

Preparation time: 20 minutes
Total cooking time: 3 hours 30 minutes
Serves 6

CHICKEN STOCK

1 kg (2 lb) chicken trimmings
　(necks, ribs, wings), fat removed
1 small onion, roughly chopped
1 bay leaf
3–4 sprigs fresh flat-leaf parsley
1–2 sprigs fresh oregano or thyme

1 1/2 cups (280 g/9 oz) brown lentils, washed
850 g (1 lb 12 oz) silverbeet
1/4 cup (60 ml/2 fl oz) olive oil

1 large onion, finely chopped
4 cloves garlic, crushed
1/2 cup (35 g/1 1/4 oz) finely chopped fresh
　coriander leaves
1/3 cup (80 ml/2 3/4 fl oz) lemon juice
lemon wedges, to serve

1　For the stock, put all the ingredients in a large saucepan, add 3 litres water and bring to the boil. Skim any scum from the surface. Reduce the heat and simmer for 2 hours. Strain the stock, discarding the trimmings, onion and herbs. You will need 1 litre of stock.
2　Skim any fat from the stock. Place the lentils in a large saucepan, add the stock and 1 litre water. Bring to the boil, then reduce the heat and simmer, covered, for 1 hour.
3　Meanwhile, remove the stems from the silverbeet and shred the leaves. Heat the oil in a saucepan over medium heat and cook the onion for 2–3 minutes, or until transparent. Add the garlic and cook for 1 minute. Add the silverbeet and toss for 2–3 minutes, or until wilted. Stir the mixture into the lentils. Add the coriander and lemon juice, season, and simmer, covered, for 15–20 minutes. Serve with the lemon wedges.
NOTE: You can freeze any leftover stock for up to three months.

CARROT AND CORIANDER SOUP

Preparation time: 15 minutes
Total cooking time: 1 hour 10 minutes
Serves 4

2 tablespoons olive oil
1 onion, chopped
800 g (1 lb 10 oz) carrots, roughly chopped
1 bay leaf
1 teaspoon ground cumin
1 teaspoon cayenne pepper
1 teaspoon ground coriander
2 teaspoons paprika
1.25 litres chicken or vegetable stock
1/2 cup (250 g/8 oz) thick natural yoghurt
2 tablespoons chopped fresh coriander leaves
fresh coriander leaves, extra, for garnish

1　Heat the olive oil in a saucepan, add the onion and carrot and cook over low heat for 30 minutes.

2 Add the bay leaf and spices and cook for another 2 minutes. Add the stock, bring to the boil, then reduce the heat and simmer uncovered for 40 minutes, or until the carrot is tender. Cool slightly, then blend in batches in a food processor. Return to the saucepan and gently reheat. Season, to taste.

3 Combine the yoghurt and coriander in a bowl. Pour the soup into bowls and top with a dollop of the yoghurt mixture. Garnish with fresh coriander.

KOUSA MIHSHI BI LABAN
(Stuffed zucchini/courgettes with yoghurt sauce)

Preparation time: 20 minutes
Total cooking time: 1 hour 10 minutes
Serves 4

4 zucchini (courgettes)
1½ cups (375 ml/12 fl oz) chicken stock

FILLING
1 tablespoon olive oil
1 onion, finely chopped
1½ tablespoons pine nuts
125 g (4 oz) lamb mince
¼ cup (55 g/2 oz) short-grain rice
1 ripe tomato, seeded and chopped
2 tablespoons chopped fresh flat-leaf parsley
½ teaspoon ground allspice
½ teaspoon ground cinnamon

YOGHURT SAUCE
250 g (8 oz) thick natural yoghurt
1 teaspoon cornflour
1 clove garlic, crushed
1 teaspoon dried mint

1 Cut each zucchini in half lengthways. Scoop out the flesh from each piece, leaving a 2 mm (⅛ inch) border on each shell. This can be done with an apple corer, but be careful not to pierce the skins of the zucchini. Soak the zucchini in salted water for 10 minutes, then drain and pat dry.

2 For the filling, heat the oil in a frying pan, add the onion and cook over medium heat for 5 minutes, or until soft. Add the pine nuts and cook for 3–4 minutes, until golden. Cool slightly, then transfer to a large bowl. Add the remaining filling ingredients and combine well.

3 Spoon filling into each zucchini half and carefully place in a wide, heavy-based saucepan or casserole. Cover with the chicken stock then invert a dinner plate over the top. Gently simmer over low heat for 1 hour.

4 About 15 minutes before the zucchini is ready, make the sauce by warming the yoghurt in a saucepan over medium heat. Stir the cornflour into 1 tablespoon water in a small bowl until smooth, then add to the yoghurt and stir well. Bring to the boil and add the crushed garlic and mint. Season well, then reduce the heat and simmer for 8–10 minutes, stirring regularly.

5 Remove the zucchini from the casserole and serve the yoghurt sauce poured over the top. Serve hot with steamed rice.

BELOW: Kousa mihshi bi laban

KIBBEH

Use two tablespoons of burghul mixture to make each sausage shape.

Push your index finger through the middle of each sausage to form a cavity for the filling.

Spoon two teaspoons of the filling into the cavity of each sausage and close the open end.

Mould each sausage into a smooth torpedo shape with slightly pointed ends.

KIBBEH

Preparation time: 45 minutes
  + 2 hours refrigeration
Total cooking time: 25 minutes
Makes 15

1 1/3 cups (235 g/7 1/2 oz) fine burghul
150 g (5 oz) lean lamb, chopped
1 onion, grated
2 tablespoons plain flour
1 teaspoon ground allspice

FILLING
2 teaspoons olive oil
1 small onion, finely chopped
100 g (3 1/2 oz) lean lamb mince
1/2 teaspoon ground allspice
1/2 teaspoon ground cinnamon
1/3 cup (80 ml/2 3/4 fl oz) beef stock
2 tablespoons pine nuts
2 tablespoons chopped fresh mint
oil, for deep-frying

1　Cover the burghul with boiling water and leave for 5 minutes. Drain in a colander, pressing well to remove the water. Spread on paper towels to absorb any moisture.

2　Process the burghul, lamb, onion, flour and allspice until a fine paste forms. Season well, then refrigerate for 1 hour.

3　For the filling, heat the oil in a frying pan, add the onion and cook over low heat for 3 minutes, or until soft. Add the mince, allspice and cinnamon, and cook, stirring, over high heat for 3 minutes. Add the stock and cook, partially covered, over low heat for 6 minutes, or until the mince is soft. Roughly chop the pine nuts and stir in with the mint. Season well with salt and cracked pepper, then transfer to a bowl and allow to cool.

4　Shape 2 tablespoons of the burghul mixture at a time into a sausage 6 cm (2 1/2 inches) long. Dip your hands in cold water, and, with your index finger, make a long hole through the centre of each sausage and gently work your finger around to make a cavity for the filling. Fill each with 2 teaspoons of the filling and seal, moulding it into a torpedo shape. Smooth over any cracks with your fingers. Place on a foil-lined tray and refrigerate, uncovered, for 1 hour.

5　Fill a deep pan one third full of oil and heat until a cube of bread dropped into the oil browns in 15 seconds. Deep-fry the kibbeh in batches for 2–3 minutes, or until browned. Drain on paper towels. Serve hot.

RIGHT: Kibbeh

Despite their size, these miniature nuts are expensive as the harvesting is labour intensive. Coming from several varieties of pine tree, the nuts are actually kernels found inside the pine cone, which must be heated so the nuts can be obtained. Pine nuts have a high fat content so they turn rancid quite quickly and it is best to buy them as you need them. If necessary, they can be refrigerated in an airtight container for up to three months or frozen for nine months. Their flavour is greatly enhanced by dry roasting them in a frying pan or under a grill. They are used in the making of pesto and are widely used in both sweet and savoury Middle Eastern dishes. The choice of nut can help identify the nationality of the cook or the dish — pine nuts and almonds tend to denote Syrian or Egyptian dishes, while walnuts usually appear in Turkish ones.

ROAST CHICKEN STUFFED WITH PINE NUTS AND RICE

Preparation time: 30 minutes
Total cooking time: 2 hours 30 minutes
Serves 4–6

STUFFING
60 g (2 oz) clarified butter (see Note)
  or ghee, melted
1 onion, chopped
1 teaspoon ground allspice
1/3 cup (60 g/2 oz) basmati rice
1/4 cup (30 g/1 oz) walnuts, chopped
1/3 cup (50 g/1 3/4 oz) pine nuts
1/3 cup (55 g/2 oz) sultanas
1/2 cup (125 ml/4 fl oz) chicken stock

1.6 kg (3 1/2 lb) chicken
2/3 cup (170 ml/5 1/2 fl oz) chicken stock

1 Preheat the oven to moderate 180°C (350°F/ Gas 4). Pour half the butter into a large frying pan, then add the onion and cook for 5 minutes over medium heat until the onion is transparent. Stir in the allspice.
2 Add the rice and nuts to the pan, then cook for 3–4 minutes over medium–high heat. Add the sultanas, stock and 1/4 cup (60 ml/2 fl oz) of water. Bring to boil, then reduce the heat and simmer for 8–10 minutes, until the water is absorbed. Allow to cool.
3 Rinse the cavity of the chicken with cold water and pat dry inside and out with paper towels.
4 When the stuffing is cool, spoon the stuffing into the cavity. Truss the chicken, using string, then place in a deep baking dish, then rub 1/2 teaspoon salt and 1/4 teaspoon freshly ground black pepper into the skin using your fingertips.
5 Pour the rest of the butter over the chicken, then add the stock to the pan. Roast for 2 hours 10 minutes, basting every 20–25 minutes with juices from the pan. Rest the chicken for 15 minutes before carving. Serve with the stuffing.
NOTE: To clarify butter, melt it in a saucepan over low heat, then remove from the heat and let the milk solids drop to the base. Only use the yellow liquid part of the butter. Discard the white milk solids at the base of the saucepan.

ABOVE: Roast chicken stuffed with pine nuts and rice

CORIANDER

Said to be the world's most commonly used herb, this Mediterranean native is grown for its roots, stems, leaves and seeds. The fresh leaves and dried seeds taste completely different from each other and cannot be substituted for each other in recipes. Fresh coriander is used in Middle Eastern stews, sauces, soups and salads and included in plates of fresh herbs that are placed on the table for people to pick at during their meal. The seeds are actually the plant's ripe, dried fruit. They have been found in Egyptian tombs dating as far back as 960 BC and are also mentioned in the Bible. Used whole or ground, they are a distinct feature of Cypriot cooking and an important component of dukkah, the Middle Eastern spice and ground nut mix widely eaten in Egypt, where it is sold in paper cones at street stalls and used to sprinkle over bread, or as a dip for hard-boiled eggs.

ABOVE: Lemon and coriander baked lamb

LEMON AND CORIANDER BAKED LAMB

Preparation time: 15 minutes
Total cooking time: 1 hour 20 minutes
Serves 4–6

1.8 kg (3 lb 10 oz) leg of lamb
2 cloves garlic, sliced
3 large strips lemon rind, cut into 1 cm pieces
1/2 cup (25 g/3/4 oz) chopped fresh coriander
3 tablespoons chopped fresh flat-leaf parsley
2 tablespoons olive oil

1 Preheat the oven to moderate 180°C (350°F/ Gas 4). Trim the lamb of excess fat and sinew. Using a sharp knife, make deep cuts in the flesh and place a slice of garlic and a piece of lemon rind into each cut.
2 Combine the coriander, parsley, oil and 1 teaspoon ground black pepper. Coat the lamb with the herb mixture and place on a rack in a baking dish. Pour 1 cup (250 ml/8 fl oz) water into the dish and bake for 1 hour 20 minutes, or until the lamb is cooked to your liking. Add extra water to the pan while cooking if the lamb starts to dry out. Serve the lamb in slices with pan juices and vegetables in season.

SHISH BARAK
(Meat dumplings in yoghurt sauce)

Preparation time: 40 minutes
  + 30 minutes standing
Total cooking time: 35 minutes
Serves 4–6

☆ ☆ ☆

250 g (8 oz) plain flour
60 g (2 oz) clarified butter, melted, for baking
40 g (1 1/4 oz) clarified butter, extra, for serving
2 cloves garlic, crushed, for serving
1 tablespoon dried mint, for serving

FILLING

20 g (³/₄ oz) clarified butter
I small onion, finely chopped
2 tablespoons pine nuts
250 g (8 oz) lamb mince
pinch of ground allspice

YOGHURT SAUCE

3 cups (750 g/1¹/₂ lb) natural yoghurt
2 teaspoons cornflour
I egg white, lightly beaten

1   For the dough, sift the flour and 1 teaspoon salt into a bowl and add ³/₄ cup (185 ml/6 fl oz) water a little at a time and combine until the mixture comes together in a ball. Cover and allow to rest for 30 minutes.

2   For the filling, melt the clarified butter in a deep heavy-based frying pan and cook the onion over medium heat for 5 minutes, or until soft. Add the pine nuts and allow them to brown, stirring constantly. Increase the heat to high and add the mince and allspice, stirring until the meat changes colour. Season, to taste, and allow to cool.

3   Preheat the oven to moderate 180°C (350°/Gas 4). Lightly grease two baking trays.

4   Roll out the dough on a floured board, to about 5 mm (¹/₄ inch) thick and cut into rounds using a 5 cm (2 inch) cutter. Place a teaspoon of filling in the centre of each round and fold the pastry over into a crescent. Press the edges together firmly and then wrap the crescent around one finger and press the two ends together to make a hat shape. Place on the baking trays and brush lightly with the clarified butter. Bake for 10 minutes, or until lightly browned. The pastries do not have to be completely cooked.

5   Place the yoghurt in a large, heavy-based saucepan and stir until smooth. Combine the cornflour with 1¹/₂ cups (375 ml/12 fl oz) of water, stir until smooth, then add to the yoghurt with the egg white and 2 teaspoons salt. Cook over medium heat, stirring constantly until the mixture thickens. Add the dumplings to the pan, stir very gently, then cook, uncovered, over low heat for 10 minutes, stirring occasionally and being careful not to boil the sauce.

6   Just before serving, melt the extra clarified butter in a small frying pan and fry the garlic gently for a few seconds. Stir in the mint and remove from the heat. Pour over the dumplings and serve with rice.

CLARIFIED BUTTER

Clarified butter or samna, as it is known in the Middle East, as well as olive and vegetable oils, have generally replaced rendered lamb fat as a cooking medium in kitchens across the Middle East. It was traditionally made from buffalo milk butter which was slowly melted over boiling water and strained through damp muslin. This separates the milk solids, eliminating impurities as well as the water content. Clarified butter is a favoured frying medium due to its distinct flavour and high smoking point. While an Indian form of clarified butter called ghee is now readily available in supermarkets, it is relatively simple to make your own. Melt unsalted butter slowly over a low temperature, skimming off any foam that forms on the top. The remaining clear butter is then strained through a fine cloth into a jar.

LEFT: Shish barak

287

SPICY SEPHARDI BAKED FISH WITH VEGETABLES

Preparation time: 15 minutes
  + 30 minutes marinating
Total cooking time: 45 minutes
Serves 4–6

☆ ☆

1 tablespoon cumin seeds
4 cloves garlic
1 small red chilli, roughly chopped
60 g (2 oz) fresh coriander leaves, stems
  and roots, chopped
1 tablespoon lemon juice
2 tablespoons olive oil
1.5 kg (3 lb) whole fish such as red snapper
  or coral trout, cleaned and scaled
  (get your fishmonger to do this for you)
450 g (14 oz) new potatoes, sliced
2–3 Roma tomatoes, cut in half lengthways,
  then sliced into 1 cm (1/2 inch) pieces
100 g (3 1/2 oz) green olives, pitted
  and halved
1/4 cup (60 ml/2 fl oz) olive oil, extra

BELOW: Spicy Sephardi baked fish with vegetables

1 Dry-fry the cumin seeds in a frying pan over medium heat for 2–3 minutes, or until fragrant. Grind the seeds to a fine powder in a mortar and pestle or spice grinder. Put the ground cumin, garlic, chilli, coriander, lemon juice and 1 teaspoon salt in a food processor, and process to a smooth paste. With the motor running, gradually add the oil.

2 Using a sharp knife, make 3 diagonal incisions through the thickest part on both sides of the fish to ensure even cooking. Rub the spice mixture over the fish, cover with plastic wrap and leave to marinate in the refrigerator for 30 minutes.

3 Preheat the oven to very hot 240°C (475°F/ Gas 9). Lay the fish in the centre of a large roasting tin and scatter the potato, tomato and olives around the fish. Pour 1/4 cup (60 ml) water and the extra olive oil over the fish and vegetables. Bake, basting often, for 40 minutes, or until the fish and vegetables are cooked through.

CHICKEN WITH ONIONS ON FLATBREAD

Preparation time: 25 minutes + overnight
  marinating
Total cooking time: 1 hour 20 minutes
Serves 6–8

☆ ☆

1.5 kg (3 lb) chicken
1 teaspoon ground cinnamon
1/2 teaspoon ground white pepper
3 tablespoons lemon juice
1/2 cup (125 ml/4 fl oz) olive oil
2 tablespoons sumac
1/2 teaspoon cardamom pods, lightly bruised
750 g (1 1/2 lb) onions, thinly sliced
1 cup (250 ml/8 fl oz) chicken stock
2 large pitta breads, split open and separated
125 g (4 oz) pine nuts, toasted
extra sumac, for garnish

1 Cut the chicken into 8 even-sized pieces, removing the giblets and any excess fat. Combine the cinnamon, white pepper, lemon juice and 1 teaspoon salt and rub into the chicken pieces, then cover and refrigerate in a ceramic dish overnight.

2 Heat the oil in a large saucepan over medium heat then add the sumac, cardamom pods, onion and stock and cook for 40 minutes, or until soft and the onion is purplish red. Remove from the

heat and carefully discard the cardamom pods.

3 Preheat the oven to moderately hot 200°C (400°F/Gas 6). Place the onion mixture in the base of a ceramic baking dish, then top with a single layer of chicken pieces, skin-side-down, and cover tightly with foil. Bake for 20 minutes then remove from the oven.

4 Tear the pitta into even-sized pieces about 8 cm (3 inches) across and place in the base of a clean, lightly oiled 30 x 25 cm (12 x 10 inch) ceramic baking dish. Lift the chicken from the onion and set aside, distribute the onion and any juices evenly over the pitta bread, then add the chicken pieces, skin-side-up and bake for another 20 minutes, or until the skin is crisp and golden. Serve sprinkled with toasted pine nuts and sumac.

PSARI TAHINA
(Baked fish with tahini sauce)

Preparation time: 30 minutes
Total cooking time: 30 minutes
Serves 4

☆ ☆ ☆

1 kg (2 lb) whole white-fleshed fish (snapper, bream or barramundi), scaled and cleaned

3 cloves garlic, crushed

2 teaspoons harissa

2 tablespoons olive oil

1 lemon, thinly sliced

1 onion, thinly sliced

2 large firm, ripe tomatoes, sliced

4 sprigs fresh thyme

TAHINI SAUCE

2 teaspoons olive oil

1 clove garlic, crushed

3 tablespoons light tahini

2 1/2 tablespoons lemon juice

1 1/2 tablespoons chopped fresh coriander

1 Preheat the oven to moderately hot 200°C (400°F/Gas 6). Lightly grease a large baking dish. Make 3 diagonal cuts on each side of the fish through the thickest part of the flesh to ensure even cooking. Combine the garlic, harissa and olive oil in a small dish. Place 2 teaspoons in the fish cavity and spread the remainder over both sides of the fish rubbing it into the slits. Place 2 lemon slices in the cavity of the fish.

2 Arrange the onion in a layer on the baking dish. Top with the tomato, thyme and remaining lemon slices. Place the fish on top and bake, uncovered, for about 25–30 minutes, or until the fish flesh is opaque.

3 Meanwhile, to make the tahini sauce, heat the olive oil in a small saucepan over low heat. Add the garlic and cook over medium heat for 30 seconds, then add the tahini, lemon juice and 1/2 cup (125 ml/4 fl oz) water and stir until combined. Add more water, if necessary, to make a smooth, but fairly thick sauce. Cook for 2 minutes, then remove from the heat and stir in the coriander. Season.

4 Transfer the onion and tomato to a serving dish. Place the fish on top and season with salt. Pour some of the sauce on the fish and the rest in a serving dish on the side.

ABOVE: Psari tahina

1 Preheat the oven to moderate 180°C (350°F/ Gas 4). Score each duck breast 2 or 3 times on the skin side with a sharp knife. Cook in a non-stick frying pan over high heat, skin-side-down, for 6 minutes, or until crisp and it has rendered most of its fat. Place in a baking dish.

2 Remove all but 1 tablespoon of fat from the pan. Add the onion to the pan and cook over medium heat for 2–3 minutes, or until golden. Add the pomegranate and lemon juice, sugar, cinnamon and 1 cup (125 g/4 oz) walnuts and cook for 1 minute. Pour over the duck breasts and bake for 15 minutes.

3 Rest the duck for 5 minutes. Skim any excess fat from the sauce. Slice the duck and serve with a little sauce. Garnish with the pomegranate seeds and the remaining walnuts.

NOTE: If fresh pomegranate juice isn't available, combine 1/4 cup (60 ml/2 fl oz) pomegranate concentrate with 3/4 cup (185 ml/6 fl oz) water.

PITTA BREAD

Preparation time: 20 minutes
  + 40 minutes rising
Total cooking time: 5 minutes
Makes 12

☆☆

7 g (3/4 oz) sachet dried yeast
1 teaspoon caster sugar
3 1/2 cups (435 g/14 oz) plain flour
2 tablespoons olive oil

1 Place the yeast, sugar and 1 1/2 cups (375 ml/ 12 fl oz) lukewarm water in a bowl and stir until dissolved. Leave in a warm place for 10 minutes, or until bubbles appear on the surface. The mixture should be frothy and slightly increased in volume. If your yeast doesn't foam it is dead and you will have to start again.

2 Process the flour, yeast mixture and oil in a food processor for 30 seconds, or until the mixture forms a ball. Or, if you prefer, place the ingredients in a bowl and mix with a wooden spoon, or with your hand, until the mixture forms a smooth dough.

3 Turn the dough onto a well-floured surface and knead until smooth and elastic. Place in a well-oiled bowl, cover with plastic wrap, then a tea towel and leave in a warm place for 20 minutes, or until almost doubled in size.

4 Punch down the dough and divide into twelve equal portions. Roll each portion into

KHORESHE FESENJAN
(Duck breast with walnut and
  pomegranate sauce)

Preparation time: 15 minutes + 5 minutes resting
Total cooking time: 25 minutes
Serves 4

☆

4 large duck breasts
1 onion, finely chopped
1 cup (250 ml/4 fl oz) fresh pomegranate juice
  (see Note)
2 tablespoons lemon juice
2 tablespoons soft brown sugar
1 teaspoon ground cinnamon
1 1/2 cups (185 g/6 oz) chopped walnuts
pomegranate seeds, to garnish, optional

ABOVE: Khoreshe fesenjan

a 5 mm (2 inch) thick round. Place on greased baking trays and brush well with water. Stand and allow to rise for another 20 minutes.

5 Preheat the oven to very hot 250°C (500°F/Gas 10). If the dough has dried, brush again with water. Bake for 4–5 minutes. The pitta bread should be soft and pale, slightly swollen, and hollow inside. Eat warm with kebabs or falafel, or cool on wire racks and serve with salad.

FLATBREAD WITH ZA'ATAR

Preparation time: 35 minutes
  + 2 hours 50 minutes standing
Total cooking time: 30 minutes
Makes 10

2 x 7 g (³/4 oz) sachets dried yeast
1 teaspoon sugar
3¹/4 cups (400 g/13 oz) plain flour
¹/2 cup (125 ml/4 fl oz) olive oil
4 tablespoons za'atar (see Note and
  Glossary page 15)
1 tablespoon sea salt flakes

1 Place the yeast and sugar in a small bowl with ¹/4 cup (60 ml/2 fl oz) warm water and stir until dissolved. Leave in a warm place for 10 minutes, or until bubbles appear on the surface. The mixture should be frothy and slightly increased in volume. If your yeast doesn't foam it is dead and you will have to start again.

2 Sift the flour and ¹/2 teaspoon salt into a large bowl. Make a well and pour in the yeast mixture and 1¹/4 cups (315 ml/10 fl oz) warm water. Gradually combine to form a dough, then knead on a floured surface for 10–15 minutes, until smooth and elastic, gradually adding 1 tablespoon olive oil as you knead. Cover and set aside in a warm place for 1 hour, or until risen.

3 Punch down the dough with your fist and then knead again. Set aside and leave to rise for 30 minutes. Knead briefly and divide into 10 portions. Roll each portion until smooth and round. Roll each into a circle about 5 mm (¹/4 inch) thick. Set aside covered with a tea towel for another 20 minutes.

4 Preheat the oven to hot 220°C (425°F/Gas 7). Grease two baking trays. Place the rolls on the trays and gently press the surface with your fingers to create a dimpled effect. Brush with the remaining oil and sprinkle with za'atar and salt. Bake for 12–15 minutes. Serve warm.
NOTE: Buy za'atar mix at speciality food stores.

YEAST
This microscopic, living, single-celled organism causes food to ferment, converting it into alcohol and carbon dioxide. It is crucial for making leavened bread as it is the interaction of carbon dioxide, moisture, warmth and sugar that allows yeast to grow, enabling dough to rise. Yeast is readily available in supermarkets and is sold as either compressed fresh yeast or as active dry yeast. Fresh yeast is alive and moist and must be stored in the refrigerator. The dehydrated yeast cells of dry yeast are also alive but are dormant until they are mixed with warm liquid. Dry yeast should be stored in a cool, dry place and can be frozen or refrigerated. It must be returned to room temperature before dissolving so that it will become active.

LEFT: Flatbread with za'atar

RICOTTA
Made from the whey that remains after the making of other cheeses, ricotta in Italian literally translates as 'recooked'. It can be made from cow, ewe and goat milk and is not strictly a cheese, as cheeses are made from milk curd, not whey. Ricotta is a fresh cheese, made by boiling the whey from cooked milk, then scooping off the solid particles that float to the top and draining off the solid remnants. Like other fresh cheeses, ricotta is most often used in cooked dishes, where the delicate flavour and creamy texture are complemented by other stronger savoury flavours like spinach or sweet flavours such as citrus and dried fruit. Look for firm ricotta, store it in the refrigerator and use within a few days as it turns rancid quite rapidly. In Middle Eastern dishes it can be replaced with regional whey cheeses such as myzithra or manouri.

OPPOSITE PAGE:
Easter walnut cakes (top);
Stuffed fried pancakes

ATAIF MIHSHI
(Stuffed fried pancakes)

Preparation time: 20 minutes + 1 hour rising
Total cooking time: 1 hour
Makes about 16

☆ ☆ ☆

BATTER
7 g (3/4 oz) sachet dry yeast
1 teaspoon sugar
1 1/2 cups (185 g/6 oz) plain flour

SYRUP
500 g (1 lb) sugar
2 teaspoons lemon juice
2 tablespoons rosewater

FILLING
1 cup (250 g/8 oz) ricotta

oil, for brushing
peanut oil, for deep-frying

1   Place the yeast and sugar in a small bowl with 1/4 cup (60 ml/ fl oz) warm water and stir until dissolved. Leave in a warm place for 10 minutes or until bubbles appear on the surface. The mixture should be frothy and slightly increased in volume. If your yeast doesn't foam it is dead and you will have to start again. Sift the flour into a large bowl, make a well in the centre and add the yeast mixture and 1 1/2 cups (375 ml/ 12 fl oz) warm water. Using a wooden spoon, gradually stir in the flour and mix until smooth. Cover the bowl with a cloth and leave in a warm place for 1 hour, or until the batter has risen and the surface is bubbly.
2   Meanwhile, for the syrup, dissolve the sugar in 1 1/4 cups (315 ml/10 fl oz) water in a heavy-based saucepan over medium heat, stirring occasionally. Bring to the boil, add the lemon juice and simmer for 8–10 minutes, until the syrup is thick enough to coat the back of a spoon. It should be the consistency of thin honey. Add the rosewater and cook for another minute. Allow to cool completely.
3   To make the pancakes, lightly grease a heavy-based frying pan and place over medium heat. Stir 1/4 cup (60 ml/ fl oz) water into the batter. Pour 1 1/2 tablespoons batter into the pan, tilting it a little so the batter spreads to about 10 cm (4 inches). If the batter is too thick, add a little extra water. Cook the pancakes for about

3 minutes, or until golden on the underside and bubbles appear on the surface. Remove them from the pan, stack them on a plate and allow to cool slightly.
4   Place 1 tablespoon of the ricotta on the unfried side of each pancake. Fold each in half and pinch the edges together to seal into a half moon shape.
5   Heat the peanut oil in a deep-fryer or heavy-based saucepan to 190°C (375°F), or until a cube of bread dropped into the oil browns in 10 seconds. Fry the stuffed pancakes 3 or 4 at a time for 2–3 minutes, until golden. Remove with a slotted spoon and drain on paper towels. Dip the hot pancakes into the cooled syrup and serve warm or cold stacked on a large flat plate.

MA' AMOUL B'JOWZ
(Easter walnut cakes)

Preparation time: 15 minutes
Total cooking time: 20 minutes
Makes 28

☆

200 g (6 1/2 oz) unsalted butter, softened
1/2 cup (125 g/4 oz) caster sugar
2 tablespoons orange flower water
2 cups (250 g/8 oz) plain flour, sifted

WALNUT FILLING
1/2 cup (50 g/1 3/4 oz) walnuts, chopped
1/4 cup (60 g/2 oz) caster sugar
1 teaspoon ground cinnamon

1   Preheat the oven to warm 160°C (315°F/ Gas 2–3). Lightly grease two baking trays and line with baking paper.
2   Cream the butter and sugar in small bowl until light and fluffy. Transfer to a large bowl. Using a metal spoon, fold in the orange flower water and flour until well combined. Press with your hands until the mixture comes together to make a stiff dough.
3   For the walnut filling, combine all the ingredients in a bowl and mix well.
4   Roll heaped tablespoons of dough into balls. Press a hollow in the centre with your thumb. Place 1 teaspoon of filling into each hollow. Place on the trays and flatten slightly without folding dough over the filling. Bake for 15–20 minutes, or until golden. Cool on a wire rack and serve.

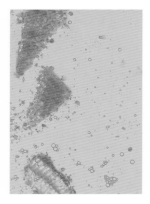

HONEY

The world's first sweetener, honey has been eaten in the Middle East since pre-Biblical times. In ancient Egypt, a form of fruit honey was extracted from dates and grapes, while Syrian bees were said to produce the best bees' honey. It is used to perfume and preserve Middle Eastern food such as pastries and cakes, which were originally soaked in honey to prevent them drying out and to refresh them once stale. The fragrance and flavour of honey depends on the flowers that the bees have fed on, not the bees themselves, as it is really processed flower nectar. This is why honey is generally classified by the name of the flower or tree from which it originates. The general rule is that the darker the colour, the stronger the flavour, so when a specific type is called for in a recipe, it can't necessarily be replaced by all other honeys. For all-purpose cooking and eating, it is best to use a pale, milder honey such as clover.

ABOVE: Mahallabia

MAHALLABIA
(Almond cream pudding)

Preparation time: 15 minutes
 + 1 hour refrigeration
Total cooking time: 40 minutes
Serves 4

☆

2 cups (500 ml/16 fl oz) milk
75 g (2¹/2 oz) caster sugar
2 tablespoons cornflour
2 tablespoons ground rice
75 g (2¹/2 oz) ground blanched almonds
1 teaspoon rosewater
2 tablespoons flower blossom honey
2 tablespoons shelled pistachio nuts, chopped

1 Place the milk and sugar in a saucepan and heat over medium heat, stirring until the sugar has dissolved.
2 Combine the cornflour and ground rice with ¹/4 cup (60 ml/2 fl oz) water and mix to a paste. Add to the milk and cook, stirring occasionally, over low heat for 20 minutes. Add the almonds and cook for 15 minutes, then add the rosewater. Spoon into shallow serving dishes and refrigerate for 1 hour. Serve drizzled with a little honey and sprinkled with pistachios.

SUFGANIYOT
(Israeli doughnuts)

Preparation time: 40 minutes + 10 minutes
 standing + overnight refrigeration
 + 30 minutes rising
Total cooking time: 25 minutes
Makes 14

☆ ☆ ☆

3/4 cup (185 ml/6 fl oz) lukewarm milk
1 tablespoon dried yeast
2 tablespoons caster sugar
2¹/2 cups (375 g/12 oz) plain flour
2 teaspoons ground cinnamon
1 teaspoon finely grated lemon rind
2 eggs, separated
40 g (1¹/4 oz) butter, softened
¹/3 cup (100 g/3¹/2 oz) plum, strawberry
 or apricot jam or conserve
oil, for deep-frying
caster sugar, extra, for rolling

1 Put the milk in a small bowl, add the yeast and 1 tablespoon of the sugar and leave in a warm place for 10 minutes, or until bubbles appear on the surface. If your yeast doesn't foam, it is dead and you will have to start again.

2 Sift the flour into a large bowl and add the cinnamon, lemon rind, egg yolks, yeast mixture, remaining sugar, and a pinch of salt. Mix well, then place the dough on a lightly floured work surface and knead for 5 minutes. Work in the butter, a little at a time, continually kneading until the dough becomes elastic. This should take about 10 minutes. Place in a large bowl and cover with a clean, damp tea towel. Leave to rise overnight in the refrigerator.

3 Place the dough on a lightly floured work surface and roll out to 3 mm (1/8 inch) thickness. Using a 6 cm (2½ inch) cutter, cut 28 rounds from the dough. Place 14 of the rounds on a lightly floured tray and carefully place 3/4 teaspoon of the jam or conserve into the centre of each. Lightly beat the egg whites, then brush a little around the outside edges of the rounds, being careful not to touch the jam at all. Top with the remaining 14 rounds and press down firmly around the edges to seal. Cover with a clean tea towel and leave to rise for 30 minutes. Make sure the dough has not separated at the edges. Press any open edges firmly together.

4 Fill a deep heavy-based saucepan one third full of oil and heat to 170°C (325°F), or until a cube of bread dropped into the oil browns in 20 seconds. Cook the doughnuts in batches for 1½ minutes on both sides, or until golden. Drain on crumpled paper towels and roll in caster sugar. Serve immediately.

MIDDLE EASTERN YOGHURT DRINK

Nearly every country in the Middle East has its own version of this yoghurt drink which is often sold both in cafes and from stalls on the streets.

Beat 2 cups (500 g/16 oz) thick natural yoghurt in a bowl until smooth, then add 2 cups (500 ml/16 fl oz) of icy-cold water, beating well until smooth. Add a pinch of salt and 1 tablespoon dried, crushed mint or to taste. Serve chilled, with ice. Serves 4.

SUFGANIYOT
Sufganiyot are the Israeli version of traditional Polish jelly doughnuts called ponchiks. Like other fried foods, they are eaten at Hanukkah, an eight-day festival also known as the festival of lights. Following the overthrow of an oppressive government, the Temple in Jerusalem was to be rededicated. However, there was only enough oil for the menorah for one day. Miraculously, the oil lasted the eight days needed to replenish supplies.

LEFT: Sufganiyot

INDEX

Page numbers in *italics* refer to photographs. Page numbers in **bold** type refer to margin notes.

ACKNOWLEDGEMENTS

HOME ECONOMISTS: Alison Adams, Renee Aiken, Kate Brodhurst, Rebecca Clancy, Ross Dobson, Justin Finlay, Jo Glynn, David Herbert, Michelle Lawton, Michaela Le Compte, Valli Little, Ben Masters, Tracey Meharg, Kate Murdoch, Justine Poole, Margot Smithyman, Angela Tregonning, Wendy Quisumbing

RECIPE DEVELOPMENT: Alison Adams, Roslyn Anderson, Janene Brooks, Jane Charlton, Rebecca Clancy, Judy Clarke, Ross Dobson, Michele Earl, Sue Forster-Wright, Jo Glynn, David Herbert, Katy Holder, Caroline Jones, Eva Katz, Kathy Knudsen, Jane Lawson, Valli Little, Barbara Lowery, Kerrie Mullins, Kate Murdoch, Christine Osmond, Sally Parker, Sarah Randell, Tracy Rutherford, Sylvia Sieff, Melita Smilovic, Margot Smithyman, Dimitra Stais, Angela Tregonning, Alison Turner, Jody Vassallo, Lovoni Welch

PHOTOGRAPHY: Jon Bader, Craig Cranko; Ben Dearnley, Joe Filshie, Oliver Ford, Phil Haley, Chris Jones, Tony Lyon, André Martin, Luis Martin, Valerie Martin, Reg Morrison, Peter Scott, Mil Truscott

STYLISTS: Marie-Hélène Clauzon, Carolyn Fienberg, Mary Harris, Michelle Noerianto, Maria Villegas, Sophie Ward

The publisher wishes to thank the following, all in NSW, for their assistance in the photography for this book:
Bertolli Olive Oil, Breville Holdings Pty Ltd; Chief Australia; MEC-Kambrook Pty Ltd